Agile and Lean Service-Oriented Development:

Foundations, Theory, and Practice

Xiaofeng Wang
Free University of Bozen/Bolzano, Italy

Nour Ali
Lero– The Irish Software Engineering Research Centre, University of Limerick, Ireland

Isidro Ramos
Valencia University of Technology

Richard Vidgen
Hull University Business School, UK

A volume in the Advances in Computer and Electrical Engineering (ACEE) Book Series

Information Science
REFERENCE

Managing Director:	Lindsay Johnston
Editorial Director:	Joel Gamon
Book Production Manager:	Jennifer Romanchak
Publishing Systems Analyst:	Adrienne Freeland
Development Editor:	Hannah Abelbeck
Assistant Acquisitions Editor:	Kayla Wolfe
Typesetter:	Nicole Sparano
Cover Design:	Nick Newcomer

Published in the United States of America by
Information Science Reference (an imprint of IGI Global)
701 E. Chocolate Avenue
Hershey PA 17033
Tel: 717-533-8845
Fax: 717-533-8661
E-mail: cust@igi-global.com
Web site: http://www.igi-global.com

Library of Congress Cataloging-in-Publication Data

Agile and lean service-oriented development: foundations, theory, and practice / Xiaofeng Wang ... [et al.], editors.
      p. cm.
   Includes bibliographical references and index.
   Summary: "This book explores the groundwork of service-oriented and agile and lean development and the conceptual basis and experimental evidences for the combination of the two approaches"-- Provided by publisher.
   ISBN 978-1-4666-2503-7 (hardcover) -- ISBN 978-1-4666-2504-4 (ebook) -- ISBN 978-1-4666-2505-1 (print & perpetual access) 1. Computer software--Development. 2. Agile software development. 3. Lean manufacturing. I. Wang, Xiaofeng, 1971-
   QA76.76.D47A379824 2013
   005.1--dc23
                          2012023354

This book is published in the IGI Global book series Advances in Computer and Electrical Engineering (ACEE) Book Series (ISSN: 2327-039X; eISSN: 2327-0403)

British Cataloguing in Publication Data
A Cataloguing in Publication record for this book is available from the British Library.

All work contributed to this book is new, previously-unpublished material. The views expressed in this book are those of the authors, but not necessarily of the publisher.

Advances in Computer and Electrical Engineering (ACEE) Book Series

Srikanta Patnaik
SOA University, India

ISSN: 2327-039X
EISSN: 2327-0403

MISSION

The fields of computer engineering and electrical engineering encompass a broad range of interdisciplinary topics allowing for expansive research developments across multiple fields. Research in these areas continues to develop and become increasingly important as computer and electrical systems have become an integral part of everyday life.

The **Advances in Computer and Electrical Engineering (ACEE) Book Series** aims to publish research on diverse topics pertaining to computer engineering and electrical engineering. **ACEE** encourages scholarly discourse on the latest applications, tools, and methodologies being implemented in the field for the design and development of computer and electrical systems.

COVERAGE

- Algorithms
- Applied Electromagnetics
- Chip Design
- Circuit Analysis
- Digital Electronics
- Electrical Power Conversion
- Optical Electronics
- Power Electronics
- Programming
- Qualitative Methods

IGI Global is currently accepting manuscripts for publication within this series. To submit a proposal for a volume in this series, please contact our Acquisition Editors at Acquisitions@igi-global.com or visit: http://www.igi-global.com/publish/.

Titles in this Series

For a list of additional titles in this series, please visit: www.igi-global.com

Agile and Lean Service-Oriented Development Foundations, Theory, and Practice
Xiaofeng Wang (Free University of Bozen/Bolzano, Italy) Nour Ali (Lero- The Irish Software Engineering Research Centre, University of Limerick, Ireland) Isidro Ramos (Valencia University of Technology) and Richard Vidgen (Hull University Business School, UK)
Information Science Reference • copyright 2013 • 312pp • H/C (ISBN: 9781466625037) • US $195.00 (our price)

Electromagnetic Transients in Transformer and Rotating Machine Windings
Editor, Charles Q. Su (Charling Technology, Australia)
Engineering Science Reference • copyright 2013 • 586pp • H/C (ISBN: 9781466619210) • US $195.00 (our price)

Design and Test Technology for Dependable Systems-on-Chip
Raimund Ubar (Tallinn University of Technology, Estonia) Jaan Raik (Tallinn University of Technology, Estonia) and Heinrich Theodor Vierhaus (Brandenburg University of Technology Cottbus, Germany)
Information Science Reference • copyright 2011 • 578pp • H/C (ISBN: 9781609602123) • US $180.00 (our price)

Kansei Engineering and Soft Computing Theory and Practice
Ying Dai (Iwate Pref. University, Japan) Basabi Chakraborty (Iwate Prefectural University, Japan) and Minghui Shi (Xiamen University, China)
Engineering Science Reference • copyright 2011 • 436pp • H/C (ISBN: 9781616927974) • US $180.00 (our price)

Model Driven Architecture for Reverse Engineering Technologies Strategic Directions and System Evolution
Liliana Favre (Universidad Nacional de Centro de la Proviencia de Buenos Aires, Argentina)
Engineering Science Reference • copyright 2010 • 460pp • H/C (ISBN: 9781615206490) • US $180.00 (our price)

www.igi-global.com

701 E. Chocolate Ave., Hershey, PA 17033
Order online at www.igi-global.com or call 717-533-8845 x100
To place a standing order for titles released in this series, contact: cust@igi-global.com
Mon-Fri 8:00 am - 5:00 pm (est) or fax 24 hours a day 717-533-8661

Table of Contents

Section 3
Practice

Detailed Table of Contents

Section 1
Foundations

Chapter 1
Juha Rikkilä, Studios 4 Future Software (S4FS), Free University of Bozen-Bolzano, Italy

A fad, hype, and a paradigm shift are often the words that are used about the agile, lean, and now also about service-oriented development. What starts as a step in evolution, grows into a mass movement in Internet and social media, and results in an avalanche of books, training, and consultancy services. Each proponent tries to differentiate from others with extreme statements of own superiority and blames of others' shortcomings. Only a next fad, hype, or paradigm shift seems to be able to override the previous. This chapter looks through the fad, hype, or paradigm shift statements and describes the principles of the agile and lean approaches to the software development. Then it introduces the service orientation that is expected to be the next major shift. If it will overshadow the agile and lean excitement in the software industry, is discussed at the end of the chapter. In addition, this chapter looks into the past in order to find a continuum between these topics till today and to the future. Further some chasms in this continuum are identified, where a new idea has made a major shift and consequently has become a major force in the field. The service orientation in the software development is in the early phase of its lifecycle. The question is: will it still go through some chasm until it settles for large use, or is it already through all of adaptations and ready to be the next wave of evolution, or the next fad, hype and paradigm shift in software industry? The last part of this chapter proposes one more adaptation that creates continuum from the agile and lean approaches but brings up also the revitalization of architecting and design methodologies.

Chapter 2

Andreas Metzger, Paluno (The Ruhr Institute for Software Technology), University of Duisburg-Essen, Germany

Elisabetta Di Nitto, Politecnico di Milano, Italy

This chapter sets out to introduce relevant foundations concerning evolution and adaptation of service-oriented systems. It starts by sketching the historical development of software systems from monolithic and mostly static applications to highly-dynamic, service-oriented systems. Then, it provides an overview and more thorough explanation of the various kinds of changes that may need to be faced by service-oriented systems. To understand how such changes could be addressed, the chapter introduces a reference service life-cycle model which distinguishes between evolution, viz. the manual modification of the specification and implementation of the system during design-time, and (self-)adaptation, viz. the autonomous modification of a service-oriented system during operation. Based on the discussion of the key activities prescribed by that life-cycle, the chapter elaborates on the need for agility in both adaptation and evolution of service-oriented systems.

Section 2
Theory

Chapter 3

Abhishek Sharma, University of Calgary, Canada

Frank Maurer, University of Calgary, Canada

This chapter presents the results of a systematic review from existing literature in software engineering for cloud-based applications and describes what the research community thinks about the effects of introducing cloud computing into a software development process. In this systematic review, the authors describe the challenges cloud computing poses for software development. They particularly investigate whether agile methodologies are beneficial or not in developing software that will be deployed in the cloud. In their results, they found that industry practitioners in their blogs and self-reported reviews indicate that agile development and cloud computing goes well together and that further investigation is required to confirm this claim.

Chapter 4

Asif Qumer Gill, University of Sydney, Australia

Deborah Bunker, University of Sydney, Australia

The emergence of Software as a Service (SaaS) has made it possible to develop dynamic and complex business processes as eServices. The development of business processes as eServices (SaaS) can be assisted by the means of adaptive or agile development processes. The development of business processes in terms of SaaS require to perform SaaS requirements engineering (RE), which is an important phase of a software development process for the success of any project. The challenge here is how best to do SaaS RE (e.g. mapping business process to eServices) and select agile development practices for developing business processes in terms of SaaS. In order to address this challenge, an integrated agile RE model for SaaS project development environments is outlined within this chapter. The purpose of the proposed RE model is to aid in iteratively determining SaaS requirements in short iterations as opposed to the "only first and onetime upfront" phase of a development process. Each identified SaaS requirement or a set of requirements for a given iteration is linked to a single or set of specific agile practices for implementation in short iterations. This model can be used as a guideline by organisations wishing to understand the challenging task of mapping business processes to SaaS and its implementation by using agile software development processes or practices.

Chapter 5

Supannika Koolmanojwong, University of Southern California, USA
Barry Boehm, University of Southern California, USA
Jo Ann Lane, University of Southern California, USA

To provide better service to customers and remain competitive in the business environment, a wide variety of ready-to-use software and technologies are available for one to "grab and go" in order to build up software systems at a rapid pace. Currently, a wide variety of Web services are available and ready to use for this purpose. Current software process models also support commercial-off-the-shelf (COTS)-based development processes. However, although COTS and Web Services are similar, they are different in many perspectives. On one hand, there are various software process models that support Web services development. Yet there is no process model that supports the project that uses services provided by others. This chapter introduces the Incremental Commitment Spiral Model (ICSM), a new generation process model that provides development guidelines, from exploring a Web service alternative to deployment and maintenance with case studies.

Chapter 6

Laura Zavala, Medgar Evers College of the City University of New York, USA
Benito Mendoza, New York City College of Technology, USA
Michael N. Huhns, University of South Carolina, USA

Although the areas of Service-Oriented Computing (SOC) and Agile and Lean Software Development (LSD) have been evolving separately in the last few years, they share several commonalities. Both are intended to exploit reusability and exhibit adaptability. SOC in particular aims to facilitate the widespread and diverse use of small, loosely coupled units of functionality, called services. Such services have a decided agility advantage, because they allow for changing a service provider at runtime without affecting any of a group of diverse and possibly anonymous consumers. Moreover, they can be composed at both development-time and run-time to produce new functionalities. Automatic service discovery and selection are key aspects for composing services dynamically. Current approaches attempting to automate discovery and selection make use of only structural and functional aspects of the services, and in many situations, this does not suffice to discriminate between functionally similar but disparate services. Service behavior is difficult to specify prior to service execution and instead is better described based on experience with the execution of the service. In this chapter, the authors present a behavioral approach to service selection and runtime adaptation that, inspired by agile software development techniques, is based on behavioral queries specified as test cases. Behavior is evaluated through the analysis of execution values of functional and non-functional parameters. In addition to behavioral selection, the authors' approach allows for real-time evaluation of non-functional quality-of-service parameters, such as response time, availability, and latency.

In agile software development, it is imperative for stakeholders such as the users and developers of an information system to collaborate in designing and developing the information system, by sharing their knowledge. Especially in development of a large-scale information system, such collaboration among stakeholders is important, but difficult to achieve. This chapter introduces a modeling method of business processes for requirements analysis and a development framework based on Web-process architectures. The modeling method makes it easier for stakeholders to agree upon requirements. It also employs a formal method to allow business process models to satisfy both understandability and accuracy. On the other hand, the development framework above enables rapid spiral development of short-term cycles through the collaboration of developers and users. This chapter also introduces an example that compares the workloads of two requirement analyses of large-scale system developments for a government service and a financial accounting service, in order to evaluate the advantages of the proposed modeling method.

The discipline of service science encourages the need to develop alternative and more scientific approaches to conceptualise modern service network environments. This chapter identifies the opportunity to apply organisational network analysis (ONA) as a novel approach to model agile service interaction. ONA also supports the visualisation of a service infrastructure which sustains agile practice. The objective of this chapter is to demonstrate how the concept of agile service network (ASN) may be examined through an unconventional method to model service operations. ONA demonstrates the exchange of resources and competencies through an ASN infrastructure. Ultimately, this chapter provides a platform to develop an audit framework with associated metrics borrowed from ONA. ONA concepts offer a new analytical approach towards ASN (for example, structural, composition, behavioural, and functional). This has a significant theoretical contribution for software engineering performance.

Chapter 9

The effective provision of security in an agile development requires a new approach: traditional security practices are bound to equally traditional development methods. However, there are concerns that security is difficult to build incrementally, and can prove prohibitively expensive to refactor. This chapter describes how to grow security, organically, within an agile project, by using an incremental security architecture that evolves with the code. The architecture provides an essential bridge between system-wide security properties and implementation mechanisms, a focus for understanding security in the project, and a trigger for security refactoring. The chapter also describes criteria that allow implementers to recognize when refactoring is needed, and a concrete example that contrasts incremental and "top-down" architectures.

Sam Chung, Institute of Technology, University of Washington, USA

Conrado Crompton, Institute of Technology, University of Washington, USA

Yan Bai, Institute of Technology, University of Washington, USA

Barbara Endicott-Popovsky, University of Washington, USA

Seung-Ho Baeg, Korea Institute of Industrial Technology, Korea

Sangdeok Park, Korea Institute of Industrial Technology, Korea

This chapter explores using service-oriented computing to reengineer non-secure legacy software applications to create new secure target applications. Two objectives of this chapter are: 1) to analyze the
architectural changes required in order to adopt new web technologies and cope with resultant vulnerabilities in source code; and 2) to measure the level of effort required to modernize software by adopting
new web technologies and adding security countermeasures. To meet these objectives, a model-driven
Scrum for Service-Oriented Software Reengineering (mScrum4SOSR) methodology was chosen and
applied to a reengineering project. Scrum is employed to manage the reengineering project, as well as
to measure implementation effort related to the modernization process. Further, a re-documentation
technique called 5W1H Re-Doc is used to re-document the non-secure software application at a high
level of abstraction in order to help project participants comprehend what is needed to identify candidate
services for service-oriented reengineering. Case studies with and without security features are created
for different types of applications - a desktop graphical user interface, a web application, a web services
application, a restful web services application, and an enterprise service bus application.

Nuno Laranjeiro, Universidade de Coimbra, Portugal

Marco Vieira, Universidade de Coimbra, Portugal

Web services are increasingly being used in business critical environments as a mean to provide a service
or integrate distinct software services. Research indicates that, in many cases, services are deployed with
robustness issues (i.e., displaying unexpected behaviors when in presence of invalid input conditions).
Recently, Test-Driven Development (TDD) emerged as software development technique based on test
cases that are defined before development, as a way to validate functionalities. However, programmers
typically disregard the verification of limit conditions, such as the ones targeted by robustness testing.
Moreover, in TDD, tests are created before developing the functionality, conflicting with the typical
robustness testing approach. This chapter discusses the integration of robustness testing in TDD for improving the robustness of web services during development. The authors requested three programmers
to create a set of services based on open-source code and to implement different versions of the services
specified by TPC-App, using both TDD and the approach presented in this chapter. Results indicate that
TDD with robustness testing is an effective way to create more robust services.

Chapter 12

Michael Felderer, University of Innsbruck, Austria
Philipp Zech, University of Innsbruck, Austria
Ruth Breu, University of Innsbruck, Austria

In this chapter, the authors present an agile and model-driven system testing methodology for service-centric systems called Telling TestStories. The methodology has a tool implementation and is based on separated system, requirements, and test models that can be validated in an integrated way. Test models contain test stories describing test behavior and test data in an integrated way. The underlying testing process is iterative, incremental, and supports a test-driven design on the model level. After a general overview of the artifacts and the testing process, the authors employ the methodology and the tool implementation on a case study from the healthcare domain.

Section 3
Practice

Chapter 13

Paul Shannon, 7digital Ltd, UK
Neil Kidd, Codeweavers Ltd, UK
Paul Barrett, Codeweavers Ltd, UK
Chris Knight, Codeweavers Ltd, UK
Sam Wessel, Esendex Ltd, UK

Following a successful adoption of lean and agile practices, the development team at Codeweavers Ltd has furthered its approach to service-oriented software development for the motor finance and insurance industry. Through iteratively inspecting and adapting their processes over the last twelve months, the team members have seen a change from their Kanban-style single piece flow to multiple work cells developing with separate swim lanes on a work in progress board and within fixed length iterations. The arrival of strong competition to their market led to a positive shift towards customer service and interaction with increased attention on lean planning and agility. This chapter reports on improvement in software craftsmanship with a focus on quality, largely achieved by the use of service-oriented architecture, combined with increased use of mocking for unit-testing. The perspective taken is from software team members, and in the chapter, the developers chart their own observations, improvements, and failures over the course of a year.

Chapter 14

David Parsons, Massey University, New Zealand
Manfred Lange, EFI, New Zealand

A number of questions have been raised by both practitioners and researchers regarding the compatibility of service oriented architectures and agile methods. These are compounded when both approaches are combined to maintain and migrate legacy systems. In particular, where test driven development is practiced as a core component of an agile development process, both legacy systems and service oriented architectures can present an incongruous set of development challenges. In this chapter, the authors provide experience reports on how legacy systems have been adapted to an agile, test driven development context by a process of decomposition into testable services. They describe two domains and technology contexts where automated agile testing at multiple interface layers has improved both quality of service and functionality.

Foreword

The Agile Manifesto, published in 2001, has been a significant milestone for the agile software movement. Individuals and interactions, working software, customer collaboration, and responding to change are the core values that have also demarcated the main directions for agile practice and research in the last decade. Recently, resurrected and claimed to be the next wave of software process, the lean approach in software development adds a new dimension to the agile methods family.

A similar manifesto exists for Service Oriented Architecture (SOA). Created in 2009, the SOA Manifesto is a set of objectives and guiding principles for a clear vision of SOA and service-orientation. The format of the manifesto resembles that of the Agile Manifesto. But this is not the only similarity between the two. Business value, strategic goals, flexibility, and evolutionary refinement are prioritized items in the SOA Manifesto which match those declared in the Agile one, resonantly and consistently.

Intriguing questions one may ask include: What happens when service orientation is used in an agile software development environment? Will we get the full potential of both worlds? If you ponder over the same questions, you should keep on reading this book. The book casts light on the overlapping area of the agile/lean approaches and service oriented development, and highlights potential synergy from the combination of both phenomena. New issues, new challenges, and new research directions have been investigated, and interesting initial outcomes are presented. I believe that the book is one of the first systematic and comprehensive endeavors to generate the useful synergy of both fields. Therefore, it offers particular value to researchers and practitioners who want to explore this intriguing avenue in more depth. It will be a roadmap to attract more researchers and university students to research and study in this area, and allow practitioners to learn from valuable previous experiences.

Pekka Abrahamsson
Free University of Bozen/Bolzano, Italy
July 30, 2012

Pekka Abrahamsson *is a full professor of computer science at Free University of Bozen-Bolzano in Italy. He is currently the academic coordinator of a large research program called Cloud Software (www.cloudsoftwareprogramme.org). This 60MEUR program enables companies to combine cloud technologies with lean software processes and new business models. One of his previous research projects, Agile Software Development of Embedded Systems, was awarded the outstanding industrial impact award in 2007 by ITEA. Pekka also received the Nokia Foundation Award that year. He is a member of IEEE, ACM, and ISERN. His practical experience involves five years in the software industry as a software developer and a quality manager. He is one of the IEEE Software advisory board members.*

Preface

The book "Agile and Lean Service-Oriented Development: Foundations, Theory, and Practice" is a collection of original research studies and experience reports covering a cross-section of software engineering issues: firstly, agile and lean software development methods and secondly, service oriented computing. Typical topics in this cross-sectional area seek to exploit the synergy that can be generated from combining knowledge from both fields. These topics include organizational adoption of agile/lean software development for service oriented development, test-driven service oriented systems, service oriented architectures driven by agile/lean principles, evolving requirements in service oriented systems, refactoring of service oriented systems, migration to service oriented systems using agile approaches, and agile/lean cloud computing. The book offers insights into the issues, challenges, patterns, and solutions for agile and lean service-oriented development, on the basis of rigorous scientific research, sound empirical evidence, and industrial experiences and lessons learnt. It will be of broad interest to agile and service research communities and practitioners alike.

WHEN AGILE AND LEAN METHODS MEET SERVICE-ORIENTATION

Modern software development projects are enacted in increasingly turbulent business environments typified by unpredictable markets, changing customer requirements, pressures of ever shorter time-to-deliver, and rapidly advancing information technologies. Two notable approaches developed in recent years - service oriented computing and agile and lean software development - present promising approaches for contemporary software development projects to deal effectively with these challenges.

Service Oriented Engineering (SOE) is an emerging software development paradigm that copes with today's organization requirements, such as shorter time to market, continuous change of business partners, integration of information systems within the organization and across organisational boundaries, distributed business and computing, and agility. Service oriented computing standards, architectures, principles and technologies are used to build applications that are currently found on the web, or mobile devices. New programming models have emerged based on service oriented principles such as cloud computing. The development of information systems based on service oriented computing suggests changes to traditional software engineering. It holds the promise of open, distributed, dynamic and adaptable systems that provide business solutions based on concepts such as loose coupling, integration and reusability.

Agile methods are a family of software development methods promoted through the Agile Manifesto, which specifies a set of agile values and principles. Agility itself is defined as "the ability to create and respond to change." Communities have formed around specific development methods, such as Scrum and eXtreme Programming (XP). Lean software development is claimed as "the next wave of software process." An increasing number of software organisations and IT departments have been adopting or are planning to adopt lean thinking and lean techniques. The agile and lean software development movement challenges the values that were held dear in conventional development methods, such as detailed upfront plans, precise prediction and rigid control strategies, preferring to emphasise the frequent delivery of working software, collaboration and communication, and the importance of people over process.

Research and practice in SOE and agile and lean methods areas have been advanced independently over the past several years. It is intriguing to explore the potential synergy that comes from a combination of both areas. For example, some may argue that SOE is based on design and architecture principles that cannot be matched with agile software development. However, as distinct as they seem to be, SOE and agile methods may have a lot in common and can inform each other. For example, agility is one of the key attributes of service oriented computing, and agile research and practice can shed light on how to achieve agility in service oriented development. Vice versa, research and practice conducted on service oriented architecture may provide valuable guidelines for agile teams to build truly agile systems that are easy to modify or extend to accommodate frequent change requests. This book is one of the first major attempts to explore this intriguing and promising cross-sectional area.

OBJECTIVES

The mission of the book is to provide a roadmap for advancing the research and practice of software engineering through the potential provided by the combination of service oriented engineering and agile and lean methods. The overall objectives of this book are: (1) to explore the foundations on which service oriented engineering and agile and lean software development can be combined; (2) to build the conceptual basis and empirical evidences for the combination of the two approaches; and (3) to provide tools, best practices and guidelines for agile and lean service oriented development in practice.

CONTRIBUTION

There is an increasing interest in investigating the values and venues of combing service orientated computing and agile and lean methods. However, very few publications have addressed this potential, and even less publications have done it in a comprehensive and systematic manner. Most of the available sources that leverage these two areas are anecdotal in nature, e.g., personal blogs. We believe that our book is a valuable contribution to the body of knowledge of both service oriented engineering and agile and lean development. It can help in establishing foundations for the combination of the two and point out directions for future software engineering research and practice.

The book advances theory by considering the intersection of agile and lean development methods and service oriented engineering. In particular it contributes to a better understanding of how adopting agile software development techniques, methodologies and practices can affect service oriented engineering and organizations that are migrating their systems into service based ones or developing them.

It also constitutes a contribution to practice. Senior IT managers who are responsible for application development and the IT infrastructure need to be aware of the potential for synergy and conflict of agile/lean and SOE. Project managers who are involved in agile development in a context of service oriented architecture will find frameworks and lessons from practice that will be valuable in understanding the architectural implications of the closer relationship between development methods and IT infrastructure. Software developers will also find this book helpful; those with an understanding of agile and SOE and how they can work together to achieve more effective business outcomes will likely be in great demand in the future.

AUDIENCE

The intended audience of the book is first of all researchers from either software engineering or information systems disciplines whose research interests lie in agile and lean methods, service computing/ service science, or both. The book will provide them with a roadmap for researching on these topics and equip them with necessary theoretical devices to conduct their studies. Secondly, software development practitioners who want to explore the potential of both agile and lean methods and service oriented computing may also find this book useful. The book will provide them with informed understanding and solutions of how to get the best out of the two worlds. Lastly, the book can also be useful for university students who specialise in software engineering or information systems. It will help them to obtain up-to-date and in-depth knowledge on agile and lean methods, service computing/service science and the overlap of the two areas.

CONTENT

The chapters of the book are divided into three sections.

Section 1: Foundations

This section has two invited introduction chapters that lay the foundation for the book and for the audience. The first chapter mainly focuses on agile and lean software development, examining the history of the agile movement as well as providing basic concepts. It touches briefly on service orientation. The second chapter takes service orientation as its primary subject, introducing relevant foundations concerning evolution and adaptation of service-oriented systems. It concludes by highlighting the need for agility in both adaptation and evolution of service-oriented systems.

Section 2: Theory

This is the main and largest section and contains ten chapters based on original research work. The topics of these chapters cover diverse, yet inter-related topics, which can be grouped into the following themes: (1) service oriented software processes (Chapter 3, 4, and 5), focusing on how agile practices are used to build service based applications; (2) agile software development and service compositions (Chapter 6, 7, and 8), describing how agile software development techniques enable service compositions and vice versa; (3) security architectural styles and agile development (Chapter 9 and 10), presenting how agile and lean approaches can benefit software architectures of secure service based applications; and

(4) testing services (Chapter 11 and 12), discussing how agile practices can be applied in service testing. The research methods used to produce the scientific results reported in these chapters range from systematic literature review, case study, and experiment to design research. Together they present the state-of-the-art of research in the cross-sectional area of agile and lean service development.

Section 3: Practice

As the section title suggests, the two chapters in this section focus more on real world experiences of agile and lean service oriented development. While Chapter 13 is a detailed and vivid recount of the agile and lean service development journey of a software development team, Chapter 14 adopts a more methodological stance reporting the experiences of test-driven decomposition of legacy systems into services. Both chapters provide valuable lessons learnt from the trenches in an easily digestible manner for practitioners.

In summary, the chapters contained in the book collectively provide a comprehensive understanding of the agile and lean service development area from different perspectives. They not only represent the knowledge of today, but also highlight the significant and promising topics that need further scientific and practical endeavours from both research communities and software practitioners.

Xiaofeng Wang
Free University of Bozen/Bolzano, Italy

Nour Ali
Lero, the Irish Software Engineering Research Centre, Ireland

Isidro Ramos
Universidad Politécnica de Valencia, Spain

Richard Vidgen
Hull University Business School, UK

Section 1
Foundations

Chapter 1
Agile, Lean, and Service-Oriented Development, Continuum, or Chasm

Juha Rikkilä
Studios 4 Future Software (S4FS), Free University of Bozen-Bolzano, Italy

ABSTRACT

A fad, hype, and a paradigm shift are often the words that are used about the agile, lean, and now also about service-oriented development. What starts as a step in evolution, grows into a mass movement in Internet and social media, and results in an avalanche of books, training, and consultancy services. Each proponent tries to differentiate from others with extreme statements of own superiority and blames of others' shortcomings. Only a next fad, hype, or paradigm shift seems to be able to override the previous. This chapter looks through the fad, hype, or paradigm shift statements and describes the principles of the agile and lean approaches to the software development. Then it introduces the service orientation that is expected to be the next major shift. If it will overshadow the agile and lean excitement in the software industry, is discussed at the end of the chapter. In addition, this chapter looks into the past in order to find a continuum between these topics till today and to the future. Further some chasms in this continuum are identified, where a new idea has made a major shift and consequently has become a major force in the field. The service orientation in the software development is in the early phase of its lifecycle. The question is: will it still go through some chasm until it settles for large use, or is it already through all of adaptations and ready to be the next wave of evolution, or the next fad, hype and paradigm shift in software industry? The last part of this chapter proposes one more adaptation that creates continuum from the agile and lean approaches but brings up also the revitalization of architecting and design methodologies.

DOI: 10.4018/978-1-4666-2503-7.ch001

INTRODUCTION

This first chapter of the book introduces the agile, lean and service-oriented approaches, and links them backwards into the history of the software development. This looking backwards enables readers to see how much of new thinking each evolutionary step contains and what radical shifts they introduce. And also see through the inevitable fad[1] and hype[2] that is included in the discussion of the new and exiting things. Further this introduction helps the reader to assess the real existence and size of the possible paradigm shifts[3] in this evolution. Understanding the technology adoption life cycle[4] and the position on it of each of the approaches presented here gives basis to assess the stability or expected change of each.

However, the software engineering is not so much in the domain of natural science than it is on that of the social sciences (Runeson & Höst, 2009). This means that though many technology and engineering characteristics are applicable in technology adoption discussion, the overall view is that of social sciences. So a definite analysis of all aspects of agile, lean and service orientation cannot be done in technical terms and one single truth of the best or most feasible cannot be determined. Instead, multi paradigm nature of social science suggests that several paradigms or patterns can be found and have applicability in any defined scope (Bryman, 2000).

This chapter is ordered according to timeline where evolution of the agile approach sets the milestones, see Figure. 1. However, as the study of the past indicates more evolution than revolution the milestones are not accurate. Though there are also some exact occasions, like the publishing of the agile manifesto or the book of the lean principles in manufacturing, they are not considered sufficient to characterize the life cycle of these approaches. Yet, they do have significant impact in the promotion of these approaches. Timelines are, by definition, always to some extent subjective. The exact dates of the events cannot be determined from the literature and the interpretations of dependences between different events and evolutionary paths may be differently viewed depending of the viewpoint. In this chapter, the proposed timeline is predominantly based on works of Larman and Basili (2003) and the author's experience in the industry since the 1970's, first in a multinational computer manufacturer and supplier, and later on in a multinational telecom vendor.

The timeline specifies the pre-agile, the agile, and the post-agile eras. The beginning of the pre-agile era is in the time when the first computers appeared and the first programs were made. The first period of the era, the early age of computers, is characterized by the batch computing, and writing of single programs. That lasted till 1970's. The second period of the pre-agile era is called Evo-IID since the debate of the evolutionary (Gilb,

Figure 1. The timeline of the agile evolution

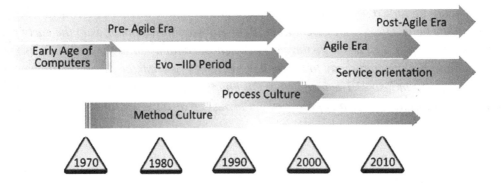

1989), and the incremental and iterative development (Larman & Basili, 2003) was the topic in the discussion about the software development and management. Particularly, it was also the basis on which the agile approach was growing. Overall, the fast growth in all aspects of computing was characteristics to this period. That is, the number of the computers increased swiftly, the size of the computers, systems and software grew fast, and the complexity of all of them increased due to the use of real time, continuously on-line integrated systems becoming dominant. The pre-agile era was turning to the end with the ending of the 1990's.

The 1990's saw also the start of the evolution of the methodologies that later became the center-pieces of the agile approach. These methodologies include XP (Beck, 2000), FDD (Coad, Lefebvre, De Luca, 1999; Palmer & Felsing, 2002) and Scrum (Schwaber, 1996; Schwaber & Beedle, 2002), just to name a few. A more comprehensive discussion is presented in the following pages. The agile era, as discussed in this paper, started at that time. Often the agile era is defined to have started with the formation of the Agile Alliance (http://www.AgileAlliance.org/) and their publication of the Agile Manifesto (http://www.agilemanifesto.org/) in February 2001, which also introduced the word agile into use in the software development. However, in this paper that is considered to be a part of the chasm in the life cycle of the agile approach, which aligned the previously separate light weight development approaches under one concept, and pushed them into the area of early adopters.

The end of the agile era is not visible yet. Though there have been statements about the end of agile, e.g. (Abrahamsson, 2008), we see it premature at this stage to declare the end of the agile era. On the contrary, there are substantial evidence of growing adoption of agile approach and practices. Forrester's latest reports indicate growth. In 2010 Forrester report (West & Grant, 2010) indicated 35% of organizations using agile,

in November 8, 2011, in Forrester blog (Grant, 2012) reported "Today, Forrester's data shows approximately 38% of developers have adopted Agile across a wide range of industries". Another similar trend can be found in the research done by Amber (2012). Thomas (2012) in his blog considered the agile practices being in the final phases on the hype curve, on the plateau of productivity. Also Project Management Institute (PMI, 2012) have started to certify the agile practitioners. So what can be said is that the agile approach has reached the early maturity, and at least some of the late majority if not the laggards. However, at the same time a report (West, 2011) indicates that many of these adoptions are far from a real agile implementation. There is no one methodology that would be the correct agile way but several exist, as can be seen from the list by the Agile Alliance. Will this diversity continue or will there be some or one approach to dominate the agile era in the future? Or will there be new concepts emerging and turning the agile era to the end? The service-oriented approach seems to have potential to do so.

In this chapter we present the hypothesis that the service orientation will be the core of the post agile era, and it has already started to emerge. But as said already above, the milestones are not distinct, so it is expected that the service orientation will grow to its maturity like the agile approach did over the many years. The service science (Alter, 2009; Spohrer & Kwan 2009), the service-dominant logic (Vargo & Lusch 2008), the service-oriented architecture (SOA) (Lankhorst & van Drunen, 2007; Bianco, Lewis, Merson & Simanta, 2011), the service-oriented application development (Chen, Kazman & Perry, 2010) are all having a growing impact to the software development. As a whole it is in the intersection of engineering, management and social sciences (Larson, 2008) and ties them closely to each other.

For the development of service-oriented software systems several different views exist. Lane and Richardson (2011) and Ramollari, Dranidis and Simons (2012) studied several design driven development models and they indicate just a minor role for agile approach. On the other hand, for example Lee, Chan and Lee (2006) and Shahrbanoo (2012) point out work done for Agile SOA development. Overall the customer centric and incremental principles of the service orientation seem to align well with the agile approach, but the actual role of the agile software development is still under debate. When the service orientation has now done a strong entrance to the software industry, it remains to be seen if it will be the next fad, hype, and paradigm shift is the software development. And what sort and size of an impact it will have on agile and lean approaches.

PRE-AGILE ERA

This chapter reviews the pre-agile era from the two views. First a timeline is presented based on the computer technology in use and the nature of the software development during it. The early age of computers were the time when the sequential computing was the dominant way of processing data. That period then turned to what is here called the Evo-IID period. That name is used in this chapter in order to emphasize the evolution of the development practices before the agile era, those of evolutionary, and incremental and iterative development methods. This naming of the period does not claim that those methods were dominant during the period, but makes referring to this period more convenient.

The second view is that of the process and engineering cultures. The word culture is used here in the meaning of "the set of shared attitudes, values, goals, and practices that characterizes an institution, organization, or group" (Wikipedia, 2012). The process culture refers to people in software organizations whose main interest is in the work steps and the work results, and managing those steps and results. The engineering culture refers to those whose main inters are in the software engineering methodologies and the ways of

doing tasks, and using methods, techniques and tools for doing them. Iivari, Hirschheim and Klein (1998) specifies methodology as "an organized collection of concepts, methods, beliefs, values and normative principles supported by material resources", and "a technique or method, in this context, consists of a well-defined sequence of elementary operations which permits the achievement of certain outcomes if executed correctly". Further, making distinction between the method and the technique is based on the definition in Oxford dictionaries (2012), where the method is defined as "a particular procedure for accomplishing or approaching something, especially a systematic or established one: the quality of being well organized and systematic in thought or action". The technique is specified as "a way of carrying out a particular task, especially the execution or performance of ... a scientific procedure". Particularly, the definition of the method contains an element of though allowing several interpretations of a topic, whereas the technique is more execution of a procedure in one and correct manner. In the following text the process culture contains management methodologies, methods, techniques and tools, and the engineering culture contains engineering methodologies, methods, techniques and tools.

The Early Age of Computers

The early age of computers, when viewed from the software development point of view can be characterized as technology being unreliable, software of limited size, processing in sequential batch mode, and software engineering as writing programs for straightforward processing of data. The focus of the software development was in the engineering. During 1970s' a large number of methodologies were published. The structured programming was based on the principle of top-down design (Wirth, 1971; Mills, 1971; Dahl, Dijkstra and Hoare, 1972; Parnas, 1972; Stevens, Myers and Constantine, 1974; Myers 1975; Yordon &

Constantine, 1975). These were largely program-focused methodologies, but similar system design methodologies were made available as well, which included means to design user tasks. ISDOS was developed in the university of Michigan, and SADT in the company called Softech. Also the ISDS/HOS methodology (Hamilton & Zeldin, 1976) was published. They all were based on the principle of reducing large problems into smaller problems, solving the small, and then build them up as the solution of the large problem. In addition to this Warnier (1974) and Jackson (1975) presented their different approaches to the program design. Logical construction of programs (LCP) and Jackson Structured Programming (JSP) were based on the analysis of the input and output data and nearly algorithmic construction of programs.

Overall, during the 1970's the engineering methodologies became very popular, if not a hype of that time. However, the human factors in the software development got attention as well. IBM was applying the chief programmer team approach (Baker, 1972). Brooks (1975) wrote the book "Mythical Man Month" which became so popular that 1995 an anniversary print of the book was taken. Further, in a research by Ramsey, Atwood and Campbell (1979) "several major human factors deficiencies and problems were identified. Formal software design methods differ in terms of: Applicability to problems of different types, size or complexity; susceptibility to design errors; and constraints and limitations imposed on the software designer. Various methods limit the designer's ability to select an appropriate problem representation, prevent the designer from utilizing relevant knowledge and experience, or impose potentially significant information loads on the designer." One of their recommendations was to consider different type of methods for different type of problems.

The process culture focused on the application of the project management to the software development. Many of the tools for the project management were already available, like the PERT charts and the critical path method, the Gantt charts, and the work break down structures. So the large projects started to apply them in practice. In 1970 Royce (1970) wrote about management of the software development, which is often interpreted as the basis of the waterfall model. The other influential document was the military standard DOD-STD-2167 published on the 4th June 1985, and its more referred update DOD-STD-2167A (DOD 1988) from 29th of February 1988. They were designed to guide the development of the US defense area projects, but were adopted by many other companies as well. When the more advanced real time systems were emerging the projects got more complex, too. The trailblazers were the military organizations that were several years ahead of the business organizations. The software development was closely integrated with the development of the hardware that was on the latest edge of innovation. There were significant controversy between the very settled project approach described in these standards and projects that progressed in interactive and incremental manner via experimentation (Larman & Basili, 2003). Contractually projects followed the standard process, but several successful cases of IID were also reported.

These successes of the IID did not, however, lead to an avalanche of it in the software development. On the contrary, many military area projects and most of the civil business area projects ended up using the waterfall model. That is, in the strict order (1) specify the scope, (2) approve the scope, (3) sign the specification project, (4) define the detailed content, (5) define the detailed project plan with resource, cost and time, (6) sign the project contract, (7) execute the project contract, (8) approve the project results, and (9) conclude the contract. This description of steps deviates the more commonly presented steps: define, design, implement, test, commission by brining in the decision and contract management points. It is not possible to firmly indicate that the ease of the business decisions and the accustoms to the traditional project management practices would have overridden the technical experience but clearly the waterfall model has been more appealing to the business management than the software development staff, from very early on. The waterfall model became the dominant approach for developing software.

In summary, the 1970's could be called a period of ordered work by disciplined people. The ordered work means doing the defined engineering tasks using the defined engineering methods, techniques, and tools. The disciplined people means executing the work in the planned and controlled manner. This is not the whole picture though. In several occasions and forums the evolutionary and incremental and iterative principles and practices were presented (Larman & Basili, 2003). It was the battle of which one is right, not of which is applicable to what.

The Evo-IID Period

The Evo-IID period was characterized with the growth of size and complexity of the systems to be built. Particularly the US defense industry was facing the challenge. The path taken to solve this problem led to ever-increasing process and management discipline that culminated in the process maturity culture. Particularly the 1990's were heavily process centric. The process maturity and models like CMM (Paulk, Curtis, Chrissis and Weber, 1993a, 1993b) and Spice or ISO15504 (ISO/IEC, 1997) were overly popular. All software organizations felt the pressure to the maturity driven process improvement (Haley, 1996; Clark, 1999; Li, Chen & Lee 2002). Models for smaller companies were developed as well (Coleman & Verbruggen 1998). The second corner stone was the project management models, the most notable reference being the Project Management Body of Knowledge (PMBOK) by Project Management Institute (PMI 1994, 1996, 1999, 2004, 2008).

The third set of processes can be found in the product line/family management (SEI/SPL, 2012; ESI/SFE, 2012) models. They extend the two previously mentioned models to cover the management of the whole product development organization. The fourth cornerstone of the process centricity is the IT infrastructure Library (ITIL, 2012) by the Office of Government Commerce (OGC), UK which has widely spread outside UK, and influenced on other standards as well. It is similar to the product line models but covers the management of the organizations internal IT infrastructure investments. Continuous assessment and improvement of processes are a part of all of these models.

Some doubts have been presented if the desire to have the maturity of processes was exceeding the capability of organizations to actually achieve them (OConnell & Saiedian, 2000). Having all processes defined was becoming more important than having them fully operational and beneficial. It is often said that the agile avalanche was the counter reaction to this stiffening process culture that the agile approach was born to cure the process paralysis (Biske, 2006; Whitten, 2008).

However, the Evo-IIP period contributed to the agile approach much more than just providing the process culture as a target to shoot at. Many of the core principles of the agile development were promoted already during the 1970's and 1980's, and even more intensively during the 1990s when the process culture was on its peak. The pre agile age had indicated the significance of uncertainty and the need for innovation during the development, not just before it. The two hallmark models from that time were the spiral model by Boehm (1986) and the evolutionary development approach defined by Gilb (1989). On top of these two, the overall list of prominent names contributing to the incremental and iterative development is long (Larman & Basili, 2003). In addition, many successes are pointed out in their article, some in very large projects.

The next step paving the agile path was the boom of Rapid Application Development (RAD), described by many, but most notably in the book by James Martin (Martin, 1991). One list of the characteristics which distinguishes a RAD project from traditional systems development projects at that time, can be found in (Hull, 1995):

- Significant business user involvement.
- The use of 'time boxes' to manage the overall project.
- A rigorously applied methodology.
- The use of automated design and build tools (CASE) to create prototypes.
- A limited number of system developers relative to the number of business users involved in the project, and significantly out of proportion to the scale of the project in business impact terms.
- An almost evangelical zeal, which you can feel within the organization as you walk through the door regarding the use of these techniques. This results in a much higher degree of user involvement than in a traditional development and consequently a RAD project approaches a PC systems development in terms of user involvement.

The RAD approach itself was developed rapidly as well. "As a generalization, we might propose that RAD as a development approach currently lacks a firm underpinning of systematically verified development principles. A substantial amount of practitioner material has been produced on RAD, but little systematic theoretical and empirical assessment of RAD approaches has been undertaken" (Beynon-Davies & Holmes, 1998).

The engineering culture saw the growth of the formal engineering methods, for the requirements specification, for the architecture design, and for the software and program design. Object orientation in the program design brought a major change to the previous procedural software design and coding. They were supported with tools. Modeling and CASE-tools (Computer Aided Software Engineering) were covering the development work from the conception to the code generation and testing. The integrated CASE (ICASE) environments, the integrated project support environments (IPSE) and the like were introduced. RAD and the jointed application development (JAD) (Carmel, Whitaker and George, 1993) were challenging the engineering method development as well, as too heavy. Discussion of the lightweight development led to reduction of the design effort and the use of design methods, and increased use of prototyping (Gottendiener, 1995). The special room as defined for JAD (Carmel et al 1993) was relying more on customers and developers working together than a strong design process.

Summary of the Pre-Agile Era

Characteristic to the Pre-Agile era was the growing number of process models for the management and engineering methods for the development. The principles of the scientific management (Taylor, 1911) were applied on specifying the work accurately, on breaking it into small tasks and on managing the tasks closely. Both the engineering methods and the management processes evolution supported this approach.

At the same time more lightweight (Miller, 2001) approaches were developed and used. Though many were successful (Larman & Basili, 2003) the heavyweight processes dominated. However, the basis for agile avalanche was created and many of the methods and techniques for them became tried in practice.

THE AGILE ERA

In the business and software engineering literature the word agile is more a common adjective and the word agility is more a common noun than the name of an accurately defined set of principles, let alone the name of a methodology with well defend set of methods and techniques. Consequently it is easy to find substantial number of definitions of these terms in different contexts. Kettunen (2009) lists seventeen different definitions for the agility in the business literature from years 1995-2008. Further he points out definitions for the strategic, business, enterprise, organization, workforce, IT, manufacturing and supply chain agility and indicates that there are several definitions of agility in the business specific areas as well.

As a summary those 17 different definitions of agility contain the change or the response to change as a key characteristic. Nearly all of them indicate the customer value or the customer involvement as a key characteristic. High quality is expressed in 5 definitions. Also innovation, effectiveness, high performance, nimbleness, competitive capabilities, profitability, simplicity of practices, dexterity of performance, cost efficiency, quickness, resiliency, robustness, adaptive, and lightness are mentioned in some definitions.

Agility in the software development is no exception to this diversity. Kettunen (2009) lists these:

- Quick delivery, quick adaptations to changes in requirements and surrounding environments (Aoyama, 1998);
- Being effective and maneuverable; Use of light-but-sufficient rules of project behavior and the use of human and communication-oriented rules (Cockburn, 2002);
- Ability to both create and respond to change in order to profit in a turbulent business environment (Highsmith, 2002);
- Ability to expedite (Anderson, 2004);
- Rapid and flexible response to change (Larman, 2004);
- Building software by empowering and trusting people, acknowledging change as a norm, and promoting constant feedback;

producing more valuable functionality faster (Schuh, 2005);
- Discovery and adoption of multiple types of ISD innovations through garnering and utilizing agile sense and respond capabilities (Lyytinen & Rose, 2006);
- Uses feedback to make constant adjustments in a highly collaborative environment (Subramaniam & Hunt, 2006);
- Iterative and incremental (evolutionary) approach to software development which is performed in a highly collaborative manner by self-organizing teams with "just enough" ceremony that produces high quality software in a cost effective and timely manner which meets the changing needs of its stakeholders (Ambler, 2007);
- Capability to accommodate uncertain or changing needs up to a late stage of the development (until the start of the last iterative development cycle of the release) (IEEE, 2007);
- Conceptual framework for software engineering that promotes development iterations throughout the life-cycle of the project Wikipedia (2007);

When the basic terminology offers such variability in definition, it is no wonder that the diversity can be found in understanding of the agile principles as well. The similar variation is also visible in the large number of agile methodologies. In this text agile is a common adjective characterizing any word it is connected with. Agile approach is common name of the agile way of developing software, complying with the agile principles. Agile methodology means some defined and named way of doing agile development, for example XP (Beck, 2000) is called a methodology.

Originally the agile approach in the software development was considered to be a team practice, which is discussed in this chapter first. Then the two dominant ways of expanding the agile approach to cover a wider scope of the software development life cycle in larger organizations are presented.

Agile Software Development

When the agile manifesto was published in 2001 it marked the start of the avalanche of the agile approach in the software development.

We are uncovering better ways of developing software by doing it and helping others do it. Through this work we have come to value:

- Individuals and interactions over processes and tools,
- Working software over comprehensive documentation,
- Customer collaboration over contract negotiation,
- Responding to change over following a "plan." (http://www.agilemanifesto.org/)

The wording of the manifesto indicates a shift of the focus, perhaps even a sharp turn of the practice, compared to then existing structured practices and defined processes. However, it cannot be considered as a declaration of a new philosophy in the software development, but more a shift in the emphasis towards principles already emerged in the pre-agile era. That said, the significance of this declaration has turned out to be industry trembling. It is the shift that a growing number of organizations are eager to follow. The manifesto has become the most referenced description of what agile is.

In the background for manifesto several methodologies were evolving, which with the manifesto were started to call as the agile methodologies. The most often referred ones are those described in the book of Highsmith (2002), Agile software development ecosystem. These are: Scrum (Schwaber, 1996; Schwaber & Beedle, 2002), Dynamic systems development method (DSDM,

1997), Crystal (Cockburn, 2002), Feature driven development (FDD) (Coad et al 1999; Palmer & Felsing, 2002), Lean development (Charette, 2002), Extreme programming (XP) (Beck, 2000), and Adaptive software development (ASD) (Highsmith, 2000). Abrahamsson, Warsta, Siponen and Ronkainen (2003) adds also Agile modeling (AM) (Ambler, 2002), Internet speed development (ISD) (Baskerville & Pries-Heije, 2001), and Pragmatic programming (PP) (Hunt & Thomas, 2000) to the list. All of these have their own application area and unique emphasis in approach.

This diversity has led to need to generate means to put these methodologies onto same continuum. Which created a large number of categorizing factors. Kettunen (2009) lists 11 sources each proposing a different classification criterion. Highsmith (2002) proposes 6 minimum practices that a methodology should contain if called as agile. Abrahamsson et al (2003) proposes additional 6 perspectives to analyze what an agile methodology may contain. Overall, it seems unlikely, that there would be one common view and one common interpretation of what agile software development is and what practices and methods it consists of. On the other hand, this diversity gives every applier the opportunity to compose his own agile methodology fully suited to his needs (Highsmith, 2002).

Agile Promise

The principles behind the Agile Manifesto documents well the initial promise the agile proponents were giving.

- Our highest priority is to satisfy the customer through early and continuous delivery of valuable software.
- Welcome changing requirements, even late in development. Agile processes harness change for the customer's competitive advantage.

- Deliver working software frequently, from a couple of weeks to a couple of months, with a preference to the shorter timescale.
- Business people and developers must work together daily throughout the project.
- Build projects around motivated individuals.
- Give them the environment and support they need, and trust them to get the job done.
- The most efficient and effective method of conveying information to and within a development team is face-to-face conversation.
- Working software is the primary measure of progress.
- Agile processes promote sustainable development. The sponsors, developers, and users should be able to maintain a constant pace indefinitely.
- Continuous attention to technical excellence and good design enhances agility.
- Simplicity--the art of maximizing the amount of work not done--is essential.
- The best architectures, requirements, and designs emerge from self-organizing teams.
- At regular intervals, the team reflects on how to become more effective, then tunes and adjusts its behavior accordingly.

As can be seen in these principles the agile approach is focused in building a co-located team and in seeing the benefits though the eyes of the team. Much of the project management tasks can be reduced to minimum due the co-location, and remaining tasks can be integrated seamlessly to the development work. Agreeing the tasks, reviewing the results, setting and striving for the task goals, solving the rising issues and other such tasks become a part of the teamwork. Similarly, external parties become an integral part or contributors of the team.

It is more difficult to achieve similar benefits in larger organizations (Kettunen, 2009) where the number of people leads to the existence of many teams and the distance between people grow bigger, even global in many occasions. Inevitably the external parties will become more distanced as well. So the agile benefits for larger organizations cannot be expected to be the same or on the same level as for small organizations. Yet the expectations are that an agile organization is responsive to the customer needs, even when the customer has difficulties in deciding on his/her own needs and changes his/her opinion frequently. In large organizations this kind of changes often have the "whip effect", similar to that in a supply chain (Lee, Padmanabhan & Whang, 1997). It creates variance and bottlenecks throughout the development and the delivery process. Keeping focus in tasks that are delivering value to the customer in the customer satisfying manner and removing the rest becomes a major challenge.

The promise of better quality is to be deemed as well (Abbas, 2009). Thought the quality in a team level means improving in a team level that does not build linearly up to better quality in larger organizations. On the contrary, the local quality optimization may lead to deterioration of overall quality due to different understanding of the optimum and conflicting implementations of the quality related practices. Having a large number of people allows the development of larger software, but requires also growing attention to the non-functional characteristics, like reliability, usability, maintainability, and other "ilities". The traditional means for the quality control, like a separate quality organization or quality gates in the process can easily lead to additional effort that may not add value to the customer.

Parallel to obtaining the customer value and the quality benefits there are business stakeholders, like owners, partners, and top management of the organization to be satisfied as well (Power, 2010). In a larger organization their distance grows to customers and also to satisfying the customer needs. Each group defines and focuses on their own interests. It becomes a challenge to achieve the customer-supplier win-win in practice. The effectiveness of an organization from its stakeholder point of view compromises the pure customer value creating interests. Particularly for the product development organizations where the product manager is "a proxy customer" distance to the customer grows bigger than what is stated in the initial agile principles.

The third interest group to satisfy is the developers and the development organization in general (Cockburn & Highsmith, 2001; Melnik & Mauer, 2006). In a large organization they easily drift away from the customers but from the business stakeholders alike. It becomes challenging to foster the customer and business knowledge, the technical and development competence, and the large-scale teamwork in a partial isolation. Consequently the demand for customer co-operation, productive self-organizing teams, growth of essential competences, and the like agile promises are not fulfilled. Yet these are the essential characteristics of an agile software development organization.

In short, the expectations have grown that the agile approach can be transformed from a team level methodology to the working and management practice of a larger organization and still retain the agile benefits. So the model of a small, co-located self-organizing team, consisting of skilled and apt people, working closely together with a customer fulfilling customer changing needs can be mapped to large organization that provides (Highsmith, 2007; Schwaber, 2007):

- Increased customer satisfaction,
- Reduced time-to-market (better "time-to-benefit"),
- Increased quality,
- Improved project portfolio and product management (project types, features),
- Improved product development investment management (control and flexibility),

- Reduced "waste" (increased efficiency, productivity, development cost),
- Better predictability (visibility),
- Better risk management (risk reduction),
- Better workforce morale (developer satisfaction, well-being).

The two main strategies for expansion are (1) inside-out and (2) outside-in. The inside-out strategy means not just expanding from the team level to the management structure but also adjusting to and with the surrounding practices, that is, expanding the agile and agile compliant principles to cover more areas of the software development life cycle as well as to the managing of the software development organization. The outside-in strategy means amalgamating the agile development with the traditional software development and the organization management sustaining both as much as possible.

INSIDE-OUT EXPANSION OF THE AGILE APPROACH

The inside-out expansion strategy keeps the original agile development approach in teams but complements the team practices for the organization wide co-operation. The main effort is put on expanding the agile approach to the other tasks of the software development and to the management. Activities in the whole software development life cycle and in the business management are transformed to be coherent with those in the agile teams. In a way the original agile principles are "kept clean". Cockburn and Highsmith suggested the following list of Methodology Design Principles (Highsmith, 2002):

1. Interactive, face-to-face communication is the cheapest and fasters channel for exchanging information,
2. Larger teams need heavier methodologies,
3. Excess methodology weight is costly,

4. Greater ceremony is appropriate for projects with greater criticality,
5. Discipline is not formality, process is not skill and documentation is not understanding,
6. Increasing feedback and communication reduces the need for intermediate deliverables,
7. Efficiency is expendable in non-bottleneck activities,
8. Think flow, not batch,
9. Greater methodology ceremony may be required to meet regulatory, security, and legal considerations.

These principles are focused in engineering. When the management change has been pursued the lean principles have become a major source for expanding the agile approach.

Heritage from the Lean Thinking

The lean thinking has its roots in Japanese culture (Womack & Jones, 2003). Before it was applied in the software development, it had gone through several interpretations. Each had done a translation, that is, trying to find right words to express the meaning, and a selection, that is, identifying the most suitable parts and ignoring some less suitable. The first interpretation took place when the Japanese tradition of the lean manufacturing was translated into English and for the western world. The source was mainly the Toyota way of manufacturing (Womack, Jones and Ross, 1991). This literature also introduced the term "lean". The difficulty of the translation can be seen in continuous use of the Japanese words in order to sustain the original meaning. The explanation of the original meaning takes often several sentences. In any case a number of words and concepts became a commonplace in the organization development: waste (muda), overburden (muri), unevenness of work (mura), automation with human touch (jidoka), just-in-time production and delivery, pull system (kanban), continuous improvement (kaizen), radical improvement (kaikoku), go-and-

see management (genchi genbutsu), self-reflection (hansei), self-study (jishuken), just to name a few.

Womack and Jones (2003) condensed the lean thinking into five key topics, value, value stream, pull, flow and perfection. The value is the starting point for all in the lean thinking, and the main purpose of any operation. The value is seen strictly from the customer point of view. The value stream is the all actions to create and deliver the value to the customer, and only those actions. All other actions are waste. The lean thinking aims at the optimization of the value steam and the elimination of all waste. That leads to the optimization of the flow, including the optimization of the item- and batch-sizes, minimizing the queues and increasing the throughput. The flow is driven by the pull by the customer, not by the push by the producer. The queuing and the intermediate stocks are minimized. The perfection means the continuous, virtuous circle of improving this all. The transparency and the immediate feedback is the basis for this perfection.

Different interpretations about the lean thinking are common. Also the selection is clearly visible in varying use of these words and interpretations in different context. This can be seen for example in Internet search using words "lean house". The lean house metaphor is often used to consolidate the essence of the lean thinking and the search brings up the many interpretations.

After the first wave in the manufacturing, the second interpretation of the lean principles took place when the context was changed from the manufacturing to the product development (Morgan & Liker, 2006). Table 1 consolidates the principles.

The culture behind the lean product development is the same Japanese culture that was first introduced with the lean in the manufacturing. Summarizing shortly, what has been emphasized in the lean is the focus on the satisfying the customer, the continuous improvement of processes, the continuous competence growth of people, and the use of tools and technology in a human man-

Table 1. The lean principles in the product development (Morgan & Liker, 2006)

The Toyota Product Development System, (Morgan and Liker, 2006)
Process: 1. Establish customer-defined value to separate value-added from waste 2. Front-load the product development process to explore thoroughly alternative solutions while there is maximum design space 3. Create a leveled product development process flow 4. Utilize rigorous standardization to reduce variation, and create flexibility and predictable outcomes **Skilled People:** 5. Develop a chief engineering system to integrate development from start to finish 6. Organize to balance functional expertise and cross-functional integration 7. Develop towering technical competence in all engineers 8. Fully integrate suppliers into the product development system 9. Build in learning and continuous improvement 10. Build a culture to support excellence and relentless improvement **Tools and Technology:** 11. Adapt technology to fit your people and process 12. Align your organization through simple, visual communication 13. Use powerful tools for standardization and organizational learning

ner. This summary does not do justice to the wealth of philosophy behind the lean but serves the purpose of understanding the expansion of agile practices for software development., which is discussed next.

Applications of Lean in the Software Development

The third interpretation has then been done when applying the lean manufacturing and product development principles for the software development. The two main schools of application can be found, one interpreting the lean principles in a comprehensive manner (Poppendieck & Poppendieck, 2003, 2007, 2010; Larman & Vodde, 2008, 2009), the other taking a selective approach (Anderson, 2010; Scotland, 2012).

When the lean principles are transferred to the software development in a comprehensive manner, it is often reduced to the main themes of continuous improvement and respect of people (Larman & Vodde, 2009; Leffingwell, 2009) and having the customer value as the main driver of the work. Using the lean house metaphor Larman and Vodde (2009) and Leffinwell (2009) combine the initial house of lean with product development principles. The two pillars of the house are the

respect of people and the continuous improvement. The value to the customer is the roof and the management practices as the basis. In the house there are the 14 principles from the lean manufacturing and the development practices condensed from the Toyota product development. So they transfer directly the lean principles as they are to the software development.

In another approach developed by Poppendieck and Poppendieck (2007, 2010) the focus was initially on the development practices but then expanded more comprehensively to the whole lean philosophy. Poppendieck and Poppendieck (2003) started applying the lean principles to the agile software development by proving the agile toolkit. That is, they translated the lean practices to be used in the agile software development.

Following this, in their next book Poppendieck and Poppendieck (2007) present more extensive translation of the lean principles. They first described the 7 principles: eliminate waste, build quality in, create knowledge, defer commitment, deliver fast, respect people, and optimize the whole, in software context. Then they translated also the waste in the manufacturing to the software terms as: partially done work, extra features, relearning, handoffs, task switching, delays, and defects and presented their removal. The eliminating the waste means identifying the non-value adding tasks and work results in the value steam and attempts to shorten the timeline by removing such a waste. This requires deep understanding of what the value is in the mind of a customer. Building quality in has the goal in doing the quality work during the development rather than during the testing at the end. It includes also minimizing the rework and partially done work during the process. Create knowledge principle considers the software development as a knowledge-creating process. In practice that means reliance on the practices that develop understanding about the technology and the product during the work, instead of locking the understanding before the work by guesses and anticipations during the planning. Related to it is the principle of deferring commitment that is based on the fact that more is known and less is uncertain later during the process, so the critical decisions are done as late as possible, not in the early planning phase. The deliver fast principle is to deliver and satisfy customers fast and consequently prevent the change. This principle connects closely to the build quality in principle and enables sustaining the high speed. The respect people principle consists of developing the good leaders, the expert technical workforce, and trust on people to enable the self-organization of teams. The principle optimize the whole refers to the whole value stream from receiving an order to addressing the customer need. Serious delays and dissatisfaction are created in the handoffs of responsibility in the process and in the local optimization of task without caring the whole.

In their following work Poppendieck and Poppendieck (2010) took a still more comprehensive view, focusing on the management of the whole software organization. The six main areas were systems thinking, technical excellence, reliable delivery, relentless improvement, great people and aligned leaders. Each of these main areas was then further divided into the four main frames. The word "frame" refers to the cognitive science where the frame means a mental construct through which we see the world. Leading the lean software development is then explained via these twenty-four frames. The style needed for the leadership is constructed piece-by-piece and the traditional management style is overturned in the process.

In a selective approach the Kanban method has become popular (Ladas, 2009; Anderson, 2010; Kniberg & Skarin, 2010; Scotland, 2012), despite of the fact it is presented to be just one of the techniques used in the lean manufacturing. However, when applied to the agile software development it has grown to a full-scale agile methodology. In fact, there are several variations of it, some as stand alone (Anderson, 2010; Scotland, 2012), some as merged with another agile methodology, like Scrumban (Ladas, 2009; Kniberg & Skarin, 2010). Anderson (2010) condenses his Kanban methodology into the six-step recipe:

- Focus on Quality,
- Reduce Work-in-Process,
- Deliver Often,
- Balance Demand against Throughput,
- Prioritize,
- Attack Sources of Variability to Improve Predictability.

It focuses with Kanban but utilizes extensively the principles and methods in the lean thinking, in the other agile approaches like FDD (Coed et al, 1999 Palmer & Felsing, 2002), in the Theory of Constraint (Goldratt, 1999, 2004), in the Product Development Flow (Reinertsen, 2009), as well as in the Complex Adaptive Systems theory (Benbya & McKelvey, 2006; Snowden & Boone, 2007). One could say it is a construction of many of the approaches described earlier in this chapter, but builds them around Kanban.

Scotland (2012) has summarized Kanban from the systems thinking point of view, which he calls Kanban Thinking. He argues that "it takes a mindset of optimizing the whole system, whatever the boundaries of that system are defined to be". So simplifying harshly he takes the system thinking as the basis, uses lean principles as the source and constructs a Kanban driven approach for the agile development. The core concepts of the value, flow and capability of people are in the goals, and studying, sharing, limiting, sensing and learning are the main themes as the means. Then he adds the understanding and dealing with the boundaries and the context as a vital element of achieving the goals.

What is shared characteristic to both Scotland and Anderson, is that they take Kanban as the dominant driver and then build all other into that context. The basic model is simple and straightforward, but there is the wealth of methods and principles to add on, when an applier's capability to use them grows.

Limitations and Contradictions

More often than not the lean and agile approaches are considered to be kin to each other. Using the lean principles and techniques to expand the agile approach and methodologies has been very popular among agile practitioners. The similarity in philosophies looks appealing and many merges have been done. Keeping the combinations true to the agile roots seem to be possible, even when the scope of application within the development life cycle is extended. The customer focus is a driving principle of both. The respect of people and the continuous learning are very visible principles in both as well. Also on practices level combining and selecting most useful ones for each need is a well-established practice in companies now.

However, the harmony between the two is not all-inclusive. When considering the engineering level, the contradiction exists with the engineering practices that traditionally have been done in the early phases of the development. The agile and lean practices push these later into the process and typically also divide them into smaller chucks. These topics include designing solutions for system performance, reliability, and efficiency; creating consistent, high quality user experience

and usability; designing for maintainability and portability; building the security and safety; standardizing interfaces to the external systems and ensuring co-operation with ecosystems; ensuring utilization of common frameworks and patterns in system development and evolution; selecting and developing hardware and firmware parallel with software; and creating overall architecture of the system and keeping it valid over the continuous system evolution during the development and maintenance. Previously with the waterfall approach these were solved before the development started. Many large and agile organizations still do them that way and don't defer decisions.

The other contradiction lies in the continuous improvement, and in the process development and control as part of it. In the agile approach the improvement is based on retrospectives, and the concluding of improvements based on that experience. Retrospectives are done frequently and as a part of the development process. The consideration is based on experience during the last short period of work, and the application of the practices during it. These practices are often informal and continuously changing. Similarly the lean approach emphasizes the continuous improvement. However, it is based on the standardization of the process and minimizing the variation in it. Tools like Six Sigma are often used to analyze and remove the variation. This may conflict with the agile principle of "we value individuals and interactions over processes and tools" when done in traditional manner.

The contradiction is, however, more challenging between the agile and lean management, and the traditional management. That is discussed next.

OUTSIDE-IN ADAPTATION OF THE AGILE APPROACH

Many large organizations have had a different approach to adapting the agile practices into their organizations. When the agile approach is brought into a larger organization, the management expectation is often to adopt an agile methodology as a software development methodology and keep the rest "as-is". Particularly, all the related management functions like the project management, product management, program management, line management, and even the quality management functions would remain the same as previously. This strategy has turned out to be controversial. The Internet search with words "agile transformation" gives plenty of hits. There are a large number of cases about transformation in teams and on developer level. There is also plenty of material about requirements to the organization management to accommodate an agile and lean change. There is even services for management to lead such an change. But it is hard to find any material about how to manage an agile and lean software organization in the agile and lean manner. What is the transformation in the management practice that needs to take place, in order to have the whole organization and all of its levels as agile and lean? Due to lack of such a material the author uses his personal experience in the domain and presents claims based on empirical observations in practice. Further research is needed to validate these claims in other case studies.

Project Management

The project management has been the dominant way of organizing the work and committing resources for tasks in the software development. A very substantial body of knowledge has been accumulated of this discipline and it is widely used both in product development and custom application development. It has become an essential part of the management structure and the main means to align development work to company goals. The hierarchical line of management is well defined and understood.

A typical project is preceded by defining the content of the desired end results, planning of the sequence of tasks to produce those end results, and allocating resources to those tasks. Each of these gets the management approval via the line management actions. After all necessary approvals the execution is started. The work continues according to the plan, and management is acting on any deviations when they occur. It is expected that the project will be completed as planned delivering the defined content with the defined level of quality. Thus both commitments to customers as well as internal business commitments are kept.

The main premise of the agile approach is that the uncertainties in the beginning and during the effort, as well as continuous changes during the execution makes this kind of the planning and execution to the plan impossible. Instead work is done in small steps that are small and shot enough to be stable, but all the rest may change so no effort is put on that. Content is produced in small increments but effort is also spend on research reducing and removing uncertainty related to the content and the effort. The content and the work reveals itself during the effort.

The dilemma with the project management arises, when an organization want to have both. It wants to plan business and internal operation based on planned and committed projects, but it wants to adjust to the uncertainty and change as agile approach allows. There have been a large number of proposals to solve the dilemma and mediate between the two management approaches, e.g. (Newbold, 1998; Shenhar, 2001, 2004; Thomsett, 2002; Schwaber, 2004; Highsmith, 2004; Boehm & Turner, 2004; Cohn, 2006; Vinekar, Slinkman and Nerur, 2006; Holcombe, 2008; Kniberg & Skarin, 2010). They present different ways to plan and manage the development and connect it with the next management layer.

One alternative to the traditional project management is based on the concept of flow (Koskela & Howell, 2002; Anderson, 2004; Reinertsen, 2009). The work is done as a continuous flow, focusing on the customer value, and delivering frequently. The working teams have a large autonomy to plan and act on the scope of their work. Instead of the project control there is the self-organizing team discipline. Overall this has full match with the flow in the lean approach, which is now also included in agile approaches. However, there are no reports yet about this approach having been implemented in a large organization.

Product and Application Management

The software product management is not a well-defined and commonly understood discipline. "The existing knowledge of software product management consists of small and unconnected pieces" (Maglyas, Nikula & Smolander, 2011). Yet, definitions can be found, e.g. "Product management is the discipline and business process governing a product from its inception to the market or customer delivery and service in order to generate the largest possible value to a business" (Ebert, 2009). The application management is similar function to product management and "helps to plan, implement and maintain a stable applications and ensure that required resources and expertise are in place to design, build, transition, operate and improve the application services and supporting technology" (itSMF, 2007).

The product management and application management are the customers of the software development. When considering the customer role in the agile and lean terms the distinction is obvious. Similarly the definition above emphasizes the value to the business, not the value to the customer. Consequently they have a responsibility to apply control over the interaction between the customers and the development teams.

When looking for compromise between the agile and lean approach and the product and application management several things will change. A large organization approach can be found in Leffingwell (2010) and Aalto (2008). It manages the product content hierarchically but with iterative process. That is, content is defined on four levels with increasing accuracy. On the top level the product requirements are defined as epics that

are on an overall level and used for business and architectural decisions. When refined to features they define the content of the releases and the release iterations. Next level of refinement results in user stories that are used to agree on all the details of the functionality. The sprint backlog items, reduced from the user stories, are then the piece of the content that are implemented in the next development cycle. So initially product can be decided in terms of epics, but final release need to be agreed by functions related to the user stories. A similar approach, but developed from a smaller company perspective can be found in (Vähäniitty, Rautiainen, Heikkilä and Vlaanderen, 2010; Vähäniitty 2012).

Adapting agility to product management raises several questions:

- Is the development team a creative participant in defining the content of a product, or just an "implementor" of the details defined by the product management?
- What kind of a role the development team has in the planning of the work, how and by whom the work is controlled, and who gives the commitments as related to the schedule for delivery?
- What are the interactions and feedback cycles for defining the content and implementing the content?
- How definite and strict are the roles in the product management and in the development, and how are they enforced?

Similar questions apply to the large-scale application management of the internal applications as well. The answers to these questions as practical implementations in software organizations will set the frame for the actual agile and lean practices in that organization. According to Vähäniitty (2012) some progress has been made in some companies. A comprehensive implementation of an agile and lean product or application management has not yet been reported.

Program Management

Program management, also called as multi-project management (see e.g. Lari, 2010), is a term used in product development for a practice to manage several projects that are needed to develop one product release for the markets. Typically product program contains one or several software projects, but often also hardware, acquisition, service channel, market channel and the like projects. The stage-gate model (Cooper, 2002) is often used to coordinate all projects. For the projects the stage gate means a defined synchronization and review point, where typically a predefined set of work product must be available.

The software project must build its life-cycle model to comply with the state-gate model. More often than not this has led to waterfall type of an approach. There has been a proposal, how to integrate agile development with the stage gate model (Karlström & Runeson, 2006).

However, the fast changes in business and operational environment as well as ever-growing complexity of products and business models has lead to growing need of new ways of developing products, as well. Several new approaches have been proposed that would radically change the traditional management and leadership practices. These include relaxation of project culture (Howell & Koskela, 2001, 2002; Schenhar 2000, 2001), Theory of Constraint (TOC) (Goldratt, 1999, 2004), Product Development Flow (Reinertsen 1997, 2009) and the Beyond budgeting movement (Hope & Frazer, 1997; Bogsnes 2008). They seem to give more agile and lean like basis for software development.

Relaxation of the project culture means the change of the very core principles of the project management. Particularly it moves focus to the appreciation of the value produced to the different stakeholders. When traditional project is considered as a failure if it exceeds its budget and schedule and produces something else than what was defined, this new thinking project may still be a glorious success if the outcome turns out to be sufficiently valuable to its stakeholders. Schenhar uses the Sidney opera house project as one example where project was total failure in traditional sense but superb success in value sense.

Another major challenge to the traditional thinking has been the theory of constraint by Goldratt and product development flow by Reinertsen. Both focus on organization throughput, removal of constraints in the process and managing the flow though the organization. Overall they are close to the lean thinking, but their origin is in the queuing theory. In practice that closeness to lean principles has made them good sources of expanding the lean approach for the development and for finding alternative ways to manage organizations that more suitable for the agile and lean development.

Beyond budgeting represents yet another approach to make management structures lighter. In the very core of it is the removal of the constraints that the financial management practices often set on the operation of the traditional organizations. In his presentation Bogsnes (2011) presents the following principles in Table 2.

As can be seen, these principles are view to internal operation and its management. However, similarity with lean principles is clearly visible.

Summary

On one hand there is a large range of agile and lean methodologies for the software development, and diverse, frequent efforts for evolving them further. A conversion towards one dominant methodology is not visible when writing this text. On the other hand management is still looking for ways to adjust management practices to align with the agile and lean transformation in their organization. Currently steps are taken to accommodate the new methodologies and the teams utilizing them but the full answer is missing what the change in

Table 2. The principles of beyond budgeting (Bogsnes, 2011)

1	Values	Govern through a few clear values, goals and boundaries, not detailed rules and budgets
2	Performance	Create a high performance climate based on relative success, not on meeting fixed targets
3	Transparency	Promote open information for self management, don't restrict it hierarchically
4	Organization	Organize as a network of lean, accountable teams, not around centralized functions
5	Autonomy	Give teams the freedom and capability to act; don't micro-manage them
6	Customers	Focus everyone on improving customer outcomes, not on hierarchical relationships
7	Goals	Set relative goals for continuous improvement, don't negotiate fixed performance contracts
8	Rewards	Reward shared success based on relative performance, not on meeting fixed targets
9	Planning	Make planning a continuous and inclusive process, not a top-down annual event
10	Coordination	Coordinate interactions dynamically, not through annual planning cycles
11	Resources	Make resources available as needed, not through annual budget allocations
12	Controls	Base controls on relative indicators and trends, not on variances against plan

management should be. Now there is a new entrant on this field. The service orientation is definitely stepped in to the software development and will have significant impact both on the engineering and teams, and on the management of the software organizations.

POST-AGILE ERA

Service orientation (Zimmermann, Schlimm, Waller & Pestel, 2005; Bianco et al, 2011) and complexity (Kautz & Madsen, 2010) have started to permeate as topics in the discussion of the future of the software development. It remains to be seen if that leads to a paradigm shift in the industry. The trends and developments in society, business and in people behavior will continue as fast as ever and that will put pressure also in the way we develop software and what software we will develop. Business has become more dominated by services than products (Lusch & Vargo, 2006; Spohrer, Maglio, Bailey & Gruhl, 2007). Software development has accommodated service orientation as core part of development philosophy (Chen et al, 2010). Even computer technology can be structured and delivered as service (Keller & Rexford, 2010). These three layers are depicted in Figure 2.

Figure 2. The three layers of the service orientation

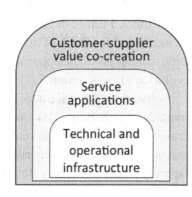 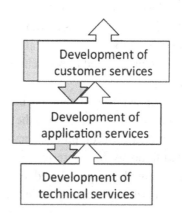

Similarly complexity as a science and particularly via Complex Adaptive Systems theory has made its way especially to agile community (Meso & Jain, 2006; Vidgen & Wang, 2009; Pelrine, 2011). It is too early to say that these are the dominant factors in this current change but they cannot go without attention either. This book is about this change.

Service-Dominant Markets and Business

The understudying of business is now converting from goods dominant logic (GD-logic) to service-dominant logic (SD-logic) (Vargo & Lusch, 2004, 2008). The entanglement of the service customer, the service provider and the system-in-use is getting ever closer, which makes developing the system and development of service inseparable. The understanding of developing software as an isolated system is slowly changing towards developing the people interaction where software is an integral part.

"Service science seeks to create a body of knowledge that accounts for value-cocreation between entities as they interact –to describe, explain, and better predict, control, and guide the evolution of value-cocreation phenomena." (Spohrer & Maglio, 2009) It focuses on man-made world where information technology has a key role tying customer and supplier in unprecedented manner. Software is becoming ubiquitous and integral part of social systems in such a way that software cannot be developed without developing the user world simultaneously. Software is not any more a separate product or application developed in a separate project and implemented as an ad-on to a system.

The traditional approach to software use has been that organizations and individuals own their software and run it on their own computers whenever they have need to do so. Software industry has taken this for granted and developed two business models, product development and custom

development. Both have been engineering and task management oriented though human aspects have been continuously grown in significance in software development. Now the balance seems to turn to human aspects, and engineering and management are becoming necessary add-ons in software development.

Software as a Service

Latest developments in technology, both in hardware and software have made it feasible to separate the software and the use of software. That is, software is provided as a service (Dubey & Wagle, 2007; Mell & Grance, 2011), instead of owning it and running it in owned environment. Many users are using the one and same software installation but each with their own data. They buy the right to use of software and the environment to store data. The vendor hosts the one version of the software, and the storage space for each user, securing the sufficient availability for each. This is often done using cloud technology that further extends the capacity to any major variation in use. Software-as-a-Service (SaaS) (Mell & Grance, 2011) has become a common delivery model for many core business applications, and many companies have become users of it. Cloud technology is likely to increase popularity of this service business model.

In addition to care-free use of service, many users are attracted to its ease of update. New releases are taken into use without much of disruption in use. Single configuration allow extensive testing applying many different use cases of different users. Further development can be based on needs and feedback of many. And doing it in agile manner gives the opportunity to continuous evolution of the solution.

Software as a service does not come without limitations and properties often considered as drawbacks. Data is stored in vendors' environment that is considered a security risk. It may reside in far away place, which may slow down the access.

There are typically many users on the same system, even on the same software, which easily create concern among users. And as the software is same for all, customization or individual solutions are typically not possible, at leas in any major scale. The development approach is often considered traditional engineering oriented (Kontogogos & Avgeriou, 2009) with little space for agile.

Service as the Solution

Service is also a valid concept in designing and implementing software solutions. The whole design process for developing software can be based on concept of service. As well as the result software can be structured with services, in so called Service-Oriented Architecture (SOA) (Bianco et al, 2011).

Looking from the top of the enterprise architecture (Lankhorst & Duren, 2007) we can separate the business, application and technology layers. Business layer design indicates the services to the customer. Application layer defines the services from the system needed to provide the services to the customer. And the technology layer services build the technical capability to run the application layer services. Methods to conduct this hierarchical architecture design process are readily available. The detailed solution building is not, however, without challenges and arbitration between options.

The latest developments in communication and Internet technologies enable elegant implementations. The capacity of broadband, the standardization of Internet protocols and stacks, the use of patterns and frameworks, the web based development environments, and the like have further enhanced the knowledge and capabilities in developing the solutions this way (Lee et al, 2006; Papazoglou & van den Heuvel, 2006). The traditional way of developing and delivering major releases can be replaced with agile and lean development of continuous enhancements and adaptations to the system. The continuous change and continuous use become inseparable.

Complexity

The word "complexity" is similar to the word "agile". It has a common every day meaning, used in daily language without any further consideration of definitions, Then there is a specialized meaning that would require definition in order to be understood as intended. Here the discussion is about conscious complexity (Geier, 2003) that focuses on human beings. Within that we confine attention to the complex adaptive systems (CAS) theory related to leadership research (Schneider & Somers, 2006). We apply it to software development as a complex adaptive system (Benbya & McKelvey, 2006).

Some agile experts have stated that agile approach has its roots in CAS (Highsmith, 2000; Schwaber, 2004; Appelo, 2011; Pelrine, 2011). Particularly they point out that the self-organization is a core common factor to all of them and a core characteristic of CAS, as well. Also adaptation, and emergence are often pointed out, particularly adaptation to change and emergence of new solutions during development. Yet, a comprehensive analysis of agile software development as a complex adaptive system is still to be made and conclusions drawn about it. Important for this text is that this new area of research is expected to bring new understanding of and possibly new practices for the software development and building software organizations (Gollery, 1999).

Complexity is also a characteristic of all social systems and they can be studied using CAS theory as a basis (Eidelson, 1997), which ties it to service-oriented thinking as well. When the fast adaptation to change and response to emergent needs becomes predominant in development, it will integrate users with developers even more closely. The agile approach can still be in a key role, but now as an enabler for new advances in the software development, which will emphasize the emergent nature of it.

The other reason for change in traditional system areas is ever growing complexity of systems. When designing these hugely complex systems, human comprehension is taken to its limits, and many current design practices are coming to the end of their problem solving capability. The traditional way of starting from the top, break the whole into details to solve them, and the build up the whole again to full system is at risk. The whole may not work as expected. In addition, often the understanding of what the whole is debatable, and reveals itself only during the process of developing solution to it. In complex world the sequential and top down problem does not always work. One tentative model for solution might be that of service orientation, having stable integrated framework to build on, and build the individual pieces of services in an agile manner.

From management perspective the focus is on managing complexity of the system framework and steering development of services as an adaptive process. New technologies, and ever-closer bind between customers and suppliers require new approaches for software development. And resulting systems need to enable loose coupling of components and continuously evolving systems, where components are phased in and phased out as needed, continuously.

SUMMARY

This chapter has been written "having agile lenses on". That is topics in the past, current and in the future are selected and presented as part of the agile life cycle. The selection and interpretation is that of the author and readers are very welcome to challenge that view. However, in the complex world only partial views can be presented. Time, space and human comprehension do not allow inclusion of all influencing factors and interpretation of all of their relationships. That said, recognizing the patterns and interpretation of their meaning will help to do decisions of the future.

When organizations have been expanding their agile competencies and adjusted their structures to accommodate agile approach, the world out-

side has not been standing still. ICT technology has taken steps advancing its performance, web technology has made advances providing new capabilities, systems development has taken steps towards service thinking, and service science is taken steps to become a new branch of science. People are getting more intimately connected and computers are becoming ubiquitous.

Understanding that customers and providers are getting more and more entangled and the new service science approach is on way to organize this closeness.

Traditional software development has seen predictability as the main goal, that is, define the target system and build it reliably according to plans. Deviations have been considered as risks and a special area for management attention. Without doubt, many applications areas will remain as such and this approach remains valid.

On the other hand, there is no doubt either that many current, uncertainty-increasing trends in business and in society will continue. The change will become ever faster, the communication and interaction will increase in volume, unexpected encounters will become more frequent and people are keeping their rights to change their minds ever faster. Businesses will see markets to grow, but competition growing even faster. Customers come closer, become more aware of also the context of products and services, and choose suppliers accordingly. That puts new requirements on customer services and systems supporting them.

In software intensive industry and service sectors agile approach has created high expectations to solve or at least relief some of the problems accompanying with this change. Its main focus has been in software development work. Partly successes in software and partly similar problems in other areas of organizations and business have lead to application of agile principles also in software development surrounding areas. There are discussion about agile project management, agile product management, agile business management, agile strategy, and so on. The generic principles of agility seem to apply to many uses.

When looking for extension of agile principles, agile practitioners have turned to lean thinking and even to complexity theory. This book paves the way to service science direction. Keeping the original ideas and philosophies, but interpreting all of these four towards common goals, seem to give a consistent new approach for organizations. Service science, service-dominant logic, as-a-Service thinking and designing of solutions feed the new understanding of customer-supplier relationship, and business interaction in between. This book opens these concepts further.

Service orientation brings, however, one major challenge. Building the customer focused service modules and technically reliable infrastructure for them seems to be two very different aspects of the service orientation. It seems that the recommendation done first time already in 1970s to adjust development approach according to the system that needs to be build, is valid. Perhaps we need agile service development, but not so agile infrastructure development for these services.

REFERENCES

Aalto, J. M. (2008). *Large scale agile development of S60 product software: A few hundred synchronized scrums –setup and experiences*. Finland: OO Days at Tampere University of Technology.

Abbas, N. (2009). *Software quality and governance in agile software development*. PhD thesis, School of Electronics and Computer Science, University of Southampton.

Abrahamsson, P. (2008). *End of agile. VTT Oliopäivät '08*. Tampere: VTT Research Center of Finland.

Abrahamsson, P., Oza, N., & Siponen, M. (2010). Agile software development methods: A comparative review. In T. Dingsøyr, T. Dybå, & N. B. Moe (Eds.), *Agile software development*, (pp. 31–59). Berlin, Germany: Springer.

Abrahamsson, P., Salo, O., Ronkainen, J., & Warsta, J. (2002). *Agile software development methods: Review and analysis. Number 478 in VTT Publications*. Espoo, Finland: VTT Technical Research Centre of Finland.

Abrahamsson, P., Warsta, J., Siponen, M. T., & Ronkainen, J. (2003). New directions on agile methods: A comparative analysis. In *Proceedings 25th International Conference on Software Engineering* (ICSE).

Alter, S. (2008). Service system fundamentals: Work system, value chain, and life cycle. *IBM Systems Journal, 47*(1). doi:10.1147/sj.471.0071

Alter, S. (2009). Mapping the domain of service science. *Proceedings of the Fifteenth Americas Conference on Information Systems,* San Francisco, California.

Amber, S. (2002). *Agile modeling: Effective practices for extreme programming and the unified process*. New York, NY: John Wiley & Sons, Inc.

Amber, S. (2012). *Surveys exploring the current state of information technology practices*. Retrieved from http://www.ambysoft.com/surveys/

Ambler, S. W. (2007). *Agile software development: Definition*. Retrieved from http://www.agilemodeling.com/essays/agileSoftwareDevelopment.htm

Anderson, D. J. (2004). *Agile Management for software engineering*. Prentice Hall PTR.

Anderson, D. J. (2010). *Kanban, successful evolutionary change for your technology business.* Blue Hole Press.

Aoyama, M. (1998). Web-based agile software development. *IEEE Software, 15*(6), 56–65. doi:10.1109/52.730844

Baker, F. T. (1972). Chief programmer team management of production programming. *IBM Systems Journal, 11*(1), 56–73. doi:10.1147/sj.111.0056

Baskerville, R., & Pries-Heje, J. (2001). Racing the e-bomb: How the Internet is redefining information systems development methodology. In Fitzgerald, B., Russo, N., & DeGross, J. (Eds.), *Realigning research and practice in IS development.* New York, NY: Kluwer.

Beck, K. (2000). *eXtreme programming explained, embrace change.* Addison Wesley.

Benbya, H., & McKelvey, B. (2006). Using co-evolutionary and complexity theories to improve IS alignment: A multi-level approach. *Journal of Information Technology,* (n.d.), 21.

Beynon-Davies, P., & Holmes, S. (1998). Integrating rapid application development and participatory design. *IEE Proceedings. Software, 145*(4). doi:10.1049/ip-sen:19982196

Bianco, P., Lewis, G. A., Merson, P., & Simanta, S. (2011). *Architecting service-oriented systems.* Carnegie Mellon University, Software Engineering Institute, CMU/SEI-2011-TN-008.

Boehm, B. (1986). A spiral model of software development and enhancement. *ACM Software Engineering Notes,* August.

Boehm, B., & Turner, R. (2004). *Balancing agility and discipline: A guide for the perplexed.* Pearson Education Inc. doi:10.1007/978-3-540-24675-6_1

Bogsnes, B. (2008). *Implementing beyond budgeting: Unlocking the performance potential.* London, UK: John Wiley & Sons.

Brooks, F. P. (1975). *The mythical man month.* Addison Wesley.

Bryman, A. (2000). *Research methods and organization studies.* Routledge. (first published 1989 by Unwin Hyman)

Carmel, E., Whitaker, R. D., & George, J. F. (1993). PD and joint application design: A transatlantic comparison. *Communications of the ACM, 36*(4).

Charette, R. N. (2002). *Foundations of lean development: The lean development manager's guide,* Vol. 2. Spotsylvania, VA: The Foundation Series on Risk Management (CD), ITABHI Corporation.

Chen, H.-M., Kazman, R., & Perry, O. (2010). From software architecture analysis to service engineering: An empirical study of methodology development for enterprise SOA implementation. *IEEE Transactions on Services Computing, 3*(2).

Coad, P., Lefebvre, E., & De Luca, J. (1999). *Java modeling in color with UML: Enterprise components and process.* Upper Saddle River, NJ: Prentice Hall.

Cockburn, A. (2002). *Agile software development.* Addison-Wesley / Pearson.

Cockburn, A., & Highsmith, J. (2001). Agile software development: The people factor. *IEEE Computer,* November.

Cohn, M. (2006). *Agile estimating and planning.* Prentice Hall PTR.

Coleman, G., & Verbruggen, R. (1998). A quality software process ofr rapid application development. *Software Quality Journal,* (n.d), 7.

Cooper, R. G., Edgett, S. J., & Kleinschmidt, E. J. (2002). *Portfolio management for new products* (2nd ed.). Basic Books.

Curtis, B., Hefley, W. E., & Miller, S. (1995). *People capability maturity model.* (CMU/SEI-95-MM-002), Software Engineering Institute, Carnegie Mellon University, September.

Dahl, O. J., Dijkstra, E. W., & Hoare, C. A. R. (1972). *Structured programming.* New York, NY: Academic Press.

Demirkan, H., Kauffman, R. J., Vayghan, J. A., Fill, H., Karagiannis, D., & Maglio, P. P. (2008). Service-oriented technology and management: Perspectives on research and practice for the coming decade. *Electronic Commerce Research and Applications, 7,* 356–376. doi:10.1016/j.elerap.2008.07.002

DOD. (1988). *Military standard, Defense system software development.* DOD-STD-2167A, Washington, US, 29 February.

DSDM Consortium. (1997). *Dynamic systems development method, Version 3.* Ashford, UK: DSDM Consortium.

Dubey, A., & Wagle, D. (2007). Delivering software as a service. *The McKinsey Quarterly,* May.

Ebert, C. (2009). Software product management. *CrossTalk, The Journal of Defense Software Engineering,* January.

Eidelson, R. J. (1997). Complex adaptive systems in the behavioral and social sciences. *Review of General Psychology, 1*(1). doi:10.1037/1089-2680.1.1.42

ESI/SFE. (2012). *System family engineering.* European Software Institute. Retrieved from http://www.esi.es/Families/famOverview.html

Geyer, R. (2003). *Europeanisation, complexity, and the British welfare state.* Paper presented to the UACES/ESRC Study Group on The Europeanisation of British Politics and Policy-Making, Department of Politics, University of Sheffield, September 19.

Gilb, T. (1989). *Principles of software engineering management.* Addison Wesley Longman.

Goldratt, E. (1999). *Theory of constraints.* North River Press.

Goldratt, E. (2004). *The goal: A process of ongoing improvement* (3rd ed.). North River Press.

Gollery, S. (1999). *Re-engineering a software development organization as a complex adaptive system.* InterSymp-99, Baden-Baden, Germany, August.

Gottesdiener, E. (1995). RAD realities: Beyond the hype to how RAD really works. *Application Development Trends,* August.

Grant, T. (2012). *What is the value of agile in your organization*? Retrieved from http://blogs.forrester.com/tom_grant/11-11-08-what_is_the_value_of_agile_in_your_organization

Grogono, P., & Shearing, B. (2008). *Preparing for paradigm shift.* Montreal, Canada: ACM. ISBN 978-1-60558-101-9/08/05

Hamilton, M., & Zeldin, S. (1976). *Integrated software development system / higher order software conceptual description.* Technical Report ECOM-76- 0329-F. Fort Monmouth, NJ: US Army Electronics Command.

Highsmith, J. (2000). *Adaptive software development: A collaborative approach to managing complex systems.* New York, NY: Dorset House.

Highsmith, J. (2002). *Agile software development ecosystems.* Addison-Wesley / Pearson.

Highsmith, J. (2004). *Agile project management, creating innovative products.* Pearson Education Inc.

Holcombe, M. (2008). *Running an agile software development project.* Wiley-Blackwell.

Hope, J., & Fraser, R. (1997). *Beyond budgeting... Breaking through the barrier to 'the third wave'. Management Accounting.* UK: Chartered Institute of Management Accountants.

Hull, E. (1995). *Systems at speed – Rapid application development in 1995. Computer Audit Update.* Elsevier Science Ltd.

Hunt, A., & Thomas, D. (2000). *The pragmatic programmer.* Addison Wesley.

IEEE. (2007). *Draft recommended practice for the customer-supplier relationship in agile software projects.* P1648/D5.

Iivari, J., Hirschheim, R., & Klein, H. K. (1998). A paradigmatic analysis contrasting information systems development approaches and methodologies. *Information Systems Research, 9*(2). doi:10.1287/isre.9.2.164

Ikonen, M. (2011). *Impacts of Kanban on lean software development.* PhD Thesis, Department of Computer Science, University of Helsinki, Series of Publications A, Report A-2011-4.

ISO/IEC. (1997). *International standard ISO/IEC TR 15504, Information technology – Process assessment- Parts 1- 5.* International Standardization Organization.

ITIL. (2012). *IT infrastructure library, Office of Government Commerce, UK.* Retrieved from http://www.itil-officialsite.com/

itSMF. (2007). *An introductory overview of ITIL,* v3. The UK Chapter of the itSMF, itSMF Ltd.

Karlström, D., & Runeson, P. (2006). Integrating agile software development into stage-gate managed product development. *Empirical Software Engineering,* (n.d.), 11.

Kautz, K., & Madsen, S. (2010). 47P. Understanding agile software development in practice. *CONFIRM 2010, Proceedings,* Paper 21. Retrieved from http://aisel.aisnet.org/confirm2010/21

Keller, E., & Rexford, J. (2010). The "Platform as a service" model for networking. *INM/WREN'10 Proceedings of the 2010 Internet Network Management Conference on Research on Enterprise Networking,* USENIX Association Berkeley, CA, USA.

Kettunen, P. (2009). *Agile software development in large-scale new product development organization: Team-level perspective.* Doctoral Dissertation, Helsinki University of Technology, Department of Computer Science and Engineering.

Kniberg, H., & Skarin, M. (2010). *Kanban and Scrum, making the most of both. C4Media Inc.* InfoQ.

Kontogogos, A., & Avgerio, P. (2009). *An overview of software engineering approaches to service oriented architectures in various fields.* 18th IEEE International Workshops on Enabling Technologies: Infrastructures for Collaborative Enterprises.

Koskela, L., & Howell, G. (2002). *The underlying theory of project management is obsolete.* Project Management Institute. doi:10.1109/EMR.2008.4534317

Kuhn, T. S. (1962). *The structure of scientific revolutions.* University of Chicago Press.

Ladas, C. (2009). *Scrumban - Essays on Kanban systems for lean software development.* Modus Cooperandi Press.

Lane, S., & Richardson, I. (2011). Process models for service-based applications: A systematic literature review. *Information and Software Technology, 53,* 424–439. doi:10.1016/j.infsof.2010.12.005

Lankhorst, M., & van Drunen, H. (2007). *Enterprise architecture development and modelling, Combining TOGAF and ArchiMate.* Retrieved from www.via-nova-architectura.org

Lari, E., Beach, J., Mazzachi, T. A., & Sarkani, S. (2010). Allocating resources in multi-project programs: Lessons Learned from the trenches. *CrossTalk, The Journal of Defence Software Engineering*, May/June.

Larman, C. (2004). *Agile and iterative development: A manager's guide*. Addison-Wesley / Pearson.

Larman, C., & Basili, V. R. (2003). Iterative and incremental development: A brief history. *Computer, 36*(6), 47–56. doi:10.1109/MC.2003.1204375

Larman, C., & Vodde, B. (2008). *Scaling lean & agile development: Thinking and organizational tools for large-scale Scrum*. Addison-Wesley Professional.

Larman, C., & Vodde, B. (2009). *Lean primer*, Version 1.5.2009. Retrieved from www.leanprimer.com

Larson, R. C. (2008). Service science: At the intersection of management, social, and engineering sciences. *IBM Systems Journal, 47*(1). doi:10.1147/sj.471.0041

Lee, L. L., Padmanabhan, V., & Whang, S. (1997). The bullwhip effect in supply chains. *Sloan Management Review*, Spring.

Lee, S. P., Chan, L. P., & Lee, E. W. (2006). *Web services implementation methodology for SOA application*. IEEE International Conference on Industrial Informatics, August.

Leffingwell, D. (2009). *Thoughts on lean thinking*. Retrieved from http://scalingsoftwareagility.wordpress.com/2009/09/15/thoughts-on-lean-thinking/

Leffingwell, D. (2010). *Agile software requirements: Lean requirements practices for teams, programs, and the enterprise*. Addison-Wesley Professional.

Li, E. Y., Chen, H.-G., & Lee, T.-S. (2002). Software process management of top companies in Taiwan: A comparative study. *Total Quality Management, 13*(5). doi:10.1080/0954412022000002081

Liker, J. K. (2004). *The Toyota way: 14 management principles from the world's greatest manufacturer*. New York, NY: McGraw-Hill.

Lusch, R. F., & Varg, S. L. (2006). Service-dominant logic: Reactions, Reflections and refinements. *Marketing Theory, 6*(3). doi:10.1177/1470593106066781

Lyytinen, K., & Rose, G. M. (2006). Information system development agility as organizational learning. *European Journal of Information Systems, 15*, 183–199. doi:10.1057/palgrave.ejis.3000604

Maglyas, A., Nikula, U., & Smolander, K. (2011). What do we know about software product management? A systematic mapping study. *IEEE Proceedings of the Fifth International Workshop on Software Product Management* (IWSPM), Trento.

Mahanti, A. (2006). Challenges in enterprise adoption of agile methods – A survey. *Journal of Computing and Information Technology, 14*(3), 197–206.

Martin, J. (1991). *Rapid application development*. New York, NY: Macmillan Publishing Company.

Mell, P., & Grance, T. (2011). *The NIST definition of cloud computing*. National Institute of Standards and Technology NIST, Information Technology Laboratory, Special Publication 800-145.

Melnik, G., & Maurer, F. (2006). Comparative analysis of job satisfaction in agile and non-agile software development teams, extreme programming and agile processes in software engineering. *Lecture Notes in Computer Science, Proceedings of the 7ᵗʰ International Conference on Extreme Programming and Agile Processes in Software Engineering*.

Meso, P., & Jain, R. (2006). *Agile software development: Adaptive systems principles and best practices*. Information Systems Management, Summer.

Miller, G. (2001). *Sizing up today's lightweight software processes. IEEE IT Professional*. May/June.

Mills, H. D. (1971). Top-down programming in large systems. In Rusting, R. (Ed.), *Debugging techniques in large systems*. Englewood Cliffs, NJ: Prentice Hall.

Moore, G. (1995). *Crossing the chasm*. New York, NY: Harper Business.

Morgan, J. M., & Liker, J. K. (2006). *The Toyota product development system: Integrating people, process, and technology*. New York, NY: Productivity Press.

Myers, G. J. (1975). *Reliable software through composite design*. New York, NY: Petrocelli/Charter.

Newbold, R. C. (1998). *Project management in the fast lane: Applying the theory of constraints*. The St. Lucie Press.

Northover, M., Northover, A., Gruner, S., Kourie, D. G., & Boake, A. (2007). *Agile software development: A contemporary philosophical perspective. SAICSIT 2007*. Sunshine Coast, South Africa: Fish River Sun.

O'Connell, E., & Saiedian, H. (2000). Can you trust software capability evaluations? Perspectives. *IEEE Computer, 33*(2).

Oxford dictionaries. (2012). Retrieved from http://oxforddictionaries.com/

Palmer, S., & Felsing, J. M. (2002). *A practical guide to feature driven development*. Upper Saddle River, NJ: Prentice Hall.

Papazoglou, M. P., & van den Heuvel, W.-J. (2006). Service-oriented design and development methodology. *International Journal of Web Engineering and Technology, 2*(4), 412–442. doi:10.1504/IJWET.2006.010423

Parnas, D. L. (1972). On the criteria to be used in decomposing systems into modules. *Communications of the ACM*, (n.d.), 15.

Paulk, M. C., Curtis, W., Chrissis, M. B., & Weber, C. (1993a). *Capability maturity model^{sm} for software*, Version 1.1. Carnegie Mellon University, Software Engineering Institute, Technical Report CMU/SEI-93-TR-024, February.

Paulk, M. C., Weber, C. V., Garcia, S., Chrissis, M. B., & Bush, M. (1993b). *Key practices of the capability maturity model*, Version 1.1. Software Engineering Institute, Technical Report CMU/SEI-93-TR-25, February.

Payne, A. F., Storbacka, K., & Frow, P. (2008). Managing the co-creation of value. *Journal of the Academy of Marketing Science, 36*, 83–96. doi:10.1007/s11747-007-0070-0

Pelrine, J. (2011). Understanding software agility: A social complexity point of view. *Emergence: Complexity & Organization, 13*(1-2).

PMI. (2008). *A guide to the project management body of knowledge* (PMBOK® Guide) — 4th ed. Retrieved from http://www.pmi.org/

PMI. (2012). *PMI agile certified practitioner^{sm}*. Retrieved from http://www.pmi.org/Certification/New-PMI-Agile-Certification/PMI-Agile-Toolbox.aspx

Poppendieck, M., & Poppendieck, T. (2003). *Lean software development: An agile toolkit*. Addison-Wesley.

Poppendieck, M., & Poppendieck, T. (2007). *Implementing lean software development: From concept to cash*. Addison-Wesley.

Poppendieck, M., & Poppendieck, T. (2010). *Leading lean software development: Results are not the point*. Addison-Wesley.

Power, K. (2010). *Stakeholder identification in agile software product development organizations: A model for understanding who and what really counts*. *AGILE 2010*. IEEE Computer Society.

Ramollari, E., Dranidis, D., & Simons, A. J. H. (2012). *A survey of service oriented development methodologies*. CiteSeer, April.

Ramsey, R. H., Atwood, M. E., & Campbell, G. D. (1979). *Analysis of software design methodologies*. Science Applications, Incorporated, U.S. Army, Research Institute for the Behavioral and Social Sciences, Technical Report 401.

Reinertsen, D. G. (1997). *Managing the design factory*. Free Press.

Reinertsen, D. G. (2009). *The principles of product development FLOW: Second generation lean product development*. Celeritas Publishing.

Royce, W. W. (1970). Managing the development of large software systems. *Proceedings, IEEE WESCON*, August.

Runeson, P., & Höst, M. (2009). Guidelines for conducting and reporting case study research in software engineering. *Empirical Software Engineering*, (n.d), 14.

Schneider, M., & Somers, M. (2006). Organizations as complex adaptive systems: Implications of complexity theory for leadership research. *The Leadership Quarterly<* (n.d), 17.

Schuh, P. (2005). *Integrating agile development in the real world*. Charles River Media, Inc.

Schwaber, K. (1996). Controlled chaos: Living on the Edge. *American Programmer, 9*(5).

Schwaber, K. (2004). *Agile project management with Scrum*. Microsoft Press.

Schwaber, K., & Beedle, M. (2002). *Agile software development with Scrum*. Upper Saddle River, NJ: Prentice Hall.

Scotland, K. (2012). *Kanban and systems thinking*. Retrieved March 12, 2012, from http://availagility. co.uk/2010/12/22/kanban-and-systems-thinking/

SEI/SPL. (2012). *Software product lines*. Software engineering Institute. Retrieved from http://www. sei.cmu.edu/productlines/

Shahrbanoo, M., Ali, M., & Mehran, M. (2012). An approach for agile SOA development using agile principles. *International Journal of Computer Science & Information Technology, 4*(1).

Shenhar, A. (2004). Strategic project leaderships toward a strategic approach to project management. *R & D Management, 34*(5). doi:10.1111/ j.1467-9310.2004.00363.x

Shenhar, A. J. (2001). One size does not fit all projects: Exploring classical contingency domains. *Management Science, 47*(3). doi:10.1287/ mnsc.47.3.394.9772

Singh, A., & Singh, K. (2010). Agile adoption - Crossing the chasm. *Proceedings of the International Conference on Applied Computer Science,* Malta.

Snowden, D. J., & Boone, M. E. (2007). A leader's framework for decision making. *Harvard Business Review,* November.

Spohrer, J., & Kwan, S. K. (2009). Service science, management, engineering, and design (SSMED): Outline & references. *International Journal of Information Systems in the Service Sector, 1*(3). doi:10.4018/jisss.2009070101

Spohrer, J., & Maglio, P. P. (2009). Service science: Towards a smarter planet. In Karwowski, W., & Salvendy, G. (Eds.), *Service engineering*. New York, NY: Wiley.

Spohrer, J., Maglio, P. P., Bailey, J., & Gruhl, D. (2007). Steps towards a science of service systems. *Computer*, *40*(1), 71–77. doi:10.1109/MC.2007.33

Stevens, W. P., Myers, G. J., & Constantine, L. L. (1974). Structured design. *IBM Systems Journal*, (n.d.), 13.

Subramaniam, V., & Hunt, A. (2006). *Practices of an agile developer – Working in the real world*. USA: The Pragmatic Bookshelf.

Taylor, F. W. (1911). *The principles of scientific management*. New York, NY: Harper & Brothers.

Teasley, S. D., Covi, L. A., Krishnan, M. S., & Olson, J. S. (2002). Rapid software development through team collocation. *IEEE Transactions on Software Engineering*, *28*(7). doi:10.1109/TSE.2002.1019481

Thomas, S. (2012). *Agile: I prefer hype to ignorance*. Retrieved from http://itsadeliverything.com/agile-i-prefer-hype-to-ignorance

Thomsett, R. (2002). *Radical project management*. Prentice Hall PTR.

Vähäniitty, J. (2012). *Towards agile product and portfolio management. Doctoral Dissertations 15/2012, Software Process Group*. Finland: Department of Computer Science and Engineering, Aalto University School of Science.

Vähäniitty, J., & Rautiainen, K. (2008). Towards a conceptual framework and tool support for linking long-term product and business planning with agile software development. In *Proceedings of the 1st International Workshop on Software Development Governance*, (SDG).

Vähäniitty, J., Rautiainen, K., Heikkilä, V., & Vlaanderen, K. (2010). *Towards agile product and portfolio management*. Aalto University, School of Science and Technology, Software Business and Engineering Laboratory (SoberIT).

Vargo, S. L., & Lusch, R. F. (2004). Evolving to a new dominant logic for marketing. *Journal of Marketing*, (n.d.), 68.

Vargo, S. L., & Lusch, R. F. (2008). Service-dominant logic: continuing the evolution. *Journal of the Academy of Marketing Science*, *36*, 1–10. doi:10.1007/s11747-007-0069-6

Vidgen, R., & Wang, X. (2009). Coevolving systems and the organization of agile software development. *Information Systems Research*, *20*(3). doi:10.1287/isre.1090.0237

Vijayasarathy, L. R., & Turk, D. (2008). Agile software development: A survey of early adopters. *Journal of Information Technology Management*, *19*(2).

Vinekar, V., Slinkman, C. W., & Nerur, S. (2006). Can agile and traditional systems development approaches coexist? An ambidextrous view. *Information Systems Management*, *23*(3). doi:10.1201/1078.10580530/46108.23.3.20060601/93705.4

Warnier, J. D. (1974). *Logical construction of programs*. Leiden, The Netherlands: Stenpert Kroese.

West, D. (2011). *Water-Scrum-fall is the reality of agile for most organizations today: Manage the Water-Scrum and Scrum-fall boundaries to increase agility*. Forrester report, July 26.

West, D., & Grant, T. (2010). *Agile development: Mainstream Adoption has changed agility*. Forrester report, January 20.

Wirth, N. (1991). Program development by stepwise refinement. *Communications of the ACM*, (n.d.), 14.

Womack, J. P., & Jones, D. T. (2003). *Lean thinking: Banish waste and create wealth in your corporation*. Free press edition.

Womack, J. P., Jones, D. T., & Roos, D. (1991). *The machine that changed the world: The story of lean production*. Harper Perennial.

Yourdon, E., & Constantine, L. L. (1975). *Structured design*. New York, NY: Yourdon, Inc.

Zimmermann, O., Schlimm, N., Waller, G., & Pestel, M. (2005). *Analysis and design techniques for service-oriented development and integration*. In INFORMATIK 2005 - Informatik LIVE! Band 2, Beiträge der 35. Jahrestagung der Gesellschaft für Informatik e.V. (GI), Bonn, September

KEY TERMS AND DEFINITIONS

Agile Approach: In software engineering, the software development approach that focuses on the customer value, and develops software in short cycles; the development teams organize themselves for work, define tasks for themselves, demonstrate results to customers, and retrospect own operation continuously.

Complexity: A common adjective characterizing either work or work results but also a branch in research focusing the complexity theory and the complex adaptive systems (CAS) research; CAS is sometimes referred to be as the theoretical basis of the agile approach.

Engineering Culture: An application of engineering methodologies, methods, techniques and tools in an organization, in this context in a software development organization.

Kanban: Initially a flow control technique related to the lean manufacturing, then applied in the software development as a work management technique which then has been develop to a full blown lean software development methodology by accommodating methods and techniques from many product, software development and management approaches.

Lean Approach: Initially developed for manufacturing to ensure economical and efficient flow of production with minimum of waste; later on expanded to product development and then also to software development. Lean software development is the name of one methodology but more often a common term meaning the application of the lean principles to software development.

Methodology: In software engineering, an organized and instructed set of methods, techniques and tools to accomplish tasks in some defined focus area, e.g. a requirements engineering methodology.

Process Culture: an application of management methodologies, methods, techniques and tools in an organization, in this context in a software development organization.

Service Oriented Approach: In software engineering, is the three level approach for using service as the key concept in the software development; it defines service in the customer-vendor relationship (business level), in the system user – system relationship (application level) and in the software application – infrastructure relationship (technology level).

ENDNOTES

[1] The fad is "an intense and widely shared enthusiasm for something, especially one that is short-lived"; (Oxford dictionaries 2012)

[2] The hype is "an ingenious or questionable claim, method, etc., used in advertising, promotion, or publicity to intensify the effect" (Oxford dictionaries, 2012). The word hype origins from the term "hype cycle", which was first used in Gartner Group report in 1995 (Fenn, 1995). The hype cycle consists of five phases: technology trigger, peak of inflated expectations, trough of disillusionment, slope of enlightenment and plateau of productivity. The common use of the word hype clearly refers to the build up of the second phase, the peak of inflated expectations.

3   The paradigm shift means in common language any profound change, but initially the term was defined by Thomas Kuhn (Kuhn, 1962) for natural sciences. He called the basic assumptions in science as paradigms, and changes in them as shifts. He also insisted that they would be a result of often a slow accumulation of new evidence and then following swift, radical, and innovative new way of thinking. The shift then takes place though fierce and lengthy debates that would end until the loosing party would extinct and one dominant paradigm would remain. In social sciences this view of converging towards one dominant paradigm is not seen feasible (Bryman, 1989). As related to software development Northover, Northover, Gruner, Kourie and Boake (2007) put doubt on applicability of Kuhnian paradigm shift. On the other hand Grogono and Shearing (2008) consider it applicable for concurrent software engineering.

4   In his technology adoption life-cycle (Moore, 1995) there are five phases described by the characteristic of users: Innovators, early adopters, early majority, late majority and laggards. The chasm is in between early adopters and early majority, meaning that any new technology have to survive through this chasm before getting though to majority of users. Often crossing the chasm requires adjustments also to the technology. Considering software and especially agile development approaches this grossing the chasm has been seen very challenging (Mahanti, 2006; Vijayasarathy & Turk, 2008).

Chapter 2
Addressing Highly Dynamic Changes in Service-Oriented Systems:
Towards Agile Evolution and Adaptation

Andreas Metzger
Paluno (The Ruhr Institute for Software Technology), University of Duisburg-Essen, Germany

Elisabetta Di Nitto
Politecnico di Milano, Italy

ABSTRACT

This chapter sets out to introduce relevant foundations concerning evolution and adaptation of service-oriented systems. It starts by sketching the historical development of software systems from monolithic and mostly static applications to highly-dynamic, service-oriented systems. Then, it provides an overview and more thorough explanation of the various kinds of changes that may need to be faced by service-oriented systems. To understand how such changes could be addressed, the chapter introduces a reference service life-cycle model which distinguishes between evolution, viz. the manual modification of the specification and implementation of the system during design-time, and (self-)adaptation, viz. the autonomous modification of a service-oriented system during operation. Based on the discussion of the key activities prescribed by that life-cycle, the chapter elaborates on the need for agility in both adaptation and evolution of service-oriented systems.

DOI: 10.4018/978-1-4666-2503-7.ch002

1. INTRODUCTION

For future software systems and software development processes, the only constant will be change. The "world" in which those future software systems operate is reaching unprecedented levels of dynamicity (de Lemos et al., 2011). Those systems will need to operate correctly in spite of changes in, for example, user requirements, legal regulations, and market opportunities. They will have to operate despite a constantly changing context that includes, for instance, usage settings, locality, end-user devices, network connectivity and computing resources (such as offered by Cloud computing). Furthermore, expectations by end-users concerning the personalization and customization of those systems will become increasingly relevant for market success (Adomavicius & Tuzhilin, 2005).

Modern software technology has enabled us to build software systems with a high degree of flexibility. The most important development in this direction is the concept of service and the Service-oriented Architecture (SOA) paradigm (Erl, 2004; Kaye, 2003; Josuttis, 2007). A service-oriented system is built by "composing" software services (and is thus also called "service composition" or "composed service" in the literature).

Software services achieve the aforementioned high degree of flexibility by separating ownership, maintenance and operation from the use of the software. Service users do not need to acquire, deploy and run software, because they can access its functionality from remote through service interfaces. Ownership, maintenance and operation of the software remains with the service provider (Di Nitto, et al., 2008).

While service-orientation offers huge benefits in terms of flexibility, service-oriented systems face yet another level of change and dynamism. Services might disappear or change without the user of the service having control over such a change.

Agility, i.e., the ability to quickly and effectively respond to changes, will thus play an ever increasing role for future software systems to live in the highly dynamic "world" as sketched above. Agility can be considered from two viewpoints:

- First, agility may concern the evolution of the system. This means that it concerns the development process and how engineering activities (such as requirements engineering and implementation) should be performed to timely address changes by evolving the software.
- Secondly, agility may concern the adaptation of the system. This means that it concerns the system itself and how the system should respond to changes (Papazoglou et al., 2007). Agility in adaptation is typically achieved through self-adaptation, i.e., the autonomous modification of a service-oriented system during operation.

In this chapter, we first sketch the historical development of software systems from monolithic and mostly static applications to highly-dynamic, service-oriented systems (Section 2). Then, we provide an overview and more thorough explanation of the various kinds of changes that need to be faced and how these could be addressed (Section 3). As reference for the remainder of the chapter, we then introduce a service life-cycle model which integrates evolution and adaptation into a coherent framework (Section 4). After elaborating on the activities prescribed by that life-cycle, we discuss the need for agility in evolution (Section 5) and adaptation (Section 6). We conclude this chapter with our perspectives on agile development for service-oriented systems (Section 7).

2. HISTORICAL DEVELOPMENT

2.1 The Emergence of the SOA Paradigm

In (Di Nitto et al., 2008) we gave an extensive account of the historical development of software technology and methods toward highly dynamic, service-oriented systems. The following paragraphs briefly summarize the major milestones along this development.

Genesis: In the late 1960s software development processes started to get disciplined through the identification of well-defined stages and criteria, which were to be met in order to progress from one stage of the process to the next. The waterfall life-cycle model as proposed by Royce in 1970 was such an attempt. It was very rigid and advocated the need for software developers to focus not only on coding but also on higher-level activities (requirements analysis and specification, as well as software design) and on verification and validation.

At the time those life-cycle models were defined, the "world" was assumed to be relatively fixed and static. Stable requirements could thus be elicited at the beginning of the development process. Additionally, most organizations were monolithic. Accordingly, solutions addressing their requirements were to a large extent also monolithic and centralized.

Enlightenment: It was soon realized that the assumption about the stability of requirements was not realistic. In most practical cases, requirements cannot be fully gathered upfront and then left untouched (Nuseibeh, 2001). Specifically, it was realized that often stakeholders do not know what they exactly expect from a system beforehand. Changing requirements should consequently be considered as an intrinsic factor that must be dealt with during development.

As a consequence, incremental and prototyping-based life-cycle models emerged. These were introduced to achieve better tailoring of solutions to requirements and to mitigate the risks involved in software development.

Industrialization: The development of software technology soon allowed dynamic bindings among modules and – even more importantly – to extend these bindings across network boundaries (examples include CORBA and Java RMI). This allowed for the distributed execution of the software.

The development of software technology was accompanied by an increased automation of software development activities. This included, for instance, automatic verification techniques and tools which reached a level of maturity that allowed them to be applied to real-life problems. Examples include model checkers or Boolean satiability checkers.

Globalization: Another major development followed regarding the ownership of software. In the beginning, software development was under the control of a single organization which ultimately owned the code completely. Then, component-based software development became dominant. Off-the-shelf components were developed and provided by third parties who were also responsible for their quality and their evolution. Software development thus became (partly) decentralized.

The development of software technology and methods further made it possible to support seamless evolution of the software in order to incorporate certain anticipated changes. These included, for instance, additional or redefined module functionality.

However, as motivated in Section 1, the demand for software to continuously respond to highly dynamic changes of its context and its requirements has reached unprecedented levels in the past few years. A further major step in the development of software technology and methods to address this dynamism was the birth of the service concept and the Service-Oriented Architecture (SOA) paradigm (Erl, 2004; Kaye, 2003; Josuttis, 2007).

2.2 What is SOA?

When referring to Service Oriented Architecture (SOA) as a paradigm, SOA typically constitutes a set of guiding principles for building service-based applications. Thanks to these principles, services can be (re-)used in many different settings and service-based applications can meet the requirements for dynamism and flexibility.

A detailed discussions of the SOA principles can be found in (Erl, 2004; Kaye, 2003; Josuttis, 2007), they include:

Loose Coupling: This principle means that a service only makes weak assumptions about its interactions with other services. For example, instead of services being tightly coupled by means of a common data model (such as was the case for distributed objects and CORBA), a small set of simple data types is used. The loose coupling principle of SOA also argues for preferring asynchronous interactions over synchronous ones, message passing instead of method invocation, as well as flexible message routing instead of fixed. Finally, late binding during deployment or even run-time (see below) is preferred over static binding during design-time.

Dynamic Service Discovery and Late Binding: This principle implies that services can be discovered and composed into a service-oriented during deployment and during run-time. The discovery of services is supported by service registries ("yellow pages") or even more powerful service search engines (see (Papazoglou et al., 2010) for more details on the latter aspect). Those facilities allow for dynamically re-configuring a service-based application by replacing services, which may have shown to be unreliable, with alternative compatible services (possibly from different service providers).

Service Interoperability and Protocol Independence: Similar to W3C's notion of Web Service, a software service may be considered a "piece" of software designed to support interoperable machine-to-machine interaction over the Internet. Existing Internet and Web Service standards allow for service interoperability by prescribing ways how services can interact, exchange messages and be located across the Internet. Those standards have led to the proliferation of services available over the Internet and described in terms of WSDL (the Web Services Description Language). As an example, at the time of writing, the seekda. com search engine has indexing almost 30.000 software services.

Self-Containment and Autonomy of Services: Self-containment and autonomy means that the logic that is governed by a service resides within an explicit boundary. The service should only have control within this boundary and should not depend on other services for it to execute its governance. This allows for keeping changes and failures isolated and will foster reusability of services.

Abstraction and Service Interfaces: The functionality that is exposed by a service naturally abstracts from the underlying implementation. In addition, the only part of a service that is visible to the outside world is what is exposed via the service interface. Typically, the underlying logic of the software, which is irrelevant to the service user and/or constitutes intellectual property of the service provider, will not be exposed via the service interface. As a consequence, this means that the service interfaces define a form of formal contract. In order to interact with the service, the service users only need to have knowledge about the service interface (and not the underlying logic or implementation). This principle thus is an application of the well-known "information hiding" principle to the realm of service-based systems.

It should be noted that a service-based application or a software service does not necessarily need to follow all of the aforementioned principles. There may be good reasons that in certain application scenarios and domains, some of the principles are not applicable. As an example, for more traditional enterprise applications it may well suffice to have static service bindings and a tighter coupling between those services by sharing more complex data structures.

2.3 The Impact of SOA

SOA enables us to build software systems with a high degree of flexibility. Software services separate ownership, maintenance and operation from the use of the software. Service users thus do not need to acquire, deploy and run software, because they can access its functionality from remote through service interfaces. Ownership, maintenance and operation of the software remains with the service provider (Di Nitto et al., 2008).

Similar to what has been enabled by globalization in the real world, third-party software services now enable organizations to flexibly outsource business functions (typically commodity functions) and to focus on the innovative functions, which differentiates one organization from another.

Thus, SOA promises huge benefits in terms of dynamism and flexibility. However, service-based applications also need to become resilient to their services changing, disappearing or violating their expected quality. Especially in the case of third-party services, the service users do not have control over such changes, thus, calling for novel solutions to address this new dimension of changes.

Luckily, the introduction of SOA technology was accompanied by another major step in the development of techniques for automating software engineering activities. Verification and measurement techniques have started to be extended to the operation phase of the systems, leading to "online" techniques (de Lemos et al., 2011; Papazoglou et al., 2010), online testing (Bertolino, 2007) and run-time verification (Bianculli et al., 2009). Those techniques provide the foundation for service-oriented systems to automatically identify and respond to certain changes (see Section 3). As an example, by continuously verifying whether the service-oriented system meets its requirements, an adaptation of the system can be triggered once a failure becomes imminent.

3. CHANGES

Adaptation and evolution of a service-oriented system are triggered by changes that may occur in three major areas: (1) the expectations that its users (or other stakeholders) have concerning the functionality and quality that the system should provide, (2) the world in which the software system is executed, (3) the system itself. The first area is the realm of requirements, the second one is traditionally called context, and the third one is often referred to as the machine (Jackson, 2001).

According to the IEEE Standard Glossary of Software Engineering Terminology (IEEE, 1990), "a requirement is: (1) a condition or capability needed by a user to solve a problem or achieve an objective; (2) a condition or capability that must be met or possessed by a system or system component to satisfy a contract, standard, specification, or other formally imposed documents; (3) a documented representation of a condition or capability as in (1) or (2)".

The term context derives from the Latin cum (with or together) and texere (to weave). It has been defined in (Dey & Abowd, 2000) as "any information that can be used to characterize the situation of entities (persons, places, objects) that are relevant to the interaction between a user and an application, including the user and the application themselves". According to (Hofer et al., 2002) context can be physical, i.e., measured by some hardware sensor or logical, i.e., captured by monitoring user interaction. When it is physical it refers to location, movement, and any environmental information. When it is logical it refers to users' goals, emotional state, business processes, etc.

Figure 1 shows typical examples of changes that may occur and trigger the need for adapting or evolving the service-oriented system.

Clearly, the examples of changes shown in the figures require different levels of intervention on the corresponding software system and its artifacts.

Figure 1. Areas for changes and examples

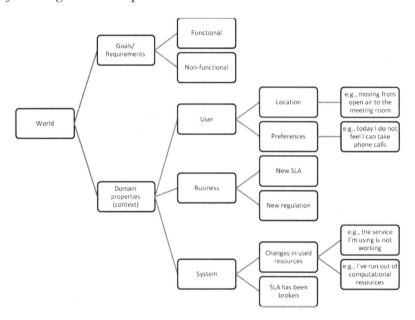

For instance, the lack of computational resources may be addressed easily, without modifying the structure of the software system, by exploiting the flexibility offered by Cloud computing (Armbrust et al., 2010). The failure of a service is also simple to address if our system is built according to the SOA paradigm that enables dynamic binding (see Section 2) of alternative and compatible services. In this case, in fact, the substitution of one service for another service can occur at runtime without performing any reprogramming activity of the software (Moser et al., 2008).

Other kinds of changes, such as the addition of new features, require a deeper intervention on the software system. In this case the system may need to be partially redesigned and re-implemented in order to address the change.

All changes that can be addressed by performing some simple reasoning (e.g., "since the user is in downtown Milano, he/she is certainly interested in knowing about free parking spaces in that area") or by modifying the bindings to services can be addressed by a service-oriented

system if it incorporates self-adaptation facilities (de Lemos et al., 2011). Vice versa, the changes that require redesign or reimplementation of the system typically have to be addressed by the intervention of human beings.

The boundary between the two kinds of changes is not necessarily defined once and for all but depends on the reasoning abilities that we are able to include in the software system while we build it. This point will be discussed in more detail in Section 4.

4. SERVICE LIFE-CYCLE MODEL

This section introduces the service life-cycle model, as defined by S-Cube, the European Network of Excellence on software, services and system (http://www.s-cube-network.eu). The S-Cube service life-cycle model (Papazoglou et al., 2010; Metzger et al., 2010) defines the relevant activities for self-adaptive service-oriented systems and integrates these into a coherent framework. Self-adaptive systems automatically and dynamically adapt to certain changes (see Section 3). The aim of self-adaptation is to reduce the need of human intervention as much as possible in order to allow those systems to quickly respond to changes.

The S-Cube service life-cycle model consists of the following two loops, which we will detail in the remainder of this chapter. The loops of the life-cycle can be executed in an incremental and iterative fashion, as follows:

- **Evolution Loop:** (see right hand side of Figure 2) Builds on the more traditional development and deployment activities, including requirements engineering, design, realization, and deployment (see Section 5.1). However, it extends those activities with "design-for-adaptation" steps, such as to define and implement how the system should monitor and modify itself when entering the left-hand side of the life-cycle (e.g., see de Lemos et al., 2011).
- **Adaptation Loop:** (see left hand side of Figure 2) Explicitly defines activities for autonomously addressing changes during the operation of service-oriented systems (see Section 6.1). The activities in the ad-

aptation loop follow the steps of the MAPE loop (Monitor-Analyze-Plan-Execute), which is typically found in autonomic systems (Salehie & Tahvildari, 2009).

It should be noted that in some cases also adaptation requires human intervention. This is often called human-in-the-loop adaptation (Papazoglou et al., 2010); Papazoglou, Pohl, Parkin, and Human-in-the-loop adaptation is different from evolution in the sense that the activities performed by the humans and the artifacts that are modified differ; e.g., the change of requirements documents certainly requires to go through the evolution loop, while the choice between two possible candidate services can be performed as human-in-the-loop adaptation.

5. EVOLUTION

When the system evolves, it goes through a re-engineering phase in which it is permanently modified. The practices used in this phase are being deeply studied in the software maintenance literature (see for instance the proceedings of the 26th International Conference on Software Main-

Figure 2. The s-cube service life-cycle model

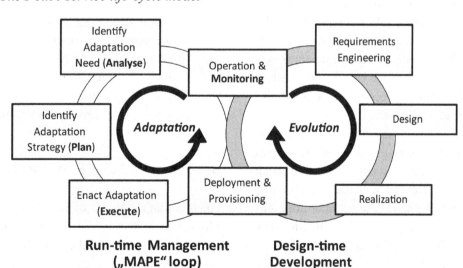

tenance (ICSM, 2010). Some of these practices have been applied to service-oriented systems as well. In this case, the main aspects which have been considered concern the issues of maintaining the interface compatibility between versions of services, of identifying the right timing for evolving services depending on the contracts currently in place, of identifying the right stakeholders for evolution and of understanding their impact to the evolution process (see Andrikopoulos, 2010 for a detailed overview).

5.1 Activities in the Evolution Loop

As mentioned above, the activities in the evolution loop follow the traditional software development activities.

- **Requirements Engineering:** During requirements engineering, the functional and quality requirements for the service-oriented system are elicited and documented. The specifics of service-oriented systems make requirements engineering a particularly relevant activity. This is related to the highly dynamic nature of service-oriented systems and to the necessity to realize the continuous adaptability of these systems. Indeed, in a context where the application is in continuous evolution and is thus characterized by rather blurred boundaries, the study of those requirements that exist a priori in the organizational and business setting and that are hence largely independent from the solution becomes very important (Cheng et al., 2009).
- **Design:** During the design phase, the workflow of the service-oriented system is typically specified using languages such as BPEL. Together with the definition of the workflow, candidate services are identified that can provide the functionality and quality to fulfill the requirements of the system. This means that those services

that provide, at least partially, the expected functionality and quality are identified. This is supported by service matchmaking techniques, such as the ones presented in (Comuzzi & Pernici, 2009). A further task is to define adaptation strategies and mechanisms which enable the application to react to adaptation needs (Bucchiarone et al., 2009), i.e., to take "design for adaptation" decisions. Finally, the conditions under which some changes will have to be enacted during the runtime have to be identified.

- **Realization:** After design, the realization and implementation of the system can start. This specifically means that contracts on quality aspects (aka. Service Level Agreements, SLAs) have to be established with the third-party service providers. Typically, this requires some form of SLA negotiation and agreement (Papazoglou et al., 2010; Comuzzi & Pernici, 2009). Moreover, the monitoring and analysis mechanisms needed to identify the conditions that require changes at runtime have to be defined together with the adaptation strategies to be executed.
- **Deployment:** Deployment comprises all the activities needed to make the system available to its users, including the deployment of internal services and software components on computing infrastructures (including Clouds [Armbrust et al., 2010]). It should be noted that the service-oriented systems itself could be offered as a service and could thus participate in other service compositions.

5.2 Towards Agile Evolution

An important element of the evolution loop is efficiency. In the age of globalization, in fact, changes need to be handled in a timely fashion. If the execution of the evolution loop is not able to quickly address changes, there is a risk of delivering a solution that addresses a certain change when this change is not relevant any longer, for instance, because it has been superseded by other new changes. Agile development approaches (Abrahamsson et al., 2003) are often mentioned as a way to address changes in a fast and interactive way, if developers are able to work in close collaboration with the owners of new requirements or with those who have a deep knowledge about the occurred context changes.

This statement has an initial evidence in the work of (Capiluppi et al., 2007), where an empirical study has been conducted which shows how the application of agile methods to support the evolution of a software system has resulted in a "smooth evolution while avoiding the problems of increasing complexity or decreasing customer satisfaction".

In the context of SOA, companies such as IBM (Krogdahl et al., 2005) and OutSystems (Sprott, 2009) are suggesting the adoption of an agile approach. Krogdahl et al. (2005) argues that refactoring is an important technique in SOA, where services and service interfaces need to be continuously adjusted to the needs of new customers. The paper also observes that management of agility in SOA is simplified by the fact that changes tend to be localized in specific parts of software systems and, in particular, in the service choreography (aka. service composition).

The adoption of an agile approach supported by a toolset called the "Agile Service Platform" is proposed in (Sprott, 2009). Among other features, this platform keeps information about components and dependencies continuously updated, thus effectively supporting the maintenance and the evolution activities, for which a 70% reduction in costs has been reported. Interaction with customers during the development and the evolution phases is strongly encouraged – facilitated by the platform by means of creating proper communication channels between customers and the project management.

A technological advancement that pushes agile development of SOA to the extreme is offered by mashups (Yu et al., 2008). Mashups constitute the integration of different web applications and services which have the purpose of serving the specific needs of some users. They are usually short lived systems intended to be built not only by expert developers but also by less-experienced people. To this end, proper development environments are being developed. These offer a specific component and composition models and are usually associated to some runtime environment. While these environments promise to shorten the development cycle in a significant way, they are still not well integrated into a proper full-fledged development methodology.

From a completely different perspective, another interesting step toward agility is the integration of service selection within the requirement engineering phase suggested by Maiden et al. (2008). They have proposed a tool called EDDIE that supports engineers in the definition of requirements and use cases, as well as in the identification of available services that fulfill such requirements with different levels of precision.

Even though it has not been designed with agile processes in mind, agile methods could be mapped to the S-Cube life-cycle. Using Scrum (Schwaber, 2004) as an example, we could assume that each iteration of the evolution loop is performed as a Sprint which aims at delivering an increment of a service-oriented system. Given that services represent a natural unit of functionality, each such Sprint could aim at incorporating a new service in the service-oriented system up to the point where the complete functionality is offered to the system's users.

Still, as the aim is to build self-adaptive systems, an agile approach targeted at service-oriented systems needs to take into account that the redesign and redevelopment of the software system has to incorporate the "design for adaptation" principle (see Section 5.1) in a seamless way. This is an issue which surely deserves further research.

6. ADAPTATION

6.1 Activities in the Adaptation Loop

As mentioned above, the activities in the adaptation loop follow the MAPE loop as known from autonomic computing.

- **Operation and Management:** Operation and management include all activities needed for running and controlling the service-oriented system. The literature also uses the term governance to describe all activities that oversee the correct execution of service-oriented system (and its constituent services).

- **The Identification of Changes, Including Problems in the Running System:** (e.g., failures of constituent services) and alteration of its context, plays a fundamental role. This identification is obtained by means of monitoring mechanism and, more generally, by exploiting techniques for run-time quality assurance such as online testing or run-time verification (de Lemos et al., 2011). Together, these mechanisms and techniques are able to detect relevant changes.

- **Identify Adaptation Need:** Certain changes trigger the service-oriented system to leave its "normal" operation and enter the adaptation or the evolution cycle. As discussed in Section 3, which of the two loops is being entered depends on the kind of observed change. The adaptation cycle is responsible for autonomously deciding whether and how the service-oriented system needs to modify itself in order to maintain its expected functionality and quality.

- **Identify Adaptation Strategy:** When the adaptation loop is entered, possible adaptation strategies are identified, selected and instantiated. Possible strategies include service substitution (rebinding), SLA re-

negotiation, and re-configuration of the workflow (Bucchiarone et al., 2009). From the set of possible strategies, the ones which fit the situation are selected and instantiated; e.g., by deciding which service to use as a substitute or which re-configuration of the workflow to perform.

- **Enact Adaptation:** After the adaptation strategy has been selected and instantiated, adaptation mechanisms are used to execute the actual adaptation. For example, service substitution, re-configuration or re-composition may be obtained using automated service discovery and dynamic binding mechanisms, while re-composition may be achieved using existing automated service composition techniques.

6.2 Towards Agile Adaptation

In addition to the degree of automation, the point in time when a change can be detected impacts on the agility of the system in responding to that change; e.g., if the system can forecast an imminent change, more time and thus more options remain for the adaptation than if the system can only detect changes once they actually occur.

The following three types of adaptation (Metzger, 2011) exemplify the impact that the point in time when changes are detected has on the agility of the system:

- **Reactive Adaptation:** The case in which the system is modified in response to external failures that have actually occurred, i.e., failures that are actually observed by the users of the system. Repair and/or compensation activities have to be executed as part of the adaptation in order to mitigate the effects of the failure; e.g., the user is paid compensation, or the workflow is rolled-back. Obviously, such a reactive adaptation can have a severe impact on how agile a system can respond to changes

(Hielscher et al., 2008). As examples, the execution of reactive adaptation activities on the running system can considerably increase execution time and therefore reduce the overall performance of the running system, or an adaptation of the system might not be possible at all, e.g., because the system has already terminated in an inconsistent state.

- **Preventive Adaptation:** The case in which an actual local failure or deviation is repaired before its consequences become visible to the user in the form of an external failure. As an example, if a local failure occurs (such as a third-party service *S1* responding too slow), the system might forecast whether this may lead to an external failure (visible by the user) and prepare repair mechanisms; e.g., a faster service *S3'* could be used instead of service *S3* in the remainder of the workflow, thereby counteracting the slow response of service *S1*. Due to the time delay between the detection of the local failure of *S1* and the observation of the external failure by the user, there is more flexibility in modifying the workflow than in the reactive case.

- **Proactive Adaptation:** The case in which the system is modified even before a local failure occurs. As an example, if the system is able to predict that a local failure is imminent (but did not yet occur), the system can be yours. A modified in advance; e.g., a service *S1*, predicted to respond too slow, can be replaced by a quicker service *S1'*. In this case, neither repair nor compensation activities would be necessary as part of the adaptation, as no failure has actually occurred.

In a nutshell, the more agile the service-oriented system is to become, the stronger the role of proactiveness in the adaptation loop becomes. This means that already during design (i.e., within the evolution loop), decisions need to be made about how to predict failures during the execution of the service-oriented system. However, selecting the right technique can be quite a challenging task due to the highly dynamic nature of service-oriented systems (see Metzger, 2011 for an in-depth discussion on this issue).

7. CONCLUSION AND RESEARCH HIGHLIGHTS

Agile methods applied in the SOA context are expected to lead to the quick and effective development and evolution of self-adaptive service-oriented systems. Self-adaptation has a strong implication on the way the agile development process is organized. Taking Scrum as an example, Sprints should not only concern the inclusion of new functionalities but also the creation of respective self-adaptation mechanisms. The challenge is therefore to understand how self-adaptation mechanisms can be developed in an incremental way, Sprint by Sprint.

Also, Sprints are more effective when associated to the creation of business value. It is thus important to identify the value that can be associated with a specific self-adaptation capability that allows the system to reliably work in a globalized environment and to execute resiliently under highly dynamic changes. How to perform such quantification is still open and should certainly be part of future research.

ACKNOWLEDGMENT

Research leading to these results has received funding from the European Community's 7th Framework Programme FP7 / 2007-2013 under grant agreement 215483 (S-Cube).

REFERENCES

Abrahamsson, P., Warsta, J., Siponen, M. T., & Ronkainen, J. (2003). New directions on agile methods: A comparative analysis. In *Proceedings of the 25th International Conference on Software Engineering*, ICSE '03, (pp. 244–254). Washington, DC: IEEE Computer Society.

Adomavicius, G., & Tuzhilin, A. (2005). Personalization technologies: A process-oriented perspective. *Communications of the ACM*, *48*, 83–90. Retrieved from http://doi.acm.org/10.1145/1089107.1089109 doi:10.1145/1089107.1089109

Andrikopoulos, V. (2010). *A theory and model for the evolution of software services*. The Netherlands: Tilburg University.

Armbrust, M., Fox, A., Griffith, R., Joseph, A. D., Katz, R., & Konwinski, A. (2010). A view of cloud computing. *Communications of the ACM*, *53*, 50–58. doi:10.1145/1721654.1721672

Bertolino, A. (2007). Software testing research: Achievements, challenges, dreams. In *FOSE '07: 2007 Future of Software Engineering* (pp. 85–103). Washington, DC: IEEE Computer Society. doi:10.1109/FOSE.2007.25

Bianculli, D., Ghezzi, C., & Pautasso, C. (2009). *Embedding continuous lifelong verification in service life cycles*. In Principles of Engineering Service Oriented Systems (PESOS 2009), co-located with ICSE 2009, DOI 10.1109/PESOS.2009.5068828

Bucchiarone, A., Cappiello, C., Nitto, E. D., Kazhamiakin, R., Mazza, V., & Pistore, M. (2009). *Design for adaptation of service-based applications: Main issues and requirements*. In Engineering Service-Oriented Applications: Supporting Software Service Development Lifecycles (WESOA) co-located with ICSOC/ServiceWave

Capiluppi, A., Fernandez-Ramil, J., Higman, J., Sharp, H., & Smith, N. (2007). An empirical study of the evolution of an agile-developed software system. In 29th International Conference on Software Engineering, ICSE 2007, (pp. 511–518). DOI 10.1109/ICSE.2007.14

Cheng, B., de Lemos, R., Giese, H., Inverardi, P., Magee, J., & Andersson, J. ... Whittle, J. (2009). Software engineering for self-adaptive systems: A research roadmap. In B. Cheng, R. de Lemos, H. Giese, P. Inverardi, & J. Magee (Eds.), *Software Engineering for Self-Adaptive Systems, Lecture Notes in Computer Science, vol 5525*, (pp. 1–26). Berlin, Germany: Springer.

Cohen, D., Lindvall, M., & Costa, P. (2004). An introduction to agile methods. *Advances in Computers*, *2004*, 2–67.

Comuzzi, M., & Pernici, B. (2009). A framework for QoS-based web service contracting. *ACM Transactions on Web, 3*(3)

de Lemos, R., Giese, H., Müller, H., Shaw, M., Andersson, J., & Baresi, L. ... Wuttke, J. (2011). Software engineering for self-adaptive systems: A second research roadmap. In R. de Lemos, H. Giese, H. Müller, & M. Shaw (Eds.), *Software Engineering for Self-Adaptive Systems*, Schloss Dagstuhl -Leibniz-Zentrum für Informatik, Germany, Dagstuhl, Germany, no. 10431 in Dagstuhl Seminar Proceedings

Dey, A. K., & Abowd, G. D. (2000). *Towards a better understanding of context and context-awareness*. In Workshop on The What, Who, Where, When, and How of Context-Awareness

Di Nitto, E., Ghezzi, C., Metzger, A., Papazoglou, M., & Pohl, K. (2008). A journey to highly dynamic, self-adaptive service-based applications. *Automated Software Engineering*, *15*(3-4), 313–341. doi:10.1007/s10515-008-0032-x

Erl, T. (2004). *Service-oriented architecture.* Prentice Hall.

Hielscher, J., Kazhamiakin, R., Metzger, A., & Pistore, M. (2008). A framework for proactive selfadaptation of service-based applications based on online testing. In *ServiceWave 2008, LNCS 5377.* Springer.

Hofer, T., Schwinger, W., Pichler, M., Leonhartsberger, G., & Altmann, J. (2002). Context-awareness on mobile devices: The Hydrogen approach. In *36th Annual Hawaii International Conference on System Sciences*, (pp. 292–302).

ICSM. (2010). *26th IEEE International Conference on Software Maintenance* (ICSM 2010), September 12-18, 2010, Timisoara, Romania. IEEE Computer Society.

IEEE. (1990). *IEEE standard glossary of software engineering terminology.* (IEEE Std 610.12-1990 ed). New York, NY: Institute of Electrical and Electronics Engineers.

Jackson, M. (2001). *Problem frames: Analysing and structuring software development problems.* New York, NY: Addison-Wesley.

Josuttis, N. (2007). *SOA in practice: The art of distributed system design.* O'Reilly Media.

Kaye, D. (2003). *Loosely coupled: The missing pieces of web services.* RDS Press.

Krogdahl, P., Luef, G., & Steindl, C. (2005). Service-oriented agility: An initial analysis for the use of agile methods for SOA development. In *IEEE International Conference on Services Computing*, (pp. 93–100). Los Alamitos, CA: IEEE Computer Society.

Metzger, A. (2011). Towards accurate failure prediction for the proactive adaptation of service-oriented systems (invited paper). In *Proceedings Workshop on Assurances for Self-Adaptive Systems* (ASAS), collocated with ESEC 2011.

Metzger, A., Schmieders, E., Cappiello, C., Nitto, E. D., Kazhamiakin, R., Pernici, B., & Pistore, M. (2010). *Towards proactive adaptation: A journey along the S-Cube service life-cycle.* In Maintenance and Evolution of Service-Oriented Systems.

Moser, O., Rosenberg, F., & Dustdar, S. (2008). Non-intrusive monitoring and service adaptation for WS-BPEL. In *Proceeding of the 17th International Conference on World Wide Web, WWW '08*, (pp. 815–824). New York, NY: ACM Press.

Nuseibeh, B. (2001). Weaving together requirements and architectures. *IEEE Computer, 34*(3), 115–117. doi:10.1109/2.910904

Papazoglou, M., Pohl, K., Parkin, M., & Metzger, A. (Eds.). (2010). *Service research challenges and solutions for the future internet: Towards mechanisms and methods for engineering, managing, and adapting service-based systems.* Heidelberg, Germany: Springer.

Papazoglou, M. P., Traverso, P., Dustdar, S., & Leymann, F. (2007). Service-oriented computing: State of the art and research challenges. *IEEE Computer, 40*(11), 38–45. doi:10.1109/MC.2007.400

Royce, W. (1970). Managing the development of large software systems. In *IEEE WESCON*, San Francisco, CA, USA, (pp. 1–9).

Salehie, M., & Tahvildari, L. (2009). Self-adaptive software: Landscape and research challenges. *ACM Transactions on Autonomous and Adaptive Systems, 4*(2).

Schwaber, K. (2004). *Agile project management with Scrum* (*Vol. 7*). Redmond, WA: Microsoft Press.

Sprott, D. (2009). Product overview: OutSystems agile SOA platform. *CBDI Journal,* 15–20.

Yu, J., Benatallah, B., Casati, F., & Daniel, F. (2008). Understanding mashup development. *IEEE Internet Computing, 12*(5), 44–52. doi:10.1109/MIC.2008.114

Zachos, K., & Maiden, N. (2008). Inventing requirements from software: An empirical investigation with web services. In *Proceedings 16th IEEE International Conference on Requirements Engineering*, (pp. 145–154). IEEE Computer Society Press.

KEY TERMS AND DEFINITIONS

Adaptation: Adaptation is a process of modifying service-based applications in order to satisfy new requirements and to fit new situations dictated by the environment on the basis of adaptation strategies designed by the system integrator. Self-adaptation requires that all adaptation steps, decisions, and actions are performed by the service-oriented system autonomously. This also assumes that all the necessary mechanisms to enact adaptation strategies are built into the application. When the adaptation process assumes any form of human intervention, this is considered human-in-the-loop adaptation.

Design for Adaptation: Design for adaptation is a design process specifically defined to take adaptation into account. It should incorporate into the system under development all those features that enable the system to meet adaptation requirements from very early design stages up to and including execution.

Evolution: Evolution of a service-oriented system is a long-term history of continuous modifications of the system after its deployment in order to correct faults, to improve performance or other quality attributes, or to address a modified environment.

Monitoring: Monitoring of services and service-oriented systems refers to checking whether certain predefined properties are satisfied by the monitored subject during its execution.

Service: Software services are not just pieces of software; instead, they represent the functionality that the underlying pieces of software offer. Rather than building a software system from scratch, or developing it by selecting and gluing together off-the-shelf components, designers can realize applications by composing services, possibly offered by third parties. This shift from adopting the piece of technology (the software) to using the functionality (the service) offers us a valuable tool to design those software systems that we call service-oriented systems at a higher level of abstraction, possibly building new value-added composed services. Services have taken the concept of ownership to the extreme: not only, as off-the-shelf components, their development, quality assurance, and maintenance are under the control of third parties, but they can even be executed and managed by third parties.

Service-Oriented System: A service-oriented system is composed of a number of possibly independent services, available in a network, which perform the desired functionalities of the architecture. Such services could be provided by third parties, not necessarily by the owner of the service-oriented system. Note that a service-oriented system shows a profound difference with respect to a component-based system: while the owner of the component-based system also owns and controls its components, the owner of a service-oriented system does not own, in general, the component services, nor it can control their execution.

Section 2
Theory

Chapter 3
A Roadmap for Software Engineering for the Cloud:
Results of a Systematic Review

Abhishek Sharma
University of Calgary, Canada

Frank Maurer
University of Calgary, Canada

ABSTRACT

This chapter presents the results of a systematic review from existing literature in software engineering for cloud-based applications and describes what the research community thinks about the effects of introducing cloud computing into a software development process. In this systematic review, the authors describe the challenges cloud computing poses for software development. They particularly investigate whether agile methodologies are beneficial or not in developing software that will be deployed in the cloud. In their results, they found that industry practitioners in their blogs and self-reported reviews indicate that agile development and cloud computing goes well together and that further investigation is required to confirm this claim.

INTRODUCTION

Cloud computing is a relatively recent term that is built upon decades of research in various fields within Computer Science from networking over distributed computing to web and software services. Cloud is emerging as a model that works on the principle of everything-as-a-service (XaaS) (Banerjee et al., 2011). While cloud-based solutions are adopted in Industry with a great pace, there appears to be little research on the impact of this new technology on software development processes.

DOI: 10.4018/978-1-4666-2503-7.ch003

There are various software engineering issues that have to be addressed when the cloud becomes the target deployment environment. For example, when we plan to migrate software testing to cloud (Parveen & Tilley, 2010) we need to decide upon the characteristic of the application that will be under test and type of testing to be performed. Another example can be the adequacy of current software process models when development involves cloud (Guha & Al-Dabass, 2010).

WHAT IS CLOUD COMPUTING?

Before presenting our review, let us understand what cloud computing is. The US National Institute of Standards and Technology (NIST) defines cloud computing as:

A model for enabling ubiquitous, convenient, on-demand network access to a shared pool of configurable computing resources (e.g., networks, servers, storage, applications, and services) that can be rapidly provisioned and released with minimal management effort or service provider interaction.-The NIST definition of cloud computing, 2011

The NIST definition is one of the most comprehensive definitions and is widely referenced. Furthermore, this definition describes cloud computing as having five essential characteristics, three service models and four deployment models. The essential characteristics are:

- **On-Demand Self-Service:** Computing resources can be acquired and used at any time without requiring human interaction with each services provider. Computing resources include processing power, virtual machines, storage etc.
- **Broad Network Access:** Above mentioned resources can be accessed over a network using heterogeneous thin or thick client platforms (e.g., mobile phones, laptops, and PDAs).

- **Resource Pooling:** The computing resources are pooled to serve multiple consumers using a multi-tenant model, with different physical and virtual resources dynamically assigned and reassigned according to consumer demand. There is a sense of transparency in it, since a consumer can decide the amount of resources that are required. The customer generally has no control or knowledge over the exact geographical location of the provided resources but may be able to specify location at a higher level of abstraction (e.g., country, state, or data center).
- **Rapid Elasticity:** A user can quickly scale out on resources, and these resources can be rapidly released to scale in. To the consumer end, the capabilities available for provisioning often appear to be unlimited and can be purchased in any quantity at any time.
- **Measured Service:** Cloud systems automatically control and optimize resource use by leveraging a metering capability on metrics like CPU hours, bandwidth, storage etc.

The above-mentioned characteristics apply to all the clouds, but abstraction at service level differ at the provider level. The level of abstraction is defined in the service models provided by NIST:

- **Software as a Service (SaaS):** Users can access the application, which is offered as a service, using thin client interfaces such as web-browsers. An example of SaaS is web-based email. Cloud users have no control at this level. The capability provided to the consumer is to use the provider's applications running on a cloud infrastructure. The consumer does not manage or control the underlying cloud infrastructure including network, servers, operating systems, storage, or even individual application capabilities. One possible exception to these rules is the presence of limited user-specific configuration settings.

- **Platform as a Service (PaaS):** The capability provided to the consumer is to deploy onto the Cloud infrastructure consumer-created or acquired applications created using programming languages and tools supported by the provider. (E.g. Google App Engine). The control and access of the underlying infrastructure is out of the reach consumer.

- **Infrastructure as a Service (IaaS):** The capability provided to the consumer is to provision processing, storage, networks, and other fundamental computing resources where the consumer is able to deploy and run arbitrary software, which can include operating systems and applications. The consumer does not manage or control the underlying cloud infrastructure but has control over operating system, storage, deployed applications, and possibly limited control of select networking components (e.g., host firewalls).

The deployment models or types of cloud on the basis of who owns and uses them come next. The NIST definitions of the four common models are:

- **Private Cloud:** The cloud infrastructure is operated solely for an organization. It may be managed by the organization or a third party and may exist on premise or off premise.

- **Community Cloud:** This can be looked upon as a shared cloud infrastructure. It supports a specific community that has shared concerns.

- **Public Cloud:** The cloud infrastructure is made available to the general public or a large industry group and is owned by an organization selling cloud services.

- **Hybrid Cloud:** As the name suggests this infrastructure is a composition of two or more clouds (private, community, or public) that remain unique entities but are bound together by standardized or proprietary technology that enables data and application portability (e.g., cloud bursting for load balancing between clouds).

The emergence of clouds seems to have caused an impact on the IT industry. Increasing interest of industry in cloud technologies and development of cloud-based applications is causing an influence on software development process and may result in changes in development process. With the introduction of cloud computing a new term has emerged – "software for the cloud" or "cloud software". Cloud software is different from the traditional web applications in a sense that customer's data and application resides on servers that provide full programmatic control, but hide the hardware level details from the customer. These applications are designed keeping in mind scalability and replication that needs to be done to reap maximum benefit out of the cloud architecture. This review basically looks at cloud computing from a software engineering perspective.

REVIEW METHODOLOGY

A systematic literature review is a secondary study that is used to identify, evaluate and interpret all available research relevant to a particular research question, or topic area, or phenomenon of interest (Kitchenham & Charters, 2007). A systematic literature review is undertaken to:

- Summarize the existing evidence concerning a treatment or technology.
- Identify any gaps in current research in order to suggest areas for further investigation.
- Provide a framework/background in order to appropriately position new research activities.

For this chapter, our main focus is to summarize existing work in the area to provide a sound basis for further research and development on software engineering for the cloud.

Protocol Development

For this review we followed the recommendations by (Kitchenham & Charters, 2007) and (Mian *et al.*, 2005) on systematic reviews. The goal of our review is to look for existing research on Software Engineering for Cloud. The research questions that guided this review are:

- What software engineering issues do the developers face while developing software for clouds?
- Are agile methodologies beneficial when we are developing software for clouds?

The research questions were used for the selection of the search keywords for our review. We decided to position keywords more towards generality on a general-specific scale, since using very specific search terms provided very limited number of results. Table 1 presents the keywords used in the search. It is evident from our list of keywords that we tried to include most of the keywords that are related to agile. This was done to reduce chances of omission of literature that discusses agile and cloud.

Table 1. Keywords used in review process

Category	Software Engineering	Cloud Computing
Keywords	Software Engineering, Agile, Scrum, Extreme Programming, Continuous Integration, Lean Development	Cloud, Cloud Computing, Cloud Development, Cloud Services, Cloud Engineering

Data Sources and Search Strategy

The search was a conjunction of Software Engineering and Cloud Computing terms. Therefore, we have the following search strings:

- Software Engineering,
- Agile or Scrum,
- Extreme Programming,
- Continuous Integration,
- Lean Development; and
- Cloud,
- Cloud Computing,
- Cloud Development,
- Cloud Services,
- Cloud Engineering.

The sources selected for search were:

- **Scopus (since it covers both ACM and Springer Digital Libraries):** A bibliographic database containing abstracts and citations for academic journal articles. Covers both ACM Digital Library and Springer Link digital libraries in inclusion with other publishing companies. Scopus includes approximately 18000 titles.
- **IEEExplore Digital Library:** Covers electrical engineering, computer science, and electronic subject areas and provides full-text and bibliographic access to IEEE transaction, journals, magazines and conference proceedings.
- **Elsevier Science Direct:** One of the largest online collections of published scientific research in the world. It contains about 10 million articles from over 2,500 journals and over 6,000 e-books, reference works, book series and handbooks issued by Elsevier.

In addition to this we hand searched proceedings of:

- ICSE Cloud workshop
- IEEE International Conference on Cloud Computing Technology and Science
- IEEE International Conference on Cloud Computing

The match domain for the string was set as "everywhere", which includes title, abstract, keywords and body. This is casting a wide search net to reduce the possibility of overlooking any relevant existing work.

Inclusion and Exclusion Criteria

We searched for literature that was peer reviewed, may it be theoretical, empirical or experimental papers. To include a paper in analysis (inclusion criteria), the paper must be in English, must be peer reviewed and reports information about cloud computing from a software engineering perspective. We, first classified the material by reading the title and abstract, and dropped all the papers that clearly did not match the inclusion criteria. The remaining papers were analyzed more carefully based on reading the introduction and conclusion. All papers whose introduction and conclusion matched our criteria were read in full. Our final list includes all papers that fulfilled our inclusion criteria even if only a small section was ful☐lling the inclusion criteria.

RESULTS

The search was conducted in digital libraries in March of 2011; this search was updated in December 2011. Since we used a wide search net, we got a total of 1353 documents. It is worth mentioning that all the papers in conference proceedings were already included in the search results from digital libraries. The results are presented in Table 2. After

Table 2. Metrics for quality attributes

Quality Attribute	Metric
Reusability	Functional Commonality, Non-functional Utilization, Coverage of Variability
Efficiency	Utilization of Resources, Time Behavior
Reliability	Service Stability, Service Accuracy
Scalability	Coverage of Scalability
Availability	Robustness of Service

the title and abstract filtering we ended up with 44 papers. For the second stage of filtering, authors read the introduction and conclusion, papers that did not satisfy the inclusion criteria were dropped, and this reduced the number of papers to 29. After reading the papers in full we decided to include 17 papers in the end. This already indicates that only a limited empirical basis exists on software engineering for the cloud.

We read all included papers and derived objective and subjective results. After collecting the information we started with classification of papers according to the phase of Software development process they were related to. The results are presented in Figure 1.

Figure 1. No. of papers after subsequent inclusion and exclusion

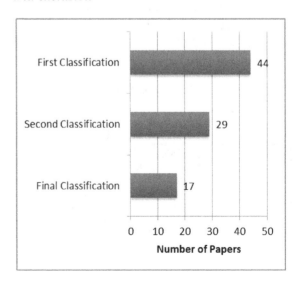

Quantitative Analysis

We did initial quantitative analysis on the gathered papers. Figure 2 shows the results that were obtained and we found that most of the papers were published in 2009 and 2010. Also it demonstrates that work in this area is just getting underway. The data also demonstrates a possible increase in the number of cloud related peer reviewed publications, which is a positive sign that research is starting in this research field.

Descriptive Information

After reading the papers we categorized them on basis of high-level topics based on stages in software development. Yara *et al.*(2009), Mei *et al.*(2009), Chabbra *et al.*(2010), and La & Kim (2009) discuss development process in general. Peng *et al.* (2010) describe migration to cloud from GIS software perspective and Guha & Al-Dabass (2010) suggest a new process model. Whereas Ju *et al.* (2010), D. Cunsolo *et al.* (2010) and Rellermeyer *et al.* (2009) have a focus over architecture and design of cloud applications. Burg *et al.* (2009) discusses about deployment

Figure 2. Papers by year

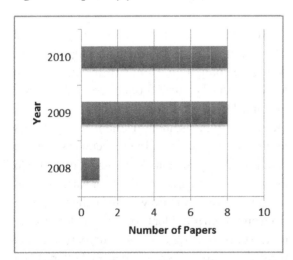

in a dynamic cloud, expressing concerns about it. Article by La *et al.*(2009) is categorized under Implementation category. Software testing in cloud is main focus of Parveen & Tilley (2010) and Riungu *et al.* (2010). The second paper is an empirical study bringing up research issues. Lee *et al.* (2009) provide insights about quality of service, Badr & Caplat (2010) talk about SaaS and versioning. We also included few papers for background information: Articles by Vouk (2008) and Lenk *et al.*(2009). Figure 3 shows these results. It clearly shows that most papers focus on process as well as design aspects.

Qualitative Results

A qualitative analysis of results produced some interesting results. In this section we will describe how research community is looking at clouds from the Software Engineering perspective. We will be using the categorization that was described in previous section. Most of the papers contained large sections describing clouds, their architecture and the benefits of using them.

Background

Two articles (Vouk, 2008; Lenk *et al.*, 2009) were included to provide a brief overview about technical details of cloud computing and related research issues. Lenk *et al.* (2009) propose stack architecture for the cloud. Further, authors try to map existing cloud landscape to the proposed architecture. The stack is described as Hardware at the bottom, then Infrastructure as a Service (IaaS), then Platform as a Service (PaaS), then Software as a Service (SaaS) and finally Human as a Service (HuaaS) at the top. This stack has included one more layer above the traditional architecture of cloud. HuaaS includes Crowdsourcing of tasks. Authors emphasize on interoperability and standardization of services being provided.

Figure 3. Categories and number of paper in each category

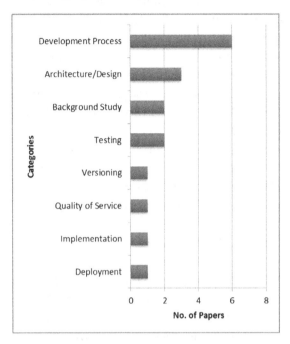

Vouk (2008) describes basic details about cloud computing, which includes short descriptions about Service-Oriented Architecture (SOA), Component based approach, Workflows and Virtualization. The author has says that key to SOA framework that supports workflow is componentization of its services. Vouk (2008) also emphasizes on reuse, customization, scalability and reliability of services. Further this article describes the importance of virtualization. Virtualization allows abstraction and isolation of lower-level functionalities and underlying hardware, providing a freedom for portability of higher-level functions and sharing and/or aggregation of hardware resources. This is important for scalability of the deployment environment. This paper discusses a number of research issues at the technical level. Prominent ones include: meta-data management, service composition and integration, portability and interoperability, optimization of resources and services, and security.

Development Process

We included 6 papers in this category. Reusability related issues were prominently brought up by these papers. Chabbra *et al.* (2010) raises issues of interoperable third party services and components which lead to problems in availability of source code for reuse. La & Kim (2009) proposed a development process for SaaS cloud services. Common software functionality and features is a primary contributor to reusability. This proposed development process is tailored keeping in mind the intrinsic characteristics and desired properties that must be possessed by a SaaS application.

Characteristics include:

- Support for common software functionalities and features,
- Internet access,
- Wide functionality,
- Multi-tenant access,
- Thin model over client side for access just from a web-browser.

Desired properties are:

- High Reusability,
- High Availability,
- High Scalability.

Mei *et al.* (2009) qualitatively compare cloud computing with service-oriented computing and pervasive computing. Comparisons are on three grounds -I/O Feature, Storage and Calculation Feature. Some interesting research issues were brought in light: standardization, reuse, access mode, concurrency model and execution states of a cloud-based application. Standardization points to the need for an abstraction layer for various cloud interfaces, which in turn will make the migration from one cloud provider to other provider, an easy task. At present migration is a cumbersome task for software teams, since cloud APIs vary from provider to provider.

P. Yara *et al.* (2009) look into Global software development with clouds. They outlined development process for a generic cloud, highlighting benefits of cloud-based platforms. According to authors (Yara *et al.*, 2009) cloud-based platforms are best solutions for distributed development, since they are best form of content collaboration spaces and are always available and accessible. Compute clouds make continuous code integrations easy and efficient. The authors indicated testing in cloud as a potential domain for future research, since testing in clouds help in verifying the system behavior in real scalability and load.

Guha & Al-Dabass (2010) raise issues regarding adequacy of prevalent software process models and framework activities when development involves cloud. The authors propose interaction with cloud provider. Currently requirements gathering phase includes customers, users and software engineers, involving cloud providers can help in answering questions related to estimations, risk management, configuration management, change management and quality assurance. Further since cloud providers are responsible for maintenance of infrastructure their involvement can be of a large benefit.

Peng *et al.* (2010) look at cloud from a GIS software perspective, stating the benefitts of migration to cloud. The authors emphasize on concept of reuse, reduction of complexity and cost reduction. Authors state that this migration will have a lot of benefits like out of the box GIS software in turn reducing the complexity of installation, on demand licensing which is important considering the cost of GIS software, last but not least scalability for GIS software since they can turn out to be extensively resource intensive.

Architecture and Design

Ju *et al.* (2010) describe the application architecture and maturity model for SaaS. Figure 4 shows the SaaS application architecture and maturity model. The application architecture is made up of different components. The process services expose interfaces that smart clients and/or the Web presentation tier can invoke, and kick off a synchronous workflow or long-running transaction that will invoke other business services, which interact with the respective data stores in order to read and write business data. Security services are responsible for controlling access to end-user and back-end software services.

Figure 4. SaaS application architecture and maturity model (Chong & Carraro, 2006)

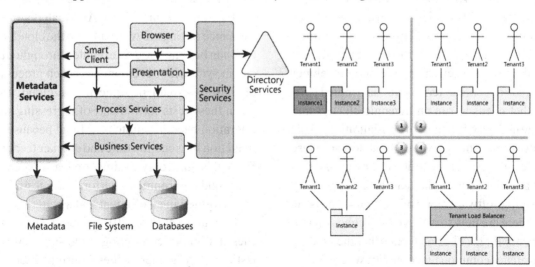

The maturity model describes four different levels: on the first level each customer has his own customized instance; second level is quite similar the only difference is that this time the instances are identical for every customer, however they are isolated from each other; on the third level customers access a single instance provided by the vendor, but they are provided unique user experience with customizable meta-data linked to customer profiles; in the fourth and the final version vendor has multiple instances running in a load-balanced farm of identical instances, here each user has unique user experience that is linked to his or her profile.

Authors also provide a comparison ASP (Application Service Provider) model with SaaS model. Some prominent differences are:

- Lack of multi-tenant services in ASP model
- ASP supported applications were simple client-server programs with simple HTML. SaaS applications are specifically designed for the Web environment, which improves usability and manageability.
- A significant difference can be seen in implementation time, ASP has a lengthy cycle in comparison to immediate implementation by SaaS.

Rellermeyer *et al.* (2009) proposed solution for challenges and difficulties of distributed and parallel software that are faced by cloud computing. The service interface hides the actual application from the remote user, the application developer still needs to come to terms with distributed software that needs to run on dynamic clusters and operate under a wide range of configurations. This paper outlines a model, which considers software modules as □rst class entities used for management and distribution that can be controlled by underlying software fabric of the cloud. The issue raised here are how to achieve high cohesion and loose coupling. Cohesion means that the module encapsulates common functionality, whereas cou-

pling corresponds to dependence of one module over internal implementation details of a second module. High cohesion and low coupling makes a module ideal candidate for reuse. They implemented an application using the ideas presented.

Testing

Parveen and Tilley (2010) and Riungu *et al.* (2010) talk specifically about Software testing in the cloud. Authors (Parveen & Tilley, 2010) discuss when to migrate software testing to cloud from two perspectives: characteristics of application under test, and the types of testing performed on the application. They look on the cloud as a cluster of virtual machines enabling a new level of testing agility. When talking about characteristics of tests, that make it feasible to be migrate to the cloud, they include:

- Test case independence so that concurrent execution is possible;
- Known operational environment so that we are familiar with components and libraries that are used;
- Programmatically accessible interface suitable for automated testing.

Further applications that require specialized hardware are difficult to be tested in the cloud. Unit Testing, High Volume Automated and Performance testing are well suited to the cloud. Unit tests can be continuously executed throughout the day in sync with development. Batch processing of these tests can be done in the cloud. Later when these tests form a part of regressing suite, migration becomes quite beneficial because of a reduction in execution time and quicker feedback. Since it is quite easy to simulate load on demand in a cloud environment, performance testing can be performed in an efficient and a better manner.

L. Riungu *et al.* (2010) gathered research issues that cloud computing impose on software testing; they gathered these during interviews with practitioners from various organizations. The obtained issues were divided into following categories application, management, legal and financial. Application issues, include:

- How to find applications suitable for on-line testing,
- Evaluate how and whether certain testing infrastructure in the cloud helps to meet a specic performance attribute,
- How to verify and validate the quality of overall testing in cloud,
- How to build highly interoperable and interactive clouds,
- How will cloud computing enhance e-business models and reduce the risks involved.

Implementation and Deployment

Article by La & Kim (2009) discusses SaaS and mash-up cloud service implementations, raising two technical issues for each and then discussing their solution spaces. For SaaS the issues raised are scalability and availability. Pre-specified level of scalability can be met by resource pooling with multi-clouds, dynamic load balancing and on-demand deployment. Availability can be improved by improving fault identifying mechanisms. For mash-ups commonality and adaptability are the issues, both are related to reusability of service. Commonality refers to common features and functionalities between various applications.

Burg *et al.* (2009) talk specifically about software deployment in a dynamic cloud, with reference to hospital environments. At present the hospital environment is device-oriented and they propose that it should be changed to service-oriented. They propose that machines should be treated as a cloud, where components of applications are automatically deployed. For example when we start a CPU intensive application (e.g. viewer for 3D scans) on a sufficiently powerful PC, the computational component of the applica-

tion will automatically be deployed on the local machine, whereas when the same application is accessed using a underpowered PDA then the computational component is deployed on a fast server sufficiently close enough to PDA in the network topology. The authors discussed following research issues:

- Need for designing applications that can be distributed across different nodes dynamically,
- A model that can automate deployment of a distributed application, by specifying the components, run-time dependencies between components and quality of service requirements.

Versioning and Quality of Service

Version control has always been an important research aspect for academia and industry. Badr & Caplat (2010) state that incremental changes in service provisions increase value, consumer satisfaction and productivity. SaaS present new challenges for revision control, since revision control helps to decide when and whether a new version of a service should be released. Badr & Caplat (2010) also raised following research issues related to SaaS:

- How can versioning be used to decide, whether a new version of e-service in particular a SaaS application should be released? And what metrics should decide the migration to a new version?
- SaaS applications are based on metered service model another question arises about cost estimation of new features

Further, with SaaS since we deal with multi-user context each user must parameterize his or her own "subjective version". Therefore versioning must deal with double multiplicity:

- Objective versioning that is linked to natural evolution of delivered services, throughout time and development.
- Subjective versioning that will take care of diversity of use by many customers.

This paper proposes a new architecture for SaaS that includes some special modules. Versioning manager module is one amongst them. It can be further sub-divided into two parts -Objective versioning management and Subjective versioning management.

Quality models play an important role in management of any kind of service, and the same is true with SaaS. Lee *et al.* (2009) presents following quality attributes:

- **Reusability:** This measures the functionality provided by the services, this includes commonality for further reuse.
- **Efficiency:** This is used to measure the amount of resources that are consumed for providing demanded functionality and level of performance under a given set of conditions.
- **Reliability:** This is used to measure the ability of SaaS to keep running with a given performance over a period of time.
- **Scalability:** This is a measure of growing demand of resource consumption.
- **Availability:** This attribute measures the ratio of the total time to the time, which a SaaS service is capable of being operable.

These are derived from features of SaaS and are further mapped to metrics.

Agile and Cloud

After analysis of peer-reviewed material, we found that it was not providing sufficient insights for our second research question. Then we decided to look into non-peer reviewed material like blog posts, articles and self-reported experience reports. A similar search strategy was used for this. We used keywords that are mentioned in Table 1. Google, Yahoo and Bing were used as the sources. Only top 100 results were taken into account for further analysis.

A couple of articles were selected for further analysis; these articles were chosen on the basis of their degree of relevance to the research questions. The understanding gained from the analysis of peer-reviewed material served as a good measure to categorize an article as relevant or irrelevant. Agile and cloud is seen as a great combination, which will reduce development costs, time to market and increase productivity (Ensell, 2011). As soon as iteration is complete the usable software can be released and the team can move to the next iteration. Agile and clouds are parallel concepts both in terms of methods and aim. Cloud speeds up the development process, eliminating the need for drawn out installation procedures, patches and reinstallations (Ensell, 2011). Ensell (2011) suggested that in future development platforms should provide capabilities in four major areas:

- Efficient on demand scaling,
- Build handling in cloud,
- Effective test capabilities,
- Production deployment leading to automatic and quick deployment.

Moreira in his article "Winning Combination of Agile and the Cloud" (Moreira, 2011), supports Ensell's (Ensell, 2011) views, since clouds do not require any on-premise installations, there is no need for installation suites or software updates. Quick deployment enables those who develop cloud products to continuously improve product functionality by using the continuous building of customer value via agile methods. And this is achieved without burdening the customer. Portelli in his article "The Beauty of Agile in the Cloud" (Portelli, 2010) states that with cloud, iterative development process is encompassing deployment into the iterations, moving from development to DevOps. DevOps is an emerging set of principles, methods and practices for communication, collaboration and integration between software development (application/software engineering) and systems administration/infrastructure professionals (Pant, 2009).

Plummer (2011) in his article "Enterprise Software Engineering to the Cloud, via Agile and DevOps", discusses how agile and DevOps when put together with cloud's capabilities, can provide a great advantage. Whether it is dynamic scaling of resources or fast delivery, this combination can be of great use. Further, he discusses about continuous deployment: a well-documented process of automating the delivery of released software through the development and operational pipeline.

The information collected from these sources was quite limited. Articles provided only an introduction on how integration of agile and cloud can be beneficial.

OVERVIEW OF GATHERED RESEARCH ISSUES

No roadmap is complete until it has a big arrow saying you are here and an indication where you should be going in the future. In the previous section, we discussed findings obtained from various papers. In this section we intend to summarize some prominent research issues that were highlighted:

Software Reuse in the Cloud: Cloud platforms support multi-tenancy. Multi-tenancy refers to a principle in software architecture where a single instance of an application running on the server supports multiple client organizations. The application is designed to virtually partition its data and configuration, providing each client organization a customized application instance. It is proposed that in this scenario code reuse can be done to a greater extent. But there are various hindrances

that need to be overcome before this can be done in an efficient manner. Absence of source code for third party components is one of the biggest challenges that need to be addressed. A need for reusability metrics and model that is specific to cloud-based application is being felt by developers.

Call For Standardization and Interoperability between Various Service Providers: Currently every service provider has APIs and platforms that have different functionalities and features. Cloud interoperability will ensure that one cloud solution will be able to work with other platforms and applications, as well as on other clouds. This will give customers the flexibility to run applications locally or in the cloud, or in a combination of different clouds.

Standardization will also help in dealing with problems that a development team faces when they decide to switch service providers and reduce vendor lock in. A proposed solution is a Universal Cloud Interface that can serve as a common interface for interactions between cloud platforms and applications. The Cloud Computing Interoperability Forum is working towards creating a common framework. But still a lot of work needs to be done. Since most of the front-runners in cloud technologies are private companies so access to code-base is quite difficult. Further it is impossible to create standardization interfaces without consensus; a clear need for more open source collaboration like OpenStack (www. openstack.org) is being felt.

Software Testing in/of the Cloud: This issue has two facets:

- **Software Testing in the Cloud:** This refers to leveraging the resources provided by the cloud infrastructure to facilitate the concurrent execution of test cases in a virtualized environment. It can be of great benefit to software testers. The cloud can replicate real world usage at a low cost and easy accessibility with its large arsenal of computing resources.

- **Testing of the Cloud:** This refers to testing of applications that are hosted or deployed in a cloud environment. This may also correspond to testing of cloud infrastructure itself. Testing of services provided by third party providers is also an important issue that needs attention of research community.

But as the introduction of software testing in/of the cloud to developers and testers was not long ago, there remain a lot of unanswered questions. What types of testing can be efficiently done on clouds, quality measures for the testing & designing applications that are suitable for cloud testing are some of them.

Agile Methodologies and Cloud: Various self-reported articles stated agile methodologies and cloud to be a good fit, but absence of peer-reviewed material clearly indicates a need for the research community to look into this. It is quite difficult to verify and validate the claims due to absence of empirical studies. Thus, empirical studies should be conducted to evaluate if the beliefs of practitioners about agile methods and cloud computing are justified or not.

Deployment Model: A deployment process that is continuous and automatic can reduce software delivery time to market. A need for a well-established model that can guide this process was expressed by some authors (Burg *et al.*, 2009).

CONCLUSION

This systematic review has a number of implications for research. First of all, it clearly indicates the need for more studies to be conducted that look upon cloud computing from a Software Engineering perspective. We need empirical and experimental studies that directly involve practitioners from industry. Relating to our findings we can answer our research questions.

Q1: What software engineering issues do the developers face while developing software for clouds?

Answer: Software Reusability, Standardization and Software testing seem to be prominent issues, but other issues like continuous deployment model, quality of service and versioning are also making their presence felt.

Q2: Are agile methodologies beneficial when we are developing software for clouds?

Answer: On the basis of self-reported articles it seems that agile methodologies can be of great advantage. It can help in reducing delivery time to market by encompassing deployment into the development and operation pipeline.

However, we identified following as the main limitations of this systematic review:

- The number of peer-reviewed sources is small. While only three digital libraries were searched, we are not aware of the papers that were missed by the search. Thus, there is a scarcity of research in the area.
- The reliability of our categorization method needs to be discussed since we did not use a pre-established classification scheme (because there is none). This issue is even more problematic due to the limited amount of primary studies and the resulting risk of important topics that are simply not yet discussed.
- There is a lack of relevant peer-reviewed papers that discuss Agile methodologies and cloud computing. This forced us to look for non-peer reviewed material that does not fulfill commonly used scientific criteria and needs to be taken with a

grain of salt. However, it seems to indicate current trends in the industry earlier than sound peer-reviewed work.

- Finally, only one researcher had fully read the final set of papers. It may have introduced bias in classification and analysis.

Despite the limitations, the results provide a current and up-to-date snapshot of the current position of research in this field and will help researchers to move forward.

This literature review provides some interesting insights about how cloud might affect software engineering practices. In our view, research community should look towards conducting empirical and experimental studies that involve industry practitioners working with cloud services.

ACKNOWLEDGMENT

Authors would like to thank Mr. Theodore D. Hellmann, Mr. Darren Andreychuk and Mr. Tiago Silva da Silva for their help during the review.

REFERENCES

Badr, Y., & Caplat, G. (2010). Software-as-a-service and versionology: Towards innovative service differentiation. *24th IEEE International Conference on Advanced Information Networking and Applications* (pp. 237–243). IEEE.

Banerjee, P., Friedrich, R., Bash, C., Goldsack, P., Huberman, B., & Manley, J. (2011, March). Everything as a service: Powering the new information economy. *Computer*, *44*(3), 36–43. doi:10.1109/MC.2011.67

Burg, S., Jonge, M., Dolstra, E., & Visser, E. (2009). Software deployment in a dynamic cloud: From device to service orientation in a hospital environment. *ICSE Workshop Software Engineering Challenges of Cloud Computing* (pp. 61-66). ACM.

CDW. (2009). *Introduction to cloud computing architecture*. Retrieved March 1, 2011, from http://webobjects.cdw.com/webobjects/media/pdf/Sun_CloudComputing.pdf

Chabbra, B., Verma, D., & Taneja, B. (2010). Software engineering issues from the cloud application perspective. *International Journal of Information Technology Knowledge Management*, *2*(2), 669–673.

Chong, F., & Carraro, G. (2006). *Architecture strategies for catching the long tail*. Retrieved from http://msdn.microsoft.com/en-us/library/aa479069.aspx

Cunsolo, D. V., Distefano, S., Puliafito, A., & Scarpa, M. (2010). Applying software engineering principles for designing cloud@home. *10th IEEE/ACM International Conference on Cluster, Cloud and Grid Computing* (pp. 618-624). Washington, DC: IEEE.

Ensell, J. (2011, April 12). *Agile development in the cloud*. Retrieved May 1, 2011, from http://www.agilejournal.com/articles/columns/column-articles/6018

Guha, R., & Al-Dabass, D. (2010). Impact of web 2.0 and cloud computing platform on software engineering. *International Symposium on Electronic System Design* (pp. 213-218). IEEE.

IBM. (2009, April). *Staying aloft in tough times*. Retrieved March 1, 2011, from ftp://ftp.software.ibm.com/common/ssi/ecm/en/ciw03059usen/CIW03059USEN.PDF

Ju, J., Wang, Y., Fu, J., Wu, J., & Lin, Z. (2010). Research on key technology in saas. *International Conference on Intelligent Computing and Cognitive Informatics* (pp. 384-387). IEEE.

Kitchenham, B., & Charters, S. (2007). *Guidelines for performing systematic literature reviews in software engineering*. Keele University and Durham University Joint Report. EBSE 2007-001.

La, H. J., Choi, S. W., & Kim, S. D. (2009). Technical challenges and solution space for developing SaaS and mash-up cloud services. *IEEE International Conference on e-Business Engineering* (pp. 359-364). IEEE.

La, H. J., & Kim, S. D. (2009). A systematic process for developing high quality SaaS cloud services. *1st International Conference on Cloud Computing* (pp. 278-289). Berlin, Germany: Springer-Verlag.

Lee, J. Y., Lee, J. W., Cheun, D. W., & Kim, S. D. (2009). A quality model for evaluating software-as-a-service in cloud computing. *ACIS International Conference on Software Engineering Research, Management and Applications* (pp. 261-266). ACIS.

Lenk, A., Klems, M., Nimis, J., Tai, S., & Sandholm, T. (2009). What's inside the cloud? An architectural map of the cloud landscape. *ICSE Workshop on Software Engineering Challenges of Cloud Computing* (pp. 23-31). ACM.

Mei, L., Zhang, Z., & Chan, W. (2009). More tales of clouds: Software engineering research issues from the cloud application perspective. *33rd Annual IEEE International Computer Software and Applications Conference* (pp. 525-530). IEEE.

Mian, P., Conte, T., Natali, A., Biolchini, J., & Travassos, G. (2005). A systematic review process for software engineering. *3rd International Workshop Guidelines for Empirical Work, Workshop Series on Empirical Software Engineering*, (pp. 1-6). Kaiserslautern, Germany.

Moreira, M. (2011, April 12). *Winning combination of agile and the cloud.* Retrieved May 1, 2011, from Agile Journal: http://www.agilejournal.com/articles/columns/column-articles/6017-winning-combination-of-agile-and-the-cloud

NIST. (2011, January). *The NIST definition of cloud computing.* Retrieved April 1, 2011, from http://csrc.nist.gov/publications/drafts/800-145/Draft-SP-800-145_cloud-definition.pdf

Pant, R. (2009, March 17). *Organizing a Web technology department.* Retrieved March 1, 2011, from http://www.rajiv.com/blog/2009/03/17/technology-department/

Parveen, T., & Tilley, S. (2010). When to migrate software testing to the cloud? *Third International Conference on Software Testing, Verification, and Validation Workshops* (pp. 424-427). IEEE.

Peng, Z., Mei, L., Fei, W., & Fei, Y. (2010). The analisis of gis software engineering pattern under the cloud computing environment. *International Conference on Educational and Information Technology* (pp. 450-452). IEEE.

Plummer, K. (2011, March 26). *Enterprise software engineering to the cloud, via agile and DevOps.* Retrieved May 1, 2011, from http://www.maestrodev.com/blogs/enterprise-software-engineering-to-the-cloud-via-agile-and-devops

Portelli, B. (2010, October 18). *The beauty of agile in the cloud.* Retrieved March 1, 2011, from http://www.cmcrossroads.com/cm-articles/columns/agile-in-the-cloud/13759-the-beauty-of-agile-in-the-cloud

Rellermeyer, J. S., Duller, M., & Alonso, G. (2009). Engineering the cloud from software modules. *ICSE Workshop on Software Engineering Challenges of Cloud Computing* (pp. 32-37). Washington, DC.: IEEE.

Riungu, M. L., Taipale, O., & Smolander, K. (2010). Research issues for software testing in the cloud. *IEEE Second International Conference on Cloud Computing Technology and Science* (pp. 557-564). IEEE.

Vouk, M. A. (2008). Cloud computing- Issues, research and implementations. *30th International Conference on Information Technology Interfaces* (pp. 31-40). IEEE.

Yara, P., Ramachandran, R., Balasubramanian, G., Muthuswamy, K., & Chandrasekar, D. (2009). *Global software development with cloud platforms* (pp. 81–95). Software Engineering Approaches for Offshore and Outsourced Development.

KEY TERMS AND DEFINITIONS

Agile Software Development: This is a process of software development that is customer centric and embraces change, rather than seeking to control it.

Cloud Computing: A model for enabling ubiquitous, convenient, on-demand network access to a shared pool of configurable computing resources (e.g., networks, servers, storage, applications, and services) that can be rapidly provisioned and released with minimal management effort or service provider interaction.

Systematic Review: Systematic Review is a literature review focused on a research question and is aimed to provide an exhaustive summary of literature relevant to a research question. This process involves systematically defining your search strategy and inclusion criteria based on predefined rules.

Chapter 4
SaaS Requirements Engineering for Agile Development

Asif Qumer Gill
University of Sydney, Australia

Deborah Bunker
University of Sydney, Australia

ABSTRACT

The emergence of Software as a Service (SaaS) has made it possible to develop dynamic and complex business processes as eServices. The development of business processes as eServices (SaaS) can be assisted by the means of adaptive or agile development processes. The development of business processes in terms of SaaS require to perform SaaS requirements engineering (RE), which is an important phase of a software development process for the success of any project. The challenge here is how best to do SaaS RE (e.g. mapping business process to eServices) and select agile development practices for developing business processes in terms of SaaS. In order to address this challenge, an integrated agile RE model for SaaS project development environments is outlined within this chapter. The purpose of the proposed RE model is to aid in iteratively determining SaaS requirements in short iterations as opposed to the "only first and onetime upfront" phase of a development process. Each identified SaaS requirement or a set of requirements for a given iteration is linked to a single or set of specific agile practices for implementation in short iterations. This model can be used as a guideline by organisations wishing to understand the challenging task of mapping business processes to SaaS and its implementation by using agile software development processes or practices.

DOI: 10.4018/978-1-4666-2503-7.ch004

INTRODUCTION

The emergence of on-demand utility service(s) or technologies provides opportunities to develop dynamic and complex business processes as eServices "Software as a Service" (SaaS) in the cloud environment (Salesforce 2008). NIST defines SaaS as "The capability provided to the consumer is to use the provider's applications running on a cloud infrastructure. The applications are accessible from various client devices through either a thin client interface, such as a web browser (e.g., web-based email), or a program interface. The consumer does not manage or control the underlying cloud infrastructure including network, servers, operating systems, storage, or even individual application capabilities, with the possible exception of limited user-specific application configuration settings" (Mell and Grance 2011). SaaS is a logical view or an abstraction of a business process such as an application or database, which is provided to the service consumer for carrying out business-level operations. The development of business processes as SaaS can be done by using the adaptive or agile development processes (Agile Manifesto 2001). The development of business processes as SaaS, however, requires carrying-out the challenging task of requirements engineering (RE), which is one of the important phases of the software development process.

RE is the process of understanding the business context and identifying and managing software system requirements. Zave (1997) states that RE is concerned with the relationship of real-world goals, needs, and constraints that is important to describe the behavior and evolution of software systems. There are a number of RE approaches (Davis 1992; Goguen and Linde 1993; Maiden and Rugg 1996; van Lamsweerde et al. 1998; Sommerville 2005; Jiang et al. 2008) that have been proposed over a period of time and it now seems agreed that RE is an integral part of a software development lifecycle. The challenge here

is how best to do SaaS RE (e.g. mapping business process to eServices) and select agile development practices for implementing SaaS requirements. There are not many studies reported on RE in agile development (Cao and Ramesh 2008) – especially how to do RE in the context of SaaS development and deployment in a cloud computing environment. In order to address this challenge, based on our recent SaaS industry projects and the analysis of different RE and agile system development approaches, this chapter presents an integrated RE model (iREM) for agile SaaS project development environments. The purpose of the proposed RE model is to aid in iteratively determining SaaS requirements in short iterations. These SaaS requirements are also iteratively integrated with the specific agile software development practices for the implementation of a given iteration. This model would be very useful for organisations wishing to understand the mapping of business processes to services; and which business processes have been developed as services by using which software development processes or practices (end-to-end traceability from business process to services and services to software process).

In summary, the focus of this chapter is:

- Concurrent just-in-time business process analysis and SaaS RE: Identification of system requirements and test cases for SaaS RE and implementation for each iteration (e.g. mapping business process to software services);
- Concurrent just-in-time evolving of agile development processes: Selection of agile development practices/roles to implement system or service requirements; and their integration at the time that the identified system requirements or services are chosen for SaaS implementation for each iteration; and
- Concurrent just-in-time evolving and management of service backlog: Put the chosen service requirements and the ag-

ile development techniques (integrated system requirements-development techniques) for SaaS implementation into the service backlog for further assessment and development.

The chapter is organized as follows: Section 3 presents research motivation and scope. Section 4 presents background and related work: business processes, service analysis, agile processes, and method engineering. Section 5 presents the proposed integrated RE model and a demonstration of the application of the proposed model for RE for an agile SaaS development. In Section 6 we discuss the iREM and agile implementation followed by a model analysis (Section 7). Section 8 provides further discussion on iREM. Section 9 presents the future research and application of the model before concluding remarks in Section 10.

RESEARCH MOTIVATION AND SCOPE

This section discusses the comparative analysis of SaaS and Traditional RE, and SaaS and Agile RE in order to highlight the research motivation and need for an agile SaaS RE and development approach.

SaaS and Traditional RE

The area of SaaS RE poses different challenges and it has been suggested that "the rapidly changing business environment in which most organizations operate is challenging traditional requirements-engineering (RE) approaches" (Cao and Ramesh 2008). Here, we summarize the comparative analysis of the traditional waterfall "only first-onetime upfront" RE approach and SaaS; and highlight the motivation and need for an agile SaaS RE approach.

1. **Agility:** Traditional waterfall approach lacks agility and assumes RE as only the first and onetime upfront phase of a development process; SaaS needs an agile, adjustable and ongoing RE approach to support the development of dynamic and complex adaptive business processes as eServices in short iterations (e.g. Stiehm et al. 2006; Berkovich et al. 2009).

2. **Abstraction:** Traditional RE approach provides the support to capture and model requirements in a number of paradigms such as objects, entities, aspects and agents etc; SaaS needs a service oriented RE approach in order to capture and model requirements as services (e.g. Tsai et al. 2007). Traditional service analysis approaches (e.g. SODA (Zimmermann et al. 2004), SOMA (Arsanjani et al. 2008) focus mainly on the fixed service behaviour components; Whereas SaaS also requires the identification of additional service management requirements such as dynamic on-demand behavior or configuration, governance limits, performance and pay-per-use pricing components of SaaS in a multi-tenant environment (e.g. Salesforce 2008; Mell and Grance 2011).

3. **Stakeholders:** Traditional RE assumes that the customer and user are the same stakeholders; Whereas SaaS clearly requires the separation of these stakeholders (e.g. a service user may be different from service customer or consumer) and also requires the involvement of a number of other stakeholders such as service providers, service developers, service integrators, software providers (software – a package of integrated services), service broker, service carrier, service auditor, to support the development, management and use of dynamic and complex business processes as eServices (e.g. Becker and Krcmar 2008; Liu et al. 2011).

4. **Sources:** Traditional RE (e.g. NFR (Chung et al. 2000), AORE (Rashid et al. 2003)) considers identifying requirements upfront from customers by using traditional RE techniques (e.g. workshops, interviews, survey, user stories, aspects, XML, CRC cards); SaaS approach requires standardization of business processes and establishing reusable business process repository (e.g. stress on business process consolidation and reusability); and iterative mapping of dynamic and complex adaptive business processes to eServices for the identification of service requirements (e.g. Tsai et al. 2007).

5. **Characteristics:** Traditional RE (e.g. NFR (Chung et al. 2000), PF (Jackson 200)) mainly focuses on the identification of traditional requirements characteristics (e.g. textual description, ownership, artifacts linking, development time, status); SaaS also needs some additional characteristics in order to specify requirements. For instance, when a SaaS is deployed in the shared cloud environment it requires additional service management requirements i.e. additional security, on-demand availability, scalability, monitoring, governance limits, performance, pay-as-you go billing, multi-tenancy (e.g. Salesforce 2008).

6. **Traceability:** Traditional approach considers RE as a first and isolated phase from the development process, which presents the partial view of a requirement (e.g. what and why to develop). For instance, traditional RE approaches such as NFR (Chung et al. 2000), PF (Jackson 2001) and Theme/Doc (Baniassad and Clarke 2004) consider traceability only at the artifact level (e.g. linking artifacts) but they do not consider traceability between the business process and development process. SaaS needs a RE approach to capture the "Service Requirements as a Whole" or service package with the appropriate development process in order to provide the end-to-end traceability and integration of business process (e.g. SaaS requirements) and development process (e.g. development practices) for the purpose of auditing and management (e.g. Berkovich et al. 2009) - i.e. which business processes have been developed as eServices (e.g. SaaS requirements) by using which software development processes or practices (e.g. traditional, agile or hybrid development process). The lack of traceability may make it difficult to identify the root causes of a problem (e.g. source of the problem or defect in the process, service etc.).

SaaS and Agile RE

A situation-specific agile approach (e.g. Poppendieck and Poppendieck 2003; Schwaber 2004) is capable of addressing the challenges and overheads often imposed by traditional approaches that lack agility (Stiehm et al. 2006). This is because "agile development cycles or sprints are mostly 2-3 weeks and provide in-built dynamism in product development. In SaaS, frequent updates are the norm. Any SaaS application must be dynamic in understanding customer needs and rolling out features. In fact, shorter release cycles have been the backbone of success of SaaS applications" (Ranjan 2011). Salesforce.com, for instance, is one of the largest SaaS vendors; they have applied the agile for SaaS development and reported the following commercial benefits (Salesforce 2008).

- Increased delivery rate;
- Increased time to market of major releases by 61 percent; and
- Increased productivity across the organization by 38 percent.

There are not many studies reported on RE in agile development (Cao and Ramesh 2008) – especially how to do RE in the context of SaaS development and deployment in a cloud computing environment, which is currently being adopted by many software development organizations worldwide (e.g. Salesforce 2008). This may be due to the fact that the Agile Manifesto (2001) values and principles mainly focus on the development of working code instead of formal requirements engineering. Agile approaches provide a number of techniques (e.g. Ambler 2009) for identifying and managing requirements such as product backlog, whiteboards, user stories, index cards etc. They do not seem to provide any guidance on service oriented RE, however, which is a core to SaaS RE (e.g. Tsai et al. 2007). For example, Scrum (Schwaber and Beedle 2002; Schwaber 2004), one of the well-known agile methods, provides the "product backlog" for managing the user stories as requirements for agile implementation but it lacks the support for the SaaS RE (e.g. how to map business process to services and then represent services in the product backlog). It has also been observed that in the original Scrum product backlog specifications, there is a potential missing view ("Requirements as a Whole") or link between the system requirements or activities and the actual system development process or techniques used by self-organizing agile teams to implement those requirements. This is important to understand the end-to-end traceability in terms of services that have been implemented by agile teams by using agile practices. The end-to-end traceability can be useful for agile process retrospectives, agile process audit, governance and continuous improvement. It has been suggested that "to address the system development challenges of the 21st century, we must integrate the processes of RE and system implementation" (Sommerville 2005).

Hence, before developing and deploying business processes as eServices (SaaS) in the cloud or non cloud computing environment, we must understand how to map business processes to eServices (e.g. SaaS RE) which then can be developed and deployed in the cloud by agile teams using situation-specific agile system development practices or techniques (e.g. just-in-time selection

of agile development process or practices). This draws our attention to the potential integration of business process (e.g. SaaS requirements) and the system implementation process or activities (e.g. development techniques) in order to understand the end-to-end traceability from business process to software process – called here an integrated RE approach.

The above-mentioned analysis also highlights a situation that may arise where sufficient SaaS requirements are not known or clear enough for selecting or tailoring an upfront agile development process. The creation or selection of a full scale method upfront for each project could be time consuming and may introduce extra overhead. To address this challenge, the scope of this chapter aims to explore the iterative selection and integration of situational agile practices by self organizing agile teams, at the time of implementation, with the individual, identified system requirements or services by using a just-in-time method engineering approach (Kumar and Welke 1992).

BACKGROUND AND RELATED WORK

This section discusses the background information and related work for the foundation for our investigation into the context of integrated RE, which poses the following research questions:

How do you map business processes to eServices for SaaS RE and then how do you integrate business process (SaaS RE - system requirements) to agile software process (development techniques) for SaaS implementation?

In order to address the above mentioned questions, based on recent research and SaaS projects, we propose an integrated RE model (iREM). As part of this research, we are developing a structured framework (Gill and Bunker 2011) to assist in the context-aware adoption of a shared cloud-enabled computing environment for developing and managing business processes (Process as a Service). The iREM is one of the components of this framework, which will be presented in detail in the later part of this chapter.

The context of the integrated RE (Figure 1) can be discussed from three perspectives: business process, agile software process and method engineering. Business process (Figure 1) with a "+" sign represents a set or repository of business processes that may be implemented as eServices. The mapping circle or event (Figure 1) indicates the iterative mapping (curved arrow represents iteration sign) of business processes to eServices (e.g. SaaS RE). Software process (Figure 1) with a "+" sign represents a set or repository of software processes (agile practices) that may be used to implement eServices. The selection circle or event (Figure 1) indicates the iterative selection of agile practices from software process repository and their integration with identified SaaS requirements by using a method engineering approach. Method engineering approach is to facilitate the iterative integration of SaaS requirements and agile development techniques for integrated SaaS RE

(represented in the green box), which is the novel contribution of this book chapter. Firstly, this section discusses the business process; secondly, the service analysis; thirdly, the agile software process; and finally, the method engineering approach in the context of integrated RE.

Business Process

A business process refers to a set of related activities that are performed to achieve desired business objectives. Davenport and Short (Davenport and Short 1990) define a business process as "a set of logically related tasks performed to achieve a defined business outcome". They further explain the business system in terms of a set of related business processes, which exhibit the behaviour of one or more business units or departments such as order material, purchase goods, produce goods, make payments etc. Hassine et al. (2002) suggest that "faced with a rough market competition, companies must increasingly change. They are constantly obliged to adapt to new needs, to make their products evolve, to change their development process and establish new collaborations. These

Figure 1. Integrated requirements engineering context

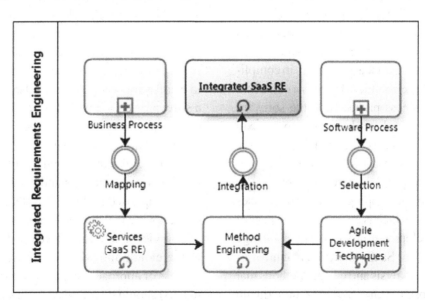

evolutions require the implementation of flexible information systems, adaptable to evolution of the business products and business processes". This dynamic and complex nature of the business process environment and large-scale enterprise applications such as embedded systems, e-health, e-government, customer relationship management, disaster management and e-business has led to the creation of an emerging SaaS in the cloud computing environment, currently being adopted by many organizations worldwide (Endrei et al. 2004; Omar and Taleb-Bendiab 2006; Salesforce 2008). The emergence of SaaS has made it possible to quickly develop and deploy business processes as services in the shared internet cloud computing environment.

Service Analysis

Service oriented paradigm is considered suitable for capturing the veiled complexity of business processes in terms of loosely coupled reusable distributed software services for large-scale business systems and for their full development (Kodali 2005). As discussed earlier, a software service is a logical view or an abstraction of a business process such as a program or database for carrying out business-level operations (Krogdahl et al. 2005; Feuerlicht 2006). A software service is a contractually defined behaviour that is developed and provided by a service provider and is used by other services or service consumers in compliance with a service contract. There is a close link between the business process and the software service. We suggest that a business process can be implemented in terms of one or more loosely coupled reusable software services (SaaS).

We need to perform SaaS requirements engineering (RE) for developing business processes in terms of SaaS, which is an important aspect of a software development process. The challenge is how to do RE for SaaS. There are a number of service oriented analysis and design methods that have been proposed: such as SODA (Zimmermann

et al. 2004) and SOMA (Arsanjani et al. 2008). These approaches discuss the use of services for the implementation of business processes, but do not seem to provide detailed guidelines for the identification and mapping of business processes to services as discussed here in this book chapter. For instance, SODA suggests (Zimmermann et al. 2004) the use of direct and indirect informal business analysis through stakeholders' interview for the identification and mapping of services. However, here, it is not clear what do we need to look for in "interviews" for the identification of services. These service oriented analysis approaches also do not consider the traceability of business processes to service mapping and its implementation processes. As discussed earlier, SaaS also needs some additional characteristics in order to specify requirements. For instance, when a SaaS is deployed in the shared cloud environment it requires additional service management requirements which are not common to traditional standard services i.e. additional security, on-demand availability, scalability, monitoring, governance limits, performance, pay-as-you go billing, multi-tenancy.

The above analysis seems to suggest that traditional service oriented analysis approaches (e.g. SOMA and SOAD) lack ability to support SaaS RE. Within this chapter, it is argued how to use or re-use business process repository (as opposed to informal interviews with stakeholders) in order to identify and map a business process to a software service (s) and also to define what a software service would need to do in order to support a business process in the cloud (SaaS RE). Notwithstanding, for developing and deploying a software service in the cloud to support a business process, we must understand what a software service is supposed to do (e.g. system requirements elicitation); which business process can be mapped to a service(s) and then developed and deployed in the cloud; and which software development process or approach (e.g. agile or non-agile techniques) should be followed to do so. Coulin et al.

(2006) stated that "the elicitation of requirements for a software system is one of the most critical and complex activities within the development lifecycle"; and also a pre-requisite for all various types of software development projects. Hence, the mapping of a business process to a software service and then its development and deployment in the cloud are not straightforward. Our proposed model (as discussed in this chapter) deals with this issue. Agile software development processes are discussed in the next section.

Software Process

Changing client requirements create new opportunities that could be met by adopting new software product development methods, tools and techniques. With modern developments in software production environments, different new software approaches, concepts, processes and methods have emerged. It has been observed that a number of new software development methods have been created to deal with the complex undertaking of modern SaaS (Arsanjani 2004; Tsai et al. 2006; Erl 2005; Zimmermann et al. 2004; Kruger et al. 2004; Zhong 2001; Castro et al. 2004). These traditional waterfall approaches (as discussed earlier) in the context of SaaS are not capable of quickly matching changing business needs and system requirements. On the other hand, an agile approach is capable for addressing the challenges and overheads often imposed by traditional approaches that lack agility (Stiehm et al. 2006; Salesforce 2008).

Agile or light-weight approaches initially originated from best practices of the software industry and emerged as a reaction to so-called "heavyweight" or traditional plan-based methodologies (Chau et al. 2003). The Agile Manifesto (2001) provides twelve agile principles and four agile values that qualitatively characterize agile methods. Agile methods focus on people competency (Cockburn and Highsmith 2001; Turk et al. 2005) rather than on reporting deliverables and are

often seen as a welcome shift of balance towards the most important factor in software development: the personnel involved. Agile methods are tagged as "people-focused" as opposed to "process-focused" plan-driven methods. Highsmith and Cockburn (2001) point out that "agile methods stress two concepts: the unforgiving honesty of working code and the effectiveness of people working together with goodwill". The use of an agile method, under optimum conditions, can indeed create a high quality environment and product (Fitzgerald et al. 2006).

There are a number of agile methods such as Extreme Programming (Beck 2000; Beck and Andres 2004), Feature Driven Development (Palmer and Felsing 2002), Adaptive Software Development (Highsmith 2000), Dynamic Software Development Method (Stapleton 1997), Lean Software Development (Poppendieck and Poppendieck 2003), Scrum (Schwaber and Beedle 2002; Schwaber 2004), and Crystal (Cockburn 2005, 2006) that have been proposed over a long period of time and that are being continually updated. Agile software development methods offer many powerful practices that provide tangible benefits over traditional plan-based methods, e.g. improved time-to-market, productivity and quality software while at the same time aiming to reduce development cost e.g. (Reifer 2002; Fitzgerald et al. 2006).

It is well acknowledged that all software development methodologies, whether traditional plan-based or agile, need to be adapted to the situation at hand (Kumar and Welke 1992; Lindvall and Rus 2000). For instance, a development team may choose to adopt Extreme Programming as their agile methodology, but their "situation-in-hand" may not allow them to use some of the standard practices such as "Pair programming", "Sit together" and "Ten minutes build" due to the constraints within their local development environment and project requirements. For instance, if at a given time only one programmer is available (e.g. due to technical expertise or resource availability reasons) for implementing the specific system requirement or service then "Pair programming" is not an option. A self organizing team may exclude or modify these practices or replace these practices with other familiar practices of agile or non-agile methods (i.e. replacing "Pair programming" with the Crystal "Side-by-side programming") at the time of implementation thus demonstrating just-in-time method engineering. A situation may also arise where sufficient project requirements are not known or clear enough for tailoring an upfront agile methodology. This study proposes an iREM therefore, to iteratively select and integrate situational agile practices, at the time of implementation, with the individual, identified system requirements or services by using a just-in-time method engineering approach. Both the agile method and system or service requirements would iteratively evolve over a period of time, as opposed to the adoption of upfront pre-defined, tailored or engineered agile software development method. Method engineering is discussed in the next section.

Method Engineering

A pre-defined software development process might not be appropriate for each and every software development project (Kumar and Welke 1992). All of these proposed agile methods (e.g. XP, Crystal) suggest the need for situationally specific method tailoring. Cockburn (2005) suggested that "each team tailors the nearest base methodology to their project's particular requirements, expertise and technology characteristics. Specific relevance to the objective of this work may necessitate the use of agile system development practices to select and then integrate the system requirements. It has been suggested (Pikkarainen et al. 2005) that "the organizations, however, need procedures and methods for supporting a systematic selection and deployment of new agile practices and for tailoring them to suit the organizational context". It has also been suggested (Mahanti 2006) that "there

is no agile methodology that can be universally applied and they all have to be tailored to integrate into existing processes".

Based on this discussion and also as per agile method analysis published in (Qumer and Henderson-Sellers 2008a), we suggest that agile methodologies are slightly different from each other, and their differences indicate how one needs to be tailored to the other by excluding, modifying and including practices of different agile methods. This highlights the need for the iterative selection and integration of situationally-specific agile system development practices or process fragments at requirement implementation time to the identified system requirements, as opposed to using a pre-defined or upfront tailored agile software development methodology. The idea of using a method engineering approach is not new e.g. (Zowghi et al. 2005; Coulin et al. 2006). Novelty resides in the proposed idea of the application of method engineering in the context of concurrent system RE, implementation and agile development process emergence.

Method engineering is concerned with the activities that may be carried out in the construction of method, tools and techniques for the development of information systems. According to Brinkkemper (1996), the method engineering approach is used to adapt, design and construct methods, tools and techniques that may be used to produce software products. The construction of a method for a specific project is called situational method engineering (SME) (Welke and Kumar 1991; Brinkkemper 1996).

In a SME approach (Henderson-Sellers 2003), small pieces of a method are identified and stored as method fragments or method chunks (ter Hofstede and Verhoef 1997) in a repository or methodbase (Ralyté 1999; Saeki 2003). The method fragments or chunks can be created or extracted from other existing methods (Beydoun et al. 2005a; Beydoun et al. 2005b) – agile method or process fragments as outlined in this paper. For each project requirement, the method fragments are then selected from the methodbase or repository. The method is thus "constructed" or engineered from its component parts in such a way that only relevant process components, as represented by the method fragments, are incorporated into the constructed method and those that are not useful can be safely ignored (Brinkkemper et al. 1998). It has been suggested (Bajec et al. 2007) that "developers often avoid to follow prescribed methods and that there is a wide gap between the organizations' official methods and the work actually performed by their developers in IT projects". Karlsson and Agerfalk (2008) have suggested the use of the SME approach, primarily originated in the context of plan-based methods, for tailoring a situation-specific agile method for information systems development project. As discussed earlier, project requirements may not be sufficiently well-known or clear for immediately tailoring of an up-front agile system development process. Eckstein (2004) suggested another approach of gradually introducing one agile practice or technique at a time. Eckstein's work (2004) highlights how to introduce unfamiliar practices (one at a time in software development environment), whereas we look at when to select and employ familiar agile practices for a specific project. We suggest iREM to iteratively select and integrate situational agile practices, within a generic process lifecycle, for the individually identified system requirements (at implementation time) or services by using a just-in-time method engineering approach. We propose to allow any number of practices to be newly introduced within a generic process lifecycle as needed [it is assumed that these agile practices would already be familiar within the development organization or team generic process lifecycle]. Notwithstanding, the software development team may be unsure about how to use a concurrent method engineering approach. The development team may select agile practices from the existing agile process fragment repository for their evolving system development process when developing

SaaS in the overall context of the proposed iREM. The structure of the proposed iREM is discussed in detail in the next section.

INTEGRATED REQUIREMENTS ENGINEERING MODEL (iREM)

This section presents the integrated RE model (iREM: Figure 2) for SaaS development. Firstly, on the left side, the iREM shows two key inputs (e.g. marked in bold and red color in Figure 2): business process and software process. It also shows the integration or link between the business and software process. Secondly, on the right-top side (e.g. marked in blue color in Figure 2), it shows the business process analysis (e.g. use case and test case analysis); and on the right-bottom side (e.g. marked in blue color in Figure 2), it shows the selection of agile software practices (e.g. agile techniques). Finally, in the right-middle side, it presents the output of iREM in terms of integrated SaaS requirement (e.g. marked in bold and green color) as the integration or link between the business and software process for the purpose of end-to-end traceability from business to software process. This model has been developed based on recent SaaS project experience and the analysis of different RE and system development approaches. The proposed integrated model addresses both the concurrent emergence of situational system requirements and the associated agile system development process for SaaS development.

The proposed iREM structure has three main elements: business, software and integrated requirements.

- The business section represents a business process (e.g. purchase goods), which is sourced from the reusable business process repository (a method engineering approach of managing reusable business process fragments); business requirements

Figure 2. Integrated requirements engineering model (iREM) (Copyright: Asif Qumer Gill)

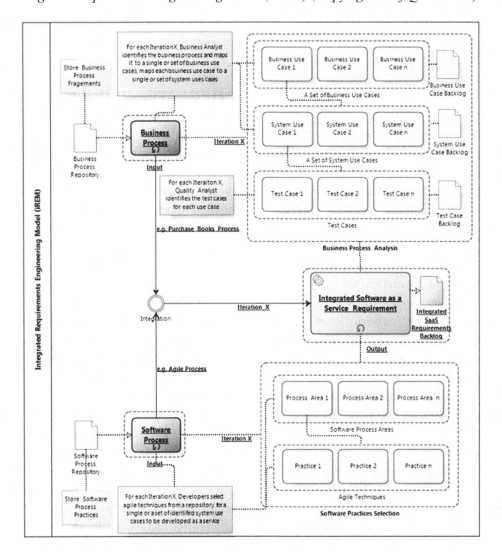

(business use cases) or activities, which are sourced from the business process and are stored in business use case backlog; system requirements (systems use cases) that represent the system capability to support the (full or part of the) business use case and are stored in system use case backlog linked to business use case backlog; and test cases that represent the desired system quality are stored in test case backlog linked to system use case backlog;

- The software section represents the agile software process (e.g. XP, Scrum, software process areas (e.g. development, management) and, also, actual practices or techniques related to the process area that are all sourced from the reusable software process repository (a method engineering approach of managing reusable software process fragments); and

- The requirements section of the iREM structure represents the integrated SaaS requirements, which are mapped to system use cases, test cases and agile practices and are stored in integrated SaaS requirements backlog for agile implementation.

The iREM also specifies the three main roles: business analyst, quality analyst and developer. The business analyst liaises with the project stakeholders and identifies the business process and related requirements in terms of business and system uses cases (for the iteration in hand). The quality analyst identifies the test cases for each identified system use case. The developer iteratively selects system development agile techniques (may consult with agile coach or consultant, if required) and integrates these with the selected SaaS requirement (e.g. selected system use cases and test cases representing the integrated SaaS requirement). The agile coach or consultant, whether external or internal, may also be engaged to educate and guide the project team on the overall agile process adoption and deployment. The requirements and development process would concurrently and dynamically evolve in project iterations as opposed to having an up-front decision about the selection or construction of the development process or techniques for overall project. The proposed approach of dynamic development process tailoring or evolving seems useful when the project requirements are not clear and it is not possible or feasible to tailor an up-front agile or non agile development process. The proposed approach would allow the self organizing project team to defer the decision of development process tailoring (selection of implementation techniques or practices) within their general process lifecycle, until the implementation time when requirements are more likely to become stable and clear. The discussion of the criteria for selecting a specific agile technique or practice for a specific system or SaaS requirement implementation is, however, beyond the scope of this chapter.

The following sections present a simple step by step example in order to explain and demonstrate how the proposed iREM is used for the engineer-

ing of integrated system requirements for a SaaS development environment. Here, for the sake of brevity and demonstration, we only consider a simplified example scenario. The scenario is that of a university book bank, which receives old books from their suppliers and offers those books for sale to students. Students can visit the book bank and purchase old books off the shelf. The following sections discuss this scenario by the means of six steps in order to explain the proposed iREM. This example does not discuss the selection criteria of agile techniques and the development platform type (cloud and non-cloud). The six steps of iREM application are: (1) business process, (2) business uses cases, (3) system use cases, (4) test cases, (5) software process, and (6) integrated SaaS requirements backlog.

Step 1: Identify Business Processes

A business process (e.g. marked in bold and red color in Figure 2) is a primary input element in the business section of the iREM structure. Štolfa and Vondrák (2004) suggested that "business process gives us an opportunity to manage project effectively by organization, simulation and realization of accurate planned processes". The first step in the structure of the iREM is the identification and pulling of the business process (project scope at high-level) from a pool or repository of business processes to be iteratively implemented in terms of software services (e.g. implementation could occur in a cloud and non-cloud environment). As discussed earlier, unlike identifying requirements upfront from customers by using traditional RE techniques (e.g. interviews, survey, user stories, CRC cards), iREM proposes the use or re-use of business processes, stored in a business process repository, as a source for the iterative identification and mapping of dynamic and complex adaptive business processes to eServices for SaaS RE.

Firstly, the key business benefits of this approach are re-usability, standardization and consolidation of the business process management in a central repository for the establishment of a single source of a truth. For instance, the updated version of same process can be re-used many times rather than mapping the same process every time for different projects and wasting resources. Secondly, as opposed to a traditional RE, iREM does not assume RE as only the first and onetime upfront phase of a development process. It is an ongoing RE approach to support the development of business processes as eServices in short iterations.

Example Scenario: Two main business processes can be identified in the example scenario of the university book bank: Receive Books (from the book bank perspective) and Purchase Books (from book banks' customer or buyer perspective). Here, the business analyst and the university book bank system user(s) collaborate and identify the "Purchase Books" business process (iteration 01) from the business process repository for the purpose of SaaS implementation in order to enable the book bank buyers to purchase old books via their online services. The buyer would visit the book bank website instead of the physical book bank retail store. Here, the business analyst would also obtain the latest version of the Purchase Books"

business map from the process repository or map (if not already mapped) and store the "Purchase Books" business process map as a benchmark for the purpose of SaaS RE and reusability in future RE ventures. A simple example of a business process pool is listed in Table 1 and a simple "Purchase Books" process map is demonstrated for the purpose of an example in Figure 3.

Step 2: Identify Business Use Cases

There is a need to analyze the business process and extract the embedded business requirements in terms of business use cases (Krebs 2005) from the business process for a current iteration in hand. A business use case describes the business requirements or capability (e.g. place order, receive goods, make payment) embedded in the business process (e.g. purchase goods). A business process may have one or more business uses cases. It has been suggested (Štolfa and Vondrák 2004) that "we can benefit from using business process for the purposes of use case specification". The second step in the structure of the iREM is the identification and extraction of business uses

Table 1. Business process pool example

ID	Business Process	Owner	Version	Iteration	Storage Location
BP001	Purchase Books	Joe Blog	V1.X	01	/business process map location
BP002	Receive Books	A Gill	V1.X	02	/business process map location
BP003	…				

Figure 3. Business process model

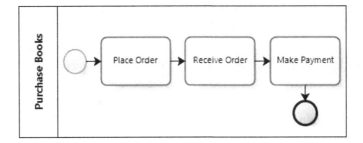

cases from the process map to store them in the business use case backlog with their status and priority that need to be implemented in terms of eServices. As discussed earlier, unlike identifying requirements upfront from customers by using traditional RE techniques (e.g. interviews, survey, user stories, CRC cards), iREM proposes the use or re-use of business processes for the identification of business use cases that need to be implemented in terms of eServices.

Here, along with agility, the key business benefits of this approach are re-usability of business processes in defining business requirements or business use cases and traceability from business process to business use case and business use case to business process in order to make sure that the requirements are not missed and are fully traceable to their origin or source.

Example Scenario: The three key business use cases can be identified and extracted from the example "Purchase Books" business process map: Place Order, Receive Order and Make Payment. Here, the business analyst and the university book bank system user(s) collaborate and select the "Place Order" business use case for iteration 1 of Purchase Books Process as a Service - SaaS implementation. Here, we may observe that a business process can be represented in terms of one or more business use cases and stored in the business use case backlog with their priority and status (please see Table 2 for an example). A business use case model (Figure 4) shows the interaction between the business (Book Bank) and the business actor (Buyer). Here, at this stage, a business use case

(subject to SaaS implementation) can be further detailed by using a use case textual description template or UML activity diagram (based on the perceived business use case complexity and situational need).

Step 3: Identify System Use Cases

A business use case or business requirement (e.g. place order) may have one or more relevant system use cases or system requirements (e.g. search goods, select goods) that need to be implemented in terms of SaaS. The third step in the structure of the iREM is the iterative identification and extraction of system use cases from the prioritized list of business use cases that should be implemented in terms of software services for current iteration in hand. The identified system use cases for the iteration in hand are stored in the system use case backlog.

Here, along with agility, the key business benefit of this approach is traceability from business use case to system use case and from system use case to business use case in order to make sure that the requirements are not missed and are fully traceable to their origin or source.

Example Scenario: The five system use cases can be identified for the "Place Order" business use case: Visit Online Store, Select Books, Search Books, Complete Order and Submit Order. Here, we may observe that a business use case or business requirement can be represented in terms of one or more system use cases. As discussed earlier, these system use cases represent system

Table 2. Business use case backlog example – Iteration 1

ID	Business Use Case	Owner	Version	Priority	Status	Business Process	Storage Location
BUC101	Place Order	Joe Blog	V1.X	1-Very High	Defined	BP001	/business use case textual description and model location
BUC102	Receive Order	Joe Blog	V1.X	2-High		BP001	
BUC103	Make Payment	Joe Blog	V1.X	3-Medium		BP001	

Figure 4. Business use case model

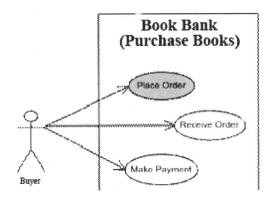

requirements and are stored in the business use case backlog with their priority and status (please see Table 3 for an example). A system use case model (Figure 5) shows the interaction between the system (Book Bank Online Services) and the system actor (Buyer). Here, the identified system uses cases are prioritized. The business analyst and the university book bank collaborate and identify the "Visit Online Store" system use case for the purpose of SaaS requirement. The description of a system requirement (identified system use case) can be found below. One system requirement represents one selected system use case:

- **Visit Online Store (System Use Case):** A buyer must be able to visit book bank on-line services website via their local browser (a system requirement).

At this stage, a system use case or system requirement statement can be further detailed by using a use case textual description template or UML activity diagram (based on the perceived system use case complexity and situational need).

Step 4: Identify Test Cases

The fourth step in the structure of the iREM is the iterative integration of the system requirement or system use case with test cases. The individual system use case can be integrated with one or more test cases for the iteration in hand. Test cases for each system requirement or system use case are identified by the quality analyst for the iteration in hand. As discussed earlier, the test cases specify the acceptable quality of the implemented system requirement (e.g. how a system use case once implemented will be tested by the user).

Here, along with agility, the key business benefit of this approach is traceability from system use case to test case and test case to system use case in order to make sure that the quality requirements are not missed and are fully traceable to their relevant use cases.

Example Scenario: The following two test cases can be identified for the "Visit Online Store" system use case. Here, we may observe that a system use case or system requirement can be tested by the means of one or more test cases. These test cases are stored in the test case

Table 3. System use case backlog example – Iteration 1

ID	System Use Case	Owner	Version	Priority	Status	Business Use Case	Storage Location
SUC101	Visit Online Store	Joe Blog	V1.X	1-Very High	Defined	BUC001	/system use case textual description and model location
SUC102	Select Books	Joe Blog	V1.X	2-High		BUC001	
SUC103	Search Books	Joe Blog	V1.X	3-Medium		BUC001	
SUC104	Complete Order	Joe Blog	V1.X	4-Low		BUC001	
SUC105	Submit Order	Joe Blog	V1.X	5-Very Low		BUC001	

Figure 5. System use case model

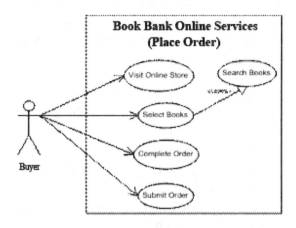

backlog with their priority, status, resolution and severity level (please see Table 4 for an example). The example of test cases attached to the "Visit Online Store" system use case or requirement is as follows:

- **Visit Online Store (Test Case 1):** A buyer enters the book bank online service website URL in a web browser(s) (e.g. IE, Mozilla). The browser(s) would then display the book bank online service home page (a test case).
- **Visit Online Store (Test Case 2):** A buyer enters the book bank online service website URL in a web browser(s) (e.g. IE,

Mozilla). The browser(s) would then display the book bank online service unavailable and retry message if the SaaS server is down (a test case).

At this stage, the business analyst, quality analyst and Book Bank project stakeholders should have collaboratively identified an integrated system use or requirement.

Step 5: Software Process-Integrated System Requirement

A software process is a primary input element (e.g. marked in bold and red color in Figure 2) in the software section of the iREM structure. Software process is a set of agile process fragments or techniques extracted from well-known agile software development methods (e.g. XP, Scrum, Crystal). These agile process fragments have been stored in the ASSF (agile software solution framework) agile process fragment repository (Qumer and Henderson-Sellers 2008b, 2010) to facilitate the situational method engineering of agile system development processes in the context of this research work. A software process may have one or more process areas (e.g. development, project management, process management) and associated best practices to support that process area. As discussed earlier, iREM does not suggest having

Table 4. Test case backlog example – Iteration 1

ID	Test Case	Severity Level	Responsible	Version	Priority	Status	Resolution	System Use Case	Attached Document
TC101	Visit Online Store (Test Case 1)	Major-1	JT	V1.X	1-Very High	Assigned	Code	SUC101	/system use case textual description and model location
TC102	Visit Online Store (Test Case 1)		JT	V1.X	2-High			SUC101	
TC102	…								

a separate upfront step in order to engineer the development process. However, it suggests that the required agile practices or techniques can be selected by the self organizing development team from the agile software process fragment repository, as required at the time of implementation, for the identified requirement or system use case or service. Here, the role of an agile coach is more like a facilitator, which may lead self organizing team when selecting and implementing agile techniques for a particular system use case or service.

Here, along with agility, the key business benefit of the proposed iREM is traceability from system use case to agile techniques and agile techniques to system use case in order to make sure that the appropriate agile techniques are not missed (e.g. pair programming, daily build) and have been applied in order to implement the system use case. It also suggests empowering the self organizing teams and eliminating the need and overhead of upfront development process selection and ongoing change management.

Example Scenario: The fifth step in the structure of the iREM is the integration of the "Visit Online Store" system requirement with the agile system implementation practices or techniques pulled from a software process for iteration in hand. The developer selects the process area, which is "Development", and then pulls two agile practices "Pair Programming"(working together on the same use case - one developing the use case and other reviewing the use case code) and "Continuous Integration" (contentiously deploying the developed self contained use case to the system integration environment) from the agile

process fragment repository. The pulled agile practices are then integrated with the "Visit Online Store" system requirement (please see Table 5 as an example). The integrated system requirement is as follows:

• **Visit Online Store (Integrated System Requirement):** A buyer must be able to visit the book bank online services website via their local browsers (a system requirement). A buyer enters the book bank online service website URL in a web browser(s) (e.g. IE, Mozilla); the browser(s) would the display the book bank online service home page (a test case). A buyer enters the book bank online service website URL in a web browser(s) (e.g. IE, Mozilla); the browser(s) would then display the book bank online service unavailable and retry message if the SaaS server is down (a test case). Agile practices "Pair Programming" and "Continuous Integration" would be used for the implementation of this system requirement. As explained earlier, the detailed discussion of the criteria for selecting a specific technique or practice for a specific requirement implementation are beyond the scope of this book chapter. The selection of a specific agile technique depends on a number of factors such as development and deployment environment, infrastructure, team capability, team agile level (please see Pikkarainen et al. 2005; Mahanti 2006; Qumer and Henderson-Sellers 2008b).

Table 5. System use case backlog and selected agile practices example – Iteration 1

ID	Agile Practices	Area	Status	System Use Case	Storage Location
LAP1001	Pair Programming	Development	Assigned	SUC101	/lean agile technique textual description location
LAP1002	Continuous Integration	Development	Assigned	SUC101	
..	..	...			

Based on the discussion and analysis in this section, integrated system requirements (Figure 6) for "SaaS" may be defined as:

"Integrated system requirement is a system use case with the embedded test cases and system development practices" whereas a system use case (Krebs 2005; Bennett et al. 2006) specifies required functional or system requirements – what the "SaaS" shall do. Paetsch et al. (2003) suggested that "use cases describe interactions between users and the system, focusing on what users need to do with the system. A use case specifies a sequence of interactions between the system and an external actor". Agile is a test-driven development (TDD) approach (e.g. test first) and Cao and Ramesh (2008) suggested that "TDD treats writing tests as part of requirements/design activity in which a test specifies the code's behavior". The associated test-cases are identified based on the desired quality aspects for the currently known system use case or system requirement. Agile system development practices specify techniques for the implementation of the system use case or requirement (SaaS requirement) with the desired quality.

At this stage, we have selected agile practices or techniques to implement the integrated system requirement or system use case. It can be observed that the developer would select agile techniques or practices (just-in-time method engineering approach) for system requirements, as opposed to having a pre-defined standard or upfront tailored agile method. Both the system requirements and system development process would iteratively evolve as the project progresses through different iterations.

Step 6: Integrated SaaS Requirements Backlog

The identified integrated SaaS requirements are mapped to the relevant software service and their interfaces; and are then pushed into the product service backlog (as per Table 6) for further assessment (which services to develop and deploy in the cloud?) and implementation (e.g. service interface and business component definition, service collaboration). The product service backlog with the integrated SaaS requirements is the main output of the iREM (e.g. marked in bold and green color in Figure 2).

The purpose of the product service backlog is to provide a repository for storing and managing the evolving services for SaaS implementation. A service may have one or more integrated system requirements or use case and each integrated system requirement has an owner or developer and shows the estimated time for the implementation of the requirement. Each service is also tagged as cloud service (to be developed or deployed in the cloud) or non-cloud service by the developer (to be developed and deployed in the local environment). It is because all the identified services may not be implemented in the shared cloud environment, which may impact (e.g. technical design, query size, effort) the implementation of the SaaS [when a service is deployed in the shared cloud environment it requires additional service management requirements i.e. additional security, on-demand availability, scalability, monitoring, governance limits, performance, pay-as-you go billing, multi-tenancy]. Further, the agile planning related attributes may be added to the proposed product service backlog such as

Figure 6. Integrated system requirement

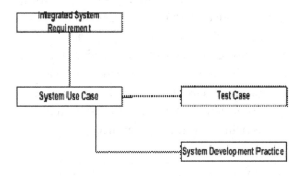

Table 6. Product service backlog example

ID	Service	Cloud Service	Priority	Status	System Use Case	Owner	Development Time
SV101	Book Bank	Yes/ No	1	In Development	SUC101	JK	36 Hours
SV102	Book	Yes/ No	1	In Development	SUC102	JK	12 Hours
SV102	Book	Yes/ No	1	In Development	SUC103	JK	10 Hours

Note: The process repository and related backlog tables have been used here to demonstrate the structure of the information that is stored and managed during RE and agile implementation. In practice, however, we use different tools to manage the business process repository, requirements, iterations and agile processes. For example, enterprise architect is used for storing and managing business process and related model artifacts; JIRA is used for managing agile iterations, requirements and issues; and ASSF repository is used for managing the agile practices. Here, we are not recommending and promoting specific tools for managing agile RE and implementation, it is up to the reader to do their own assessment about the use of available tools in the market place for their development environment.

priority (e.g. between 1 and 5), status (e.g. not started, in development, in test, completed, validated and verified), start date, end date and estimated dollar value.

Here, firstly, along with agility, the key business benefit of the proposed iREM is to enable the end-to-end traceability from business process to software service. For instance, as discussed earlier, traditional approach considers RE as a first and an isolated phase from a development process, which presents the partial view of a requirement (e.g. what and why to develop. Whereas iREM proposes an approach to capture the "Service Requirements as a Whole" or service package with the appropriate development techniques in order to provide the end-to-end traceability and integration of business process (e.g. SaaS requirements) and development process (e.g. development practices). The end-to-end traceability is important for the purpose of project post implementation review, process auditing and management - i.e. which business processes have been developed as eServices (e.g. SaaS requirements) by using which software development processes or practices. Secondly, it also allows the differentiation between cloud and non-cloud services, which may impact the technical design and implementation of the SaaS. For instance, when a service is developed and deployed in the Salesforce shared cloud platform, a

developer has to follow the governance limit set by Salesforce cloud such as the heap size for a given SaaS execution context should not be more than 3MB, DML statement can process only 10,000 records at a given time etc.

Example Scenario: The integrated system requirement "Visit Online Store" is first mapped (Figure 7) to the relevant software service and their interfaces (in this case the software service would be "Book Bank" and the software service interface would be "Book Bank Management"), and is then pushed into the product service backlog (as per Table 6) for further assessment (which services to develop and deploy in the cloud?) and implementation (e.g. service interface and business component definition, service collaboration). The other software services and their relevant interfaces that may be identified for the other system use cases are: "Book" service and "Book Management" service interface for the "Select Books" and "Search Books" use cases; "Order" service and "Order Management" service interface for the "Complete Order" and "Submit Order" use cases. A software service interface contains the signature of public methods that can be implemented by the actual software service. A service consumer may access the public methods of a particular service for their needs.

Figure 7. Software service and interfaces

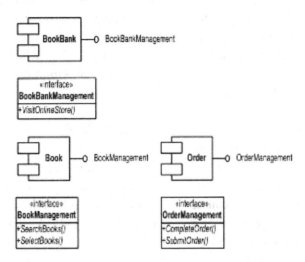

iREM AND AGILE IMPLEMENTATION

This section summarizes the proposed iREM in the overall context of agile implementation. As discussed earlier, iREM is an iterative approach of SaaS RE for the agile implementation. It facilitates the discovery of services by mapping business process to services for the agile implementation in small iterations:

- A business process (BP) is identified as an input (e.g. marked in bold and red color in Figure 2) from a pool or repository of business processes that need to be implemented in terms of software services in the agile iteration X (depending on situational circumstances, a large business process may span multiple iterations or a small number of business processes may fit in one iteration).
- The identified business process (BP) is linked or mapped to a single or set of business use cases (BUC), which are identified and stored in the business use case backlog for the iteration X.
- Each identified business use case (BUC) is linked or mapped to a single or set of sys-

tem use cases (SUC), which are identified and stored in the system use case backlog for the iteration X.

- Each identified system use case (SUC) is linked or mapped to a single or set of test cases (TC), which are identified and stored in the test case backlog for the iteration X. At this stage, the system use case backlog integrated with the test case backlog is released for the iteration X implementation by using agile practices.
- Each identified system use case (SUC) is linked or mapped to a single or set of agile practices (within their overall generic process lifecycle), which is called integrated system requirement or system use case (please see Section above for details).
- Each integrated system use case is linked or mapped to a software service (integrated SaaS requirements, which are stored in the product service backlog (e.g. marked in bold and green color in Figure 2) for the iteration X.

The business analyst and quality analyst start the next iteration X + 1 for identifying the BP and attached BUC, SUC and TC. The development team starts working on the implementation of services listed in the product service backlog for the iteration X as per their priority. If the requirements are changed during the iteration X implementation then those changes (if minor) can be considered in the current iteration X or next iteration X+n (where n= 1, 2, 3...). In the end of an iteration X, the iteration X retrospective is conducted to review the agile process (e.g. which services have been implemented by using which agile practices), and identify any issues (e.g. missed requirements, less than 50% unit test coverage) and their root-causes (e.g. continuous integration was not performed for SUC of service 1, code view review and user viewing sessions were not conducted) and then finally, the iteration X is released for further integration and user acceptance testing. Here, at this stage, the system use case backlog integrated with test case backlog for the next iteration X+1 may be released to development team by the business and quality analysts for implementation. The development team starts a work on the Iteration X+1 and also provides support for fixing any defects in the previous iteration X.

Here, we may observe how iREM supports the iterative discovery of SaaS requirements and their agile implementation. It can also be observed that there can be one or more active iterations at a given point of time (business and quality analyst working on the iteration X+1 while the development team is working on iteration X).

MODEL ANALYSIS

The RE approach may vary depending on the situation, however, the five core requirements engineering activities as specified by the literature remain the same: (1) elicitation, (2) analysis, (3) verification and validation, (4) documentation and (5) management (Paetsch et al. 2003; Sommerville 2005). Here, we present the analysis of the iREM against these five core activities and traditional RE approach. In the future, subject to

further research, we anticipate that further testing and evaluation of the iREM would be conducted against each of these activities for SaaS requirements engineering, which may raise a range of additional opportunities for research (Table 7).

DISCUSSION

While working on different agile and SaaS projects in industry, it has been found that that there are a number of service analysis and design methods (e.g. SODA, SOMA) that discuss the development of services for the implementation of business processes, however, they do not seem to provide detailed guidelines for the identification and mapping of business processes to services for RE. They suggest using direct and indirect interviews to identify the service requirements; however, interviews are textual or vocal artifacts; and therefore, are subject to human error and misinterpretation. In order to address the short comings of interview-based approach (e.g. face-to-face communication), we here proposed the use and re-use of business process repository as an input to identify the services. It would not only help consolidating, standardizing and managing the business processes in a single repository but it would also help to save the time and cost of mapping the same process again and again in different projects by different teams with different redundant versions.

These traditional service analysis methods also do not seem to discuss the additional characteristics of SaaS (e.g. governance limits, multi-tenancy, pay-as-you-go), which are different from traditional services. Here in this chapter, we explicitly mention the consideration of these additional characteristics that need to be considered during the SaaS RE and development.

As we discussed earlier, the traditional RE methods (whether service oriented or non-service oriented) discuss the traceability of different artifacts (e.g. analysis to design to code) but do

Table 7. Product service backlog example

ID	RE Activities	Cloud Service
1	Requirements Elicitation	The iREM facilitates the systematic iterative elicitation of the software service requirements (output) from re-usable business processes (input) as opposed to using the traditional RE techniques such as focus groups, user stories, and interviews. The iREM provides an end-to-end approach of requirements elicitation – from business process [business and system uses cases] to service [process as a service] while focusing on business process re-usability. The iREM is not a onetime upfront phase of a development process rather it is an agile, adjustable and ongoing requirements elicitation approach to support the development of dynamic and complex adaptive business processes as eServices in short iterations
2	Requirements Analysis	The iREM structure suggests a review and analysis of reusable business processes (input) that involve the business analyst and the system user(s). The purpose of this review is to pull the needed business requirements or activities (business use cases), for the specific project iteration in hand, from a business process map, which are then subject to implementation (system use cases or requirements). An individual system use case is analyzed and integrated with the test cases (identified by the quality analyst) and system development practice (identified by the developer). Furthermore, integrated system use cases are analyzed and mapped to software services.
3	Requirements Verification and Validation	Traditional approaches consider RE as a first and an isolated phase from a development process, which presents the partial view of a requirement (e.g. what and why to develop). Therefore, in order to make sure that the requirements are fully traceable, the iREM structure suggests to capture the "Service Requirements as a Whole" or service package with the appropriate development process in order to provide the end-to-end traceability and integration of business process (e.g. SaaS requirements) and development process (e.g. development practices) for the purpose of auditing and management i.e. which business processes have been developed as eServices (e.g. SaaS requirements) by using which software development processes or practices. For example, an identified software service can be traced back to the integrated system SaaS requirement (a package of system use cases, test cases and agile practices), integrated system requirement can be traced back to business use cases and the business use case traced back to the business process.
4	Requirements Documentation	The iREM suggests the use of a number of tools for documenting the requirements. For instance, the iREM structure suggests using the business process models, use cases, activity diagrams and textual description or artifacts at each iteration level. Based on the actual situation, a developer and user may negotiate an acceptable level of requirements detail with the business (e.g. detail textual description of system use cases, test cases) for the purpose of communication.
5	Requirements Management	The iREM suggests the use of a number of tools for managing requirements. For instance, the iREM structure suggests using the re-usable process repositories, use case, test case and service backlogs for managing versions, prioritization, status, and cloud and non-cloud service implementation information. As discussed earlier, the adoption of a shared cloud computing environment for developing and deploying services may pose several challenges. It is important to distinguish which software services would be developed and deployed in the shared cloud computing environment (cloud service); and which service would be developed and deployed in the non-cloud environment. The selection of the service development and development platform (cloud or non-cloud) is not in the scope of this chapter, and is an area for further development (e.g. a cloud adoption and improvement model).

not seem to discuss the traceability between the business process and actual development process or practices that had been used to implement the business process as a service (e.g. which service requirements had been implemented by using which agile or non-agile practices). For instance, taking an example from our experience in the industry project, when there were multiple teams working in an agile environment, business process was developed and released as a service into production environment without implementing the peer review and code review practices. After the release of the service in the production environment, it was identified that there was a missing component of the service, which had not been included in the final build of a service release (e.g. omissions or defects in production environment may lead to system downtime and may also prove very expensive to fix). Here, one may ask a key question, why that component had been missed? What is the root cause of such omission? Who is responsible for the cost and fix of this defect? Did we perform the peer review and code review practices? Which team is responsible i.e. development or test? Now, if we had stored or tracked the information about the practices that had been used to implement the business process as a service then it would had been be relatively easier to identify the root cause of the problem in hand (e.g. the root cause was that the peer review and code review practices had not been followed by the development team and therefore, development team lead was responsible for this). The lack of such traceability would not only make it difficult to identify the root cause of the problem but would also lead to distress, conflict and blame game among the teams (e.g. pointing fingers at each other i.e. your team is responsible and should bear the cost of omission fix and downtime of the system) but would also put the whole project at risk. Here in this chapter, the iREM structure suggests to capture the "Service Requirements as a Whole" or service package with the appropriate development process or practices in order to provide the end-to-end traceability and integration of business process (e.g. SaaS requirements) and development process (e.g. development practices) for the purpose of auditing.

In summary, based on our current research, experiences and challenges in different large agile and SaaS projects in industry in Australia, this book chapter presented the iREM model to guide the agile SaaS RE and implementation in short iterations (e.g. mapping business process to services and to actual development process or practices that would be used for implementing the business process as a service).

FUTURE RESEARCH AND APPLICATION

Understanding the delivery and use of SaaS in the shared cloud computing environment is an important issue in the area of crisis and disaster related situations (Smith and Bunker 2007; Bunker and Smith 2009). This is due to the fact that multiple stakeholders (i.e. emergency services agencies, community groups) must work together to prepare for, respond to and recover from, a catastrophic event. The ability to share processes and systems in a useful and sustainable way is critical during a disaster situation. A "context-aware cloud adoption (CACA)" structured framework (Gill and Bunker 2011) is being developed to assist Emergency Services Agencies (ESAs) in the systematic, context-aware adoption and improvement of a shared cloud-enabled computing environment. This framework facilitates the development and management of adaptive collaborative business processes (Process as a Service) and information systems (IS as a Service) for disaster management. The iREM, as outlined in this chapter, is a CACA framework component, and is also a first step towards the development of a comprehensive model to assist ESAs with the SaaS RE for "Process as a Service" and "IS as a Service" in a specific cloud computing environment. In future, we intend to further empirically evaluate and improve the iREM within the disaster management context, and also provide additional guidelines to support the indexing and selection of business processes and associated services to be developed and deployed in the cloud for disaster management. The example we have used here is restricted to service systems, although, in future, we also intend to show a more general applicability of the proposed model. Other issues to be addressed are: the costs associated with maintaining the process fragment repository or library and associated tools; the overhead of having to decide on the selection of agile implementation techniques for each system requirement or service; and also the overhead associated with the management (e.g. change management, regression testing) of evolving systems requirements and evolving development process in each project iteration.

CONCLUSION

This chapter has presented the iREM, which provides a novel approach to integrating agile practices to system use cases for SaaS RE. The benefits of the iREM are: end-to-end traceability to make it less difficult to identify the root causes of any problem or issue that may arise before, during and post implementation; and that a pre-defined or tailored upfront software process is not required to be constructed at the start of the project, rather, an agile system development process can dynamically evolve during the course of the project in different iterations. The iREM is intended for use by developers, business and quality analysts for iteratively integrating the system requirements with the test cases and agile system development practices for SaaS RE and implementation.

REFERENCES

Agile Manifesto. (2001). *Manifesto for agile software development*. Retrieved from http://www.agilemanifesto.org/

Ambler, S. W. (2009). *Inclusive modeling: User centered approaches for agile software development*. Retrieved from http://www.agilemodeling.com/essays/inclusiveModels.htm

Arsanjani, A. (2004). *Service-oriented modeling and architecture*. Retrieved from http://www-128.ibm.com/.

Arsanjani, A., Ghosh, S., Allam, A., Abdollah, T., Ganapathy, S., & Holley, K. (2008). SOMA: A method for developing service-oriented solutions. *IBM Systems Journal, 47*(3). doi:10.1147/sj.473.0377

Bajec, M., Damjan Vavpotič, D., Furlan, S., & Krisper, M. (2007). Software process improvement based on the method engineering principles. *IFIP International Federation for Information Processing, 244,* 283–297. doi:10.1007/978-0-387-73947-2_22

Baniassad, E., & Clarke, S. (2004). *Finding aspects in requirements with theme/doc.* Workshop on Early Aspects (AOSD 2004), Lancaster, UK.

Beck, K. (2000). *Extreme programming explained.* Boston, MA: Addison-Wesley Pearson Education.

Beck, K., & Andres, C. (2004). *Extreme programming explained: Change.* Boston, MA: Addison-Wesley.

Becker, J., & Krcmar, H. (2008). Integration von Produktion und Dienstleistung – Hybride Wertschöpfung. *Wirtschaftsinformatik, 50*(3). doi:10.1365/s11576-008-0044-y

Bennett, S., McRobb, S., & Farmer, R. (2006). *Object-oriented system analysis and design using UML.* McGraw Hill.

Berkovich, M., Esch, S., Leimeister, J. M., & Krcmar, H. (2009). Requirements engineering for hybrid products as bundles of hardware, software and service elements – A literature review. *Wirtschaftinformatik Proceedings 2009.*

Beydoun, G., Gonzalez-Perez, C., Low, G., & Henderson-Sellers, B. (2005a). Synthesis of a generic MAS metamodel. *4th International Workshop on Software Engineering for Large-Scale Multi-Agent Systems,* St. Louis, Missouri.

Beydoun, G., Hoffmann, A., Fernandez-Breis, J. T., Martinez-Bejar, R., Valencia-Garcia, R., & Aurum, A. (2005b). Cooperative modelling evaluated. *International Journal of Cooperative Information Systems, 14*(1), 45–71. doi:10.1142/S0218843005001080

Brinkkemper, S. (1996). Method engineering: Engineering of information systems development methods and tools. *Information and Software Technology, 38*, 275–280. doi:10.1016/0950-5849(95)01059-9

Brinkkemper, S., Saeki, M., & Harmsen, F. (1998). Assembly techniques for method engineering. *Proceedings Advanced Information Systems Engineering, 10th International Conference, CAiSE'98, LNCS1413,* Pisa, Italy, (pp. 381-400). Springer Verlag.

Bunker, D., & Smith, S. (2009). *Disaster management and community warning (CW) systems: Inter-organisational collaboration and ICT innovation.* Pacific Asia Conference on IS.

Cao, L., & Ramesh, B. (2008). Agile requirements engineering practices: An empirical study. *IEEE Software, 25*(1), 60–67. doi:10.1109/MS.2008.1

Castro, V. D., Marcos, E., & Cáceres, P. (2004). A user service oriented method to model web information systems. *WISE 2004: Web Information Systems, LNCS: Vol. 3306. 2004, Brisbane, Australia* (pp. 41–52). Berlin, Germany: Springer.

Chau, T., Maurer, F., & Melnik, G. (2003). Knowledge sharing: Agile methods vs. tayloristic methods. *Proceedings of the 12th IEEE International workshop on Enabling Technologies: Infrastructure for Collaborative Enterprises,* Linz, Austria, (pp. 302-307).

Chung, L., Nixon, B. A., Yu, E., & Mylopoulos, J. (2000). *Non-functional requirements in software engineering.* Kluwer Academic Publishers, 2000.

Cockburn, A. (2005). *Crystal clear: A human-powered methodology for small teams.* Addison-Wesley.

Cockburn, A. (2006). *Agile software development: The cooperative game.* Addison-Wesley.

Cockburn, A., & Highsmith, J. (2001). Agile software development: The people factor. *Computer, 34*(11), 131–133. doi:10.1109/2.963450

Coulin, C., Zowghi, D., & Sahraoui, A. (2006). A situational method engineering approach to requirements elicitation workshops in the software development process. *Software Process Improvement and Practice, 11*(5), 451–464. doi:10.1002/spip.288

Davenport, T. H., & Short, J. E. (1990, July 15). The new industrial engineering: Information technology and business process redesign. *Sloan Management Review.*

Davis, A. (1992). Operational prototyping: A new development approach. *IEEE Software, 9*(5). doi:10.1109/52.156899

Eckstein, J. (2004). *Agile software development in large. Diving into the deep.* New York, NY: Dorset House Publishing.

Endrei, M., Ang, J., Arsanjani, A., Chua, S., Comte, P., & Krogdahl, P. (2004). *Patterns: Service-oriented architecture and web services.* IBM Redbooks.

Erl, T. (2005). *Service-oriented architecture: Concepts, technology, and design.* Upper Saddle River, NJ: Pearson Education Inc.

Feuerlicht, G. (2006). System development life-cycle support for service-oriented applications. In Fukita, H., & Mejri, M. (Eds.), *New trend in software methodologies, tools and techniques (Vol. 147,* pp. 116–126). Quebec, Canada: IOS Press.

Fitzgerald, B., Hartnett, G., & Conboy, K. (2006). Customising agile methods to software practices at Intel Shannon. *European Journal of Information Systems, 15*(2), 200–213. doi:10.1057/palgrave. ejis.3000605

Gill, A. Q., & Bunker, D. (2011). *Conceptualization of a context aware cloud adaptation (CACA) framework.* Ninth IEEE International Conference on Dependable, Autonomic and Secure Computing, Sydney.

Goguen, J., & Linde, C. (1993). Techniques for requirements elicitation. *1st IEEE International Symposium on Requirements Engineering (RE'93),* San Diego, USA, (pp. 152-164).

Hassine, I., Rieu, D., Bounaas, F., & Seghrouchni, O. (2002). *Towards a resuable business components model.* A Workshop of the 8th International Conference on Object-Oriented Information Systems OOIS, Montpellier, France.

Henderson-Sellers, B. (2003). Method engineering for OO system development. *Communications of the ACM, 46*(10), 73–78. doi:10.1145/944217.944242

Highsmith, J., & Cockburn, A. (2001). Agile software development: The business of innovation. *Computer, 34*(9), 120–122. doi:10.1109/2.947100

Highsmith, J. A. I. (2000). *Adaptive software development: A collaborative approach to managing complex systems.* New York, NY: Dorset House Publishing.

Jackson, M. (2001). *Problem frames: Analyzing and structuring software development problems.* ACM Press.

Jiang, L., Eberlein, A., Far, B. H., & Mousavi, M. (2008). A methodology for the selection of requirements engineering techniques. *Software Systems Models, 7*(3), 303–328. doi:10.1007/s10270-007-0055-y

Karlsson, F., & Ågerfalk, P. J. (2008). Method configuration: The eXtreme programming case. *Agile Processes in Software Engineering and Extreme Programming. Lecture Notes in Business Information Processing, 9,* 32–41. doi:10.1007/978-3-540-68255-4_4

Kodali, R. R. (2005). *What is service-oriented architecture: An introduction to SOA.* Retrieved from www.javaworld.com

Krebs, J. (2005). *Dissecting business from software requirements.* Retrieved from www.ibm.com/developerworks/rational/library/aug05/krebs

Krogdahl, P., Luef, G., & Steindl, C. (2005). *Service-oriented agility, Methods for successful service-oriented architecture (SOA) development,* Part 1. IBM. Retrieved from http://www-128.ibm.com/

Kruger, I. H., Gupta, D., Mathew, R., Praveen, M., Phillips, W., Rittmann, S., & Ahluwalia, J. (2004). *Towards a process and tool-chain for service-oriented automotive software engineering.* ICSE 2004 Workshop on Software Engineering for Automotive Systems, Edinburgh.

Kumar, K., & Welke, R. J. (1992). Method engineering: A proposal for situation-specific methodology construction. In Senn, C. A. (Ed.), *Systems analysis and design: A research agenda* (pp. 257–269). John Wiley and Sons.

Lindvall, M., & Rus, I. (2000). Process diversity in software development. *IEEE Software, 17*(4), 14–18. doi:10.1109/MS.2000.854063

Liu, F., Tong, J., Mao, J., Bohn, R., Messina, J., Badger, L., & Leaf, D. (2011). *NIST cloud computing reference architecture.* National Institute of Standards and Technology, US Department of Commerce.

Mahanti, A. (2006). Challenges in enterprise adoption of agile methods – A survey. *Journal of Computing and Information Technology, 14*(3), 197–206.

Maiden, N., & Rugg, G. (1996). ACRE: Selecting methods for requirements acquisition. *Software Engineering Journal, 11*(3), 183–192. doi:10.1049/sej.1996.0024

Mell, P., & Grance, T. (2011). *The NIST definition of cloud computing.* National Institute of Standards and Technology, US Department of Commerce.

Omar, W. M., & Taleb-Bendiab, A. (2006). Service oriented architecture for e-health support service based on grid computing overlay. *IEEE International Conference on Services Computing,* (pp. 135-42). IEEE Computer Society.

Paetsch, F., Eberlein, A., & Maurer, F. (2003). Requirements engineering and agile software development. In *Proceedings of the Twelfth international Workshop on Enabling Technologies: Infrastructure for Collaborative Enterprises, WETICE,* (p. 308). Washington, DC: IEEE Computer Society.

Palmer, S. R., & Felsing, J. M. (2002). *A practical guide to feature-driven development.* Upper Saddle River, NJ: Prentice-Hall Inc.

Pikkarainen, M., Sal, O., & Still, J. (2005). Deploying agile practices in organisations: A case study. *The Proceedings of the EuroSPI, LNCS, 3792,* 16–27.

Poppendieck, M., & Poppendieck, T. (2003). *Lean software development: An agile toolkit.* Addison-Wesley, Inc.

Qumer, A., & Henderson-Sellers, B. (2008a). An evaluation of the degree of agility in six agile methods and its applicability for method engineering. [IST]. *Information and Software Technology, 50*(4), 280–295. doi:10.1016/j.infsof.2007.02.002

Qumer, A., & Henderson-Sellers, B. (2008b). A framework to support the evaluation, adoption, and improvement of agile methods in practice. *Journal of Systems and Software, 81*(11), 1899–1919. doi:10.1016/j.jss.2007.12.806

Qumer, A., & Henderson-Sellers, B. (2010). *Framework as software service (FASS) - An agile e-toolkit to support agile method tailoring.* International Conference on Software and Data Technologies, Athens, Greece.

Ralyté, J. (1999). Reusing scenario based approaches in requirements engineering methods: CREWS method base. *Proceedings of the 10th International Workshop on Database and Expert Systems Applications (DEXA'99), 1st International REP'99 Workshop,* Florence, Italy, (p. 305).

Ranjan, J. (2011). *SaaS and agile – Match made in heaven.* Retrieved from http://www.mindtree.com/blogs/saas-agile-match-heaven

Rashid, A., Moreira, A., & Araujo, J. (2003). *Modularisation and composition of aspectual requirements.* International Conference on Aspect Oriented Software Development (AOSD), Boston, USA.

Reifer, D. (2002). How good are agile methods? *IEEE Software, 19,* 16. doi:10.1109/MS.2002.1020280

Saeki, M. (2003). CAME: The first step to automated software engineering. In C. Gonzalez-Perez, B. Henderson-Sellers & D. Rawsthorne (Eds.), *Proceedings of OOPSLA 2003 Workshop on Process Engineering for Object-Oriented and Component-Based Development,* Anaheim, CA, (pp. 26-30).

Salesforce. (2008). *Agile development meets cloud computing for extraordinary results.* Retrieved from salesforce.com

Schwaber, K. (2004). *Agile project management with Scrum.* Redmond, WA: Microsoft Press.

Schwaber, K., & Beedle, M. (2002). *Agile software development with SCRUM*. Prentice Hall.

Smith, S., & Bunker, D. (2007). *Community warning systems: An information process and ICT architecture approach for emergency incident response*. Issue paper (submitted to the State Emergency Management Committee).

Sommerville, I. (2005). Integrated requirements engineering: A tutorial. *IEEE Software, 22*(1), 16–23. doi:10.1109/MS.2005.13

Stapleton, J. (1997). *DSDM: The method in practice*. Addison-Wesley, Inc.

Stiehm, T., Foster, R., & Hulen, R. (2006). *SOA, meet agile: Adopting SOA with agile teams*. Digital Focus – a Command Information Company.

Štolfa, S., & Vondrák, I. (2004). A description of business process modeling as a tool for definition of requirements specification. *Proceedings of System Integration*, (pp. 463-469).

ter Hofstede, A. H. M., & Verhoef, T. F. (1997). On the feasibility of situational method engineering. *Information Systems, 22*, 401–422. doi:10.1016/S0306-4379(97)00024-0

Tsai, W. T., Jin, Z., Wang, P., & Wu, B. (2007). *Requirement engineering in service-oriented system engineering*. IEEE International Conference on e-Business Engineering, ICEBE 2007.

Tsai, W. T., Malek, M., Chen, Y., & Bastani, F. (2006). Perspectives on service-oriented computing and service-oriented system engineering. In *Proceedings of the Second IEEE International Symposium on Service-Oriented System Engineering,* (pp. 3-10).

Turk, D., France, R., & Rumpe, B. (2005). Assumptions underlying agile software development processes. *Journal of Database Management, 16*(4), 62–87. doi:10.4018/jdm.2005100104

van Lamsweerde, A., Darimont, R., & Letier, E. (1998). Managing conflicts in goal-driven requirements engineering. *IEEE Transactions on Software Engineering, 24*(11), 908–926. doi:10.1109/32.730542

Welke, R., & Kumar, K. (1991). Method engineering: A proposal for situation-specific methodology construction. In *Systems analysis and design: A research agenda*. Wiley.

Zave, P. (1997). Classification of research efforts in requirements engineering. *ACM Computing Surveys, 29*(4), 315–321. doi:10.1145/267580.267581

Zhong, J. (2001). *Step into the J2EE architecture and process*. Retrieved from www.JavaWorld.com

Zimmermann, O., Krogdahl, P., & Gee, C. (2004). *Elements of service-oriented analysis and design*. IBM.

Zowghi, D., Firesmith, D. G., & Henderson-Sellers, B. (2005). Using the OPEN process framework to produce a situation-specific requirements engineering method. *Proceedings of SREP*, Paris, France, (pp. 59-74).

ADDITIONAL READING

Armbrust, M., Fox, A., Griffith, R., Joseph, A. D., Katz, R., & Konwinski, A. … Zaharia, M. (2009). *Above the clouds: A Berkeley view of Cloud Computing*. UC Berkeley EECS. Retrieved from http://www.eecs.berkeley.edu/Pubs/TechRpts/2009/EECS-2009-28.pdf

Bunker, D. (2010). *Information systems management (ISM): Repertoires of collaboration for community warning (CW) and emergency incident response (EIR)*. IEEE Conference on Technologies for Homeland Security, Boston.

Bunker, D., Kautz, K., & Anhtuan, A. (2008). An exploration of information systems adoption: Tools and skills as cultural artefacts – The case of a management information system. *Journal of Information Technology, 23*(2), 71–78. doi:10.1057/palgrave.jit.2000134

Bunker, D., Kautz, K., & Nguyen, A. (2007). The role of value compatibility in IT adoption. *Journal of Information Technology, 22*, 69–78. doi:10.1057/palgrave.jit.2000092

Daneshgar, F., Bunker, D., & Mawson-Lee, K.(2006). An e-business collaborative process integration framework for the Australian health insurance sector (AHIS*). International Journal of Business Process Integration and Management, 1.*

Economist. (2008, October 23). Corporate IT special report: Let it rise. *The Economist.* Retrieved from http://www.economist.com/specialreports/displayStory.cfm?story_id=12411882

Goldstein, P. (2009). The tower, the cloud, and the IT leader and workforce. In R. Katz (Ed.), *The tower and the cloud: Higher education in the age of cloud computing.* Educause. Retrieved from http://www.educause.edu/thetowerandthecloud

Henderson-Sellers, B., & Ralyte, J. (2010). Situational method engineering: State-of-the-art review. *Journal of Universal Computer Science, 16*(3), 424–478.

Järvinen, P. (2001). *On research methods.* Tampere, Finland: Juvenes-Print.

Kasanen, E., Lukka, K., & Siitonen, A. (1993). The constructive approach in management accounting research. *Journal of Management Accounting Research, 5*, 243–264.

Keenan, F. (2004). Agile process tailoring and probLem analYsis (APTLY). In *The Proceedings of the 26th International Conference on Software Engineering (ICSE 2004),* Edinburgh, Scotland, IEEE, (pp.45-47).

Powell, J. (2009). *Cloud computing – What is it and what does it mean for education?* Retrieved from erevolution.jiscinvolve.org/wp/files/2009/07/clouds-johnpowell.pdf

Smith, S., Winchester, D., Bunker, D., & Jamieson, R. (2010). Circuits of power: A study of mandated compliance to an information systems security de jure standard in a government organization. *MISQ: Special Issue on Information System Security in the Digital Economy, 34*(3), 463–486.

Van Toorn, C., Bunker, D., Yee, K., & Smith, S. (2007). The barriers to the adoption of e-commerce by micro businesses, small businesses and medium businesses. *The International Journal of Knowledge, Culture and Change Management, 6.*

Venable, J. R., Pries-Heje, J., Bunker, D., & Russo, N. L. (2010). *Creation, transfer, and diffusion of innovation in organizations and society: Information systems design science research for human benefit.* IFIP WG 8.2/8.6 International Working Conference, Perth, Australia.

Whyld, D. C. (2010). *Moving to the cloud: An introduction to cloud computing in government.* Retrieved from www.businessofgovernment.org

KEY TERMS AND DEFINITIONS

Agile Method: A light-weight people focused and an adaptive approach for developing and managing software systems.

Business Process: A set of business roles, activities, and rules that are executed to achieve desired business value.

Method Engineering: An approach to assemble software methods from small method chunks or fragments.

Requirement Engineering: An approach for gathering and managing requirements for building a software system.

Software as a Service (SaaS): A logical view or an abstraction of a business process or a program or for carrying out business-level operations or activities.

Software Process: A set roles, activities and rules that are executed for developing and managing software systems.

Use Cases: A technique to model or represent business and system requirements.

Chapter 5
The Incremental Commitment Spiral Model for Service–Intensive Projects

Supannika Koolmanojwong
University of Southern California, USA

Barry Boehm
University of Southern California, USA

Jo Ann Lane
University of Southern California, USA

ABSTRACT

To provide better service to customers and remain competitive in the business environment, a wide variety of ready-to-use software and technologies are available for one to "grab and go" in order to build up software systems at a rapid pace. Currently, a wide variety of Web services are available and ready to use for this purpose. Current software process models also support commercial-off-the-shelf (COTS)-based development processes. However, although COTS and Web Services are similar, they are different in many perspectives. On one hand, there are various software process models that support Web services development. Yet there is no process model that supports the project that uses services provided by others. This chapter introduces the Incremental Commitment Spiral Model (ICSM), a new generation process model that provides development guidelines, from exploring a Web service alternative to deployment and maintenance with case studies.

DOI: 10.4018/978-1-4666-2503-7.ch005

INTRODUCTION

The expeditious and fast growing of Internet and Web applications create a variety of available services over the Internet. Services or Web Services or Software as a service are software functionalities that are available online to be accessed by users using a web browser over the internet. Approximately 80% of the world economy provides services in various forms (CMMI 2009). Each day, there are roughly 3 new mashups or Web service extensions created and listed at programmableweb.com (Programmable 2009). The same increasing trend can be seen through the increasing demand for Web services usage in real-client software development projects for the graduate level software engineering course at University of Southern California (CSCI577ab 2011). New opportunities, such as using mashups or services, also come with new risks. The process user should not follow the same set of activities or use the default process model when the project has a new risk pattern (Boehm 2008). As a result, the Web services consumers need to know how to select the appropriate service and utilize the service properly. Various process models such as CMMI-SVC (CMMI 2009) provide great support for a Web-services development project and CMMI-COTS (Tyson et.al 2003) supports the COTS-based development. However, there is no process model for the software development project that uses services provided by others or service-intensive development. Although COTS and web services are both non-developmental items (NDI) and they are similar in numerous aspects, they are fairly different in detail. Moreover, based on our preliminary study (Koolmanojwong 10), a pure COTS-based development process does not fit well for services-intensive project. Hence, there is a need for a process model that could specifically support services-intensive or services-based development projects.

The ICSM (Boehm 1996) (Boehm and Lane 2007) is a new generation process model. ICSM covers the full system development life cycle, consisting of an exploration phase, valuation phase, foundations phase, development phase, and operations phase. It has been evaluated to be a reasonably robust framework for systems development. One of the main focuses of the ICSM is feasibility analysis; evidence must be provided by the developer and validated by independent experts. The ICSM combines the strengths of various current process models and limits their weaknesses. The ICSM, like the V-Model (V-Model 2009), emphasizes early verification and validation, but allows for multiple-incremental interpretation and alleviates sequential development. Compared to the Spiral Model (Boehm 1998), the ICSM also focuses on risk-driven activity prioritization, but offers an improvement by adding well-defined in-process milestones. While ICSM, RUP, and MBASE (Boehm 1996) perform concurrent engineering that stabilizes the process at anchor point milestones, ICSM also supports integrated hardware-software-human factors oriented development. Compared with Agile methods (Agile manifesto 2001), ICSM embraces adaptability to unexpected change perspective and concurrently allows scalability.

Based on the risk pattern, size, complexity, change rate, criticality, available NDI support, and organizational and personnel capability, projects could be categorized into eleven process patterns ranging from a very small scale project such as Use Single NDI to a very large scale multi-owner system of systems. This chapter focuses on one of the eleven process patterns called NDI-intensive process pattern by pinpointing to a services-intensive sub process pattern. Later, the chapter will layout the process decision framework and flow of activities in the service-intensive project development. Additionally, this chapter will discuss success case studies of e-services projects that follow services-intensive process pattern and how they improve project performance, especially in terms of faster-time-to-market and higher client satisfaction.

THE INCREMENTAL COMMITMENT SPIRAL MODEL (ICSM)

Key Principles

Based on several analyses of the strengths and difficulties of current process models (Pew and Mavor 2007), key principles are developed to emphasize the strengths and to address the challenges. The four underlying principles of the ICSM include:

1. **Stakeholder Value-Based System Definition and Evolution:** The project should be developed based on win-win conditions for all success-critical stakeholders, otherwise the stakeholders often will not commit to the project and this gradually leads to project rejection or ignorance.
2. **Incremental Commitment and Accountability:** The success of the project must be built upon the participation, commitment, and accountability of the success critical stakeholders, otherwise the final product will not be the system that is most needed.
3. **Concurrent Interdisciplinary Definition and Development:** Contrary to sequential development, the concurrent development of requirements, solutions, hardware, software, human factors, and economic considerations allow the project to move faster and be more flexible in order to yield optimal results.
4. **Evidence and Risk-Based Decision Making:** At each milestone review—in order to show the progress of the project and to avoid the "Death by PowerPoint and UML" phenomenon—the development team uses evidence of project feasibility as the key ingredient to avoid risks and determine the future of the project. This can also serve as a means to successfully synchronize and stabilize the

concurrent activities and system artifacts and upgrade feasibility evidence as a first-class deliverable.

The life cycle starts with the innermost phase—or exploration phase—where a project: identifies its objectives, constraints, and alternative solution approaches (OC&A); evaluates the alternatives; and makes a risk-driven determination for a course of action. If one alternative is clearly superior and feasible, the project segues to detailed requirements, designs, and plans, then proceeds to implementation. On the other hand, if there are uncertainties or risks, the project addresses the risks before proceeding to the next level. If the risks are high but manageable, such as in the user interface look and feel, the project proceeds to developing a series of elaborated prototypes. However, as seen in the lower left of Figure 1, the fourth kind of risk, the fourth dashed-line, represents risks that are too high and not addressable—perhaps it was not worthwhile for project to continue with the current commitment, or the project needs to adjust its scope, its OC&A, or possibly the project needs to be terminated. Each spiral follows a concurrent approach rather than sequentially addressing all activities of project development. Requirements and solutions, products and process, hardware, software, human factors, business case analysis are all considered concurrently in every spiral. Not only the documents, all of the evidences or artifacts will be synchronized and stabilized and assessed at the various stakeholder commitment decision milestones by independent experts. Shortfalls, uncertainties, and risk exposure will be carefully analyzed and then addressed by a risk mitigation plan.

When the spiral is unrolled, the ICSM (see the phase view, in Figure 2) represents activities in each phase. In the exploration phase, a development team focuses on initial scope, current system, and alternative systems. Some of the activities in the valuation phase include developing the operational concept, prioritizing the requirements,

Figure 1. The incremental commitment spiral model – Spiral view (Koolmanojwong 2010)

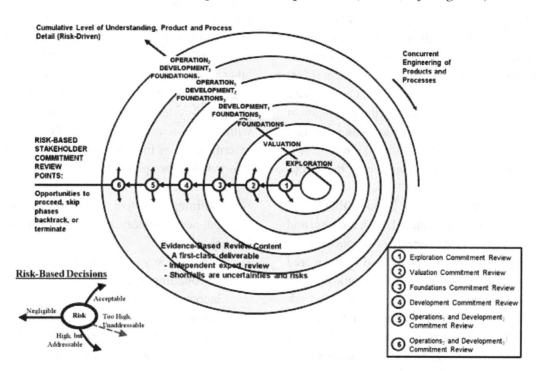

Figure 2. The incremental commitment spiral model – Phased view (Koolmanojwong 2010)

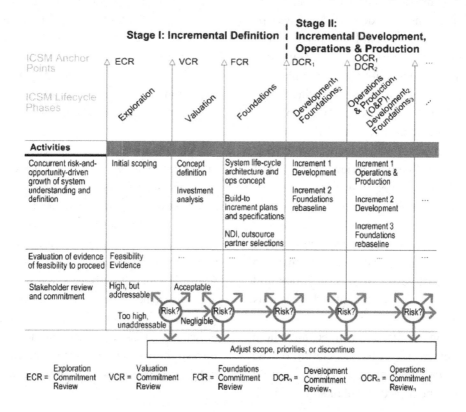

assessing the non-developmental products, and reviewing the business case analysis. In the foundations phase, the development team focuses on building the system and software architecture, acquiring the non-developmental items, and creating a development iteration plan. One or more development increments occur in the development phase. Additionally, the transition plan is defined in the development phase. Finally, the project is delivered, deployed, and maintained in the operations phase.

The lower part of Figure 2 shows that ICSM is a risk-driven process model. Risk analysis and management is used to decide on a course of action. If the risks are acceptable and well covered by risk mitigation plans, the project would proceed into the next spiral. If the risks are high but addressable, the project would remain in the current spiral until the risks are resolved or acceptable. If the risks are negligible, the current phase and the next phase can be combined. For example, this can happen if the exploration spiral finds that the solution can be easily produced via an online service product rather than developing a customized solution. Hence, the exploration phase and the valuation phase can be combined. If the risk is too high and unaddressable (for example, if it is found at any point that the market window for such a product has already closed), the project should be terminated, or rescoped if there is a different market sector whose market window is clearly still open. The phase view of the ICSM also shows the two major stages of the overall lifecycle process. Stage I, incremental definition, covers the system understanding, definition, feasibility assurance, and stakeholder commitment and leads to a larger Stage II commitment to implement a feasible set of specifications and plans for incremental development and operations of the desired system.

The duration of Stage I can be anywhere from one week to five years, depending on the capability and compatibility of the proposed system's components and stakeholders. A small,

compatible, and agile developer-customer team who operates on a mature infrastructure can form and begin incremental development using Scrum, eXtreme Programming (XP), Crystal or other agile methods within a week. An ultra-large, unprecedented, multi-mission, multi-owner system-of-systems project needing to integrate with numerous independently-evolving legacy or external systems may take up to five years. Main efforts would be spent on:

- Defining a system vision through sorting out needs, opportunities, and organizational roles.
- Maturing key technologies.
- Reconciling infrastructure incompatibilities.
- Reducing uncertainties and risks via models, simulations, prototypes, advanced technology demonstrations, and operational exercises.
- Evolving a feasibility-validated set of specifications and plans for Stage II at the build-to level for the initial increment, but only elaborated for later increments where there can be high-risk elements to resolve or expected downstream changes in mission objectives, technology, and interoperating systems to accommodate.

As shown in Figure 2 at each anchor point milestone review, the project's activity path will be determined by the arrows resulting from the risk assessments and stakeholder commitment decisions. A project that plans to use available Web services could spend more time in exploration and valuation phases, but spend little to no time in the foundations phase since the architecture and infrastructure are provided by the service providers. Or, in some cases, the reviews might indicate that certain essential technologies or infrastructure incompatibilities need more work before proceeding into the next phase.

Stage II. For Stage II (incremental development and operations), the development commitment review determines the length of the increments to be used in the system's development and evolution. A small agile project can use two-to-four week increments. However, an ultra-large SoS project such as a metropolitan-area crisis management system with independent evolving elements or external systems would need increments of up to two years to develop and integrate an increment of operational capability, and would include several internal integration sub-increments. Some very large, non-subsettable hardware systems would take even longer to develop their initial increments and would be scheduled to synchronize their deliveries with concurrently-evolving infrastructure or software increments.

Comparison to Agile and Lean Principles

Agile, Lean, and ICSM address best practices in a similar manner. A comparison of the 4 key ICSM principles (Boehm and Lane 2008; Poppendieck and Poppendieck 2003; Agile Manifesto 2001) with characteristics of lean and agile principles has been conducted and a summary of the results are shown in Table 1. Although there are differences in the level of detail in each set of principles specified, there are no substantial differences in general concepts. All principles focus on efficiently performing value-adding activities at the appropriate point in the development life cycle and eliminating activities that don't add value. The ICSM core principles are all recognized on both agile and lean principles.

Table 1. Key principles comparison

ICSM Principles	Related Lean Principles (Poppendieck and Poppendieck 2003)	Related Agile Principles (Boehm 2007; Agile Manifesto 2001)
1. Stakeholder value-based system definition and evolution	• Joint customer-developer iteration planning • Value stream mapping	• Joint customer-developer iteration planning • Satisfy the customer through early and continuous delivery of valuable software
2. Incremental commitment and accountability	• Respected leaders and champions • Team commitment • Master developers to guide decisions, make rapid progress, and develop high-quality software	• Business people and developers must work together daily throughout the project • Provide the developers with environment and support they need
3. Concurrent interdisciplinary definition and development	• Decide as late as possible to support concurrent development while keeping options open • Ensure emergence of a good architecture through reuse, integrated problem solving, and experienced developers • Balance experimentation with deliberation and review • Iteration planning with negotiable scope and convergence	• The best architectures, requirements, and designs emerge from self-organizing teams • Deliver working software frequently • Working software is the primary measure of progress
4. Evidence and risk-based decision making	• Eliminate waste • Value stream mapping	• Team reflects periodically on how to become more effective, then tunes and adjusts its behavior accordingly • Simplicity—the art of maximizing the amount of work not done—is essential

Process Patterns of Software Development Project

Because of the diversity and the complexity of software systems, the ICSM has been developed to assist users in applying the framework in order to create a development process appropriate for their system of interest. The differences in their risk pattern or opportunity pattern determine different courses of action throughout each life-cycle phase. The following eleven common cases cover the very small to the very large project, as well as the use of non-developmental item such as COTS or Web-service products to develop a large, complex, customized system or to maintain developed systems. Eleven common cases of the ICSM are as follows:

1. Use single non-developmental (NDI)
2. Agile, architected agile
3. Formal methods
4. SW embedded HW component
5. Indivisible initial operational capability
6. NDI- intensive
7. Hybrid agile/plan-driven system
8. Multi-owner system of systems
9. Family of systems
10. Brownfield major upgrade
11. Maintenance

More information can be found in (Boehm et.al 2009).

This chapter is going to focus on case 6 above, the NDI-intensive. NDI, or non-developmental item, is a previously developed component that includes COTS, open source software, or Web service. When an appropriate NDI solution is available, it is an option to use either the existing NDI or to develop a version by oneself, or to outsource such a development, which generally incurs more expense and takes longer to begin to capitalize on its benefits. On the other hand, an NDI may come with high volatility, complexity, or incompatibility. Major effort is thus spent on appraising the

NDI. In 2006, Yang (Yang 2006) proposed the COTS-based development framework whereby a COTS-intensive system is a system in which 30% of end-user functionality is provided by COTS. A great deal of attention goes into appraising the functionality and interoperability of COTS, COTS tailoring, COTS integration, and COTS upgrade synchronization and evolution (Yang 2006; Li 2006; Morisio 2000). Development of such capabilities involves much more prototyping and much less documentation than is needed for more programming-oriented applications; for example, the internals of the COTS packages are generally unavailable for architectural documentation, and the resulting system capabilities are more driven by COTS capabilities than by pre-specified requirement documents.

SERVICES-INTENSIVE PROCESS PATTERN

Although Web services is a kind of NDI, to develop a service-intensive application, the development team may use the COTS-based development process, but they have to be aware of the differences between COTS and Web services. Risks from using COTS are different from risks from Web services. For example, the Web-services products are always platform and language independent, but users have no control over the revisions in future versions. On the other hand, most NDI products are platform dependent and the users are fully entitled to the version they own. This section will discuss differences between COTS and Web services and the life-cycle activities of services-intensive development projects.

Differences between COTS and Services

COTS and services are both readily available NDIs with many functionalities that consumers may or may not need. Examples of COTS are Microsoft

Office Package, TurboTax, SAP, and QuickBooks. Examples of services are Google 3D Warehouse, Salesforce, NetSuite Package, and Paypal. Since both COTS and Services are developed by external partners, consumers have very limited control over the capability modifications. Although COTS and services are very similar in various ways, they are not identical. The difference between COTS and services can be explained below:

- **Payment:** COTS are generally not free and since they are developed by for-profit organizations, they tend to have high monetary cost in various aspects such as package fees, training fees, enhancement fees, and tailoring fees. These fees can be negotiated with the COTS vendor. On the other hand, not all Services are free either. Many of them charge by transaction, such as Paypal, or by subscription fee, such as Salesforce. For hardware requirements, some COTS require a dedicated server machine, while Services require the Internet and client machines only. In general, Services has a lower initial cost to start with.
- **Platform:** COTS are developed based on a specific platform and language, such as Windows, hence Mac OS users will need to select a different package, if available. Services are built on standard Web protocols, such as XML and http standards, and are easily accessible from different client platforms.
- **Integration:** With platform specific, tightly-coupled technology, and black box package, COTS are more difficult to integrate. In some cases, the COTS providers may charge additional fees for tailoring and integration. With platform independent technology, Services are easier for integration options. Mashups are good examples of new functionalities that are integrated from more than one Services provider.

- **Changes:** The consumers own a specific version of the COTS once they acquire them. Hence, there are pros and cons for owning them. The consumers will be able to freeze the changes that might happen to the COTS. But on the other hand, the consumers will not own the latest update of the COTS. In various cases, the COTS providers may stop providing support to outdated versions of the COTS. To upgrade to the new version, it requires end-user intervention and usually has an additional cost. For Services, the consumers have no control over the changes. The changes from the server side are reflected in the client side. These changes are unpredictable, unavoidable, and do not require user intervention.
- **Extensions:** COTS extensions can be done only if the source code is available and the license permits. The extension that is developed at the consumer site may not be compatible with a COTS's future release. For Services, an extension is do-able but is limited to data provided by the services. Popular in-house extensions and/or integrations are wrapper and mashup.
- **Evaluation Criteria:** General evaluation criteria for both COTS and Services are similar, such as provided functionalities, usability, support, cost, and reliability. Specific evaluation criteria may vary from project to project. COTS consumers may need to pay more attention to platform compatibility, upgrades, code-escrow consideration, extensibility, and support services, while Services consumers should pay more attention to security, reliability, availability, speed, predicted longevity of the service-provider, and feature-data controllability.
- **Support Services:** COTS vendors usually provide support services, such as training, tailoring, a helpdesk, and upgrades, with arrangement-dependent charges. Services

providers, however, generally do not provide support services or customized software for a specific organization. FAQ and helpdesk generally come as an online discussion board. Upgrade services will be done online without end-user intervention.

- **Data:** COTS data is stored locally and the owner has total ownership of the data. COTS data format depends on the COTS platform. Access to data that is stored locally is very fast. On the other hand, Services data is stored on the server's side by using a cross-platform, cross-language data model. Data security and data-retention are two major concerns for Services. Access to data over the internet can be slow at times.

With these differences, it is not appropriate for Service-intensive application developers to select potential services by using COTS selection criteria or to follow COTS-intensive development guidelines. Table 2 summarizes the differences between COTS and Services.

Services-Intensive Process Decision Framework

When the project starts, one may not know which process pattern one should follow. After understanding the project scope and realizing the possible service consuming opportunity, one should consider following the service-intensive process pattern. Major activities, pitfalls and possible activity decision consideration of the Service-Intensive development project are shown in Figure 3.

- **P1: Identify Object Constraints and Priorities (OC&P):** Identify the goals the proposed system is trying to achieve and compare the improvements of the proposed system with the current system. Detailed information can be found in Figure 4.

- **P1.1 - P2: Identify OC&Ps and Explore Alternatives:** As shown in Figure 4, various inputs can be used to support the OC&P identification. The output of this process is the candidate Services, which could be a single Service or a combination of Services.

  ○ **Identify Capability Goals:** Provide a brief enumeration of the most important operational capability goals. A "capability" is simply a function or set of functions that the system performs or enables users to perform.

  ○ **Identify Level of Service Goals:** Identify the desired and acceptable goals for the proposed new system's important levels of service, or in other words, the system's quality attributes or "-ilities" such as reliability, usability, and interoperability. Capability goals address what the system should do: level of service goals address how well the system should perform. Indicate the desired and acceptable levels of service of the new system.

  ○ **Identify Organizational Goals:** List briefly the broad, high-level objectives and aspirations of the sponsoring organization(s) and any organization that will be using and maintaining the new system.

  ○ **Identify Constraints:** Identify constraints of the project. Constraints will be derived from your WinWin negotiation and/or client meetings. Constraint is a limiting condition that you have to satisfy when selecting or evaluating the services or when developing the system. Examples of constraints are CO-1: Windows as an Operating System: The new system must be able to run on Windows platform; or CO-2: Zero Monetary

Table 2. Differences between COTS and services

Category	COTS	Services
Payment	• Non-commercial items usually have no monetary cost • Expensive initial costs, moderate recurring fee, training fee, licensing arrangement-dependent	• Not all services are free, mostly pay per transaction • Low initial costs, moderate marginal cost, duration dependent license
Platform	• Specific and limited to specific platform / language • Generally supported on a subset of platforms or multiple platforms but with different editions	• Platform and language independent • Server and client can work on different platform • Interaction between machines over a network
Integration	• Generally more tightly coupled • Not very flexible on existing legacy systems when proprietary standard is used • Difficult when it is platform dependent and different technologies are involved. • Detailed documentation and on-site extensive support	• Generally more loosely coupled • Common Web standards, flexible, easy to integrate • Requires Internet access • Supports forums and API documentation • This integration could be done merely in code, without additional installation of external components
Changes	• Able to freeze the version • Designed for specific use, thus is costly for customization and change • Change on server side doesn't impact the client side • Major releases occasionally • Requires end-user intervention to upgrade	• Changes are out of developers' control • Not easy to predict change, cannot avoid upgrade, end-user has the latest version • Change on the server side can result in change on the client side • Minor releases frequently (through patching) • Does not require end-user intervention
Extensions	• Only if source is provided and the license permits • Extension must be delivered to and performed at the end-user's site • Custom extensions may not be portable across COTS or may not be compatible with future releases	• Extension is limited to data provided by the Web services • In-house extension such as wrapper or mashup • Little control over performance overhead
Evaluation Criteria	• Maintenance, extensibility, scalability, reliability, cost, support, usability, dependency, ease of implementation, maintainability, upgrades, size, access to source and code-escrow considerations • Upfront costs opposed to subscription • Platform compatibility, feature controllability	• Reliability, availability, cost, available support, speed, predicted longevity of the service provider, release cycle, bandwidth • Recurring costs to use the service and future functionality offered • Standards compatibility, feature-data controllability
Support Services	• Vendor support for integration and training; and tailoring/modification sometimes available for a fee • Help topics or FAQs would likely not be updated after installation • Upgrades/patches and data migration support • Sometimes can be customized for specific user • Upgraded by purchasing new releases, self-install	• Support for tailoring/modification and training generally not available • Help topics would generally be frequently updated; self-learning • Usually not customized for a specific user • Patching on service provider's side; generally does not require installation on client side
Data	• Data often stored locally. Backups generally the responsibility of the user • Data access is generally fast • Possible variety of proprietary formats • May be inflexible for change, but more secure • Platform-dependent data format • Can process data offline	• Data stored on servicehost servers. Backups by the provider. Introduces privacy and data-retention • Data access could be slower since it is Internet based • Common XML using Web-standard protocols • Data from different Web services can be used by a single client program • Process data online

Budget: The selected services should be free of or have no monetary cost.

○ **Compare to Current System:** Summarize the relationship between the current and new systems in a table. Include key differences between the current and new roles, responsibilities, user interactions, infrastructure, stakeholder essentials, etc.

○ **After Reading a Project Proposal:** The development team should investigate alternatives in the development project. Quite often, an appropriate service solution or partial solution is available. Even if a better solution is produced (frequently not the case), more expense and longer time to capitalize on its benefits will result. Oftentimes, the Service has features

Figure 3. Service-intensive process decision framework (Koolmanojwong 2010)

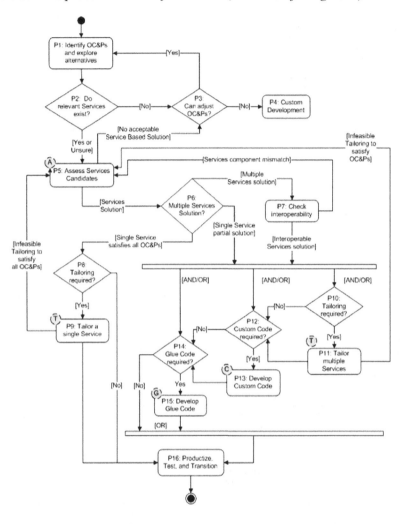

Figure 4. Identify OC&Ps and explore alternatives (Koolmanojwong 2010)

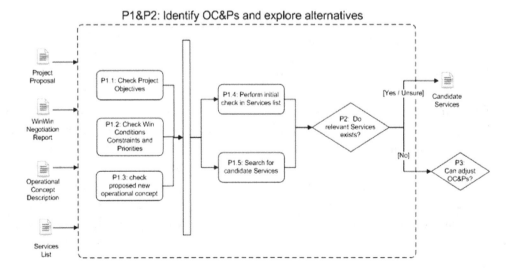

that one hadn't realized would be needed, but are there when one needs them.

○ **Check Project Objectives:** Analyze project proposal, identify the project objectives.

○ **Check Win Conditions, Constraints, and Priorities:** After WinWin Negotiation, study all the win conditions, especially capability/product win conditions and level of service win conditions; use them to investigate or explore possible Services solutions.

○ **Check Proposed New Operational Concept:** Consider what has been proposed to the client, how can their business workflow change, or how can new technologies or any improvement to the project be introduced.

○ **Perform Initial Check in Services List:** Look at the commonly used components in List of Services, check to see if there is any component that can be used in the project.

○ **Search for Candidate Services:** Search for possible Service components in the market, both in the commercial-product sector and the free-product sector.

• **P2: Do Relevant Services Exist?:** Given the OC&P, explore all possible related alternatives, such as commercial products, freeware, open-source software, reuse library, reuse component, or Web service. It is possible that one product could satisfy all the desired functionalities, or it could be a combination of multiple products. To support the Services selection, gather all available information, such as functionalities and costs.

• **P3: Can Adjust OC&Ps?:** One of the main differences between the architected agile process and Services-intensive pro-

cess is that the Services-intensive process does not start with requirements, but with OC&Ps. If there is no Services application that could contribute the required functionalities to the final product deliverable, or if there are some Services that conditionally satisfy the win conditions, the development group should discuss with all critical stakeholders in order to adjust the OC&Ps to accommodate the possible Services.

• **P4: Custom Development:** If the OC&Ps are not adjustable, the project should move on with custom development.

• **P5: Assess Services Candidates:** With the possible alternatives, use the objectives, constraints, and priorities to establish weights for all Services attributes. To assign weights, all team members should talk to the client to find out how important each attribute is. Examples of Services features include: report module, discussion board module, and show pictures/video module. Initial assessment should attempt to quickly filter out the unacceptable Services with respect to the evaluation criteria. The objective of this activity is to reduce the number of Services candidates needing to be evaluated in detail. If no available Services products pass this filtering, this assessment element ends up at the "no acceptable Service based solution," and continues with P3: Adjust OC&Ps. Detailed information is shown in Figure 5.

• **P5.1 – P5.7 Assess Services Candidates:** With the possible alternatives, the development should evaluate each alternative solution based on the given objectives, constraints, and priorities (OC&P)

○ **Establish Evaluation Criteria and Weights By Using Services Attributes:** After the task of identifying organizational and operational transformation, use objectives, constraints, and priorities from the opera-

Figure 5. Assess services candidates (Koolmanojwong 2010)

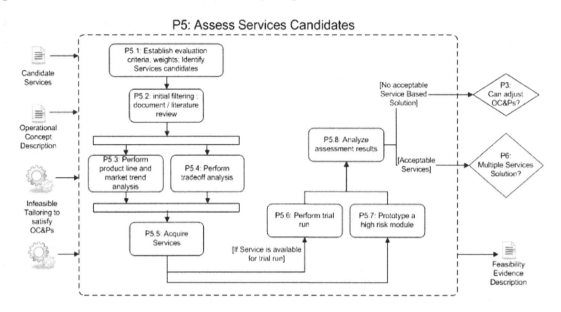

tional concept description document to establish weights for each Services attribute. To assign weights, all team members should talk to the client to find out how important each attribute is.

○ **Establish Evaluation Criteria and Weights By Using Services Features:** After the task of Identify organizational and operational transformation, use objectives, constraints, and priorities from the operational concept description document to establish weights for each Services feature. To assign weights, all team members should talk to the client to find out how important each attribute is.

○ **Perform Initial Filtering:** Initial assessment tries to filter out the unacceptable Services packages quickly with respect to the evaluation criteria. The objective of this activity is to reduce the number of Services candidates needing to be evaluated in de-

tail. If no available Services products pass this filtering, this assessment element ends up at the "none acceptable" exit.

○ **Perform Product Line and Market Trend Analysis:** Briefly analyze the market trend, product popularity, product market standpoint, predicted longevity of the company, etc. Also, analyze the related products that are developed/launched by the same company/organization. For example, if a company has been in the market for quite some time, and this company is very popular for the product that you are considering, this component may get a higher score or higher credit.

○ **Perform Tradeoff Analysis:** Compare scores from each evaluation criteria, market trend, and product line and analyze pros and cons for each component or component combination.

○ **Acquire Services:** After scoping out and filtering out the alternatives, you should have a small list of potential components or a component combination. If the component is available to download or install, either in a trial version, open source version, or free version, you should acquire and try to use it. If the candidate component is not free for trial, it is a decision between your client and you as to whether you need to have a hands-on trial for that particular component.

○ **Perform Trial Run:** When the component or the component combination is available, try to use the functionalities that will be required or related to the project scope.

○ **Analyze Assessment Results:** Data and information about each Services candidate are collected and analyzed against evaluation criteria in order to facilitate trade-offs and decision making. In this step, a screening matrix or analytic hierarchy process is a useful and common approach to analyze the collected evaluation data

• **P6: Multiple Services Solution?:** Although interoperability between services is minimal compared to COTS interoperability, the development team should raise this question when the solution contains more than one service.

• **P7: Check Interoperability:** See Figure 6.

• **P7.1 – P7.4: Check Interoperability:** When there is more than one component involved in the project, the development team must be active in mitigating the component mismatch risk by checking whether the components are interoperable. This might not be a concern with Services because the components are platform independent and they use the standard XML to communicate among components.

○ **Check Services based Architecture:** One should have a draft system-architecture that identifies the potential system structure, case use, artifacts, hardware, and software.

○ **Identify Potential Services Component Combinations:** Identify all the possible choices of the Service and/or their combination.

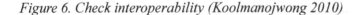

Figure 6. Check interoperability (Koolmanojwong 2010)

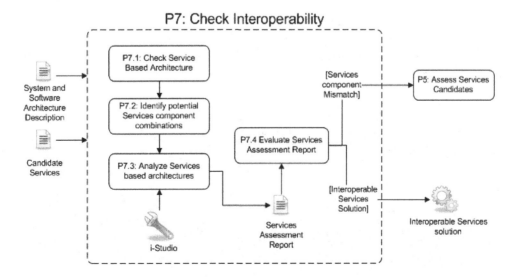

○ **Analyze Services based Architectures:** Analyze the interoperability of finding mismatches between your architecture and component combination choices.

○ **Evaluate Services Assessment Report:** Evaluate the result reported, recheck the potential mismatches, and find the best alternative architecture.

• **P8, P10: Tailoring Required?:** Although this is not the case usually for a ready-to-use product, in some instances the Web services can be tailored to fit your requirements. Hence, in a case involving a single Service, or multiple Services, the development team must check whether the Service needs to be tailored to satisfy the requirements.

• **P9: Tailor a Single Service, P11: Tailor Multiple Services:** When a certain Services product satisfies all of the requirements, there is no need to develop a custom code or glue code. However, the selected Services product may need to be tailored in order to provide proper functionalities for the specific system context. More details can be found in Figure 7 and Figure 8.

• **P12: Custom Code Required?:** – The development team should identify the missing functionalities that the Services do not provide, then develop additional functionalities or coding in order to satisfy the requirements. The functionalities are derived from stakeholders' win conditions and capability goals.

• **P13: Develop Custom Code:** – The architecture of each component is modeled in the software architecture document. Compared to architected agile process, it may be more challenging to identify the component architecture for Services as the Service architecture is frequently unknown. One way to mitigate the risk of component mismatch is to check for the components' interoperability or to develop the prototype for component integration. The development team should identify which components will be developed within which iteration of the iteration plan.

• **P14: Glue Code Required?:** When there is more than one component needed in the project development, it is highly likely that the glue code needs to be developed.

Figure 7. Tailor a single NDI/ service (Koolmanojwong 2010)

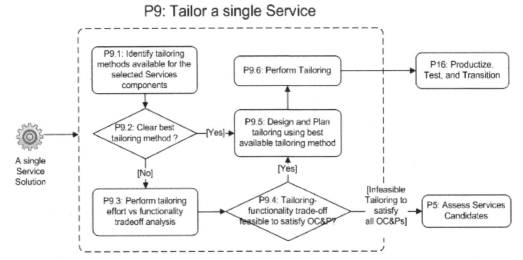

Figure 8. Tailor multiple services (Koolmanojwong 2010)

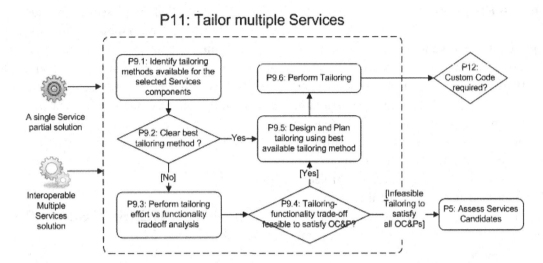

- **P15: Develop Glue Code:** Glue code is used to develop an interface between Services and other components. More information can be found in Figure 9.
- **P15.1 – P15-3: Develop Glue Code:** In order to get the service provided, or to be able to integrate Services to the system, or to integrate the multiple Services, one must develop some code to interface or coordinate with Services. This is so that the Services can properly pass the data to other software components, which could be an-

other Service or component that is developed from scratch.

- **P16: Productize, Test, and Transition:** After all components are identified and integrated, the development team should thoroughly test the product by using both verification and validation techniques. Furthermore, the team should prepare for the transition, such as data preparation, site preparation, and human resource preparation.

Figure 9. Develop glue code (Koolmanojwong 2010)

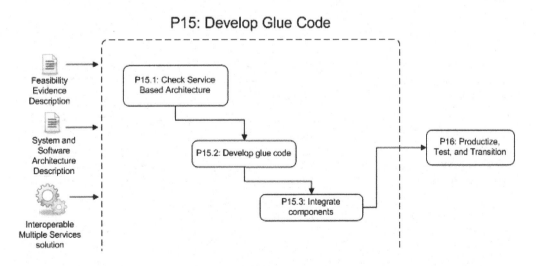

Level of Activities in Services-Intensive Projects

To represent the overview of the main activities for a service-intensive development process, Figure 10 illustrates the concurrency view for the main activities and the level of effort required in each phase by comparing the service-intensive development activities with traditional software development activities. The solid line represents the level of activities in service-intensive projects, while the dashed line represents the traditional approach. While most activities are common and similar to both project types, there are some differences, such as:

- **Develop System Architecture and Develop Architecture of Components:** While architecture in traditional software development is mainly developed in the foundations phase, the architecture of a service-intensive system is defined earlier in the process in order to help explore the Web service candidates. Additionally, the service-intensive projects expend less ef-

fort since the majority of the architecture is pre-specified by the service provider.

- **Develop Components and Integrate Components:** Since the majority of the end-user functionality for service-intensive projects are provided by Services, it only requires the development team to do minor custom coding, tailoring, and possibly glue coding and less integrating.

SERVICES-INTENSIVE SUCCESS CASE

The service-intensive development process was introduced to a graduate-level software engineering class. Students were asked to apply software engineering theories to a real-client software development project. With teams of 8 students per group, for a 24 week period, the development teams began by studying the clients' proposal in the exploration phase in order to deliver and deploy a final product in the operation phase. There were various instances in which the development

Figure 10. Prototyping and implementing levels of activities (Koolmanojwong 2010)

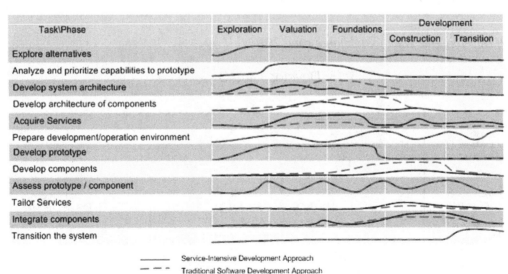

teams could have followed the traditional software development process. Instead, they successfully delivered the products with less effort, better performance, and high customer satisfaction.

- **Social Networking Tools for Librarians:** The client is looking for a tool that would be similar to social networking sites like Facebook or MySpace that fit the special requirements for librarians, such as sharing resources with selected users. Required functionalities include an authorization system, a discussion board, blogs, online profile management capabilities, resource sharing, search options, multiple profile views, an email system, and end-user management capabilities. The development team has two alternatives; (a) develop all these capabilities from scratch, (b) pick and choose one service or a combination of service items. After struggling with the traditional process, the mentor suggested that they follow the tailored version of a COTS-based development process to fit with the service-based project. Hence, the team successfully delivered the product with very high client satisfaction.

- **Client Information Management Project:** The client is looking for an online tool to collect various types of customers and customer-related information. With a limited schedule, the first team followed a traditional process. After 24 weeks, the team delivered a product that did not meet the client's requirements. When the second team took over, they found various online services including Salesforce. The second team followed the service-intensive approach and carefully selected the most appropriate online service. At the end of 12 weeks, they had a product ready to use that was tailored to their client's requirements—and it was delivered with less effort, a shorter schedule, and high client-satisfaction.

- **Client/Donor/Partner Communications and Project Tracking Tool Development:** An organization is looking for a tool that would provide a centralized and organized database for client contact information, project-progress tracking, donation tracking, and sponsor/partner mass-mailing capabilities. The project was originally developed in-house using a COTS-based development process with 4 different COTS packages. The COTS-based project is rudimentary and most of the data that is used on a day-to-day basis is stored in Microsoft Excel files. In addition, some data is stored in Microsoft Access or a shared e-mail module. Most of the data is not updated in timely fashion and eventually is outdated. The organization is interested in revamping the project. The new development team elects to follow the Incremental Commitment Spiral Model with an NDI-intensive common case. After the initial exploration of potential COTS and Services based on the client's win conditions, the development team follows the steps suggested by the Services-Intensive Process Decision Framework. After discussing the pros and cons and the differences between COTS and Services, the client decides to go with the Services option. The candidate Services are Salesforce, eTapestry, Convio Common Groun, Zoho, Sugar CR, and HighRise. At the end of 12 weeks, the development team delivered the intricate system that satisfied the client's requirements.

These three case studies have shown that Services-intensive applications are different from COTS-intensive applications; as a result, it needs a Services-specific process model. In addition, these three cases are the feasibility evidence that the Services-Intensive Process Decision Framework can be used as a process model to improve the project performance and client satisfaction by developing faster, better, and cheaper Services-intensive applications.

FUTURE RESEARCH DIRECTIONS

Project cost, schedule, and effort estimation are essential ingredients for project management, project planning, and project budgeting. The majority of the estimation tools in the marketplace support build-from-scratch development projects, such as COCOMO II, SEER, and TrueS, while COCOTS and Price-S support COTS-based development projects. As shown in Table 2, COTS and Web Services are different, especially with regard to payment option, component interoperability, support services, and data location. Hence, to achieve an accurate project estimation, Services-intensive projects needs a proper tool whereby the algorithmic model is developed based on the historical service-intensive project data and project characteristics.

CONCLUSION

As technology evolves, various ready-made software components can be used to speed up software development, especially for rapid-fielding projects, where time-to-market is a key factor in gaining an advantage over the competition. The Incremental Commitment Spiral Model (ICSM) builds on experience-based, critical-success, factor principles such as stakeholder satisficing, incremental definition, iterative evolutionary growth, concurrent engineering, and risk management and the strengths of the existing V, concurrent engineering, spiral, agile, and lean process models to provide a framework for concurrently engineering system-specific critical factors into the systems engineering and systems development processes. The ICSM provides capabilities for evaluating the feasibility of proposed solutions and for integrating feasibility evaluations into decisions on whether to proceed further into systems development and operations. One of the common cases for the ICSM is NDI-intensive, which focuses mainly on the project for which more than 30% of end-user functionalities are provided by NDI such as COTS, open source, or Web services. To develop a Services-intensive system, one can follow COTS-Intensive development framework to some extent, but as mentioned in Table 1, COTS and Services are different. The Services-Intensive applications have their own issues and risks and therefore need a different development framework. The Services-Intensive Process Decision Framework emphasizes exploring and comparing the Services alternatives available in the market and performing interoperability among multi-component alternatives. The Services-Intensive Process Decision Framework helps process-users save time and effort in unnecessary tasks, while successfully delivering products that satisfy a client's requirements.

REFERENCES

Beck, K., et al. (2001). Principles behind the agile manifesto. *Agile Manifesto*. Retrieved August 4, 2009, from http://agilemanifesto.org/principles. html

Boehm, B. (1996, July). Anchoring the software process. *IEEE Software*, *13*(4), 73–82. doi:10.1109/52.526834

Boehm, B. (1998, May). A spiral model of software development and enhancement. *IEEE Computer*, *21*(5), 61–72. doi:10.1109/2.59

Boehm, B., & Bhuta, J. (2008, November). Balancing opportunities and risks in component-based software development. *IEEE Software*, *25*(6), 56–63. doi:10.1109/MS.2008.145

Boehm, B., & Lane, J. A. (2007, October). Using the incremental commitment model to integrate systems acquisition, systems engineering, and software engineering. *Cross Talk*, (pp. 4-9)

Boehm, B., & Lane, J. A. (2008). *Incremental commitment model guide*, Version 0.5. Center for Systems and Software Engineering Technical Report. Retrieved August 4, 2009, from http://csse.usc.edu/csse/TECHRPTS/2009/usc-csse-2009-500/usc-csse-2009-500.pdf

Boehm, B., Lane, J. A., Koolmanojwong, S., & Turner, R. (2010). *Architected agile solutions for software-reliant systems*. Paper presented at the 20th International Symposium of INCOSE, Chicago, IL.

CMMI Product Team. (2009). *CMMI for services,* Version 1.2. Retrieved January 11, 2010, from ftp://ftp.sei.cmu.edu/pub/documents/09.reports/09tr001.doc

CSCI577ab (2011). *CSCI577ab – USC software engineering course*. Retrieved June 11, 2011, from http://greenbay.usc.edu/csci577/spring2011/

Koolmanojwong, S. (2010). *The incremental commitment spiral model process patterns for rapid-fielding projects*. Doctoral dissertation, Department of Computer Science, University of Southern California.

Li, J. (2006). An empirical study of variations in COTS-based software development processes in Norwegian IT industry. *Journal of Empirical Software Engineering, 11*(3), 433–461. doi:10.1007/s10664-006-9005-5

Morisio, M., Seaman, C. B., Parra, A. T., Basili, V. R., Kraft, S. E., & Condon, S. E. (2000). Investigating and improving a COTS-based software development. *Proceedings of the 22nd International Conference on Software Engineering* (pp. 32-41).

Pew, R. W., & Mavor, A. S. (2007). *Human-system integration in the system development process: A new look*. Washington, DC: National Academy Press.

Poppendieck, M., & Poppendieck, T. (2003). *Lean software development, an agile toolkit*. Boston, MA: Addison Wesley.

Programmable Web. (2009). *Mashups*. Retrieved November 11, 2009, from http://www.programmableweb.com/mashups

Tyson, B., Alberts, C. J., & Brownsword, L. (2003). *CMMI for COTS-based systems*. Software Engineering Institute. Retrieved August 4, 2009, from http://www.sei.cmu.edu/publications/documents/03.reports/03tr022.html

V-Model. (2009). *V-model lifecycle process model*. Retrieved October 9, 2009, from http://www.v-modell.iabg.de/kurzb/vm/k_vm_e.doc

Yang, Y. (2006). *Composable risk-driven processes for developing software systems from commercial-off-the-shelf (COTS) products*. Doctoral dissertation, Department of Computer Science, University of Southern California, California.

ADDITIONAL READING

Boehm, B. (2007, October). Future challenges and rewards for software engineers. *DoD Software Tech News* (pp. 6-12).

Boehm, B. (2010, July). The changing nature of software evolution. *IEEE Software, 27*(4), 26–29. doi:10.1109/MS.2010.103

Boehm, B., & Lane, J. A. (2010). Lecture Notes in Computer Science: *Vol. 6195. Evidence-based software processes. New Modeling Concepts for Today's Software Processes* (pp. 62–73). doi:10.1007/978-3-642-14347-2_7

Boehm, B., Lane, J. A., & Koolmanojwong, S. (2009). *A risk-driven process decision table to guide system development rigor*. Paper presented at the 19th International Symposium of INCOSE, Singapore.

Boehm, B., Lane, J. A., Koolmanojwong, S., & Turner, R. (2010). Architected agile solutions for software-reliant systems. In Dingsory, T., Dyba, T., & Moe, N. B. (Eds.), *Agile software development: Current research and future directions*. Springer.

Boehm, B., & Turner, R. (2003). *Balancing agility and discipline: A guide for the perplexed*. Boston, MA: Addison Wesley. doi:10.1007/978-3-540-24675-6_1

Koolmanojwong, S., & Boehm, B. (2010). *The incremental commitment model process patterns for rapid-fielding projects*. Paper presented at the International Conference on Software Process Paderborn, Germany.

Koolmanojwong, S., & Boehm, B. (2011). *Educating software engineers to become systems engineers*. Paper presented at the 2011 24th Conference on Software Engineering Education and Training, Waikiki, HI.

Selby, R. (2007). *Software engineering: Barry W. Boehm's lifetime contributions to software development, management, and research*. Hoboken, NJ: Wiley-IEEE Computer Society Press.

(2011). Some future software engineering opportunities and challenges. InNanz, S. (Ed.), *The Future of Software Engineering* (pp. 1–32). Berlin, Germany: Springer.

Yang, Y., Boehm, B., & Clark, B. (2006). Assessing COTS integration risk using cost estimation inputs. *Proceedings of the 28th International Conference on Software Engineering* (pp. 431-438).

KEY TERMS AND DEFINITIONS

COTS: Commercial-Off-the-Shelf. A product that is: sold, leased, or licensed to the general public; offered by a vendor trying to profit from it; supported and evolved by the vendor, who retains the intellectual property rights; available in multiple identical copies; used without source code modification.

Development Phase: Phase in which systems components are procured, developed, tested, integrated, and tested. Typically performed in an iterative manner, with selected iterations targeted for migration to operations.

Exploration Phase: Initial phase that identifies and clarifies system capability need(s) and options for providing the capabilities. Also determines likely feasibility and process choices for options.

Foundations Phase: Phase in which management and technical foundations are developed for the selected option/alternative. Technical foundations include a fully developed system architecture, prototypes, and evidence of technology maturity for those technologies that are key to the selected option/alternative. Note that more than one option/alternative may be under development at this point in the lifecycle.

ICSM: A "cradle to grave" risk-driven system lifecycle model that describes key activities starting with initial system need and ending with either the discontinuation of development or system retirement. The key incremental phases are exploration, valuation, foundations, development, and operations.

Non-Developmental Item: (a) Any product that is available in the commercial marketplace; (b) any previously developed product in use by a U.S. agency (federal, state, or local) or a foreign government that has a mutual defense agreement with the U.S.; (c) any product described in the first two points above that requires only modifications to meet requirements; (d) any product that is being produced, but not yet in the commercial marketplace, that satisfies the above criteria.

Operations Phase: During this phase, the system is in use. Usage and performance data are often collected to determine operational adequacy, needed capability changes, and/or new capabilities.

Service-Intensive Project: A project that at least 30% of end user functionalities are provided by Web services.

Valuation Phase: Second phase of development lifecycle that analyzes alternative solutions. Often includes a return on investment (ROI) and total cost of ownership analyses for key alternatives.

Chapter 6
A Test–Driven Approach to Behavioral Queries for Service Selection

Laura Zavala
Medgar Evers College of the City University of New York, USA

Benito Mendoza
New York City College of Technology, USA

Michael N. Huhns
University of South Carolina, USA

ABSTRACT

Although the areas of Service-Oriented Computing (SOC) and Agile and Lean Software Development (LSD) have been evolving separately in the last few years, they share several commonalities. Both are intended to exploit reusability and exhibit adaptability. SOC in particular aims to facilitate the widespread and diverse use of small, loosely coupled units of functionality, called services. Such services have a decided agility advantage, because they allow for changing a service provider at runtime without affecting any of a group of diverse and possibly anonymous consumers. Moreover, they can be composed at both development-time and run-time to produce new functionalities. Automatic service discovery and selection are key aspects for composing services dynamically. Current approaches attempting to automate discovery and selection make use of only structural and functional aspects of the services, and in many situations, this does not suffice to discriminate between functionally similar but disparate services. Service behavior is difficult to specify prior to service execution and instead is better described based on experience with the execution of the service. In this chapter, the authors present a behavioral approach to service selection and runtime adaptation that, inspired by agile software development techniques, is based on behavioral queries specified as test cases. Behavior is evaluated through the analysis of execution values of functional and non-functional parameters. In addition to behavioral selection, the authors' approach allows for real-time evaluation of non-functional quality-of-service parameters, such as response time, availability, and latency.

DOI: 10.4018/978-1-4666-2503-7.ch006

INTRODUCTION

A methodology for software development based on services as fundamental building blocks, known as service-oriented computing, has become widely used in building enterprise systems, because it greatly enhances their flexibility and adaptability. As a further incentive for this methodology, the number of publicly available services is continuing to increase and the Internet is becoming an open repository of such atomic heterogeneous software components. Multiple services can be integrated to facilitate cooperation between various business parties, achieve agility of the business integration, and even provide value-added services for service consumers. Essential to these capabilities is the detection of entities, services, and other resources that can be used for satisfying a specification of desired functionality. The precision of the selection process improves the possibility of having services that find, connect, and communicate with one another automatically, sharing information and performing tasks without human intervention.

Web services are the current most promising instantiation of the service-oriented methodology. Web services comprise infrastructure for describing service structure, via WSDL (Christensen, Curbera, Meredith, & Weerawarana, 2001); specifying semantics and functionality via WSDL-S (Akkiraju et al., 2005), OWL-S (Martin et al., 2004), and WSMO (Roman et al., 2006)); supporting a service repository, via UDDI (Clement et al., 2004) or some less structured registry; interacting with services, via SOAP (Gudgin et al., 2007); and scheduling and orchestrating, via WSCL (Banerji et al., 2002) (Barry, 2003; Wombacher, Fankhauser, & Mahleko, 2004). The relationships among these components are depicted in Figure 1.

There are three orthogonal dimensions for describing a service at the knowledge level (Table 1): (1) structure, (2) function, and (3) behavior. Current approaches for automating discovery and selection of services make use of only the first two. Syntactic and semantic search based on keywords on the structural definition of the service, usually the WSDL content, are used for service discovery in repositories. Semantic descriptions of service inputs and outputs are used for the selection of services. WSDL-S, OWL-S, and WSMO are the most significant standards for such semantic descriptions.

Figure 1. The general architectural model for Web services

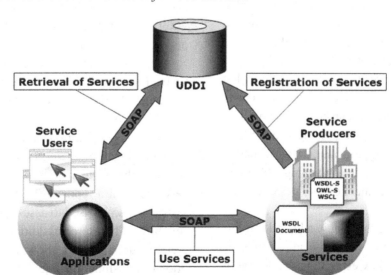

Table 1. Different levels of description for a Web service

Description of Service	Current Representation Standard/ Technique
Structure: syntactic	WSDL
Structure: semantic	WSDL and OWL, WSDL-S, OWL-S, WSMO
Function	WSDL-S, OWL-S, WSMO
Behavior	Unit Testing (our approach)

WSDL-S, OWL-S, and WSMO are also used in attempts to describe the functionality of a service or a composition of services. They describe inputs, outputs, message flows, sequences of actions, etc., which constitute a *static* model for the services being selected. They do not have the capability to describe the dynamics of the services and how they will behave when they are invoked. Behavioral selection of services should be used to provide a more precise selection. That is, it is important to know not only *what* a service will do, but also know *when* the service will provide its functionality and *how well* it will be provided. "When" and "how well" are descriptive parts for the *behavior* of a service. Behavior is difficult to specify prior to a service's invocation and often can only be described accurately based on experience with the execution of the service. Built-in tests are one way to acquire the needed experience. The underlying idea is to furnish service clients with the ability to test the services to validate not only that they do what has been stated in their specifications, but also that what they do is indeed what the client needs them to do. Additionally, services can be tested at runtime to assure that they have not changed or, if they have, they are still appropriate. That is, behavioral tests have the added advantage of being useful for the management of services over their lifetimes.

Take for example the widely adopted similar-parameters technique for the semantic matching of services. It works by estimating the degree of similarity between the expected and the actual service's input and output parameters. However, even if these parameters are semantically similar, their execution values would still provide valuable guidance for a decision-making process determining service adequacy for the task. WSDL-S attempts to deal with this problem by providing a reference from each input and output parameter to a mutually agreed upon ontology. But this requires the existence of such an ontology or a way to reconcile the independently developed ontologies of the service requestor and the service provider, neither of which might be widely available. Moreover, ontologies rarely include constraints on the execution values of those parameters and, if such constraints were made available, the values would be context dependent and generalizable only with great difficulty.

Over time, even if a developer initially selects a correct service, the provider might update the service, such as by requiring an additional input. The application using this service would then fail, and the offending service would have to be identified and replaced. Frequent retesting of services or a more complex monitoring mechanism can help avoid such situations and retesting of previously discovered services can lessen the incurred overhead of adaptation. Further, dynamic reconfiguration facilitates the building of self-healing systems (Brazier, Kephart, Parunak, & Huhns, 2009) that adapt to changes in the environment and in requirements.

We present an approach, inspired by agile software development (Martin, 2002), to the behavioral selection of services based on the use of test cases to evaluate a service's behavior (through the analysis of execution values of functional and non-functional parameters), enabling an informed decision about which of the discovered candidate services from a repository are appropriate. The tests can also be used to assess performance and reliability. Therefore, in addition to behavioral selection, our framework allows for real-time evaluation of non-functional quality-of-service (QoS) parameters (e.g., response time, availability, and latency), scalability, and dynamism (a change in the client's requirements and/or the service's API). Finally, the approach can be applied for runtime behavior monitoring and adaptation of service oriented applications, thus providing a foundation for autonomic, self-managing, self-healing, self-optimizing, and self-adaptive applications.

BACKGROUND

Our approach builds upon the existing general architectural model for Web services and uses existing service discovery and selection mechanisms to find candidate Web services. It is inspired by agile software development and uses concepts and tools from test driven development to verify the behavior of the candidate Web services initially found. It allows for runtime adaptation given changes in the availability, interaction, and behavior patterns of the services. In this section we provide an overview of the key concepts in these areas, particularly the ones used in our work, and provide pointers to the reader to more comprehensive explanations.

Semantic Service Discovery and Selection

Service discovery is the process of finding a set of suitable services for a given task. Selection consists of choosing, from the discovered set of services, the one that best matches the requirements for the task. The search and selection can be done manually or automatically.

In order to make services discoverable to potential consumers, a provider can explicitly register a service with a registry, which is sometimes based on UDDI. In order that a consumer can use a service, providers usually augment a service endpoint with an interface description using the Web Services Description Language (WSDL).

Approaches to service discovery and selection are based on syntactic and semantic matching of a service specification with representations of the structural and/or functional description of a candidate service. Syntactic approaches match service descriptions based on keywords or interfaces. Semantic approaches extend and adapt the vocabulary used to describe services in order to give semantic meaning to the terms used in the description (e.g., input and output parameters and the names of operations). This is usually achieved through the use of semantic annotations and ontologies, as well as logical reasoning mechanisms. In general, these semantic matching solutions have provided important research directions in overcoming the limitations present in prior purely syntactic approaches for service matching. A more detailed discussion on service discovery and selection can be found in (Singh & Huhns, 2005). It covers the principles and practice of Web services and relates all concepts to practical examples and emerging standards. Barry (2003) contains a higher level view of Web Services and Service-Oriented Architectures and general discussion on implementing Web service projects. Existing works and approaches to service discovery, selection, and composition are discussed in the *Related Work* section.

Test-Driven Development

Agile software development is an iterative and incremental approach that proposes the development of software in small incremental releases or iterations. Each iteration is like a miniature software project of its own and includes all of the tasks necessary to release the mini-increment of new functionality: planning, requirements analysis, design, coding, testing, and documentation. The goal is to write code faster while increasing code quality (Martin, 2002). The best known agile method is Extreme Programming, which comprises several core practices, such as Simple

Design, Continuous Integration, Collective Code Ownership, Pair Programming, Design Improvement, Small Releases, and Test-Driven Development (Ron, 2011).

Test-driven development (Beck 2002) is an evolutionary (iterative and incremental) approach to software development that relies on the repetition of a very short development cycle: before writing any piece of functional code, developers write a failing automated test case that defines a desired improvement or new function, then write just enough code to fulfill that test and finally refactor (restructure) the new code to acceptable standards.

Test-driven development breaks testing into two levels: developer tests and acceptance tests (also known as customer tests). Developer tests are unit tests written by the developers as the production code is written. The tests can be thought of as white-box testing. Inspection of the state of the code in the unit under test is important in this type of testing. Acceptance tests are more like black-box tests. They test that a feature is functioning properly. For example, a customer test for an application that has a feature to generate a graph could be: given inputs x and y, the graph should appear like z. Acceptance tests are usually specified by customers in a high level specification language, such as FitNesse[1] and FIT[2], and generally involve testing the whole system (e.g. interactions between system and user, testing multiple screens, etc.) instead of single units. If only a single entry point needs to be tested, acceptance tests can also be expressed as unit tests. In fact, some acceptance test frameworks (e.g., FIT) use JUnit[3] on the backend but allow the users to define test cases in some high level format (e.g., HTML tables), which are later converted to unit cases in JUnit.

Various xUnit frameworks (e.g., JUnit for Java, nUnit for .NET, and PyUnit for Python) have been developed to facilitate the creation of unit tests for specific programming languages. With the use of these frameworks, all a developer must do is set up a minimal program structure and call the function being tested. The program structure is very intuitive and comprises actions to be performed before and after the test, as well as preconditions and post-conditions. A unit test can be run automatically and, as it checks the results it obtains, it can provide simple and immediate feedback as to whether the tests on the unit passed or failed.

Test-driven development has the advantage that it separates the unit test from the module being tested. The unit tests can be written even before the module to be tested is coded. In this way, developers do not have to modify their program to include debugging statements within the program itself. Because the debugging statements are in a separate program, they can be changed without having to recompile the program. With acceptance tests, the test cases do not even have to be written by the developer of the program; someone other than the original developer can write the tests, execute them, and interpret the results. Indeed, it is possible to combine tests from various developers and run them together without concern about interference.

Runtime Service Behavior Monitoring and Adaptation

The management of service-oriented applications is a complex task due to the lack of central control that results from combining services from different providers. Changing the availability, interaction, and behavior patterns of services, results in undesired failures in the applications. Runtime service verification aims at detecting such problems, rather than detecting implementation errors within services, and is therefore validation-oriented rather than verification-oriented. Boehm (1984) distinguishes verification and validation as follows: "When a service user is connected to a service provider it needs to determine whether it is using the *right* service rather than whether the service it is using is *right*."

BEHAVIORAL SERVICE SELECTION AND MAINTENANCE

Looking only into the structural and functional aspects of the services does not suffice to discriminate between functionally similar but disparate services. We suggest the use of behavioral selection of services to provide more precise results. Service behavior, that is, how the service behaves when invoked, is difficult to specify *prior* to its execution and often can only be described accurately based on experience with the execution of the service.

Since acceptance test-driven development (i.e. based on acceptance tests) allows for verification of behavior conformance at runtime, it provides a basis for behavioral selection of Web services.

In (Zavala Gutierrez, Mendoza, & Huhns, 2007), we have proposed an approach to behavioral service selection and maintenance based on behavioral queries specified as test cases. The test cases are expressed in a high-level specification formalism and automatically mapped to unit tests. The unit tests are for validation —lightweight checking of behavior conformance at runtime, as opposed to verification of correct execution to detect errors in the implementation. We assume that the services have been adequately tested during development and any identified faults fixed. When services are selected at runtime, therefore, any problems that arise will more likely be due to behavior misunderstandings about the functionality of the services than implementation errors in them. Behavior is evaluated through the analysis of execution values of functional and non-functional parameters. Our approach not only improves the accuracy of selecting services, but also could work as a mechanism for runtime adaptation. In this section, we provide a discussion of our approach, a formal model for specifying expected service behavior, and two examples of the application of the model.

Test-Driven Evaluation of Service Behavior

The specific part of test-driven development that we are using is acceptance tests, since we do not want to inspect the state of the code in the service under test, which would likely not be available anyhow. We are only interested in verifying whether the service is behaving as expected. Behavior is evaluated through a defined set of behavioral constraints. The behavioral constraints verify that the execution values of functional and non-functional parameters are in the expected range for a particular chosen set of scenarios (the values of input parameters). The behavioral constraints are expressed in validation-oriented unit tests as preconditions and post-conditions. In addition to behavioral selection, our framework allows for real-time evaluation of non-functional QoS parameters, such as response time, availability, and latency.

Formal Model for Expressing Expected Behavior

Service behavior is defined as the performance of the service (outputs values, response time, etc.) under different scenarios (i.e., assignment of values to the input parameters). We have developed a formal model for expressing the expected behavior of a Web service. For this model, we define a Web service, *WS*, as a tuple <*I, FP, NFP, scenario, constraints*>, where:

- *I* is the set of input parameters
- *FP* is the set of functional parameters (the Web service outputs)
- *NFP* is the set of non-functional parameters (e.g., response time and availability)
- *Scenario* is an assignment of values to the input parameters
- *Constraints* is a conjunction of restrictions or behavior, $B_1 \wedge B_2 \wedge \ldots \wedge B_n$, that must hold under *scenario*.

Each constraint B_i is a tuple containing the following elements {*parameter*, *expectedRange*, *relevance*} where:

- *Parameter* is an element of either *FP* or *NFP*
- *ExpectedRange* is a pair of values (*min*, *max*)
- *Relevance* is an indicator of the importance of the constraint

I and *FP* are used for semantic matchmaking in a UDDI-based repository of available Web services. *Scenario* and *constraints* make use of *I*, *FP*, and *NFP* to specify the expected behavior of the service by indicating expected ranges of values (*expectedRange*) for functional and non-functional parameters (*FP* and *NFP*) under specific situations (*scenarios*). Figure 2 shows how the test cases and ranking table are incorporated in the application part of the general model for Web services.

Stock Quoting and Purchasing Example

Suppose we want to find a service for purchasing financial stocks. Using current discovery techniques, we might find a list of candidate services

Figure 2. Extensions to the general architectural model for services to support behavioral queries

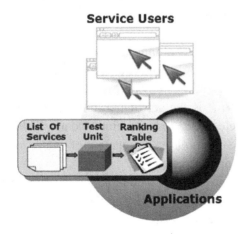

with two inputs (a string identifying the stock and an integer specifying the number of units) and an output (a real specifying the price). There is no guarantee that all the services do in fact correspond to the financial domain. One of the services could, for example, provide a quote for purchasing livestock (the string input identifying the type of livestock). If you invoke the service for a particular stock (e.g., "IBM") for which you wish to know its price, you would expect the result to be in a certain range (e.g., between 120.0 and 180.0), while the price for livestock would be in a different range.

Using our formalism for expressing expected behavior and giving the same relevance to each of the constraints, a particular instance of WS for this example is:

```
I = {stockSymbol, numberOfUnits},
FP = {price}, NFP = {availability,
responseTime},
scenario = {stockSymbol="IBM", num-
berOfUnits=10}, and
constraints = {B₁, B₂, B₃}, where:
B₁= {price, (120, 180), 1}
B₂= {responseTime, (0, 5000), 1}
B₂= {availability, (80, 100), 1}
```

Hotel Search Example

Suppose a developer wants to find a service that maintains a catalog of hotels along with a search component that accepts hotel criteria as inputs. Also suppose that there exists a local travel agency and a local basketball association that provides semantically equivalent services based on the hotel service.

However, there is a potential difference between the two. The first one returns all the hotels available to tourists that match the search criteria, while the second one returns only those hotels that both match the search criteria and have special arrangements with the local basketball association.

Using our formalism for expressing expected behavior, a particular instance of WS for this example is:

```
I = {zipcode, distance},
FP = {number_of_hotels_found}
scenario = { zipcode ="21250", dis-
tance=10},
and constraints = {B1}, where:
B1= { number_of_hotels_found, (10,
15), 1}
```

This example sets the constraint based on the number of hotels found by the service for a particular zip code. We could also set constraints on other features, such as the price given for each hotel and the availability of other methods for reserving or getting further information. In the rest of this chapter we focus on a stock quoting and purchasing example.

Service Selection and Maintenance

Two phases are involved in the selection and maintenance of services:

- **Design-Time Phase:** A unit test for a WS is created from its expected behavior specification.
- **Run-Time Phase:** The unit test is used for either selection of Web services from a list of candidates or maintenance of the system.

Service Selection: Our approach builds upon the existing general architectural model for Web services (Figure 1). Syntactic and semantic structural searches are first performed to find candidate Web services in a repository, which is possibly UDDI-based. A syntactic search is basically a keyword search on the structural definition of the service (the WSDL content). A semantic search performs a semantic match on the operation, input, and output elements, possibly represented

in OWL or RDFS. Then, the behavior of each candidate Web service is compared with the expected behavior. This is done by running a unit test for each candidate. A sound analysis of the results obtained from the test is used to determine the relevance of the candidates. Specifically, the candidate Web services are ranked according to a similarity measure that represents the similarity of the candidate to the expected service behavior specification. The similarity is a function of the number of behavioral constraints met and their relevance. Figure 3 shows a sequence diagram of this process.

Service Maintenance: The ranked list of candidate services obtained during the selection phase can be stored and used later for maintenance purposes. Specifically, if at some point in the future a service that was selected as the most relevant one causes problems during execution (due probably to temporary or permanent removal of the service by the provider), the next candidate is selected automatically. Alternatively, the service that caused the problem could be retested with the unit test created for it during the original selection process to detect possible causes of the failure.

Issues and Applicability

An issue that needs to be considered when using the approach described herein is that some scenarios would have to be constantly reevaluated, since the expected execution values might be valid only for some time period (e.g., hotel rates and stock quotes), after which the tests would need to be revised and updated. This could be addressed by using a central authority (third party) to provide mostly cached results for test queries that clients can execute to test the service. For queries whose results frequently change (like stock quotes), the queries could be updated on a daily basis and only a small set of queries would be allowed (e.g., only queries for a small predetermined set of stocks). The advantage of a third party is that it could ad-

Figure 3. A sequence diagram showing the process of requesting, testing, and selecting a service

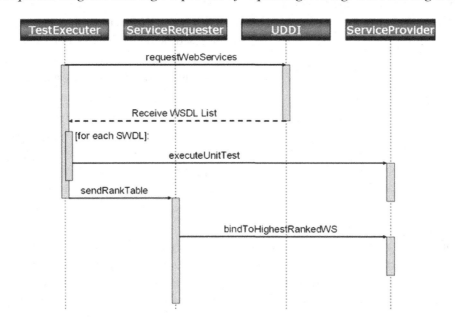

ditionally allow the incorporation of reputation mechanisms, so that clients could rank the services based on results obtained from them. There have been some efforts addressing this idea, such as (Vu, Hauswirth, & Aberer, 2005) and (Wang & Vassileva, 2007).

Evaluating service behavior through the analysis of execution values of functional and non-functional parameters provides the basis for a new type of service selection paradigm. The approach works in scenarios where users have an idea of what the output values for specific cases should be. Additionally, it allows specifying constraints for the evaluation of non-functional QoS parameters. Its applicability for some other situations, however, would require modification of existing business models so that clients can run behavioral queries. Such is the case of commercial services that require payment for access to them. Commercial providers would need to provide a way for requesters to execute test queries without having to pay. For example, tokens can be granted for testing purposes and expire after a certain number of uses or after a specified period

of time. Allowed queries could be restricted to only a few for testing purposes. Security, trust, and other issues arise, which have to be considered and investigated to assure that the mechanism is not being abused (free riders). Some commercial service providers currently offer an option for testing the service by invoking allowed method calls under testing mode. Such is the case for the stock quoting Web services found at *xmethods.net*.

Another issue regarding commercial services is the cost of the service. Even if there was a mechanism in place for allowing behavioral queries, clients would need to know the cost of using the service if it turned out to be a good match for their needs. To make use of the cost of a service would require a contracting protocol with a legal authority, which is not part of the service's behavior. Therefore, the issue is out of the realm of a behavioral service selection approach.

One case where the applicability of the behavioral queries might not be adequate is the search for Web services that perform actions and have side effects, such as printing documents or buying products. However, this is a common issue in current approaches to automated service selection and composition. In theory, the behavioral queries or any other automated selection approach could be used but certain effects might be undesired for testing purposes.

The use of validation-oriented test units to specify behavioral constraints provides a means not only to conduct selection of semantically discovered services, but also to achieve the self-healing capability envisioned in autonomic computing (Brazier, Kephart, Parunak, & Huhns, 2009). By having dynamic reconfiguration using the service ranking table, the system would adapt to changes in the environment and requirements (runtime adaptation). For example, when the highest ranked candidate service does not behave as expected (e.g., it is temporarily unavailable, there are changes in the API, or there are login and payment requirements), the next service in the ranking could be selected. Furthermore, the first one could be retested to find the cause of the problem and a report could be sent to the administrator or stored in a log file.

AN EXAMPLE IMPLEMENTATION IN JUNIT

The fundamental aspect of our behavioral approach is the specifications of service behavior in the proposed formalism and the semantics of such specifications. The parsing of the specifications, as well as the implementation of the test cases to verify behavior compliance does not have to follow any specific methodology or use any specific language.

A search for "Stock Quoting" services with $I =$ {*stockSymbol*}, $FP =$ {*lastPrice*}, $NFP =$ {*responseTime*} returned the Web services available at:

1. http://www.webservicex.net/stockquote.asmx?WSDL
2. http://www.restfulwebservices.net/wcf/StockQuoteService.svc?wsdl

3. http://ws.cdyne.com/delayedstockquote/delayedstockquote.asmx?WSDL
4. http://www.gama-system.com/webservices/stockquotes.asmx?WSDL

These are the discovered services to which behavioral selection is applied to verify and select the one(s) with the expected behavior. The expected behavior and behavioral constraints expressed in our formal model are: *scenario* = {*stockSymbol*="IBM"}, and *constraints* = {B_1, B_2, B_3, B_4, B_5, B_6, B_7, B_8, B_9, B_{10}}, where B_1={*price, (120, 180), 10*}, B_2={*responseTime, (0, 1000), 9*}, B_3={*responseTime, (0, 1500), 8*}, B_4={*responseTime, (0, 2000), 7*}, B_5={*responseTime, (0, 2500), 6*}, B_6={*responseTime, (0, 3000), 5*}, B_7={*responseTime, (0, 3500), 4*}, B_8={*responseTime, (0, 4000), 3*}, B_9={*responseTime, (0, 4500), 2*}, B_{10}={*responseTime, (0, 5000), 1*}.

This behavioral information was captured in an XML file (Figure 4), which is passed as input to the unit test generator. More visual means could be used to capture the behavioral specification, such as HTML tables as used in existing frameworks for acceptance tests (e.g., FitNesse). The XML could then be automatically generated.

We used JUnit for the implementation of the unit cases and Apache Axis WSDL2Java[4] for the automatic generation of client stubs to invoke the Web services. The behavioral constraints are expressed as assertions in the unit test. Figure 5 shows the source code of the unit test in JUnit. *Client* is an instance of the service requester class, which is the one tested by the unit test. Figure 6 shows the source code in Java for the service requester class.

After executing the unit test, we have a list of which assertions (behavioral constraints) were met by each candidate service. We calculate the similarity of the candidate to the expected behavior with a function, *rank(WS)*, of the relevance of the behavioral constraints met:

$$rank(WS) = \sum_{1 \leq i \leq n | WS(B_i)=true} relevance(WS(B_i))$$

Among the four candidate services found for this example, the first three satisfied the first constraint, B_1. The fourth service did not satisfy B_1. This service returns -4 when getting a quote for "IBM". It turns out that this service only provides quotes for two stock exchanges, NASDAQ and LJSE (Slovenia Stock Exchange). IBM is listed on the NYSE and thus is not found by this service, returning an error code instead. The corresponding *responseTime* for each of the tested services was 1: 922ms, 2: 1287ms, 3: 1595ms,

Figure 4. A fragment of an XML document containing the representation of the constraints for the stock quote example

```
<?xml version="1.0" encoding="ISO-8859-1"?>
<scenario>
   <parameter>
      <name>stockSymbol</name>
      <value>IBM</value>
   </parameter>
</scenario>

<constraints>
   <constraint>
      <id>B1</id>
      <parameter>lastPrice</parameter>
      <type>double</type>
      <range>
         <min>120</min>
         <max>180</max>
      </range>
      <relevance>50</relevance>
   </constraint>

   <constraint>
      <id>B2</id>
      <parameter>responseTime</parameter>
      <type>integer</type>
      <range>
         <min>0</min>
         <max>1000</max>
      </range>
      <relevance>9</relevance>
   </constraint>
   .
   .
   .
</constraints>
```

and 4: 1254ms. Only the first candidate passed all the tests, obtaining the highest rank, 95. The other services missed one or two constraints giving them a lower ranking, as shown in Table 2. Since we would like to maintain as candidates only those services that find the testing *stockSymbol* within the corresponding price range and with a maximum *responseTime* of 5000ms, we discard all the services with a ranking equal to or less than 50. That is, a Web service could be used only if it satisfies B_1 and at least one of the other constraints.

RELATED WORK

Semantic Service Discovery and Selection

There have been a number of efforts that use ontologies, description logic (DL), and logic reasoning approaches for semantically matching services. The matchmaking framework presented in (Chakraborty, Perich, Avancha, & Joshi, 2001) uses a DAML-S based ontology for describing the services. A DL reasoner is used to classify the matches for a given request in order to get an indication of how good a match is. Matches are classified into one of its five degrees of match, which are: exact, plug-in, subsume, intersection, and disjoint. This is achieved by computing the subsumption relationship of the request description with respect to all the advertisement descriptions. The issue of semantic ambiguity between the terms used to describe services is addressed in (Akkiraju, Srivastava, Ivan, Goodwin, & Syeda-Mahmood, 2006). Using cues from domain-independent and domain-specific ontologies, they compute an overall semantic similarity score between ambiguous terms in order to find matching service descriptions. Chakraborty et. al. (2001) proposed semantic matching approaches for pervasive environments, which use ontologies to describe the services and a Prolog-based reasoning engine to facilitate the semantic matching. They define an

Figure 5. A fragment of the JUnit code of a test case for the stock quote example

```
import java.util.Date;
import org.junit.AfterClass;
import org.junit.BeforeClass;
import org.junit.Test;
import static org.junit.Assert.*;

public class StockQuoteClientTest {
    static StockQuoteClient client;
    static double price;
    static long responseTime;

    public StockQuoteClientTest() {
    }

    @BeforeClass
    public static void setUpClass() throws Exception {
        price = 0.0;
        responseTime = 0;
        client = new StockQuoteClient();
    }

    @AfterClass
    public static void tearDownClass() throws Exception {
        price = 0.0;
        responseTime = 0;
    }

    @Test
    public void testB1() {
        System.out.println("getQuote");
        assertEquals(0.0, price, 0.0);
        price = client.getQuote("IBM");
        assertTrue(price >=120.0 && price <= 180.0);
    }

    @Test
    public void testB2() {
        Date d1 = new Date();
        System.out.println("testResponseTime");
        assertEquals(0.0, responseTime, 0.0);
        price = client.getQuote("IBM");
        Date d2 = new Date();
        responseTime = d2.getTime() - d1.getTime();
        assertTrue(responseTime >= 0 && responseTime <= 1000);
    }
    .
    .
    @Test
    public void testB10() {
    .
    .
    \
```

ad hoc heuristic-based criterion for judging the closeness between the service advertisements and the request, and provide approximate matches if no exact match exists for the given request. Ontologies are used in (Wang & Stroulia, 2003) to describe and select Web services for composition by comparing the Web service output parameters with the input parameters of other available Web services. Similarly, (Paolucci, Kawamura, Payne, & Sycara, 2002) presents a service discovery approach based on DAML-S, where the semantics of input and output parameters of the provided and required services are compared in order to

calculate the degree of similarity between the two services. A markup language called USDL (Universal Service Description Language) has been proposed for describing the semantics of Web services formally (Simon, Mallya, Bansal, Gupta, & Hite, 2005). This approach uses WSDL to give a syntactic description of the name and parameters of a service, while a specialized universal OWL ontology is used to formally describe what these mean on a conceptual level. In (Ye & Zhang, 2006), semantic annotations based on domain-oriented functional ontologies are proposed to discover Web services with functional semantics. Predefined terms are used in (Sivashanmugam, Verma, Sheth, & Miller, 2003) to express pre- and post-conditions.

Ontologies are used in (Xiao, Zou, Ng, & Nigul, 2010) to define the elements of contexts that are relevant to find users' needs and recommend appropriate services. Ontologies are also used in (Bandara, Payne, De Roure, Gibbins, & Lewis, 2008) to describe the requests and to facilitate the discovery of device-based services in pervasive environments. The approach includes a ranking mechanism that orders services according to their suitability and also considers priorities placed on individual requirements in a request during the matching process.

Some approaches aim at modeling the function of a service using automata or another mechanism that allows specifying the sequence of execution. In (Lei & Duan, 2005), the OWL-S process model specifying the "behavior" of a Web service is transformed into an extended deterministic finite-state automaton (EDFA). The approach in (Shen & Su, 2005) combines the use of automata for handling input and output messages with the use of OWL-S for describing semantics. A query language and query evaluation algorithms for the proposed formalism are also provided. Agarwal and Studer (2006) present a formalism based on pi-calculus to describe the functionality of Web services in annotated WSDL documents. A matchmaking algorithm that makes use of such

Figure 6. A client in Java for the stock quote example

```
import javax.xml.ws.WebServiceRef;
import net.restfulwebservices.servicecontracts._2008._01.StockQuoteService;
import net.restfulwebservices.servicecontracts._2008._01.IStockQuoteService;
import net.restfulwebservices.datacontracts._2008._01.StockQuote;

public class StockQuoteClient{
    @WebServiceRef(wsdlLocation = "WEB-
INF/wsdl/www.restfulwebservices.net/wcf/StockQuoteService.svc.wsdl")
    private StockQuoteService service;

    public double getQuote(String stockSymbol){
        double lastPrice = 0.0;
        StockQuote result;
        try {
            service = new StockQuoteService();
            IStockQuoteService port =
service.getBasicHttpBindingIStockQuoteService();
            result = port.getStockQuote(stockSymbol);
            lastPrice = Double.valueOf(result.getLast().getValue());
        }
        catch (Exception e) {
            System.out.println(e.getMessage());
            e.printStackTrace();
        }
        return lastPrice;
    }
}
```

Table 2. Ranking table for the Web services in the stock quote example

WS	B_1	B_2	B_3	B_4	B_5	B_6	B_7	B_8	B_9	B_{10}	rank(ws)
1	50	9	8	7	6	5	4	3	2	1	95
2	50	0	8	7	6	5	4	3	2	1	86
3	50	0	0	7	6	5	4	3	2	1	78
4	0	0	8	7	6	5	4	3	2	1	36

annotations is also described. An approach for ranking semantic Web service advertisements with respect to a service request is presented in (Skoutas, Simitsis, & Sellis, 2007). Ranking is based on the use of a domain ontology to infer the semantic similarity between the parameters of the request and the advertisement. The approach is applicable to several types of ontologies, ranging from simple taxonomies to highly expressive ontologies, such as OWL ontologies.

Another commonly studied paradigm is to model the sequence of messages in the conversation protocol that the Web service follows. In (Grigori, Corrales, & Bouzeghoub, 2006), graphs representing the conversation protocol or model are used to specify interactions with a service. The problem is thus reduced to a graph matching one. An error-correcting matching algorithm allows an approximate matching. An approach in (Wang & Vassileva, 2007) makes use of message sequences to describe the interactions with services; therefore, messages can be exchanged successfully between the compatible services. However, this approach must be performed under an assumption that elements of two message sequences to be compared must come from the same WSDL document to guarantee that the same message names have identical semantics. Moreover, if the messages describe objects instead of simple data types, then consideration of how objects are serialized into the messages is crucial.

Finally, some approaches focus on QoS parameters. The work in (Srivastava & Sorenson, 2010) introduces a technique that compares functionally equivalent services on the basis of customers' perceptions of the QoS attributes rather than the actual attribute values. The goal is to assign weights that reflect not only the actual QoS attribute values, but also their importance on the basis of the customers' preferences. In (Vu, Hauswirth, & Aberer, 2005), it is assumed that providers advertise the service quality and that users provide feedback on the actual levels of the QoS delivered to them. They address the issue of detecting and dealing with false ratings by dishonest providers and users. Non-functional properties are used in (Braun, Strunk, Stoyanova, & Buder, 2008) to describe QoS as well as context of service execution. They consider two types of context information: measurable data with a certain range and a certain unit, such as the resolution in dots per inch and the queue length of a printer service; non-measurable data such as the quality (laser or inkjet), and the color depth of printed documents. A QoS broker-based architecture for Web service selection in (Serhani, Dssouli, Hafid, & Sahraoui, 2005) defines a broker entity for the verification and certification of service qualities. Details of how selection is done are not specified, but rather left to the client that would use the information that the broker holds. The broker makes multiple concurrent calls to the Web service to check that the operations described in the service interface are available and, at the same time, calculate QoS metrics (availability, response time, and processing time). This related work is the closest to our approach. However, the work only considers non-functional parameters (QoS metrics). The values of functional parameters obtained during execution are not used and, thus, behavior is observed only from a performance point of view.

Other initiatives, such as the Business Process Execution Language for Web Service (BPEL4WS) and the OWL-S Service Model, are focused on representing service compositions (i.e., plans) where flow of a process and bindings between services are known a priori. Furthermore, approaches to automated service composition address the problem of automatically generating the plan and usually combine AI planning algorithms with semantic approaches. The focus in this paper is on service selection and runtime adaptation. Service selection is performed after discovery and prior to composition. Runtime adaptation is used when some of the selected services fail or become unavailable. Interested readers should look at (Rao & Su, 2004) for a survey of approaches to automated Web service composition.

Runtime Service Behavior Monitoring and Adaptation

Irmert, Fischer, and Meyer-Wegener (2008) present a framework, a middleware that allows replacing service implementations at runtime; that is, to add new functionality or change the functionality of a service in a Service-Oriented Architecture (SOA) environment at runtime without any side effects on the applications that are currently using it.

Atkinson, Brenner, Falcone, and Juhasz (2008) present an approach that aims to complement the semantic based service composition methods with test sheets that software engineers write and read and explicitly describe specific sequences of operation invocations representing one more usage scenarios in a visual and intuitive way. The test sheets are human readable and help application engineers, at design time, to carry out tests for quality assurance. Additionally, the authors argue that these semantically self-contained tests can be directly executed at runtime to validate a service provider's contract compliance qualitatively or to assess a service provider's reliability quantitatively.

Cardellini and Iannucci (2010) present a framework architected as a service broker that supports the QoS-driven runtime adaptation of SOA applications offered as composite services to users. It acts as an intermediary between users and concrete services, performing a role of service provider towards the users and being in turn a requestor to the concrete services used to implement the composite service. Its main task is to drive the adaptation of the composite service it manages to fulfill the Service Level Agreements (SLAs) negotiated with its users, given the SLAs it has negotiated with the concrete services.

FUTURE RESEARCH DIRECTIONS AND CONCLUSION

Semantic formalisms that capture the functional description of Web services provide a way for automating the discovery, selection, and matchmaking of services. However, the accuracy of such an automatic composition mechanism largely relies on how soundly the formal methods working on such semantic descriptions consume them.

This chapter described an agile approach to the behavioral selection of services that builds on top of existing semantic discovery approaches. Our approach works with the current characterization and technologies for a SOA; it does not suggest any modifications to any of the SOA components. Importantly, it is very easy to implement for existing services, many of which are freely available on-line. The case for commercial Web services would require some appropriate business model, because they could not simply be tested as we have done herein without some form of compensation. We envision the appearance on the Web of third party brokers authorized to run tests on a provider's service. Similarly, if a service had side effects, such as performing transactions, e.g., buying and selling, a means for distinguishing between test executions and real executions would be needed.

Behavioral constraints are expressed in validation-oriented (as opposed to verification-oriented) unit tests.

We have presented examples of the analysis that can be made with the execution values of the service parameters using range constraints. However, this analysis might have to be much more complex than just verifying conformance to a range. We plan to modify the model so that other type of constraints (e.g., exact value) can be expressed over service parameters or even properties of those parameters (e.g., size of a string parameter) Further, we envision intelligent agents reasoning about the service behavior based on the execution values of functional and non-functional parameters. This would even allow for discovery of contextual information that could later be used to provide added value services.

Service-Oriented Computing has recently been considered by the Grid community as a useful emerging paradigm to adopt. According to the Open Grid Services Architecture (OGSA) framework, the service abstraction may be used to specify access to computational resources, storage resources, and networks in a unified way. Hence, a computer service may be implemented on a single-processor or multiprocessor machine; however, these details might not be directly exposed in the service contract. The granularity of a service can vary and a service can be hosted on a single machine, or it may be distributed. Dynamic discovery and selection of services in this case will be essential for interoperability (Singh & Huhns, 2005). Our behavioral selection approach provides the means to have precise results without having access to the hidden implementation of the service.

REFERENCES

Agarwal, S., & Studer, R. (2006). Automatic matchmaking of Web services. *Proceedings of the IEEE International Conference on Web Services* (pp. 45-54).

Akkiraju, R., Farrell, J., Miller, J., Nagarajan, M., Schmidt, M.-T., Sheth, S., & Verma, K. (2005, November 7). *Web service semantics - WSDL-S.* Retrieved from http://www.w3.org/Submission/WSDL-S/

Akkiraju, R., Srivastava, B., Ivan, A.-A., Goodwin, R., & Syeda-Mahmood, T. (2006). SEMAPLAN: Combining planning with semantic matching to achieve Web service composition. *Proceedings of the IEEE International Conference on Web Services* (pp. 37-44).

Astels, D. (2003). *Test driven development: A practical guide.* Prentice Hall Professional Technical Reference.

Atkinson, C., Brenner, D., Falcone, G., & Juhasz, M. (2008). Specifying high-assurance services. *IEEE Computer, 41*, 64–71. doi:10.1109/MC.2008.308

Bandara, A., Payne, T., De Roure, D., Gibbins, N., & Lewis, T. (2008). A pragmatic approach for the semantic description and matching of pervasive resources. *Proceeding of the 3rd International Conference on Grid and Pervasive Computing* (pp. 434-446).

Banerji, A., Bartolini, C., & Beringer, D. Chopella. V., Govindarajan, K., Karp, A., . . . Williams, S. (2002, March 14). *Web services conversation language* (WSCL) 1.0. Retrieved from http://www.w3.org/TR/wscl10/

Barry, D. K. (2003). *Web services and service-oriented architectures (The savvy manager's guides).* San Francisco, CA: Morgan Kaufmann Publishers.

Beck, K. (2002). *Test driven development by example* (1st ed.). Addison-Wesley Professional.

Boehm, B. (1984). Verifying and validating software requirements and design specifications. *IEEE Software, 1*(1), 75–88. doi:10.1109/MS.1984.233702

Braun, I., Strunk, A., Stoyanova, G., & Buder, B. (2008). ConQo - A context- and QoS-aware service discovery. *Proceedings of the IADIS International Conference WWW/Internet* (pp. 432-436).

Brazier, F. M. T., Kephart, J. O., Parunak, H. V. D., & Huhns, M. N. (2009). Agents and service-oriented computing for autonomic computing: A research agenda. *IEEE Internet Computing, 13*(3), 82–87. doi:10.1109/MIC.2009.51

Cardellini, V., & Iannucci, S. (2010). Designing a broker for QoS-driven runtime adaptation of SOA applications. *Proceedings of the 2010 IEEE International Conference on Web Services* (pp. 504-511). Miami, Florida, USA.

Chakraborty, D., Perich, F., Avancha, S., & Joshi, A. (2001). Dreggie: Semantic service discovery for m-commerce applications. *Proceedings of the Workshop on Reliable and Secure Applications in Mobile Environment, Symposium on Reliable Distributed Systems.*

Christensen, E., Curbera, F., Meredith, G., & Weerawarana, S. (2001, March 15). *Web services description language* (WSDL) 1.1. Retrieved from http://www.w3.org/TR/wsdl

Clement, L., Hately, A., von Riegen, C., Rogers, T., Bellwood, T., Capell, S., et al. (2004, October 19). *UDDI spec technical committee draft.* Retrieved from http://uddi.org/pubs/uddi_v3.htm

Grigori, D., Corrales, J. C., & Bouzeghoub, M. (2006). Behavioral matchmaking for service retrieval. *Proceedings of the IEEE International Conference on Web Services* (pp. 145-152).

Gudgin, M., Hadley, M., Mendelsohn, N., Moreau, J.-J., Nielsen, H. F., Karmarkar, A., & Lafon, Y. (2007, April 27). *SOAP version 1.2 part 1: Messaging framework* (2nd ed.). Retrieved from http://www.w3.org/TR/soap12-part1/

Irmert, F., Fischer, T., & Meyer-Wegener, K. (2008). Runtime adaptation in a service-oriented component model. *Proceedings of the 2008 International Workshop on Software Engineering for Adaptive and Self-Managing Systems* (pp. 97-104). Leipzig, Germany.

Lei, L., & Duan, Z. (2005). Transforming OWL-S process model into EDFA for service discovery. *Proceedings of the IEEE International Conference on Web Services* (pp. 137-144).

Martin, D., Burstein, M., Hobbs, J., Lassila, O., McDermott, D., McIlraith, S., et al. (2004, November 22). *OWL-S: Semantic markup for Web services*. Retrieved from http://www.w3.org/Submission/OWL-S/

Martin, R. C. (2002). *Agile software development: Principles, patterns, and practices* (1st ed.). Prentice Hall, Inc.

Paolucci, M., Kawamura, T., Payne, T. R., & Sycara, K. (2002). Semantic matching of Web services capabilities. *Proceedings of the International Semantic Web Conference* (pp. 333-347).

Rao, J., & Su, X. (2004). A survey of automated Web service composition methods. *Proceedings of the First International Workshop on Semantic Web Services and Web Process Composition*.

Roman, D., Lausen, H., Keller, U., de Bruijn, J., Bussler, C., Domingue, J., et al. Michael Stollberg. (2006, October 21). *D2v1.3. Web service modeling ontology* (WSMO). Retrieved from http://www.wsmo.org/TR/d2/v1.3/

Ron, R. (2011). *XProgramming.com: An agile software development resource*. Retrieved March 1, 2011, from http://www.xprogramming.com

Serhani, M. A., Dssouli, R., Hafid, A., & Sahraoui, H. (2005). A QoS broker-based architecture for efficient web services selection. *Proceedings of the IEEE International Conference on Web Services* (pp. 113-120).

Shen, Z., & Su, J. (2005). Web service discovery based on behavior signatures. *Proceedings of the IEEE International Conference on Services Computing* (pp. 279- 286).

Simon, L., Mallya, A., Bansal, A., Gupta, G., & Hite, T. D. (2005). A universal service description language. *Proceedings of the IEEE International Conference on Web Services* (pp. 824-825).

Singh, M. P., & Huhns, M. N. (2005). *Service-oriented computing: Semantics, processes, agents*. West Sussex, UK: John Wiley & Sons, Ltd.

Sivashanmugam, K., Verma, K., Sheth, A., & Miller, J. (2003). Adding semantics to Web services standards. *Proceedings of the IEEE International Conference on Web Services* (pp. 395-401).

Skoutas, D., Simitsis, A., & Sellis, T. (2007). A ranking mechanism for Semantic Web service discovery. *Proceedings of the IEEE Congress on Services* (pp. 41-48).

Srivastava, A., & Sorenson, P. G. (2010). Service selection based on customer rating of quality of service attributes. *Proceedings of the 8th International Conferences on Web Services*.

Vu, L.-H., Hauswirth, M., & Aberer, K. (2005). QoS-based service selection and ranking with trust and reputation management. *Proceedings of the Cooperative Information System Conference*.

Wang, Y., & Stroulia, E. (2003). Flexible interface matching for web-service discovery. *Proceedings of the 4th International Conference on Web Information Systems Engineering* (pp. 147- 156).

Wang, Y., & Vassileva, J. (2007). Toward trust and reputation based Web service selection: A survey. *International Transactions on Systems Science and Applications*, *3*(2), 118–132.

Wombacher, A., Fankhauser, P., & Mahleko, B. (2004). Matchmaking for business processes based on choreographies. *Proceedings of the IEEE International Conference on e-Technology, e-Commerce and e-Service* (pp. 359-368).

Xiao, H., Zou, Y., Ng, J., & Nigul, L. (2010). An approach for context-aware service discovery and recommendation. *Proceedings the 8th International Conference on Web Services*.

Ye, L., & Zhang, B. (2006). Web service discovery based on functional semantics. *Proceedings of the Second International Conference on Semantics, Knowledge, and Grid* (pp. 57-57).

Zavala Gutierrez, R. L., Mendoza, B., & Huhns, M. N. (2007). Behavioral queries for service selection: An agile approach to SOC. *Proceedings IEEE International Conference on Web Services*, (pp. 1152-1153).

KEY TERMS AND DEFINITIONS

Functional Parameters: The inputs required by the service as well as the service outputs.

Non-Functional Parameters: The properties that capture other aspects of a service aside from functionality; e.g., security, price, temporal availability, and quality.

Quality of Service (QoS) Parameters: Nonfunctional parameters related to the quality of the functionality provided by the service; e.g., performance, throughput, accuracy, reliability, availability, and trust.

Service Behavior: The performance of the service (outputs values, response time, etc.) under different scenarios (i.e., assignment of values to the input parameters).

Service Composition: The development of customized services often by discovering, integrating, and executing existing services. Existing services are orchestrated into one or more new services that fit the desired functionality of a composite application.

Service Discovery: Searching over service repositories, usually by exploiting the services' metadata, to find the services satisfying a specification of desired functionality.

Service Selection: The ranking mechanism used to choose a service among a list of discovered services with comparable functionalities.

Services: Unassociated, loosely coupled, reusable units of functionality that have no calls to each other embedded in them, but provide descriptive metadata about their structure, functionality, and interface, so that can be used for meeting a specification of desired functionality.

Test-Driven Development: An approach for software development that involves repeatedly writing a unit test and implementing only the code necessary to pass the test.

Unit Test: The smallest testable part of an application. Unit testing is a method by which individual units of source code are tested to determine if they are fit for use.

Web Services: Services accessible over standard Internet protocols independent of platforms and programming languages.

ENDNOTES

[1] www.fitnesse.org
[2] fit.c2.com
[3] www.junit.org
[4] ws.apache.org/axis/java

Chapter 7

User–Centered Business Process Modeling and Pattern–Based Development for Large Systems

O. Takaki
Japan Advanced Institute of Science and Technology, Japan

T. Seino
Maebashi Kyoai Gakuen College, Japan

N. Izumi
National Institute of Advanced Industrial Science and Technology, Japan

K. Hasida
National Institute of Advanced Industrial Science and Technology, Japan

ABSTRACT

In agile software development, it is imperative for stakeholders such as the users and developers of an information system to collaborate in designing and developing the information system, by sharing their knowledge. Especially in development of a large-scale information system, such collaboration among stakeholders is important, but difficult to achieve. This chapter introduces a modeling method of business processes for requirements analysis and a development framework based on Web-process architectures. The modeling method makes it easier for stakeholders to agree upon requirements. It also employs a formal method to allow business process models to satisfy both understandability and accuracy. On the other hand, the development framework above enables rapid spiral development of short-term cycles through the collaboration of developers and users. This chapter also introduces an example that compares the workloads of two requirement analyses of large-scale system developments for a government service and a financial accounting service, in order to evaluate the advantages of the proposed modeling method.

DOI: 10.4018/978-1-4666-2503-7.ch007

INTRODUCTION

In agile software development, it is imperative for stakeholders in the development of an information system to collaborate in designing and developing the information system. "Stakeholders" includes business modelers, software developers, users, and system administrators who must agree on specifications, features, and many other items (Highsmith, 2001; Cohn, 2005). However, such collaboration is particularly difficult in the development of a large-scale information system, because such development has many stakeholders and the process, and outcomes of the development tend to be so complex that many agile approaches are hard to apply (Boehm, 2004; Erdogmus, 2003; Stephens, 2003).

In order to address the problem of collaboration among all the stakeholders in large-scale system development, this chapter introduces a modeling method of business processes for requirements analysis, and a development framework based on Web-process architectures. The modeling method makes it easier for stakeholders to agree upon requirements. Moreover, it employs a formal method to verify consistency properties of business processes. On the other hand, the development framework enables rapid spiral development through short-term cycles based on patterns of routine tasks in services.

The modeling method employs a diagram to represent a business process, business forms used in the business process and the lifecycles of business forms. The diagram is a workflow with business form lifecycles (BFLs). In order to collaborate in requirements analysis among users and developers of an information system, it is important to use a modeling language that is easily understandable to both users and developers. For example, office workers who use information systems for their services tend to grasp the details of the services based on the process of how they offer the service to their customers. Therefore, it is easier for such office workers to represent the

details of their services with business process models, which must be accurate. By verifying a correctness property of BFLs in a workflow, the model is assured to be correct from the perspective of not only the control flow but also the outputs of the business process that are represented by the workflow. Thus, workflows with BFLs have the advantages of both readability and accuracy.

We also introduce a development framework based on Web-process architectures, which helps in dealing with the conceptual diversity of service operations on the Web (e.g., business activities, business processes, workflow applications, software components, and service primitives) as well as the extensive variety of component repositories available (e.g., UDDI registry, WSDL specification, enterprise data stocks, and software library resources). This framework eventually reduces the cost of information system development. We describe the framework based on Web-process architectures, in which customer processes, front-office processes, and back-office tasks interoperate in a business process model based on workflows with BFLs.

The proposed method and the framework have been applied to the real development of a large-scale information system for local (province) government services. We explain the advantages of the modeling method based on workflows with BFLs of a requirements analysis for large-scale developments from the perspective of agile software development.

Overview of this Chapter

The main body of this chapter consists of a modeling method of business processes and a development framework. Prior to explanation of them, we briefly explain the relationship between the modeling method and the development framework.

The method and the framework above are used to realize a type of SOA development. First, users and developers of an information system that will be developed collaborate in performing requirements analysis with the modeling method. They here develop workflows with BFLs that are explained in Section 2, through iteration of composition and verification of the workflows. In the iteration, users check and/or compose workflows, while developers compose, check and/or support users to compose workflows. Next, they develop the information system from the workflows, by using the developing framework that is explained in Section 3. Developers here develop the information system based on software components that have been developed in a series of development projects by AIST (2006), while users check the information system regularly (Figure 1).

We mention the relationship above from the viewpoint of SOA, as follows:

1. Through requirements analysis based on business process modeling with workflows with BFLs, necessary software components and how to combine them are determined.
2. According to the determination above, developers select, adjust and combine software components by using the development framework based on Web-process architectures.

The remainder of this paper is organized as follows. Section 2 explains the modeling method of business processes based on workflows with BFLs. Section 3 introduces a development framework based on Web-process architectures. Section 4 introduces an example of an application of the modeling method in the requirements analysis of large-scale information systems. The final sections provide related work, the conclusions and prospectus of this research.

BUSINESS PROCESS MODELING BASED ON WORKFLOWS WITH BUSINESS FORM LIFECYCLES

Rapid technological progress in our society has made businesses, organizations, and their information systems large and complex. Moreover, the case in which an organization offers a single service has become rare, while combination of services, organizations, and information systems is becoming widespread. Thus, in order to design an information system, the service that an organization offers with the information system must be defined in explicit detail.

Figure 1. Relationship between the modeling method and the development framework

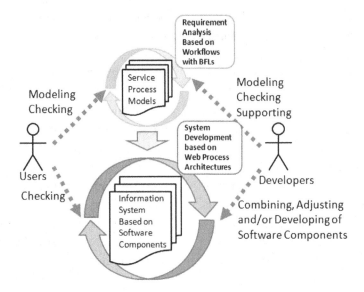

In many cases, however, such a service cannot be easily defined in explicit detail. On the other hand, it is often easier to formalize how to perform a service than to formalize what the service is. In fact, many workers, who are also users of information systems involved in these services, can easily determine the processes to perform the service as flows of their tasks. Therefore, we focus on the business process instead of the service itself. We often call a business process by an *event-flow*, which is a process consisting of events along temporal orders (note that we often refer to a task or a service in SOA as "an event").

Moreover, we focus on *business forms* in the business process, where a "business form" is a resulting document used in some event(s) in the business process. For example, Figure 2 describes a prescription business process (a prescription event-flow) in a hospital, where nine events are denoted by rectangles, and four business forms

in this schema are denoted by C (medical chart), P (prescription), M (medicine),[1] and T (tutorial).

In a service provided collaboratively by several workers (e.g., a government service or a medical service), they perform their tasks to provide the service according to several business forms inherent to the service, or they use business forms as intermediates to perform their tasks. Thus, it is often useful to check the *life-cycles* of business forms in an event-flow in order to verify validity of the event-flow, where the "life-cycle" of a business form means a series of states of the business form at an event that represent how to compose, refer to, re-write, judge, store, distribute, or dump the business form at the event.

The event-flow model enables users and developers to collaborate in modeling the business process and in checking that the process achieves the service goals. It also helps stakeholders share all services, and defines the specifications of the

Figure 2. Prescription business process

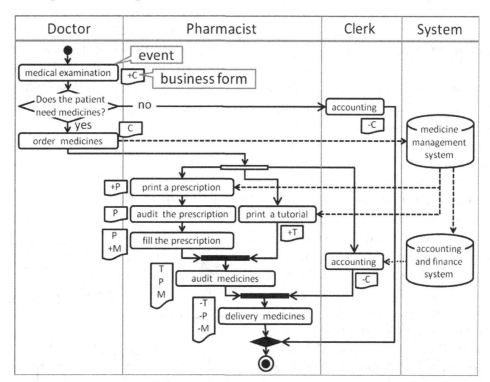

information system based on business forms as outputs of services. Here an event-flow model is called a *workflow*. While workflows are easy for users to understand, it is not easy to verify the event-flows in them. Such models tend to contain omissions, leaks, and inconsistent descriptions that are difficult to detect. To overcome these shortcomings, we introduce a workflow in which we can describe life-cycles of business forms. We call it by a *workflow with BFLs* (Business Form Lifecycles). We also define the correctness of the event-flows and lifecycles of business forms along event-flows, and verify workflows with BFLs by checking the correctness properties. By considering graph-theoretic properties corresponding to the correctness, one can apply a formal method for the verification of event-flow models (Takaki 08-A, Takaki 09, Takaki 10).

In the rest of this section, we explain a workflow that describes event-flows of a business and lifecycles of business forms that are created and/or used in the business, and then we explain the correctness of lifecycles of business forms in a workflow.

Workflow and Correctness

Previous research has defined several kinds of workflows (Aalst, 1997; 1998; 2005; Andrews, 2003; WfMC, 2002). For simplicity, we consider only acyclic workflows. Please see (Aalst, 1997; 1998; 2005; Takaki, 2008A; Takaki, 2010) for cyclic workflows. One can also refer to previous research for the language, semantics, and correctness properties of workflows in detail.

A workflow denotes a directed graph that consists of *nodes* and *arcs*. Here, a node denotes an event or a symbol controlling some flows of events, while an arc denotes an order relation of events and control flow nodes. Each node is categorized as one of the following types: trigger, terminal, event, XOR-split, XOR-join, AND-split, and AND-join. Here, XOR-split can be regarded as a branch, and AND-split as a fork. Note that the trigger of a workflow W is the unique start-

ing node of W, and that the terminal of W is the unique ending node of W. Whenever an arc f has a node x as the target (or the source), x has f as an *incoming arc* (or an *outgoing arc*). The number of arcs of a node is determined by the type of node (see Figure 3).

Next we define the operational semantics of workflows, that is, we define how to execute events according to a given workflow, as follows. In order to define the semantics, we employ *tokens* that stay on the arcs of the workflow and that show the events that are executed at each time point.

1. At the first point, there is a single token at the outgoing arc of the trigger of the workflow.
2. When a token is at the incoming arc of an event, the task is executed, and the token proceeds to the outgoing arc of the event.
3. When a token is at the incoming arc of an XOR-split, it proceeds to one of outgoing-arcs of the XOR-split.
4. When a token is at the incoming-arc of an XOR-join, it proceeds only to the outgoing arc of the XOR-join.
5. When a token is at the incoming arc of an AND-split, it is copied as often as the number of outgoing arcs of the AND-split minus one, and the tokens concurrently proceed to all its outgoing arcs.

Figure 3. Types of nodes

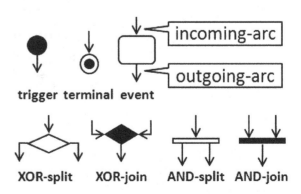

6. When a token is at the incoming arc of an AND-join, it stops there and waits until all other incoming-arcs of the AND-join have tokens. When all incoming arcs have tokens, the tokens are put together into a single token that proceeds to the outgoing arc of the AND-join.

7. When a token is at the incoming arc of the terminal, it just stops there.

For a workflow W, the tokens on W show the events that are executed at each time point. The set of locations of tokens in W at a time point T is called the *state* of W at T. The *initial state* of W is the state in which there is only a single token at the outgoing arc of the trigger of W at the initial time point. If a state H of W at T is changed into H' at the next time point of T by one of the conditions 2–7 above, then we represent this as $H{\rightarrow}H'$. For states H and H' of W, if there exist states $H_1, ..., H_n$ of W satisfying $H=H_1{\rightarrow}H_2{\rightarrow}H_3{\rightarrow}...{\rightarrow}H_n=H'$, or if $H=H'$, then H' is said to be *accessible from* H (and H is said to be *accessible to* H') and this is represented by $H{\rightarrow}{\rightarrow}H'$.

We finally define the correctness of a workflow, which is equivalent to the existing correctness property of an acyclic workflow (Aalst, 2002; Sadiq, 2000; Takaki, 2010). A workflow W is said to be correct if for any state H of W that is accessible from the initial state of W, there exists a state H_e satisfying the condition that $H{\rightarrow}{\rightarrow}H_e$ and that there is only a single token at the incoming flow of the terminal of W. The correctness of W shows that regardless of the number of events executed according to W, there is a process that safely completes the rest of the events with no redundant execution of an event.

One can verify the correctness of an acyclic workflow W by checking the graph theoretic property of the sub-graphs of W, i.e., *instances*, which are defined as follows. A subgraph V of W is called an *instance* if V satisfies the following properties.

1. V contains the trigger of W.
2. For any node x in V, there exists a path on V from the trigger to x.
3. If V contains an XOR-split x, then V contains just one outgoing-arc of x.
4. If V contains a node x other than XOR-split, then V contains all outgoing-arcs of x.

An instance of a workflow W denotes the log or story of what events have been executed to perform the service that is described by W, according to the semantics of W. For example, the workflow in Figure 2 is shown as two instances in Figure 4 as two patterns of stories: the first instance denotes the story of executing events in the case where the patient needs medicine, and the second instance denotes another story where the patient does not need medicine.

We could define the semantics and consistency based on Petri Nets. In fact, as far as acyclic workflows are concerned, the consistency property we defined in this chapter is equivalent to Aalst's soundness property of workflows (workflow-nets) (Aalst, 1997; 1998). However, since it needs a lot of preliminaries to define semantics and consistency (soundness) of workflows based on petri-nets, we selected a simpler way to define them without petri-nets.

To verify the correctness of an acyclic workflow, the graph theoretic properties of all instances of the workflow are verified as follows.

Theorem (Takaki, 2010): A workflow W is correct if every instance V of W is *deadlock free* and *lack of synchronization free*, that is, every instance V of W satisfies the following conditions:

1. For any AND-join x on V, V contains all incoming-arcs of x.
2. For any XOR-join x on V, V contains a single incoming-arc of x.

Figure 4. Two instances of the workflow in Figure 2

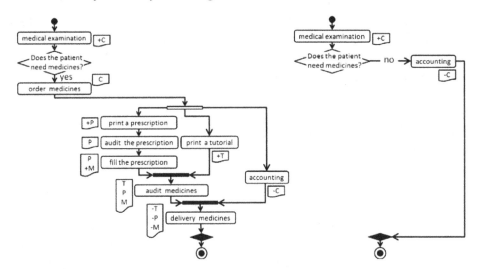

For example, the workflow in Figure 2 has two instances in Figure 4, both of which are deadlock free and lack of synchronization free. Therefore, the workflow is correct.

Correctness of BFLs

In this subsection, we briefly explain lifecycles of business forms and their correctness. Their detailed definitions are introduced in (Takaki, 2008A; Takaki, 2008B).

"Business forms" in workflows are usually paper documents or the data files of documents. In this chapter, we regard a business form as a paper document that is composed, referred to, re-written, judged, stored, distributed, or dumped in some events. Unlike data files, a business form is a tangible thing. Although it can be copied, the copy is regarded as not the same as the original business form. Moreover, unlike data in a system that multiple people can access simultaneously, a business form cannot be used by multiple people at the same time.

In formulating workflows, particularly human workflows, business forms are still very important, even though paper documents have been replaced by data (data files) in information systems. In a

workflow, business forms used in an event are explicitly described in the event, in order to verify life cycles of business forms more correctly.

We now define business forms in workflows, their life cycles, and their correctness. A business form is described at an event. For example, the event "fill the prescription" in Figure 5 has two business forms, P (Prescription) and M (Medicine). The prefix symbol "+" of the label of a business form shows that the business form is created at the event. On the other hand, another symbol "-" shows that the business form has been checked off at the event. In many cases, a business form with symbol "-" is stored, passed to external people of the workflow or dumped at the event. For example, the business form M in Figure 4 is created at the event "fill the prescription", and checked off at the event "delivery medicines."

Roughly, the lifecycle of a business form means a series of states of the business form, and correctness of the lifecycle means consistency in the order of the states. For example, for a business form B, there should not be a state using B earlier than the state creating B nor later than the state storing B. If a given workflow is correct, every lifecycle of a business form can be described as a sequence of events using the symbols of the

Figure 5. Business forms in a workflow

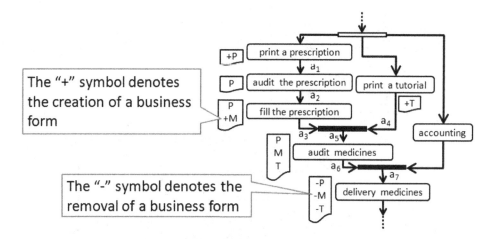

business form. For example, the business form C has a lifecycle that is described as a sequence of events "medical examination," "order medicines," and "accounting," which have the symbols "+C," "C," and "-C," respectively," as the states of C at the events. Figure 6 shows four sequences as the lifecycles of four business forms.

For a correct workflow, correctness of the lifecycle of a business form is determined by the order of states of business forms in the lifecycle. Although there are many kinds of states of business forms, for simplicity we here consider only three kinds of states:

1. Creation of a business form B, which is denoted by "+B."
2. Use or keeping of a business form B, which is denoted just by "B".
3. Store, pass or dumping of a business form B, which is denoted by "-B".

By using the above three states, we now roughly explain the correct lifecycles of business forms. See (Takaki, 2008A) for a more accurate definition.

Let W be a workflow. Then, a *line* in W is a sequence L of arcs

$$L := (A_1 \xrightarrow{f_1} A_2 \xrightarrow{f_2} \dots \xrightarrow{f_{n-1}} A_n),$$

where A_1 and A_n are events in W, while no A_i $(i=2, \dots, n-1)$ is an event.

Let V be an instance of W and B a business form in W. Then, the *correct lifecycle* of B on V is the sequence π of lines in V

$$\pi := (A_1 \xrightarrow{L_1} A_2 \xrightarrow{L_2} \dots \xrightarrow{L_{n-1}} A_n),$$

which satisfies the following properties:

1. Every event A_i has B.
2. B is created on A_1, that is, A_1 has the state "+B".
3. For any i with $i>1$, no A_i has the state "+B".
4. B is stored, passed or dumped at A_n, that is, A_n has the state "-B".
5. For any i with $i<n$, no A_i has the state "-B".

A correct workflow W is said to *have correct BFLs* if, for each instance V of W, each event A in V and for each business form B on A, there is an essentially unique correct life cycle π of B on V that contains A.

Figure 6. Four lifecycles of business forms

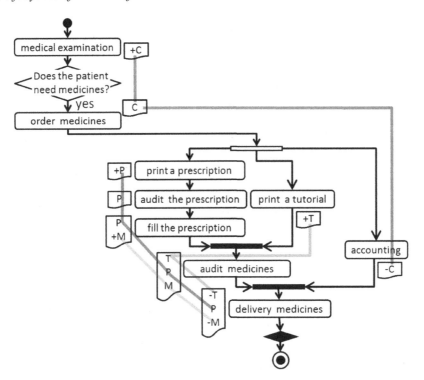

For example, all lifecycles of *C*, *T*, *P*, and *M* in the example shown in Figure 6 are correct. In fact, the workflow in Figure 2 also shows correct business form lifecycles.

Note that one can consider correctness of the lifecycle of a business form to be defined based on a compiler technology that checks states of a variable in a block in a program (AHO, 2006). Here, a block in a program corresponds to an instance in a workflow, while a series of states of a variable including variable-declaration and variable-consumption corresponds to a lifecycle of a business form.

Design and Verification of Workflows with BFLs for Agile Development

In the previous sub-sections, we explained the correctness of a workflow from the perspective of the control flow and correctness of BFLs in a workflow. The correctness properties of a work-

flow can be reduced to graph theoretic properties of instances of the workflow. In fact, for a correct workflow *W* the correctness of BFLs of *W* is shown to be equivalent to a property that is defined by local conditions called *local evidence conditions*, which are defined by using instances of *W* (see Definition 5.5 and Lemma 5.6 in Takaki, 2008A). Actually, algorithms have been developed that verify the correctness properties and implementations of them (Takaki, 2008A). Figure 7 shows a snapshot of composing workflows with BFLs by using a tool that is obtained by implementing the algorithms above. For details on the algorithm that verifies correctness of BFLs in a workflow or on its implementation, see Section 6 and Section 8 in (Takaki, 2008A), respectively.

Although this chapter deals with acyclic workflows only, there are also algorithms that can deal with cyclic workflows (Takaki, 2008A). Moreover, although we define a business form lifecycle based on only three states—creation of the business

Figure 7. Snapshot of composing workflows with BFLs by using a tool

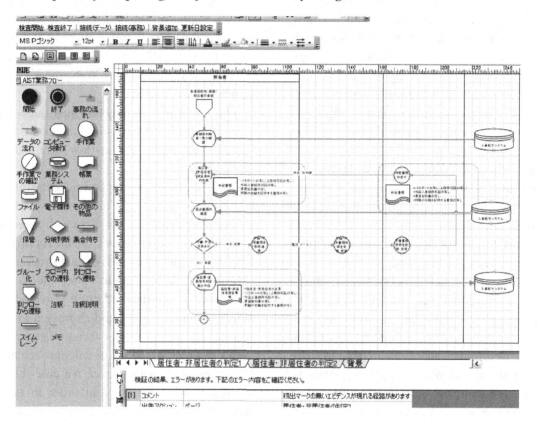

form, its use or holding, and its release—one can extend the definition of BFLs and their correctness by adding new states such as review, audit, revision, or imprint.

The method to model business processes based on workflows with BFLs enables modelers to consider business forms as significant outputs of the services, and to construct or refine models based on event-flows that are needed to achieve the services. By using this method, one can construct a business process model that has both of good readability for the users of information systems (who are also service providers) and accuracy, which is obtained by verifying that the service outputs are unproblematic. It also prevents them from making mistakes when they construct or refine business process models. In this sense, this

method assists agile software development in the requirements analysis of a large-scale information system.

DEVELOPMENT FRAMEWORK BASED ON WEB-PROCESS ARCHITECTURES

After modeling processes of services that an organization provides to its customers, we classified tasks in the business processes into either knowledge-intensive tasks or routine tasks. While knowledge-intensive tasks are achieved by workers' flexible responses, routine tasks have stable patterns that indicate how to achieve the tasks. This section introduces a framework to develop an information system that assists routine tasks according to Web-process architectures (Izumi, 2009). The framework enables developers to adjust and compose software components selected through the requirements analysis with the modeling above while reflecting the specifications obtained through the requirements analysis to the information system obtained by composing the components above.

The architecture consists of three layers. The top layer describes the structures of tasks obtained from event-flows. The middle layer defines Web layouts as user interfaces, the data structure, and the control structure of Web processes. The bottom layer describes rules on Web page transitions. As a result, a business model of routine tasks is implemented as a thin client application. The development framework enables rapid spiral development of short-term cycles because business modelers, software developers, and users are able to share the same framework of description and systems.

In the following sub-sections, we will explain a framework based on Web-process architectures, by which one can extract patterns from routine tasks and model them.

Overview of the Proposed Framework

To execute Web processes as user tasks, systems need to be able to complete the following tasks:

- Interact with customers and various servers,
- Configure user tasks by using Web resources,
- Coordinate and cooperate with different Web processes.

With regard to Web process interoperation, we use an ontology-based approach (Studer, 1998) that mediates the different sorts of resource semantics. To implement this approach and prepare machine accessible resources on the Web, we base the design of the Web application architecture on a multi-grain-size repository (Izumi, 2002), which is a special architecture for integrating different sorts of resources. Figure 8 shows an overview of our proposed framework of Web processes based on a layered repository.

Our proposed architecture has three levels corresponding to the following descriptions: business-task level, subtask-flow level, and page-transition level.

As the top level corresponding to the information architecture of EA, the *business-task level* provides us with the task structure obtained from business process definitions. On the *subtask-flow level*, we define three kinds of data structure. The first one is a Web layout as a user interface, and the second is the data structure provided in an object-oriented manner and expressed as JAVA objects. The third kind is the control structure of Web processes based on pi-calculus semantics. On the *page-transition level*, we describe rules about exception handling in order to manage system error, and we provide fine-grain software components as JAVA codes.

Building Business Object Ontology for Task Structure

In order to share the same framework of description and systems among modelers, developers, and users, it is important to bridge the differences between not only viewpoints but also the business descriptions as both natural language texts and in proper process repositories that are available for software development. We construct the business activity repository by using WordNet (Fellbaum, 1998) as a general lexical repository.

We classify the noun concepts appearing in business forms by using WordNet as a general ontology that contains over 17,000 concepts. If we were to use WordNet as it is, however, the number of candidates would explode because of the variety of word meanings and the ambiguity of words. To construct an ontology, nouns and

Figure 8. Framework of three-level architecture for service coordination of Web process

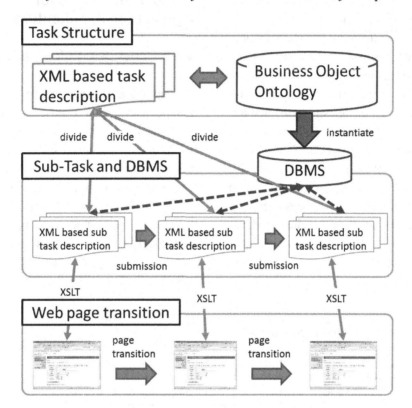

verbs are especially important. Moreover, as compared to verbs, nouns are often easier to use for constructing an ontology. In fact, WordNet has relationships between words, whose structures differ from one word class to another. Moreover, the structure of relationships between nouns is simpler and more useful to construct an ontology than other structures in WordNet (Fellbaum, 1998). Thus, to construct an ontology based on WordNet, nouns concepts described in business forms are especially useful to construct a business object ontology.

Using WordNet to classify the noun concepts appearing in business forms, we choose major concepts with respect to the degree of abstraction and frequency. In determining the criteria for selecting a major noun concept, we pay attention to the roles of input-output objects in the definition of business processes. We thus construct a business object ontology in the following way:

1. Consider the case-study models of workflow definitions and extract the taxonomy.
2. Evaluate the frequency of the appearance of each noun concept.
3. Compare the noun hierarchies of WordNet and the obtained taxonomy, and total the appearance frequencies of concepts that have similar meanings.
4. Select as upper noun concepts those with high scores, and build upper ontologies by giving all those nouns the formal is-a relation.
5. Merge all the noun hierarchies extracted from the business forms in this way.

According to WordNet's structure, we define the substructure of the concepts obtained above as an upper ontology, provided that priority of meaning is given to a business domain. However, when we fix the upper ontology to construct a business domain ontology, concept drift (semantic shift in a specific domain) often occurs and makes the building of ontologies inefficient.

Figure 9 shows the structure of business object ontology of medical services. To construct the ontology, we first gather business forms such as clinical charts, nursing reports, prescriptions and receipts, and extract characteristic terms that appear frequently from each kind of business forms (Steps 1 and 2). Next we construct small ontologies from the sets of terms above, based on taxonomies that are defined in WordNet according to semantic similarity and frequency score (Steps 3 and 4). Finally we merge the small ontologies (Step 5).

Using business object ontology as taxonomy, we define a user's task in the XML format based on RDF data model.

Model Refinement for Application Architecture

Web Page Design for the User Interface

To capture a business process from the user's perspective as a Web process, we model a personal work process as Web page transition. To formalize the captured Web process, we use the business object ontology shown in Figure 9 as the taxonomy for XML task descriptions.

The top-level task structure is determined first by using business object ontology. This task structure specifies, in XML format, which properties are to be obtained, assigned, exchanged, or stored in the execution of work processes.

Figure 9. A business object ontology (Partial)

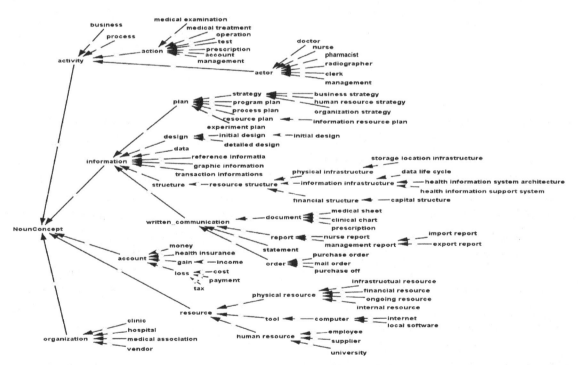

The semantic structures of business forms that are exchanged in the work process are obtained by dividing the top-level task into subtasks. Because the task structure is based on a business object ontology, the subtask structures obtained from the top-level task structure are also based on this ontology.

The Web page design can be described by assigning an XSLT description to each subtask structure in XML. Due to the business object ontology and its instance in a data base management system (DBMS), the obtained Web page is strongly connected to read and write in DBMS. Our development methodology thus enables us to check the sufficient condition of the Web process and DB schema in an early stage of development.

Building a WS Object Ontology for Data Structures

In the same way as the business object ontology is constructed, the WS (Web service) object ontology in Figure 10 is constructed as a domain-independent ontology from the implementation of Web processes. Although we do not explain the content of the WS object ontology here, it should be noted that the ontology includes words for expanding domain ontologies (such as building a set, picking up an element of a set, and indicating a calculation stage) as well as data structures for implementation details and so forth.

For developing business applications from the Web page transition model obtained above, we need a detailed data structure of each XML-described subtask for native JAVA execution. In order to give the subtask description the operational data structure that is used for application development, we base the preparation of the JAVA library on the application template, which maps XML documents and JAVA objects in relation to each other, according to the business and WS object ontologies. Figure 11 provides the JAVA code for transforming JAVA objects corresponding to an XML document of subtask description.

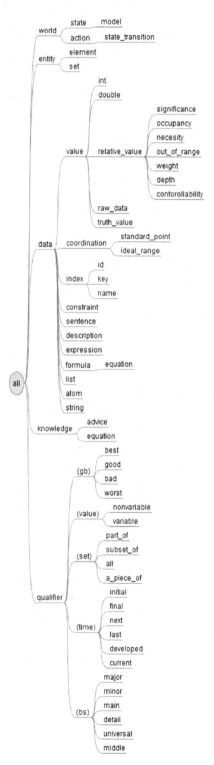

Figure 10. WS (Web services) object ontology (partial)

Figure 11. Java code for mapping XML documents and Java objects to each other

- JAVA code type definition

```
import jp.aist.samples.userlist.User;
import jp.aist.samples.userlist.UserList;
```

- From XML data (string) to JAVA object

```
XmlObjConverterImpl xmlObjConverter =
                            new XmlObjConverterImpl();
String sdoc = XMLdata(string);
UserList userList = (UserList) xmlObjConverter.convert( sdoc );
// storing data in JAVA object: userList
```

- From JAVA object to XML data (string)

```
XmlObjConverterImpl xmlObjConverter =
                            new XmlObjConverterImpl();
UserList userList = UserListObject;
String sdoc = xmlObjConverter.convert( userList );
// storing XML data in sdoc
```

Assigning Data Interchange Type for Control Structure

In order to perform the semantic coordination of Web processes, we need to implement the framework for various interoperations of work processes to obtain approval of a decision. To exchange data between different kinds of work processes, we introduce tuple space semantics based on the pi-calculus. The tuple space enables us to exchange data between input and output processes through matched tuples. However, since we deal with not only just input and output processes but also the best practices for the reuse of personal work processes, we require detailed control structure for the deployment of data exchange in tuple space.

To bridge the gap between the best practices of work processes and the control structure in tuple space, we analyzed the case studies in the MIT Process Handbook [MIT] and obtained the business trading structures as shown in Figure 12, which constitute a business interoperation repository. Diagrams in Figure 12 give typical patterns of tuples. Thus, by using the business interoperation repository, we are able to clarify in detail the type of data exchange in tuple space on the application servers. Furthermore, the model obtained from the business interoperation repository enables application developers to select and reuse the control structure of Web process implementation, such as wait, suspend, conditional, and so forth.

Architecture of Service Coordination Environment

To perform service coordination of Web processes based on pi-calculus semantics, we developed an environment for managing the top-level task model of business process in the execution with the business software components. Figure 13 shows our developed architecture of Web application server that is reinforced tuple space and workflow engine. This architecture enables us to execute task models described as the work process script in work process script interpreter based on pi-calculus semantics. In the final step of Web process coordination, the refinement models obtained are transplanted to the software application architecture. The architecture we use is a Java runtime environment platform.

Figure 12. Business interoperation repository for control taxonomy

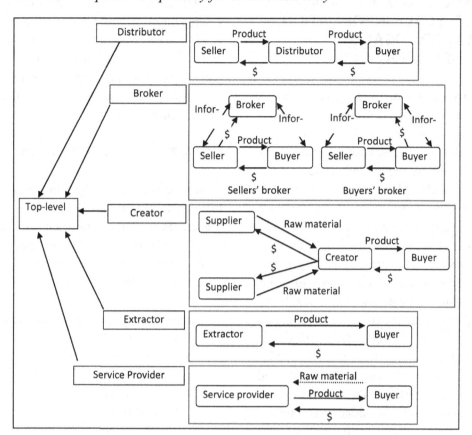

Figure 13. Service coordination architecture based on the Java runtime environment

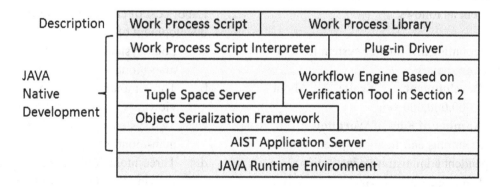

APPLICATION TO DEVELOPMENT OF LARGE-SCALE INFORMATION SYSTEMS FOR LOCAL GOVERNMENT SERVICES

The method and the framework explained in this chapter have been applied to the real development of large-scale information systems for local government services. Based on the results of (Takaki 08-B), we explain advantages of the modeling method based on workflows with BFLs of the requirements analysis for large-scale system development from the perspective of Agile software development.

In order to validate the method for requirements analysis based on workflows with business form lifecycles, which we abbreviate to "workflows with BFLs," we report an experimental result that we obtained through requirements analysis of real large-scale information systems in 2007. One information system used workflows with BFLs, and one did not use BFLs. Both of the two information systems are supposed to have thousands or tens of thousands of users, and they are developed based on open source software developments.

Two System Developments

We explain the two information systems used in the experiment as follows:

- **N:** Accounting and finance system for a local government:
  - **Development Scale:** About 1,000,000,000 yen[2]
  - **Number of Files of Workflows:** 120.
- **T:** Accounting and finance system for an independent administrative institution:
  - **Development Scale:** About 850,000,000 yen.
  - **Number of Files of Workflows:** 187.

Our framework was used in the system development of N, while it was not used in that of T. Both N and T are large-scale information systems. Although their scales cannot be compared precisely, one would be able to consider that they are similar from the viewpoint of their system development costs.

Comparison of Labor Costs

As the main comparison criterion, we deal with labor costs of composing workflows in N and T. We are particularly concerned with the people who composed the workflows, and the time it took to compose them. We show the labor costs of composing wo rkflows as follows.

1. Labor cost of composing workflows in the development of N
   a. Two office workers (Total of 12 man-months)
   b. Five months for composing (As Is) workflows.
   c. One month for reviewing workflows above.
   d. Two system engineers (Total of 2 man-months)
   e. One month for reviewing the above workflows.
2. Labor cost of composing workflows in the development of T
   a. Four system engineers (Total of 12 man-months)
   b. Three months for composing and reviewing (To Be) workflows.
   c. Two system administrators (Total of 6 man-months)
   d. Three months for composing and reviewing the above workflows.

An interesting point is that the main designers of the workflows in the case of N were government office workers who actually worked with the information system. Since they did not have any knowledge of workflow composition, a software engineering researcher taught them how to compose workflows with BFLs. Before composing the above As-Is workflows, they practiced composing workflows with BFLs for about one month, while carrying out their primary tasks. In the beginning, they often composed workflows with many defects. However, the practice workflows enabled them to modify such defects, and they progressed to compose workflows with few defects. Moreover, since they could clearly recognize the flows of business forms in workflows with BFLs, they often noticed defects in the lifecycles of business forms before checking them using the verification tool. In contrast, professional system engineers and administrators composed workflows in the requirements analysis of the development of T.

Although it was difficult to compare the labor costs of composing workflows, we confirmed that office workers who composed workflows with BFLs in the development of N, produced about the same level of describing workflows on workflows as that produced by professional system engineers and administrators in development of T. Therefore, the method based on workflows with BFLs is certainly helpful in enabling office workers—who use information systems well but are not familiar with system development—to analyze jobs with information systems as competently as professional system engineers.

From the perspective of agile software development, the above result has a greater significance than the problem of labor costs. In the case of N, the office workers functioned as designers of business process models to directly compose workflows. This learning experience helped them to understand more deeply the specifications of the information system and what they wanted from the system. The office workers also came to understand the issues developers faced, and they shared what should have been made clear in the requirements analysis. Therefore, user-centered requirements analysis stimulates both

users and developers of the information system to collaborate in its design. The result shows that workflows assist in realizing user-centered requirements analysis.

Workflows with BFLs, which are described based on event-flows, are easy for office workers to deal with, since they are familiar with the idea of event-flows. Moreover, they can verify that a user can easily obtain the output of the system through the event-flows in a workflow with BFLs by checking the correctness of the lifecycles of business forms described therein. A workflow with BFLs may be easily composed and its correctness preserved. Therefore, workflows with BFLs are useful for users to directly model their business process and collaborate with developers in requirements analysis for information systems.

RELATED WORK

Many workflow languages have been developed, such as BPEL4WS (BPEL) (Andrews, 2003), XPDL (WfMC, 2002) and YAWL (van der Aalst, 2005). There have been also systems that help create business process models. For example, in [Koschmider 11] the authors have presented a modeling support system suggesting users process models related to them based on users' profiles. Our workflow language has been developed to describe human workflows, and the main feature of our workflow is that one can easily describe and understand life cycles of business forms in workflows. In the last subsection of Section 2, we also give a brief explanation of a tool (Takaki, 2008A; Takaki, 2008B) that helps describe the workflows in the workflow language proposed in this chapter.

There have been several investigations of document-centric workflows such as (Botha, 2001; Dourish, 2000; Krishnan, 2001; Wang, 2005). However, our definition of consistency of business form life cycles in a workflow diagram, which is based on instances of the workflow diagram, is very clear, and AWDE can verify consistency of structure and business form life cycles over a workflow diagram rigorously, at least when the workflow diagram is acyclic. Moreover, our language makes it easy for workflow designers to describe what business form is used in an event described in a workflow. Compared with other verification tools, AWDE can verify new properties of workflow diagrams, that is, it verifies correctness and consistency of business form life cycles in a workflow diagram.

The Use case Responsibility Driven Analysis and Design methodology (URDAD) is a service-oriented analysis and designing methodology (Solms, 2010; 2011). From service requirements, URDAD can generate a technology neutral UML-based model in a language consists of process, contract, core and constraint. The authors focus their attention on quality of modeling language from the viewpoints of completeness, consistency and complexity and they aim to increase agility of URDAD at a high level of abstraction. They also design URDAD based on semi-formal method, by balancing the quality of models and costs of modeling. URDAD and the modeling method in this chapter have strong similarity in the respects of balancing formality and understandability. On the other hand, our modeling method avoids using UML because of easily understandability for users of information systems, and hence, our method can be considered to relatively value understandability, compared with URDAD.

CONCLUSION AND PROSPECTUS

This chapter introduces a modeling method by using workflows with BFLs (Business Form Lifecycles), and a framework based on Web-process architectures, which consist of three major layers. Verifying correctness of the BFLs of a workflow helps not only professional designers but also users of the information system check validity of

the workflow. The modeling method makes possible the development of large-scale information systems based on collaboration among the stakeholders, since they can obtain a clear consensus about business processes. On the other hand, the development framework based on Web-process architectures enables rapid spiral development through short-term cycles, since stakeholders can share the same framework of descriptions and systems. From the viewpoint of SOA, the modeling method and the development framework also assist developers to select, to adjust and to combine system components to develop an information system by collaborating with users.

This chapter also discusses an example comparing requirement analyses for two large-scale information systems. Results show that the modeling method helps users of information systems to model business processes on their own initiative, which implies that the method is useful not only for user-centered requirements analysis, but also for the collaboration of users and developers in the development of information systems.

Future work will focus on a method to model services based more closely on their objectives. While the novel method discussed in this chapter models services based on event-flows, it also represents services in terms of ontologies of business tasks and constraints on business forms plus relationships among them. The method is yet to be improved to support more declarative models which minimize the stipulation of business processes and highlight service objectives and shared values so that stakeholders will be better able to collaborate and communicate more clearly aiming at mutual benefits.

ACKNOWLEDGMENT

The authors would like to thank the reviewers for their many helpful advices.

REFERENCES

van der Aalst, W. M. P. (1997). Verification of workflow nets. In *Application and Theory of Petri Nets, LNCS 1248,* (pp. 407-426). Springer.

van derAalst, W. M. P. (1998). The application of petri nets to workflow management. *The Journal of Circuits. Systems and Computers, 8*(1), 21–66.

van der Aalst, W. M. P., Hirnschall, A., & Verbeek, H. M. W. (2002). An alternative way to analyze workflow graphs. In *Proceedings of the 14th International Conference on Advanced Information Systems Engineering (CAiSE), LNCS 2348,* (pp. 535-552). Springer.

van derAalst, W. M. P., & Hofstede, A. H. M. (2005). YAWL: Yet another workflow language. *Information Systems, 30*(4), 245–275. doi:10.1016/j.is.2004.02.002

Aho, A. V., Lam, M. S., Sethi, R., & Ullman, J. D. (2006). *Compilers: Principles, techniques, and tools* (2nd ed.). Prentice Hall.

Andrews, T., Curbera, F., Dholakia, H., Goland, Y., Klein, J., & Leymann, F. … Weerawarana, S. (2003). *Business process execution language for Web services, version 1.1.* Technical report, BEA Systems, International Business Machines Corporation, Microsoft Corporation.

Boehm, B., & Turner, R. (2004). *Balancing agility and discipline: A guide for the perplexed.* Addison-Wesley. doi:10.1007/978-3-540-24675-6_1

Botha, R. A., & Eloff, J. H. P. (2001). Access control in document-centric workflow systems an agent-based approach. *Computers & Security, 20*(6), 525–532. doi:10.1016/S0167-4048(01)00613-7

Cohn, M. (2005). *Agile estimating and planning.* Prentice Hall.

Dourish, P., Edwards, K. K., Lamarca, A., Lamping, J., Petersen, K., & Salisbury, M. (2000). Extending document management systems with user-specific active properties. *ACM Transactions on Information Systems, 18*(2), 140–170. doi:10.1145/348751.348758

Erdogmus, H. (2003). Let's scale agile up. *Agile Times, 2*(1), 6–7.

Fellbaum, C. (Ed.). (1998). *WordNet.* Cambridge, MA: MIT Press.

Highsmith, J., et al. (2001), *Manifesto for agile software development.* Retrieved from http://agilemanifesto.org/

Izumi, N., Takaki, O., & Hasida, K. (2009). Service system development based on web process ontology. *Proceedings of the 4th International Conference on Software Engineering Advances (ICSEA 2009),* (pp. 222-228). IEEE Computer Society Press.

Izumi, N., & Yamaguchi, T. (2002). Integration of heterogeneous repositories based on ontologies for EC applications development. *International Journal of Electronic Commerce Research and Applications, 1*(1), 77–91. doi:10.1016/S1567-4223(02)00007-8

Koschmider, A., Hornungb, T., & Oberweis, A. (2011). Recommendation-based editor for business process modeling. *Data & Knowledge Engineering, 70*(6), 483–503. doi:10.1016/j.datak.2011.02.002

Krishnan, R., Munaga, L., & Karlapalem, K. (2002). XDoC-WFMS: A framework for document centric workflow management system. [Springer.]. *Conceptual Modeling for New Information Systems Technologies, LNCS, 2465,* 348–362. doi:10.1007/3-540-46140-X_27

Sadiq, W., & Orlowska, M. E. (2000). Analyzing process models using graph reduction techniques. *Information Systems*, *25*(2), 117–134. doi:10.1016/S0306-4379(00)00012-0

Social Intelligence Technology Research Laboratory (SITR). (n.d.). *Outline of AIST-framework.* Retrieved from http://www.sitr.jp/index/activities/aistfw

Solms, F., Gruner, S., & Edwards, C. (2011). *URDAD as quality-driven process.* 10th International Conference on Intelligent Software Methodologies, Tools, and Techniques (SOMET 2011).

Solms, F., & Loubser, D. (2010). URDAD as a semi-formal approach to analysis and design. *Innovations in Systems and Software Engineering*, *6*(1-2), 155–162. doi:10.1007/s11334-009-0113-4

Stephens, M., & Rosenberg, D. (2003). *Extreme programming refactored: The case against XP.* APress.

Studer, R., & Benjamins, V. R., & Fensell, D. (1998). Knowledge engineering: Principles and methods. *Data & Knowledge Engineering*, *25*, 161–197. doi:10.1016/S0169-023X(97)00056-6

Takaki, O., Seino, T., Takeuti, I., Izumi, N., & Takahashi, K. (2008). Verification of evidence life cycles in workflow diagrams with passback flows. *International Journal on Advances in Software*, *1*(1), 14–25.

Takaki, O., Seino, T., Takeuti, I., Izumi, N., & Takahashi, K. (2008). Workflow diagrams based on evidence life cycles. *Proceedings of the 8th Joint Conference on Knowledge - Based Software Engineering 2008 (JCKBSE 2008), Frontiers in Artificial Intelligence and Applications*, (pp. 145-154). IOS Press.

Takaki, O., Takeuti, I., Izumi, N., & Hasida, K. (2010). Syntax and semantics of workflows that include passbacks. *Proceedings of the 5th International Conference on Software Engineering Advances (ICSEA 2010)*, (pp. 169-177). IEEE Computer Society Press.

Takaki, O., Takeuti, I., Seino, T., Izumi, N., & Takahashi, K. (2009). Incremental verification of consistency properties of large-scale workflows from the perspectives of control flow and evidence life cycles. *International Journal on Advances in Software*, *2*(1), 145–159.

The MIT process handbook project. (n.d.). Retrieved form http://ccs.mit.edu/ph/

The National Institute of Advanced Industrial Science and Technology (AIST). (2006). *AIST has embarked developments of large scale information systems without vendors' locks-on (in Japanese).* Retrieved from http://www.aist.go.jp/aist_j/press_release/pr2006/pr20061219/pr20061219.html

Wang, J., & Kumar, A. (2005). A framework for document-driven workflow systems. *Proceeding of 3rd International Conference on Business Process Management (BPM), LNCS 3649*, (pp. 285–301). Springer.

Workflow Management Coalition (WfMC). (2002). *Workflow standard: Workflow process definition interface - XML process definition language (XPDL). (WfMC-TC-1025).* Lighthouse Point, Florida, USA: Technical Report, Workflow Management Coalition.

KEY TERMS AND DEFINITIONS

Business Form Lifecycles: A series of states of a business form that represent how to compose, refer to, re-write, judge, store, pass, or dump the business form.

Business Process Model: A model describing how to perform a service, where the service denotes what an organization provides to its customers such as a medical service and a government service.

EA: Abbreviation of Enterprise Architecture, which denotes a methodology to standardize business processes and information systems for huge enterprises such as big company and government, in order to optimizing and efficiently managing the organizations.

Formal Method: A methodology to resolve problems by using approaches based on mathematical science.

Ontology: An explicit specification of conceptualization. It can be regarded as a framework to collect proper concepts and to construct definitions of them to accomplish a certain purpose.

Petri Net: A type of transition systems, which is described by a finite directed graph and tokens. Petri Nets are often used to describe process models or to make semantics of process models.

UDDI: An abbreviation of Universal Description, Discovery and Integration, which denotes a retrieval system for web services.

User-Centered Requirements Analysis: A requirements analysis where users have the initiative.

Web-Process Architecture: A three layered architecture describing business-task level, subtask-flow level and page-transition level. This architecture differs from a Web Service based architecture in SOA.

Workflow: A diagram describing business processes or a business process model. By using a workflow, one can describe a process to perform a service. Usually, a workflow is identified with a business model. Write, judge, store, pass, or dump the business form.

WSDL: An abbreviation of Web Services Description Language, which denotes a language to describe web services or a generic name of a definition file that is described in the language.

ENDNOTES

[1]   Though medicines should not be regarded as business forms, this chapter treats some products such as medicines as business forms.

[2]   One yen was nearly equivalent to 1/160 euro as of April 2007.

Chapter 8
Service Science:
Exploring Complex Agile Service Networks through Organisational Network Analysis

Noel Carroll
University of Limerick, Ireland

Ita Richardson
University of Limerick, Ireland

Eoin Whelan
National University of Ireland Galway, Ireland

ABSTRACT

The discipline of service science encourages the need to develop alternative and more scientific approaches to conceptualise modern service network environments. This chapter identifies the opportunity to apply organisational network analysis (ONA) as a novel approach to model agile service interaction. ONA also supports the visualisation of a service infrastructure which sustains agile practice. The objective of this chapter is to demonstrate how the concept of agile service network (ASN) may be examined through an unconventional method to model service operations. ONA demonstrates the exchange of resources and competencies through an ASN infrastructure. Ultimately, this chapter provides a platform to develop an audit framework with associated metrics borrowed from ONA. ONA concepts offer a new analytical approach towards ASN (for example, structural, composition, behavioural, and functional). This has a significant theoretical contribution for software engineering performance.

DOI: 10.4018/978-1-4666-2503-7.ch008

1. INTRODUCTION

Promoting software engineering methodologies is one of the key challenges for Ireland, yet a vital one to sustain our economic competitiveness (Ryan, 2008). Agile software engineering is a methodology which continues to gain increasing levels of academic and industrial attention. Agile software development is a collaborative approach which supports iterative and incremental methods within software engineering teams (Abrahamsson et al. 2003). The key factors which foster the value of agile software development include human interactions, developing improved software solutions, customer collaborations, and responding to change (Beck et al. 2001). Thus, the composition and organisation of agile teams has a direct influence on the functionality of agile software development. While the software industry is currently undergoing a fundamental change with the transition to agile and lean methods, there is a lack of integrated research efforts towards understanding the dynamics of agile and lean methods in an effort to optimise agile capabilities (for example, Vidgen and Wang, 2009). One of the key issues within agile software is understanding how the dynamics of team collaboration impacts on service performance. The aim of this chapter is to demonstrate how we can apply organisational network analysis (ONA) as an agile software engineering modelling method which improves the visualisation of team dynamics. This will allow managers to monitor the impact of service relational structures on performance through a service network performance analytics framework (Carroll et al. 2010). The output of employing ONA is to develop a theoretical and practical approach to monitor and measure how collaborative efforts across teams can be structured to optimise agile software development outcomes. This chapter provides a theoretical foundation to develop an audit framework with associated metrics of agile practice. This research is also grounded in the emergence of service science developments to examine value co-creation across agile teams.

2. SERVICE SCIENCE

Agility has become an important service strategy to respond to the dynamic business environment. Defined by van Oosterhout et al. (2007), agility is "an innovative response to an unpredictable change". It is concerned with taking greater "control" of unpredictable changes. Therefore, the design, management and delivery of complex service systems suggest that we need to develop a scientific understanding regarding the configuration of resources to deliver service excellence. In order to extend our understanding on service delivery, particularly within an agile environment, there is a need to establish alternative methods to examine service formation and the value propositions which connects them. Within the service-dominant environment (Normann, 2001; Vargo and Lusch, 2008), organisations are faced with increasing challenges to develop their capabilities in complex service models (Vargo et al. 2008). The emergence of "service science" as a discipline in recent years confirms the fundamental change which continues to alter the nature and application of technology within business environments. Service science is an attempt to understand the complex nature of service systems and acts as an interdisciplinary umbrella which incorporates widely diverse disciplines to construct, manage, analyse and evolve service systems (Spohrer et al, 2007). This suggests that we need a more systematic, analytical, and overarching approach to examine service co-production operations to generate knowledge regarding the overlap between the social, business, and technology factors within a service environment (i.e. bridging service management and service computing). As services become more "open", collaborative, flexible, agile, and adaptive, there are greater pressures on business to reconfigure and meet change through strategic realignments (Carroll et al., 2010). In doing so, managers should develop an understanding as to how this impacts the "value" of the service system. A service system comprises of a provider(s) and a client(s) who collaborate to deliver (i.e. co-create) and benefit from a service (Vargo et al. 2008). A service system may be defined as (IfM and IBM, 2007; p. 5):

...a dynamic value co-creating configuration or resources, including people, technology, organisations and shared information (language, laws, measures and methods), all connected internally and externally by value propositions, with the aim to consistently and profitably meet the customer's needs better than competing alternatives.

The environment in which the configuration of resources is achieved is described as a service network. A service network comprises of clear linkages which define the service structure and interactions in which it co-ordinates its tasks to achieve a certain business objective. Since it accounts for the collective effort of all service interactions to generate and realise value, co-creation is an important concept within a service network. Merging the concept of agility and co-creation together derives the concept of service networks.

2.1 Service Networks

Nowadays, through the affordance of technology, services are becoming part of a networked service environment (Carroll et al. 2010), for example, agile project management. While the literature suggests that although there are many benefits from the use of agile methods to develop service networks, there appears to be a lack of research developments on agile practice in management theory (e.g. Abrahamsson et al, 2009; Conboy, 2009). Thus, our focus here is to provide an analytical lens to examine the underlying agile service infrastructure. We envisage that this will support managers' ability to examine the service network and how its interactions align with project management activities. As we argue in this chapter, it is extremely difficult to manage and

orchestrate an intangible asset, i.e., a service, and reconfigure an "invisible" service infrastructure. It is increasingly important that managers gain a scientific understanding of the service environment to optimise service operations and examine innovative strategies to evolve the service (Spohrer et al. 2007; Chesbrough, 2011). In today's service-dominant world, a service is typically part of a network which supports the co-creation of service value. Value is created through the complex and intertwining nature of services. This draws our attention to the notion of "service as a network", where a service relies on collaboration through continuous interaction executed by people, software, and service logic (see Figure 1), for example, an agile software engineering team.

The nine service relationships of an ASN illustrated in Figure 1 may be categorised as follows (Zhao et al., 2008):

1. Organisation to people;
2. Organisation to software;
3. Organisation to organisation;
4. People to organisation;
5. People to software;
6. People to people;
7. Software to organisation;
8. Software to people;
9. Software to software.

As illustrated, service computing is largely concerned with organisational and software components, while service management is mainly concerned with organisational and people components. However, both service computing and management are required to successfully deliver a service. This figure also shows the unification of these broad concepts which makes communication between service engineers and managers more effective as they are aligned with service technological initiatives. Such initiatives are central to the emergence of ASN.

Figure 1. The service network (adapted from Zhao et al., 2008)

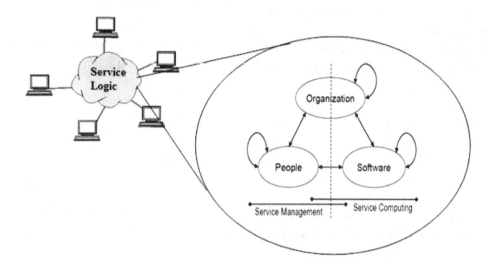

2.2 The Concept of Agile Service Networks

Nowadays, service networks are forced to adapt their processes at a much faster pace than before. In addition, managers must also be proactive, reactive and more decisive at a faster rate than ever before. Thus, agility requires an efficient communication system to support decision-making tasks while understanding the value of the relational infrastructure of a service network. Agile practices rely on flexibility to address novel software engineering approaches, and on technologies while adapting to the service environment. In this sense, people enable the co-creation and co-production of an ASN. ASNs are networks which foster collaborative service interactions across agile teams or business applications. What is of importance here is the relational structure which stabilises the ASN, often through the reconfiguration of actors and resources. ASNs may be described as emergent and dynamic service networks which provide some form of business value by reacting to change. This suggests that ASNs are spontaneous in nature and rely on business partners' collaborative strengths to deliver service value as a network.

Thus, an ASN relies on continuous interactions and exchanges to support the co-evolution of the service environment through the mobilisation of business processes (Carroll et al. 2010).

Agility within a service network is the collective ability to adapt rapidly, be as cost efficient and economical as possible, without jeopardising the quality of the product or service. Identifying changes within business processes is critical for either preventing or encouraging certain agile practice workflows. An ASN comprises of large numbers of long-running, highly dynamic complex end-to-end service interactions reflecting asynchronous message flows that typically transcend several organisations and span geographical locations (Mancioppi et al. 2008; Dubois, 2008; van den Heuvel et al. 2009). However, what is apparent across literature is that there is a significant void in understanding how the underlying relational infrastructure of service networks impacts or influences service operations and performance (Carroll et al. 2010). Kawalek and Greenwood (2000), describes an abstract model of the organisation, and how one can develop an understanding of "value" through the addition of three models when applied to a service network:

1. **A Model of the System:** A high level, structural view of actor interactions (who and/or what interacts);
2. **A Model of Goals:** Having identified patterns of interaction in the model, how can we describe the interactions (why do they take place);
3. **A Model of Methods:** Having identified what interacts and why, a model is developed to determine why and how goals are achieved.

These models also complement our understanding of ASN. Carroll et al. (2010) suggests that we should add two additional steps (Figure 2). A fourth step, from a service network perspective, is to implement a "model of action", i.e. a model which would allow us to explore service strategic possibilities to simulate a "what-if" approach to understanding the influence of each relationship across service processes. A fifth step would include a "model of evaluation" which introduces service performance analytics to learn how interactions and ASN innovations influence performance.

We propose that while adopting this view of ASN, we can gain a better understanding of the dynamic nature of an agile environment. There is continued interest in researchers' ability to bridge the fields of service management and service computing and explore how both fields may support business relationships across service processes (for example, Zhoa et al. 2008). Thus, it is important that managers explore "how" service networks maintain the ability to adjust relational structures within a service system to meet customer demands. In addition, network dynamics plays a central role in monitoring agile activities and allowing the service system to learn and reconfigure operations for further tasks to take advantage of future opportunities. Service science highlights the need to theorise the "modern" concept of service on a scientific level (Vargo and Lusch, 2008). The nature of service activities involve negotiated and often co-created

Figure 2. Abstract view of service network analysis (Carroll et al. 2010)

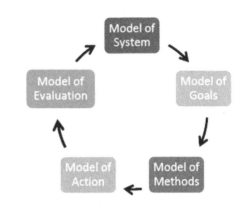

exchanges between a provider and a client in the provision of largely intangible assets, as well as the collective coordination and integration of knowledge in service delivery (Vargo et al. 2008). We need to understand service business models and service value for the organisation within the 21st century IT-enabled service economy. Service value, in this case, refers to "the adaptability and survivability of the beneficiary system" (Vargo et al., 2008, p.148) creating "opportunities for reinvestment and cross-subsidisation of activities that may potentially benefit people not involved in the original transaction" (Auerswald, 2009, p.53). ASN shares a similar logic and we introduce the need to model the dynamic ASN environment.

3. RESEARCH JUSTIFICATION

Information exchanges are a vital resource to support decision-making within agile software service teams (Abrahamsson et al. 2003). In short, there is a need for more sophisticated methods in data management and usage by agile software development teams to facilitate higher quality decision-making (Abrahamsson et al. 2003; Vidgen and Wang, 2009; Conboy and Morgan, 2011). We address this gap by introducing a novel method which assists teams through targeted and focused decision support mechanisms by mapping service behaviour. Supporting service actions through cross-organisational organisations and teams may be described through ASN. ASN rely on message flows that typically transcend several organisations and span geographical locations (Mancioppi et al. 2008; Dubois, 2008; van den Heuvel et al. 2009). However, understanding how information is disseminated across teams and geographical locations is considered problematic, especially across agile service developments (Bruegge et al. 2006). From a management perspective it would be more practical to understand the service characteristics (Chesbrough, 2011), such as structural, compositional, and behaviour to identify (Carroll et al. 2010). For example, it would be useful to identify where bottlenecks exist or where structural holes exist across the network. Agility has therefore become an important service factor to respond to the dynamic business environment particularly to sustain innovation within the software industry. The design, management and delivery of complex service systems suggest that we need to develop a scientific understanding regarding the configuration of resources to deliver service excellence. In order to extend our understanding on service delivery, particularly within an agile environment, there is a need to establish alternative methods to examine service formation and the value propositions which connects them.

4. ORGANISATIONAL NETWORK ANALYSIS

Organisational network analysis (ONA) has been used since the mid-1930s to advance research efforts in social and behavioural sciences (Wasserman et al. 2005). In the 1980's and 1990's, ONA was employed to examine more "technical" characteristics of networks including, "reciprocity, structural balance, transitivity, clusterability, and structural equivalence" (Wasserman et al.

2005). ONA developments stem from the network science and social science disciplines. Lewis (2009) defines network science as the study of the theoretical foundations of network structure/dynamic behaviour and its application to many subfields, such as ONA. In addition, to incorporate the dynamic nature of networks, one must avail of the information which informs us how the service interaction results in a specific outcome. Using ONA, we can define the structure of a system in terms of vertices (nodes) and edges (links) to represent a "real world" environment. In addition, Lewis (2009) suggests that the best way to describe a network is by what it does, i.e. "the study of the structure of the collection of nodes and the links that represent something real", and the "study of dynamic behaviour of the aggregation of nodes and links" (p. 6). Using ONA, we can study the exchange of resources and competencies (for example, information) among actors. We can identify patterns of relations among nodes such as people, groups, organisations, or information systems and visualise the value of ties and relationships between each node. Consequently, OSA provides us with an approach to detect, describe, and analyse relationships which support ASN. Another benefit of ONA is its ability to provide a methodology to gain deeper insight of how structural regularities influence behaviour. Structures may be altered to optimise service network outcomes. Therefore, ONA is a very fitting technique to deploy to uncover more "truths" as to ASN activities, interaction, and exchanges.

ONA focuses on pairs or groups of individuals who share some kind of relational tie such as within ASN. ONA typically begins with one specific community and examines the relational infrastructure which stabilises the network, for example, an organisation. Adopting ONA is a significant contribution within the agile research domain. There are many difficulties in modelling the intertwining complexity and dynamic service configuration (IfM and IBM, 2008) of people, knowledge, activities, interactions, and decisions which create and deliver value. This presents a starting point upon which this research explores how to model an ASN and supports how we describe an ASN as "the exchange of resources or competencies". There is a large body of literature which suggests that ONA can present us with a unique method to model and monitor the dynamics of ASN (for example, Berkowitz, 1982; Wellman and Berkowitz, 1988; Scott, 1991; Wasserman and Faust, 1994; Tichy, et al., 1979; Hansen, 1999; Watts, 2004, Hassan, 2009; Carroll et al. 2010). It is claimed that managers have ignored the "dynamic characteristics of networks and the ways that dynamic qualities of networks affect organisations' flexibility and change" (Cross and Parker, 2004). This has unavoidably led to organisations failing to capture the "health" of their service networks dynamics and performance (for example, behavioural, functional, compositional, and structural) and the overall contributory value of service linkages (relational structures). ONA focuses on exchange patterns of relations among actors (Freeman et al., 1992) and presents an opportunity to model the relational ties between each node to model service network behaviour. To understand the dynamic nature of ASN and its impact on service performance, it is critical to explore the underlying principles in service behaviour and analyse both how and why services perform in a specific manner from the socio-technical viewpoint. This is necessary as Spohrer et al., (2007) posit that the success of service science will be achieved through the introduction of general theories of service interaction and co-creation of value. Mapping a representation of an ASN is important as managers realise that the key to continued success is within their understanding of how workflows and business processes can be optimised (e.g. Linder and Cantrell, 2000).

4.1 ONA Methodology

ONA is an approach and set of techniques which can assist us study the exchange of resources and competencies (for example, information) among actors. ONA focuses on patterns of relations among nodes such as people, groups, organisations, or information systems. ONA also demonstrates the value of ties and relationships between each node to provide a visual and mathematical representation of interaction. Mapping representation of ASN interaction is important to support the development of an audit framework with associated metrics and training materials. Therefore, ONA offers a powerful modelling technique for ASN. Marsden (2005) explains that, as a technique, ONA data collection practices throughout literature typically involve survey methods. A common method of analysis has been to use implicit or explicit snowball sampling. To develop an understanding of service networks, we had to undertake a rigorous description of the relationship patterns of the network population as the starting point of analysis. Investigating the relationships which exist within a service network is a tedious task, for example, data gathering, analysis, manipulation, and calculation using matrices to record data and represent interactions. ONA software is vital to support these tasks and to provide a visualisation which represents the relational descriptions. There are a number of software packages available to support ONA, for example, UCINET, Pajek, and NetMiner. Adopting formal methods allows us to mathematically represent the network data and learn of structural characteristics of the ASN environment. Formal methods also provide graphing rules and mathematical notation which presents further insights on network data which may not be clear in descriptive text form.

The majority of social network studies apply either "whole-network" research design where a set of interrelated actors which are considered for analytical purposes or "egocentric" research design where the focus is on a focal actor and the relationships in their loyalty (Marsden, 2005). In matrix terms, a study may examine one set of actors which are linked through one set of relationships at a specific period of time which provides a sociomatrix (i.e., one-mode data). Data which examines more than one set of relationships at various periods of time (i.e., to examine change) is described as one-mode (Wasserman and Faust, 1994). Deciding on which actors lie within the network is a difficult task for whole-network studies (Marsden, 2005). Laumann et al. (1989) list three possible approaches to adopt as network boundary specification strategies:

1. **Positional Approach:** Based on characteristics of network membership, e.g. employment;
2. **Event-Based Approach:** Participation in a certain class of activity, e.g. meeting specific goals;
3. **Relational Approach:** Based on social connectedness, e.g. social network (professional and/or friendship).

In this chapter we introduce service network analytics to model service network behavioural changes. We achieve this by monitoring the impact of change on service relational structures using ONA. For example, we can examine the cohesion of a network by examining the density and distance of relational structures. If, for example, we want to examine the impact of implementing technology on a service network, we can re-examine the relational structure post-technological implementation to determine the effect of technology on the service relational structure. We use UCINET6 to generate ONA measures, and by comparing pre- and post-IS measures, we can generate metrics to determine the impact on the service structure. As a simple example of gathering data, and examining an ASN, the next section provides an overview of the main concepts which support ASN.

4.2 Analysing ASN: Main Concepts

The major characteristics of ASN analysis are that the unit of analysis to describe the behaviour of the ASN is the network which unites actors (person, group, organisation, etc.) and its variables (i.e. values associated with interaction). Normann

(2001) suggests that co-ordinating efforts by different actors towards a common whole is not new, for example, he explains how economics describes the logic leading to complementary specialisation as that of "competitive advantage". However, Normann (2001) adds that what is new is the way it now expresses itself in terms of role patterns and modes of interactivity and organically reshapes co-productive roles and patterns. This is true in the case of ASN. Therefore, understanding the main principles of network structures is critical towards our quest to model ASN. We apply Lewis's (Lewis, 2009; p. 20-21) list of the key characteristics of network science which are applicable in ASN (see Table 1).

An analysis of ASN may be simply described as an x-ray of a service network structure which highlights the importance of relational structures to support service performance. According to Tichy et al., (1979), network analysis is concerned with the structure and pattern of these relationships and seeks to identify both their causes and consequences. Therefore, an ASN can be viewed on an abstract level as social groupings with relatively stable patterns of interactions over time. ONA allows us to explore techniques to model the system relational structures though a coherent framework and methods of analysis which capture both emergent process patterns between a specific set of linkages and their properties among a defined set of actors. Tichy et al. (1979) provides an overview of network concepts and network properties as listed in Table 2.

The transactional content explores what is exchanged by actors (e.g. information) during the formation and evolution of the ASN. The nature of the links considers the strength and qualitative nature of the relation between two or more nodes, while the structural characteristics examine the overall pattern of relationships between the actors. For example, clustering, network density, and special nodes on the network are all structural characteristics. Watts and Strogatz (1998) report that real-world networks are neither completely

Table 1. General principles of an ASN

Characteristic	Description
Structure	A collection of nodes and links that have a distinct format or topology which suggests that function follows form.
Emergence	Network properties are emergent as a consequence of a dynamic network achieving stability.
Dynamism	Dynamic behaviour is often the result of emergence or a series of small evolutionary steps leading to a fixed-point final state of the system.
Autonomy	A network forms by the autonomous and spontaneous action of interdependent nodes that "volunteer" to come together (link), rather than central control or central planning.
Bottom-Up Evolution	Networks grow for the bottom or local level up to the top or global level. They are not designed and implemented from the top down.
Topology	The architecture or topology of a network is a property that emerges over time as a consequence of distributed – and often subtle – forces or autonomous behaviours of its nodes.
Power	The power of a node is proportional to its degree (number of link connecting to the network), influence (link values), and betweenness or closeness; the power of a network is proportional to the number and strengths of its nodes and links.
Stability	A dynamic network is stable if the rate of change in the state of its nodes/links or its topology either diminishes as time passes or is bounded by dampened alternations within finite limits.

Table 2. ONA properties

Property	Explanation
Transactional	
Transactional Content	Four types of exchanges: 1. Expression of effect (e.g. initiate a transaction) 2. Influence attempt (e.g. negotiating a SLA) 3. Exchange of information (e.g. terms and conditions) 4. Exchange of goods and services (e.g. payment)
Nature of Links	
Intensity	The strength of the relations between individuals (i.e. intensity of service interactions)
Reciprocity	The degree to which a relation is commonly perceived and agreed on by all parties to the relation (i.e. the degree of symmetry)
Clarity of Expression	The degree to which every pair of individuals has clearly defined expectations about each other's behaviour in the relation, i.e. they agree about appropriate behaviour between one another (i.e. SLA)
Multiplexity	The degree to which pairs of individuals are linked by multiple relations. Multiple roles of each member (e.g. consumer, supplier, negotiator, etc) and identifies how individuals are linked by multiple roles (the more roles, the stronger the link).
Structural Characteristics	
Size	The number of individuals participating in the network (i.e. service eco-system)
Density (Correctedness)	The number of actual links in the network as a ratio of the number of possible links
Clustering	The number of dense regions in the network (i.e. network positioning, structural holes)
Openness	The number of actual external links of a social unit as a ratio of the number possible external links
Stability	The degree to which a network pattern changes over time (i.e. level of innovation)
Reachability	The average number of links between any two individuals in the network.
Centrality	The degree to which relations are guided by the formal hierarchy
Star	The service with the highest number of nominations
Liaison	A service which is not a member of a cluster but links two or more clusters
Bridge	A service which is a member of multiple clusters in the network (linking pin)
Gatekeeper	A star who also links the social unit with external domains (i.e. knowledge diffusion and service network analyst)
Isolate	A service which has uncoupled from the network.

Table 3. Example of employing ONA as service network analytics

Metric	Explanation of it Measure
Betweenness	Examines the connectivity of node between two other nodes in a network and determines the number of actors a particular node connects other nodes indirectly.
Bridge	Is the link which, if it was removed, it would move the nodes to an alternative structural position in the sociogram/graph.
Centrality	Provides an indication of the 'power' of actors based on their overall connection with other actors.
Centralisation	Identifies the difference between all of links for each nodes divided by maximum available links.
Closeness	Determines how resources may flow from one actor to another, i.e. it measures how close actors are to one another in a network.
Clustering coefficient	Examines the likelihood that two associates of an actor are associates themselves. The higher the value the greater the clique.
Cohesion	Measures the degree to which actors are connected to one another, for example, the strength of cliques.
Degree	Counts the number of ties to other actors across a network.
Eigenvector centrality	Measures the importance of actors within a network based on their connectivity.
Path length	Measures the distance between two nodes in the network.
Radiality	Examines the degree of an actors 'reach' into the network which is informs and influences.
Reach	Measures the degree in which an actor within the network can reach another actor in the network.
Structural equivalence	Examine which nodes have a common set of link connections to other actors within the network.
Structural hole	Identifies network holes which may be strategically filled by connecting one or more actors. This may, for example, improve communication within a network.

ordered nor completely random, but rather exhibit properties of both. In addition, they claim that the structure of network can have dramatic implications for the collective dynamics of a system, whose connectivity the network represents, and that large changes in dynamic behaviour could be driven by even subtle modifications to the network structure. Therefore the orchestration of structural relations (emergent property of the connection, the exchange process) or attributes (intrinsic characteristics, e.g. value of an exchange) becomes a central concept to analyse an ASN structural properties. ONA assumes that actors are interconnected, with real consequences for behaviour and performance. Thus, structures may be altered to optimise the networks outcomes which present an opportunity to model service network analytics (i.e., offers us a blueprint of ASN).

Table 3 summarises how we can borrow ONA concepts as service metrics to examine ASN. In the next section, we examine some of these to demonstrate how they may be applied in an ASN scenario.

5. ASN SCENARIO

This scenario examines the impact of service technology on the relational infrastructure of a service network. In our research, we examine how we could develop an audit framework with associated metrics and training materials which will have significant contributions towards software engineering performance. A fictitious agile organisation, Agile Inc., wishes to examine their ASN in the hope to gain a better understanding of the relational structure which supports their agile activities. Agile Inc. are interested in learning about ASN characteristics (as listed in Tables 1 and 2) in order to gain a deeper understanding of how their agile practice performance may be improved. They also want to examine how technological innovation may influence their service structure and consequently, team performance. The organisation wishes to foster an interactive agile environment between the international software engineering teams and is interested in learning how agile leaders across an international service network interact with other team leaders across the team. Management are particularly interested in understanding the exchange of resources and competencies among actors. This scenario demonstrates how the organisation can examine how performance is influenced by the relational structure of the agile team.

6. MAPPING THE ASN

An ASN typically comprises of numerous entities in the form of organisations, groups, or teams. The actors distributed across Agile Inc. are represented as nodes within a network. Between each node, interaction is facilitated by the exchange of resources and/or competencies in various agile practices. The organisational headquarters is represented by the yellow node (see Figure 3). The exchanges between nodes are represented as edges or links within the graph. This links are vital as they represent the value of the relational infrastructure which supports the co-creation of service "value". It is critical to understand that each node in the network is not fixed, but rather, represents its position within a given time (i.e. a snapshot). Interaction involves at least two

nodes within any exchange which represents their reaction to specific business processes. These exchanges may comprise of a number of factors, for example, knowledge diffusion through various ASN partners in a decision-making problem. Modelling the ASN may highlight who is the greatest influence, who emerges as a leader within the ASN, or where "structural holes" exist across the network. Therefore, ONA concepts and measures (Table 3) allow us to examine the relational structure of the ASN to uncover truths of service interactions (i.e. compare the differences between Figures 3 and 4). For the purpose of this study, we provide an abstract representation of the ASN. Node identifications have been removed from both Figures 3 and 4 as this example scenario is employed for demonstrative purposes.

Figure 3 illustrates the relational structure of ten main agile teams which interact on a regular basis during various software engineering practices. These teams are dispersed across Europe in various locations, all of which are linked to the headquarters office (i.e. yellow node). The yellow node illustrates the position of the organisational headquarters and the blue nodes represent the managers of each organisation while the red nodes

Figure 3. ONA map of ASN (before IT-innovation)

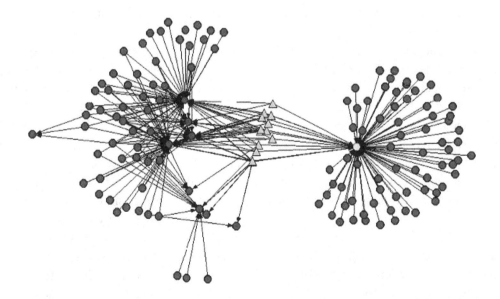

Figure 4. ONA map of ASN (after Web-based system)

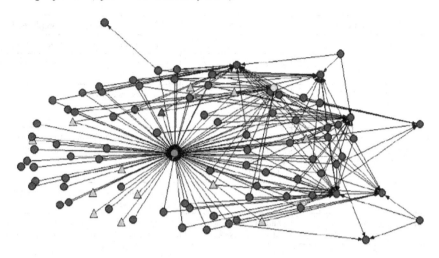

represent the software developers. The links illustrate the connection or relationship each actor has with other team members within the environment. This data may be gathered through the distribution of a survey to all staff members within this ASN. Each staff member may be asked to indicate their level of interaction with employees across the ASN for various tasks.

Upon further inspection, Agile Inc. notices that there is a lack of network cohesion across the ASN. They suspect that this may hamper agile practices, for example, it becomes more difficult to transmit information which threatens service quality. As a result, this can have a negative impact on their service reputation. Ultimately, this prevents them from optimising performance. The organisation also identify that there are 13 nodes (triangle nodes) which appear to be dominant within the centre of the network as they occupy a powerful position. This would be known as a bridge or a broker between service providers. Agile Inc. are considering innovative methods to centralise agile practice through a more united application of agile practices. They implement a central communication forum which allows actors exchange resources and competencies with other actors for agile software practices. While the implementation of service innovation is often considered to

be beneficial, the organisation wishes to employ a method which would examine how service relations have altered as a result of the service communication forum. Figure 4 demonstrates the impact of implementing service innovation technology on the service structure, highlighting how the service has become more centralised by removing service bottlenecks through the service. This approach supports the diffusion of innovation across the network and enhances the exchange of information to support decision-making tasks. In addition, one can clearly see how the headquarters has been relieved of decision-making tasks which optimise efficiency and performance of the network. The service brokers have also become more integrated in the ASN which provides greater support to various international organisations.

To examine how this change impacts on the ASN, Table 4 lists some of the ONA concepts and summarises the impact of implementing technology on a service network relational structure. This examines the impact of service technology on the relational infrastructure of the service network. It also demonstrates how ONA concepts may be introduced as service network analytics to examine change to service dynamics within an ASN and develop service network performance analytics for technological innovation.

Table 4. Examples of service network analytics metrics

Metrics	Old ASN	New ASN	Difference explained
No. of Ties	254	208	Reduced number of structural ties to deliver a service.
Density	0.061	0.072	Increased density of network making the network more connected.
Distance	Average: 1.97 Cohesion: 0.514 Fragmentation: 0.49	Average: 1.13 Cohesion: 0.73 Fragmentation: 0.28	Distance reduced as a result of technological innovation and improved the cohesiveness of the ASN.
Krackhardt GTD Measures	Connectedness: 1.00 Hierarchy: 0.00 Efficiency: 0.97 LUB[1]: 1.00	Connectedness: 1.00 Hierarchy: 0.38 Efficiency: 0.10 LUB: 0.95	The "horizontal differentiation" of the service structure have reduces to improve 'connectivity'.
Hybrid Reciprocity:	0.0031	0.00	The reciprocity of ties has reduced which suggests greater service efficiency.
Degree (Centralisation)	Outdegree: 0.54% Indegree: 25.34%	Outdegree: 5.48% Indegree: 94.88%	IT service innovation introduces greater cohesion and efficiency and is less dependent on other individuals.
Eigenvector Centrality	55.02%	8.31%	IT innovation provides more equal service structures as it adopts the central position.
Distance-Weighted Fragmentation	0.486	0.28	Reduces the distance between all nodes of a service through increased cohesion.
2-Mode Cohesion Measures	Density: 0.03 Avg Dist: 2.48 Radius: 3.00 Diameter: 4.00 Fragmenta: 0.00 Transitiv: 0.56 Norm Dist: 0.60	Density: 0.68 Avg Dist: 1.62 Radius: 2.00 Diameter: 4.00 Fragmenta:0.23 Transitiv: 0.98 Norm Dist: 1.18	Service IT innovation increases the service density, and transitivity, while it reduces the average distance, radius, diameter, fragmentation, and normalised distance across the network. Interestingly, the diameter remains the same in both networks suggesting that there was no significant impact on the actor-network boundary.

While some of the metrics we incorporate to examine the impact of technological innovation on ASN are listed in Table 4, we can also incorporate the use of key performance indicators in agile software development through predefined service performance targets. These are ONA measures which are employed in the context of ASN metrics. There are many measures (see Table 3) which a manager may apply to an ASN to examine various factors of a service network. The example provided here generates many measures to inform management of the service structure and how ONA provides insights on the ASN dynamics. The metrics employed in this chapter are for demonstration purposes to explain how we can develop service network analytics metrics to examine agility across software engineering teams. The metrics compare the impact of technology on the service relational structure to allow managers determine the "value" and "success" of

ASN change. From such insights, it becomes evident that ASN are not engineered and but rather become the emerging product of collaboration to co-create and co-stabilise an ASN. Although, the purpose of this scenario is to provide an example of how one might demonstrate the application ONA to model ASN, while using large data sets it becomes more obvious as to the power of ONA as an analytics method.

7. CONCLUSION AND FUTURE WORK

Agile software development is a collaborative approach which supports iterative and incremental methods within software engineering teams. The key factors which foster the value of agile software development include human interactions, developing improved software solutions, frequent customer collaborations, and the ability to rapidly respond to change. Thus, the composition and organisation of agile teams has a direct influence on the functionality of agile software development. Decision-making plays a critical role within a complex service environment to stabilise software development teams. Thus, information exchanges are therefore a vital resource to support decision-making within service teams. The material used to guide decisions on service actions is influenced by socio-technical factors. Understanding how information is disseminated across teams is considered problematic, especially across agile service developments. Technology is often implemented to enhance service efficiency and enhance performance. However, in many cases, managers have little insights as to "how" technology influences service relational structures. This chapter introduces an agile software engineering modelling method which improves the visualisation of team dynamics through using ONA graphs. This method allows managers to monitor the impact of service relational structures on performance. This may be achieved through a service network performance analytics framework which is supported by the application of ONA. ONA is a novel approach to model ASN interaction and visualise the agile service infrastructure. This chapter discusses the importance of developing greater insights into ASN and examining alternative methods to visualise the relational structure which stabilises networks. The scenario highlights that the ONA method of studying service patterns is critical to examining service systems. We explain how ONA offers a fitting technique to study relational patterns which support ASN infrastructures. This chapter provides a significant platform to extend theoretical developments on ASN and developing additional methods to map agility within the service environment.

As part of our future work, we will build on this approach from both a theoretical and practical approach through numerous case studies in agile software development. We anticipate that this work will lead to the construction of an audit framework which will assist the process of monitoring ASN and provide significant contributions to the emergence of service science. Our work will pay particular attention towards the foundation of performance analytics for ASN and continue to test the application of ONA in developing ASN performance indicators within the audit framework. We anticipate that this approach will harness more open innovation within agile software engineering developments.

ACKNOWLEDGMENT

The research leading to these results has received funding from the European Community's Seventh Framework Programme FP7/2007-2013 under grant agreement 215483 (S-Cube). This work was supported in part by Science Foundation Ireland grant 03/CE2/I303_1 to Lero – the Irish Software Engineering Research Centre (www.lero.ie).

REFERENCES

Abrahamsson, P., Conboy, K., & Wang, X. (2009). Lots done, more to do- The current state of agile method research: Challenges and opportunities. *European Journal of Information Systems*, *18*(4), 281–284. doi:10.1057/ejis.2009.27

Abrahamsson, P., Warsta, J., Siponen, M. T., & Ronkainen, J. (2003). New directions on agile methods: A comparative analysis. In *Proceedings of the 25th International Conference on Software Engineering* (ICSE'03), IEEE Press.

Auerswald, P. (2009). Creating social value. *Stanford Social Innovation Review*, *7*, 50–55.

Balkundi, P., & Kilduff, M. (2006). The ties that lead: A social network approach to leadership. *The Leadership Quarterly*, *17*, 419–439. doi:10.1016/j.leaqua.2006.01.001

Beck, K. et al. (2001). *Manifesto for agile software development*. Retrieved November 29, 2011, from agilemanifesto.org

Berkowitz, S. D. (1982). *An introduction to structural analysis: The network approach to social research*. Toronto, Canada: Butterworth.

Bruegge, B., Dutoit, A. H., & Wolf, T. (2006). *Sysiphus: Enabling informal collaboration in global software development*. International Conference on Global Software Engineering. Florianopolis, Brazil.

Carroll, N., Whelan, E., & Richardson, I. (2010). Applying social network analysis to discover service innovation within agile service networks. *Service Science, 2*(4), 225–244. doi:10.1287/serv.2.4.225

Chesbrough, H. (2011). Bringing open innovation to services. *MIT Sloan Management Review, 52*(2), 85–90.

Conboy, K. (2009). Agility from first principles: Reconstructing the concept of agility in information systems development. *Information Systems Research, 20*(3), 329–354. doi:10.1287/isre.1090.0236

Conboy, K., & Fitzgerald, B. (2004). Toward a conceptual framework of agile methods: A study of agility in different disciplines. In *Proceedings of XP/Agile Universe*. Springer Verlag. doi:10.1007/978-3-540-27777-4_11

Conboy, K., & Morgan, L. (2011). Beyond the customer: Opening the agile systems development process. *Information and Software Technology, 53*, 535–542. doi:10.1016/j.infsof.2010.10.007

Cross, R. L., & Parker, A. (2004). *The hidden power of social networks: Understanding how work really gets done in organizations*. Harvard Business Press.

Dove, R. (2001). *Response ability – The language, structure, and culture of the agile enterprise*. New York, NY: Wiley.

Dubois, D. J. (2008). *An approach for improving business process management in agile service networks*. Minor Research Report. Retrieved from http://home.dei.polimi.it/dubois/papers/bpm4asn09.pdf

Freeman, L. C., White, D. R., & Romney, A. K. (1992). *Research methods in social network analysis*. New Brunswick, NJ: Transaction Publishers.

Goldman, S. L., Nagel, R. N., & Preiss, K. (1995). *Agile competitors and virtual organizations: Strategies for enriching the customer*. Van Nostrand Reinhold.

Hansen, M. (1999). The search-transfer problem: The role of weak ties in sharing knowledge across organization subunits. *Administrative Science Quarterly, 44*(1), 82–111. doi:10.2307/2667032

Hassan, N. R. (2009). Using social network analysis to measure IT-enabled business process performance. *Information Systems Management, 26*(1), 61–76. doi:10.1080/10580530802557762

Hooper, M. J., Steeple, D., & Winters, C. N. (2001). Costing customer value: An approach for the agile enterprise. *International Journal of Operations & Production Management, 21*(5/6), 630–644. doi:10.1108/01443570110390372

IfM and IBM. (2007). *Succeeding through service innovation: A discussion paper*. Cambridge, UK: University of Cambridge Institute for Manufacturing.

IfM and IBM. (2008). *Succeeding through service innovation: A service perspective for education, research, business and government*. Cambridge, UK: University of Cambridge, Institute for Manufacturing.

Kawalek, P., & Greenwood, R. W. (2000). The organization, the process, and the model. In Bustard, D., Kawalek, P., & Norris, M. (Eds.), *Systems modeling for business process improvement* (pp. 61–80). Artech House Publishers.

Knoke, D., & Kuklinski, J. H. (1991). Network analysis: Basis concepts. In G. Thompson, J. Frances, R. Levačić, & J. Mitchell (1991). *Markets, hierarchies and networks: The coordination of social life*. Sage Publications.

Laumann, E. O., Marsden, P., & Prensky, D. (1989). The boundary specification problem in network analysis. In Freeman, L. C., White, D. R., & Kimball Romney, A. (Eds.), *Research methods in social network analysis*. Fairfax, VA: George Mason University Press.

Lewis, T. G. (2009). *Network science – Theory and application*. Hoboken, NJ: John Wiley & Sons.

Linder, J. C., & Cantrell, S. (2000). *Changing business models: Surveying the landscape*. Institute for Strategic Change, Accenture. Retrieved from http://www.riccistreet.net/dwares/lane/mba600/linder.pdf

Mancioppi, M., Carro, M., van den Heuvel, W.-J., & Papazoglou, M. P. (2008). Sound multi-party business protocols for service networks. In *6th International Conference on Service-Oriented Computing (ICSOC 2008), Volume 5364 of Lecture Notes in Computer Science*, (pp. 302–316).

Marsden, P. V. (2005). Recent developments in network measurement. In Carrington, P., Scott, J., & Wassermann, S. (Eds.), *Models and methods in social network analysis* (pp. 8–30). Cambridge, UK: Cambridge University Press. doi:10.1017/CBO9780511811395.002

Normann, R. (2001). *Reframing business: When the map changes the landscape*. Chichester, UK: Wiley.

Ryan, K. (2008). Engineering the Irish software tiger. *Computer*, *41*(6), 66–71. doi:10.1109/MC.2008.186

S-Cube. (2009). *Initial models and mechanisms for quantitative analysis of correlations between KPIs, SLAs and underlying business processes.* Retrieved from http://www.s-cube-network.eu/results/deliverables/wp-jra-2.1

Salancik, G. R. (1995). Wanted: A good network theory of organization. *Administrative Science Quarterly*, *40*, 345–349. doi:10.2307/2393642

Scott, J. (1991). *Social network analysis: A handbook*. London, UK: Sage.

Spohrer, J., Maglio, P. P., Bailey, J., & Gruhl, D. (2007). Steps toward a science of service systems. *IEEE Computer*, *40*(1), 71–77. doi:10.1109/MC.2007.33

Tichy, N. M., Tushman, M. L., & Frombrun, C. (1979). Social network analysis for organizations. *Academy of Management Review*, *4*, 507–519.

van den Heuvel, W. J. A. M. (2009). *Changing the face of the global digital economy: What smart service systems means for people's everday life, enterprises and societies*. Tilburg, The Netherlands: Tilburg University Press.

van Oosterhout, M., Waarts, E., van Heck, E., & van Hillegersberg, J. (2007). Business agility: Need, readiness and alignment with IT strategies. In Desouza, K. C. (Ed.), *Agile information systems: Conceptualization, construction, and management*. Elsevier Inc.

Vargo, S. L., & Lusch, R. F. (2008). From goods to service (S): Divergences and convergences of logics. *Industrial Marketing Management*, *37*, 254–259. doi:10.1016/j.indmarman.2007.07.004

Vargo, S. L., Maglio, P. P., & Akaka, M. A. (2008). On value and value co-creation: A service systems and service logic perspective. *European Management Journal*, *26*, 145–152. doi:10.1016/j.emj.2008.04.003

Vidgen, R., & Wang, X. (2009). Coevolving systems and the organization of agile software development. *Information Systems Research, September*, *20*(3), 355-376

Wadhwa, S., & Rao, K. S. (2003). Flexibility and agility for enterprise synchronization: Knowledge and innovation management towards flexagility. *Studies in Informatics and Control Journal, 11*(2), 29–34.

Wasserman, S., & Faust, K. (1994). *Social network analysis: Methods and applications*. Cambridge, UK: Cambridge University Press. doi:10.1017/CBO9780511815478

Watts, D. J. (2004). The "new" science of networks. *Annual Review of Sociology, 30*, 243–270. doi:10.1146/annurev.soc.30.020404.104342

Watts, D. J., & Strogatz, S. H. (1998). Collective dynamics of 'small-world' networks. *Nature, 393*(6684), 440–442. doi:10.1038/30918

Wellman, B., & Berkowitz, S. D. (1988). *Social structures: A network approach*. Greenwich, CT: JAI Press.

Zhao, J. L., Hsu, C., Jain, H. K., Spohrer, J. C., Tanniru, M., & Wang, H. J. (2008). ICIS 2007 panel report: Bridging service computing and service management: How MIS contributes to service orientation. *Communications of the Association for Information Systems, 22*, 413–428.

KEY TERMS AND DEFINITIONS

Agile Service Network (ASN): An emergent and dynamic service networks which provide some form of business value by reacting to change which is spontaneous in nature and rely on business partners collaborative strengths to deliver service value as a network.

Agility: An innovative response to an unpredictable change.

Business Agility: The ability of a service environment to decide how to react to change by exploiting its relational infrastructure to execute actions which optimise on resource and competence exchanges across a service network to meet specific service goals.

Organisational Network Analysis (ONA): An approach and set of techniques which examines the exchange of resources (for example, information) among actors. ONA also demonstrates the value of ties and relationships between each node to provide a visual and mathematical representation of interaction and exchanges which influence behaviour.

Service Network: A service network may be defined as a set of complex interactions which co-create value through the support of a socio-technical relational infrastructure to stabilise a service environment through the exchange of resources, competencies and capabilities to benefit the performance of another actor though the generation and realisation of value.

Service Science: An interdisciplinary umbrella which incorporates widely diverse disciplines to construct, manage, analyse and evolve service systems through systematic and overarching approaches to examine service co-production operations between business and technology (i.e. service management and service computing).

Service System: A service system is defined as a dynamic value co-creating configuration or resources, including people, technology, organisations and shared information (language, laws, measures and methods), all connected internally and externally by value propositions, with the aim to consistently and profitably meet the customer's needs better than competing alternatives.

Service Value: Concerned with the adaptability and survivability of the beneficiary system creating opportunities for reinvestment and cross-subsidisation of activities that may potentially benefit people involved in the service network.

ENDNOTES

[1] Least Upper Bound

Chapter 9
Agile Development of Security–Critical Enterprise System

Xiaocheng Ge
University of York, UK

ABSTRACT

The effective provision of security in an agile development requires a new approach: traditional security practices are bound to equally traditional development methods. However, there are concerns that security is difficult to build incrementally, and can prove prohibitively expensive to refactor. This chapter describes how to grow security, organically, within an agile project, by using an incremental security architecture that evolves with the code. The architecture provides an essential bridge between system-wide security properties and implementation mechanisms, a focus for understanding security in the project, and a trigger for security refactoring. The chapter also describes criteria that allow implementers to recognize when refactoring is needed, and a concrete example that contrasts incremental and "top-down" architectures.

INTRODUCTION

An enterprise system is an information system that promises a seamless integration of all the applications that process the information in an organisation. It provides a technical platform that enables organisations to integrate and coordinate their business processes. The concept and adaption of enterprise systems have attracted increasing interests as organisations have been seeking how they do their business more efficiently. However, if an organisation rushes to install an enterprise system without first having a clearing understanding of the business implications, the dream of integration can quickly turn into a nightmare. To avoid the problems, it is necessary to have a good understanding of aspects related to the applications, including the business characteristics; processes and architecture of the applications. Service oriented architecture (SOA) is an archi-

DOI: 10.4018/978-1-4666-2503-7.ch009

tectural style promoting the concept of business-aligned enterprise service as the fundamental unit of designing, building, and composing enterprise business solutions. The primary goal of SOA is to align the business world with the world of information technology (IT) in a way that makes both more effective. SOA is a bridge that creates a symbiotic and synergistic relationship between the two that is more powerful and valuable than anything that we've experienced in the past. Moreover, SOA is about the business results that can be achieved from having better alignment between the business and IT. It represents a set of architectural principles that position software services as the primary means through which business services are offered by the organisation to its ecosystem. SOA is also becoming an important concept in the development of software applications. It provides a systematic solution to transform the development of a software application from a heavyweight process to an iterative and incremental one.

Securing access to information is important to any business. For a long time, security has been one of the major concerns in the development and the operation of all types of information systems (Amoroso 1994; Anderson 2001; Pfleeger and Pfleeger 2003; McGraw 2006). Security is a system issue that takes into account both security mechanisms (such as access control) and the engineering of security (such as a robust design that makes it difficult for software attacks to succeed). Sometimes these overlap, but often they do not. Security engineering is concerned with building secure system, and it has a layered architecture (Ge 2007). On the top of this architecture, it is the application security. The focus of this monograph is application security, which can be seen as a software engineering problem where the system is designed to resist attacks. The engineering of application security relies heavily on the discipline of software engineering, liberally borrowing methods that work and making use of critical engineering artefacts. A sound software engineering method

is a prerequisite to sound software security. After decades of efforts, it is well accepted that security considerations should be taken into account at every stage of the application (system) development life cycle (Eric A. Fisch 2000; Anderson 2001; Viega and McGraw 2002; Grance, Hash et al. 2003; Pfleeger and Pfleeger 2003; Apvrille and Pourzandi 2005; McGraw 2006).

Security becomes even more critical for implementations structured according to service-oriented architecture (SOA) principles, due to loose coupling of services and applications, and moreover their possible operations across trust boundaries. On the other hand, to enable a business so that its processes and applications are flexible, changes to both process and application logic, as well as to the policies associated with them, including security access policies, are expected. The topic on this chapter is an agile development/ integration of a secure enterprise system which has a service-oriented architecture. It covers three fields: enterprise system security, agile development, and SOA. In this chapter, we will focus on the relationship of these three elements from the perspective of security engineering, since the discussions from different angles are covered in other chapters in this book.

The rest of this paper is divided into two main parts. The first part provides a criterion for architectural security: what constitutes an iterative architecture, what properties it should uphold, and how it fits into an agile development process. The second part of the paper gives a concrete example, drawn from the practical work that motivated this approach.

BACKGROUND

In recent years, the principles and practices of agile software development have aroused enormous interests. The driver of developing software systems using agile software methods is to better manage different kinds of change. Agile development naturally matches stakeholders' needs for incremental delivery, and is therefore becoming the method of choice; however, little has been done to understand how security can be fully integrated in an incremental development. Several researchers have contrasted Agile or XP developments with traditional security engineering processes (Baskerville 1993; Abrahamsson, Warsta et al. 2003; Baskerville 2004), and while these are generally favourable to XP they also highlight the gap between the documentation requirements of traditional engineering and the lightweight approach of agile methods. Unfortunately the gap is wider than merely aligning documentation practice: traditional security engineering is built on traditional design methods, which are qualitatively and quantitatively different; for example, the documentation requirements of classical security engineering provide a firewall of independence between development and review, but XP has a completely different approach to quality assurance. What is needed is the development of new, agile, security practices.

The notion of "*good enough security*" has been suggested by Beznosov (Beznosov 2003) who reviews XP practices from the security perspective. Of course, the traditional security community practices "good enough security", simply because security is not an absolute property or function: it must be cost-justified in terms of the system, its assets, stakeholders concerns, and the threat environment. Typically, risk based methods are used to judge the value of security in a system (Anderson 2001; Stoneburner, Goguen et al. 2002) and determine what security features are justified. The research problem of this monograph is about the security-critical systems, which is a system whose security requirements are not specified only by customers or security engineers. The security-critical systems have to satisfy a set of security requirements usually set by third party certification authorities with the reference to the international security evaluation criteria, for example Common Criteria (Criteria 2005). In such

case, the security requirements of an information system are fixed up in the front of development process, and are nonchangeable. The examples of a security critical system are very common in our daily life, such as systems in banks, hospitals, etc. A development project of security critical systems has a number of facets, including how to establish what security features are necessary and efficient, when the features should be implemented in an iteration, and how to manage the overall development process.

As the conclusions in Boehm and Turner's book (Booch, Cockburn et al. 2004), there is no silver bullet of agile or plan-driven development method, and balanced agile-discipline methods are emerging. It is generally claimed that iterative application security, especially is difficult: the system-wide nature of security properties mean that security may be prohibitively expensive to retrofit (Jaquith 2001; Amey and Chapman 2003) and refactoring is essentially a bottom-up process that may break system properties (Baskerville 2004); even Fowler comments that security may be hard to refactor (see Design Changes that are Difficult to Refactor at (Fowler, Beck et al. 1999)). This is a bleak perspective for agile security, and highlights two critical questions:

- How can developers satisfy themselves that security mechanisms, which may be scattered through the system, provide useful system level security features?
- What factors have to be considered in an iteratively developing system, to ensure that new security features are not prohibitively expensive?

In this chapter, we will discuss those questions in details and give our answers. In short, we will introduce an approach of argument-based development to deal with the incremental security architecture. Unlike the conventional security architecture, an iterative architecture remains true to agile principles by including only the essential features needed for the current system iteration -it does not try to predict future requirements -but it does deal with both these questions directly: it provides a link between local functions and system properties, and it provides a basis for the undergoing review of the system from a security perspective. In addition, we will discuss several existing techniques that can be used in order to support the overall iterative development process. Based on these, we propose an *"agile enough development process"* to develop security-critical enterprise systems, especially those with a service oriented architecture. The proposition of our research is that there is a feasible and agile enough process for the development of security-critical enterprise systems with a service oriented architecture, and we should be able to give a concrete example of such an agile process, including the process model and related techniques in practice. The agile development process should have all characteristics of existing agile software development, which are (Abrahamsson, Salo et al. 2002):

- **Incremental:** Small software releases, with rapid cycles,
- **Cooperative:** Customer and developers working constantly together with close communications,
- **Straightforward:** The method itself is easy to learn and to modify, well documented, and
- **Adaptive:** Able to make last moment changes.

In next section we review a typical development process of security critical systems and compare it with Agile processes for the purposes of identifying commonalities and areas of incompatibility. This in turn will help us to derive the key challenges that must be overcome to allow security software development to benefit from the principles and practices of agile development.

Security-Critical Software Development Process

The typical process of developing a security-critical software system is generally time-consuming. Most such processes are based on the V-model, which is illustrated diagrammatically in Figure 1. The model identifies the major elements of the development process and indicates the structured, and typically sequential, nature of the development process. The sequential nature of development is generally considered essential for reasons of managing communication and scale, for scheduling different phases and disciplines, for managing traceability (which is mandated by relevant safety standards) and for certification purposes.

The last phase in the V model is a phase of certification, which is often the most important concern of the critical system development process. In order for a security-critical system to be put in service, it must be tested and evaluated by independent third parties (i.e., a certifying authority) against demanding and standardised criteria, in order to obtain a certificate for release to service; we refer to this as certification although the terminology used may vary between sectors. The need for assuring the quality of systems in critical applications has led governments and international regulatory organisations into developing *consensus* standards or guidelines, which must be adhered to before any system of a critical nature is commissioned. Those standards and guidelines are means of specifying how critical systems *should be* developed, based on best practices and past experience gathered over many years. In order to certify the quality of software application, different standards or guidelines are applied for different application domains. For example, Common Criteria (Criteria 2005). In general, standards and guidelines have at least two purposes. On one hand, they aim to provide a way for the producers of critical systems to

Figure 1. The V model of security-critical system development (Grance, Hash et al. 2003)

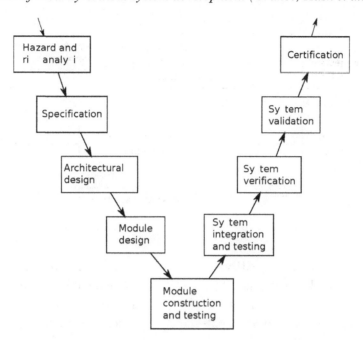

determine whether the system they are acquiring is free (to the greatest technical extent possible) from defects which may result in losses; on the other hand, they provide the developers of critical systems with guidelines on how to develop such systems, so that the resulting products will perform according to the stakeholders' expectations.

Figure 2 illustrates the Common Criteria model. In this model, a customer wishing to evaluate the security of an IT product first defines the *target of evaluation (TOE)*. Next, a *security target* for that target of evaluation is developed. Whether bespoke or derived from a *protection profile (PP)* intended to apply to all targets of evaluation of a given type, the security target contains four elements:

1. An identification of the assets and threats to those assets;
2. A description of the information technology countermeasures (called the *security objectives*) and a rationale demonstrating that the countermeasures are sufficient to counter the threats;

3. An operationalization of the information technology countermeasures in the form of security functional requirements that the target of evaluation must satisfy;
4. A set of security assurance requirements sufficient to give adequate confidence that the target of evaluation does not contain implementation errors that lead to vulnerabilities.

To aid the security developer in enumerating a sufficient set of security functional requirements, Part 2 of the Common Criteria contains a standard set of template security functional requirements. These template security functional requirements are used as part of a guided enumeration process: security template writers consider each template security functional requirement and, if applicable, instantiate it with appropriate parameters. Similarly, to aid the security developer in enumerating a sufficient set of security assurance requirements, Part 3 of the Common Criteria contains a standard set of template security assurance requirements. Part 3 of the Common Criteria also defines a set

Figure 2. Common criteria model

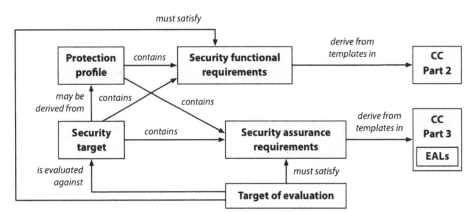

of seven standard, hierarchically-organised Evaluation Assurance Levels (EALs), each naming a set of security assurance requirement components that compliant systems must satisfy. Complementing parts 1, 2, and 3 of the Common Criteria is a separate standard describing how evaluators should conduct evaluations of protection profiles, security targets, and targets of evaluation.

Actually, Common Criteria does not specify any particular process or sequence of system development. Instead it emphasised that *"the development is a refinement process of the security requirements into a TOE (Target of Evaluation) summary specification expressed in the security target. Each lower level of refinement represents a design decomposition with additional design de-tail. The final representation is the TOE implementation itself."*

In addition, there should be *sufficient* design representations presented at a sufficient level of granularity to demonstrate where required (Criteria 2005):

A. "That each refinement level is a complete instantiation of the higher levels (i.e. all TOE security functions, properties, and behaviour defined at the higher level of abstraction must be demonstrably present in the lower level);"

B. "That each refinement level is an accurate instantiation of the higher levels (i.e., there should be no TOE security functions, properties, and behaviour defined at the lower level of abstraction that are not required by the higher level)."

There are three separate processes addressed in Common Criteria that comprise most life cycles and describes the interactions between them: a planning process, a technical development process, and an integration process. While Common Criteria does not specify a concrete process, it does identify objectives that any process must meet. For each software product to be developed according to Common Criteria, a software life-cycle(s) is constructed that includes these three processes. In practice, it is easy to understand why heavyweight development processes currently dominate industrial security critical software development. Such processes are widely accepted, are integrated with certification standards, and are generally based on well-defined principles (e.g., waterfall life-cycle model). Heavyweight processes also share a common view of the phases that make up an ideal software development life-cycle, namely analysis, design, implementation, and testing and integration.

There have been several research works that contrasted general agile methods (Baskerville 2004; Paige, Cakic et al. 2004; Ge, Chivers et al. 2005; Siponen, Baskerville et al. 2005) or XP development (Wayrynen, Boden et al. 2004) with traditional security engineering processes. These research works highlight the gap between the traditional security engineering methods and existing agile methods in several areas of development, such as the requirement of documentation. These approaches can be classified to the school of agile methods for *"good enough security"* (Beznosov 2003). The concept of *"good enough security"* shifts the responsibility of defining what security is good enough from security engineers to the customers, and then the customers are allowed to change the definition as much as they want. Based on this principle, the software developers can tailor an existing agile method with security practices. The approach from the school of *"good enough security"* agile methods is suitable for the development of information systems of which the customers can define the security requirements. However it is not the case of what our research is focusing on. In next section, we will briefly introduce the development processes presented in existing Agile methods.

Overview of Agile Development Processes

Agile processes are in effect a family of development processes. Typical Agile development methods include eXtreme Programming (XP) (Beck and Andres 2004), Feature Driven Development (FDD) (Palmer and Felsing 2002; Last accessed on Oct. 2006), and Scrum. Table 1 briefly summarises the common features of these three agile development methods.

In terms of development process, each agile development method introduces its own life-cycle model. For example, the XP process consists of five phases: Exploration, Planning, Iterations to release, Productionizing, Maintenance and Death. By comparison, a Scrum process has only three: pre-game, game, and post-game. We will not explore the details of these phases. We observe that, despite different names for these phases in different agile development methods, there is commonality, and it is not difficult to produce a generic software development life-cycle model (SDLC) for Agile methods, which is based on the tasks and activities in each phase. We illustrate this generic life-cycle model in Figure 3. The generic life-cycle model consists of four phases: preparation, planning, short iterations to release, and integration.

Table 1. General features of agile methods (derived from (Abrahamsson, Salo et al. 2002))

Method	Key Points	Special Features	Identified Shortcomings
XP	Customer driven development, small teams, daily builds.	Refactoring -the ongoing redesign of the system to improve its performance and responsiveness to change.	While individual practices are suitable for many situations, an overall system view and management practices are given less attention.
FDD	Five-step process, Object-oriented component (i.e. feature) based development. Very short iterations: from hours to 2 weeks.	Method simplicity, design and implementation the system by features, object modelling.	FDD focuses only on design and implementation, and needs other supporting approaches.
Scrum	Independent, small, selforganising development teams, 30-day release cycles.	Enforce a paradigm shift from the "defined and repeatable" to the "new product development view of Scrum."	While Scrum details specifically how to manage the 30-day release cycle, integration and acceptance tests are not detailed.

Figure 3. Generic SDLC of agile development process

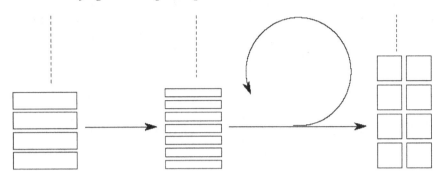

Different agile development methods may have different names for the *preparation* phase, For example Exploration in XP, Pre-game in Scrum, and Develop an overall model in FDD. The development task in this phase is to understand the blueprint and environment of the system. The product of this phase is a package of current requirements or user stories which provide materials for the next phase, *planning*, in which the whole system is disassembled into pieces according to an appropriate priority index. For example, in XP the user stories are prioritised and allocated to the development iterations in phase Planning; and the planning job is done in *Pre-game* phase of Scrum and the stage Build a feature list and Plan by feature of FDD. Once the objectives of every iteration are clear, the system is constructed iteratively through many *short iterations of release*. The phase *Short iterations of release* is a key characteristic of all agile development methods, although it goes by different names. For example in Scrum, it is called the game phase, whereas in XP it is called iterations to release. Each development iteration is short, usually 2 to 4 weeks. At the end of each iteration, tests are carried out to verify and validate the release. When the last iteration is completed, the system is ready for *integration*. In the *integration* phase, the system undergoes additional testing and checking of

satisfaction of environmental variables, e.g., requirements. This phase is instantiated in phases Productionizing, and Maintenance and Death of XP, and Post-game in Scrum.

There are commonalities between the generic agile lifecycle model and the steps carried out in a plan-driven process (which consists of four activities: analysis, design, implementation and testing). More specifically, at the beginning and the end of an agile development process, software engineers have to do the same sort of development activities (i.e. analyse and design at the beginning, and test at the end), and in the iterations the four activities are performed in the same sequence. Figure 4 shows the commonalities and differences between plan-driven and Agile processes.

Figure 4. Plan-driven development model vs. agile development model

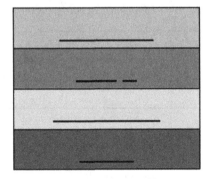

The core differences between Agile and plan-driven processes are thus as follows:

1. Plan-driven processes have an up-front design (including the analysis activity). Instead of planned design, the design in agile processes is evolutionary. Compared with plan-driven processes, the shape of the system rather than its details is designed at the beginning of an Agile process, which makes up-front design in an agile process lighter.
2. In plan-driven processes, implementation is normally a monolithic activity, which also entails a monolithic testing phase. In an agile process, implementation (and hence testing) is iterative and incremental.

In order to enable the development of security critical systems using an agile process, there are thus two key requirements:

- "Lighten" the amount of effort required in up-front design of a security-critical system, and
- Perhaps more significantly, support iterative development.

Experience shows that there are few planned development iterations in industrial security-critical system development projects; these iterations occur typically at later stages of the development process, e.g., coding and testing. In this monograph, we discuss the activities that occur at early stage of development, i.e., designing and planning, which seem to be a more constructive way to emphasise the benefits of agile development. In the next section, we describe our efforts towards achieving these two requirements.

TOWARDS AN ACCEPTABLE AGILE PROCESS FOR DEVELOPMENT OF SECURITY CRITICAL SOFTWARE

We are aware of companies who say that they apply agile practices, however these are not well-documented (i.e., in the public domain) and the notion of "incremental certification" remains an aspiration, albeit one which is being actively researched. Although there are as of yet no detailed, evidenced reports of an application of an established Agile process successfully applied to a real-world, security-critical software project that requires certification, there have been a number of research papers arguing that an Agile process, with some customisation, can be applied to critical systems. This includes work on developing both security-and safety-critical software systems, and generally involve modifications to agile practices (e.g., inclusion of greater use of model-based design and auto-coding) (Beznosov 2003; Booch, Cockburn et al. 2004). However, current practices and current methods have been informed by decades of experience on long-lived projects; the ability to change current practice on projects that may take 20-30 years to deliver and deploy is both technically and politically difficult. Thus, direct adoption of *any* new method is difficult, though agile development methods offer their own distinctive challenges. In principle, agile software development is intended to lead to a development process that is more responsive than traditional plan-driven methods to customer needs. At the same time, Agile processes aim to create software of better quality[2]. The quality of the target software is based not only the functionality, but also other aspects, such as reliability and other non-functional properties. In principle, therefore, there is no conflict between the principles of agile development processes and the requirements of security-critical software projects. Earlier, we identified two key challenges in adopting agile development methods for building security-critical software: managing up-front architecture; and carrying out iterative and incremental development. We now discuss each challenge in turn and explain how these challenges can be overcome.

Incremental Security Architecture

The word architecture is often avoided in agile development, because of its traditional association with top-down design; however, it is not completely discounted as a concept. Kent Beck relates a system architecture to the idea of a metaphor, but stresses that it has to be "*the simplest thing that could possibly work*" (Beck and Andres 2004). Practical XP projects have also found that it is useful to build an architecture as the system develops: "we lacked a clear overall vision… Eventually we decided to put up posters that showed sketches of the architecture" (Murru, Deias et al. 2003).

Our concept of an incremental security architecture is exactly in conformance with these views (Chivers 2005):

An incremental security architecture is one that develops with the system, and includes only features that are necessary for the current iteration or delivery. The architecture is a working vision for developers, which encapsulates important security features of the existing design.

We deliberately avoid the question of documentation for independent security assurance. Our aim is to build fit-for-purpose security within an agile development framework; experience will later allow us to speculate how we can best distinguish successful from unsuccessful security implementations.

However, we do need to make judgments about systems as they are developed. Functional developers refactor code because its structure is not fit for purpose: the existing code base inhibits the addition of new features, or is developing in a way that is structurally undesirable. Fowler describes Bad Smells, which allow developers to recognize situations that demand refactoring (Fowler and Beck 1999). If security is to be developed iteratively, then it is similarly necessary to have security criteria that allow the development team to distinguish good from bad practices.

Criteria for Good Security Architectures

Shore's work on Continuous Design (Shore 2004) includes the addition of features that he describes as pervasive (i.e. not local): fine grain access control, transactional processing and internationalization. The access security was added to a conventional project -it was tedious and extensive but not difficult; the other features were added in an XP project and required only limited changes to the code, because effective refactoring had already resulted in a target system with low functional duplication.

In Shore's work the features already present in the system included wrappers or interface functions (e.g. for HTML templates and persistence). The property that makes these structures effective is not just the avoidance of functional duplication, but reduced coupling between system functions: these design patterns reduce the number and type of function calls between modules. Low coupling is well established as a design principle, and we suggest that it is of critical importance to allow the subsequent introduction of security features.

This is consistent with security design principles that have been understood for some time; for www.agilemanifesto.org example, Viega and McGraw (Viega and McGraw 2002) listed ten principles, three of which are particularly relevant to security architectures:

- Be Reluctant To Trust.
- Execute all parts of the system with the least privilege possible.
- Keep it Simple.

To trust is to place reliance on something; any service constrained by a security control is relied on to support the security of the system, so the parts of the system that are security critical should be minimized. *Privilege* is the degree of access, or authority, that any process has; protection of the integrity of the system itself is the most significant privilege issue: a fundamental part of any security architecture is to identify how the system is administered, and minimize the number of users, or system functions, that can exercise that authority. The "keep it simple" principle is a reminder that security guarantees and functional complexity are not easily combined; complex applications should not be security critical, and interfaces to security functions should be as simple as possible (coupling, again).

The security architecture must allow the project team to review the current implementation against these principles. It must also bridge the gap between local and sys-tem level properties; again we can draw advice from established security practice by proposing that the architecture should:

- Partition a system, identifying which parts are security-sensitive, and in what way.
- Show how security components combine to provide useful system level security.
- Communicate the structural logic of security; for example, ensuring that team members do not inadvertently build functionality that bypasses security.

Partitioning a system separates security relevant parts from those that are security-neutral. In practice this often means that an effective design places security in the infrastructure, which then constrains the behaviour of security-neutral applications.

How Should an Incremental Security Architecture Be Used?

In an agile project, building a security architecture (i.e., summarizing which components contribute to security, and how) supports these design principles by provoking a discussion, which may highlight the need for refactoring. This is the primary principle that we seek to establish: in each iteration the implementers must have space and reason to consider security; if not, the *"bad smells"* simply accumulate to a level that is too difficult to refactor away when the system is presented with a demanding requirement. Security can only be developed iteratively if the development team continuously monitors its design.

In summary:

- An agile security architecture should be produced as the code is produced: it is a security view of the current system, and should not anticipate future iterations.
- The architecture should be as simple as possible, and be documented in such a way that it communicates the security intent to the whole development team (e.g. posters, simple UML diagrams).
- As the architecture is produced it should be reviewed against the criteria outlined in section 2.1. As with functional code, refactoring may be necessary to re-establish a system that satisfies the architectural criteria.

Many security architectures come ready-made, for example those of operating systems and web-servers; often these are well designed and implemented, and form a good basis for a security infrastructure. Without an explicit security architecture, however, as new security requirements are added the danger is that they will simply be adsorbed into application code. The use of ready-made security infrastructure is commendable, but it should not be used as a reason to defer making the system security architecture explicit.

How is an Incremental Security Architecture Built?

Security development is an exercise in risk management. Model with a purpose is a core agile principle. In (Ambler 2002; Viega and McGraw 2002), Ambler states:

with respect to modelling, perhaps you need to understand an aspect of your software better, perhaps you need to communicate your approach to senior management to justify your project, or perhaps you need to create documentation that describes your system to the people who will be operating and/or maintaining/evolving it over time. If you cannot identify why and for whom you are creating a model then why are you bothering to work on it all?

In agile projects, the plan for iterative development effectively constitutes a form of up-front design. This plan is normally incomplete and focuses more on the shape (or abstract architecture) of the software system rather than its detailed design; FDD and Scrum both take this approach. However, for security-critical projects, the up-front design/plan needs to be sufficiently detailed to serve as input to risk analysis/management, which in turn informs the certification processes later. Systematic security techniques such as Checklists (Baskerville 1993) are carried out at the start of the development. As design progresses, more detailed analyses are carried out using techniques such as Fault tree analysis (FTA); there are usually feedback cycles between the design and analysis processes, with issues found in analysis leading to design changes. In the early stages of security critical development, the preliminary risk analysis is based on an architectural model of the system. Thus, an up-front plan for security-critical software development must include not only up-front architectural design but also up-front risk analysis, and as the architecture evolves, the risk analysis must be extended. The question we must answer is: for a specific project, how can we lighten its up-front design load, while still achieving acceptable levels of detail in our risk analysis? Already, this gives us a precise notion of sufficiency for our planning and up-front design.

Underpinning this question is a general issue about assessing the sufficiency and adequacy of software models in general. It is difficult to define general-purpose criteria about whether or not an up-front model is sufficiently accurate and detailed in an agile security-critical software project, because different projects have different requirements for the rigorous risk analysis. However, as shown in Figure 1, the last phase of the development process of a security-critical system is certification. Certification is a process whereby the system is evaluated by a certifying authority against demanding criteria. To demonstrate that the system is acceptably security, a document, presenting a detailed security argument of how the security characteristics of the system are achieved, is normally required. Taking the ideas from safety engineering domain, we propose an argument-based approach in order to help the definition of criteria about what an up-front architecture model is sufficiently accurate and detailed. In safety engineering domain, languages and tools exist for constructing and validating safety arguments (Kelly 2004; Kelly 2007). In an argument-based certification regime, a certifying agency (or its agent) must examine the submitted assurance argument and either accept it — thereby clearing the system for deployment and use — or reject it. The standards upon which existing argument-based certification regimes are built require that an assurance argument have specific properties, for example the security assurance level defined in Common Criteria (Criteria 2005).

Kelly has proposed a four-step process for argument review (Kelly 1998; Kelly 2007). According to Kelly, the sufficiency of an inductive argument step depends upon six factors:

1. The extent to which the argument / evidence presented "covers" the conclusion;
2. The independence of multiple grounds given for a single conclusion;
3. The range of situations under which evidence or a conclusion is thought to hold;
4. The degree to which the argument or evidence "directly" addresses the conclusion;
5. The degree to which evidence / argument is relevant to the conclusion;
6. The degree to which the argument is sensitive to changes in the evidence.

Kelly tasks the reviewer with auditing the evidence presented to verify that the evidence exists and has the claimed properties. Reviewers are asked to assess four factors:

1. The degree of "buggy-ness" of the evidence;
2. The level of peer review to which the evidence has been subjected;

3. The experience and competence of the personnel hand-generating the evidence;
4. The qualification and assurance of tools used to produce the evidence.

In our approach, the argument for security assurance can also be used as a driving force of development planning. When developing a security critical software system, evidence should be produced and a security argument can still be constructed to demonstrate how the system is accepted as a secure system. The security architecture then shows the blueprint of the security features required as the evidence in the argument. However, in an agile project, we must find a way to incrementally build security arguments so that we can reuse security arguments of previous releases in producing an argument for the current release. This is difficult because arguments are generally monolithic and are constructed for complete software systems (Kelly 2004). Considering the development of safety argument in safety engineering domain, in order to construct safety arguments for large systems, an approach of modular safety argument structure was proposed (Kelly 2004; Hawkins 2006). This

Figure 5. Modular argument structure

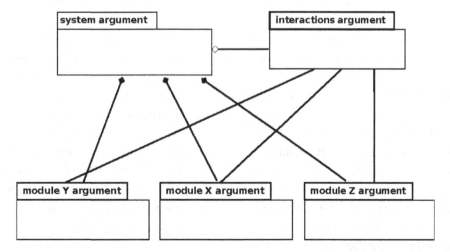

approach allows safety arguments to be developed in terms of modules with argument dependencies. An example of a modular argument structure is shown in Figure 5. In this structure, a safety argument for the whole system main contains three sub-arguments for arguing over a particular module in the system. An argument about all the (software) module interactions is made in a separate (argument) module. There are no longer any links between the module arguments as these no longer have the responsibility to reason about their effect on other modules.

We identified that this technique can be adapted in an agile security-critical software project as one of references for the plan of iterative development because the plan must take the anticipated security argument structure into account, i.e. a package of security arguments should be produced in one iteration. However, this introduces a potential point of tension. Existing agile development methods suggest that iteration should be short, normally taking 2~4 weeks. However, the requirement to produce a security argument structure sometimes will need to override the other requirements of iteration planning in order to ensure that the release of each iteration is acceptably secure. In other words, iterations may need to be extended in order to satisfy requirements for producing a security argument, since without this argument the software cannot be deployed.

In iteration, the software components are developed while in parallel the security argument is produced (in typical security critical software development, the security argument is not produced by the software development team). Taking the example of Figure 4, the security argument for the entire system requires four parts: the arguments for individual components X, Y, and Z, and an argument for the interactions between modules. Therefore, the system can be developed in at least three iterations: iteration produces a module and its security argument. The security argument of interactions is produced when the system is integrated at the completion of the third iteration.

Establishing Essential Quality of Security Argument

The security argument is vital because it is the foundation where the security architecture is built. The essential qualities that a security argument must have are established by the phased inspections within iterations. The specific qualities are as follows:

- **Terminology Understood Identically By All Users:** The security experts cannot evaluate a security argument adequately if security experts and software architects do not share a common understanding of the terms in which the argument is written. Serious security consequences might result if security experts and software architects understand a term differently but are unaware of the difference. Techniques have been developed to deal with this problem in other contexts (Wasson 2006); these can be applied to a greater or lesser extent. Security experts should require a definition for any term that is not common knowledge or that they know has been used to convey different meanings in similar contexts. When the meaning of a term appears to be central to the meaning of a critical portion of the security argument, the security experts should insist upon its definition and test this definition by inquiring about hypothesized examples. Completion of this phase yields both the greatest practical confidence that the security experts and software architects share a vocabulary and, secondarily, confidence that a later third-party users will also understand the terms used in the security argument.

- **Absence of Vagueness:** As with terminology, the security experts cannot evaluate a security argument adequately if the natural-language text used within the various documents is vague. Elimination of vagueness can be based upon the removal of sentence forms that are known to be problematic and upon the security experts' own experience.

- **Document Syntactic Validity:** A security argument comprises a number of documents. Each of these documents must follow a prescribed format and style. Of particular concern is the security argument itself, which must conform to the syntactic rules of the language in which the argument is encoded. In safety engineering domain, Goal Structuring Notation (GSN) (Kelly 1998; Kelly 2004) has been widely used to construct safety arguments. In the GSN, for example, the arrows must point in the correct direction, the argument graph must be acyclic, the text in a strategy parallelogram must describe an argument strategy, etc.

- **Evidence Availability and Sufficiency:** Evidences citations in a security argument take the form of an identifier for a security feature in the security architecture and its brief description. The security experts should ascertain whether the given identifier is sufficient to uniquely identify a particular version of a security feature from among the project's many artefacts, whether the identified artefact is available in the security argument, and whether it has the claimed property. Determining whether an artefact has the claimed property might be difficult for many reasons. The process of verifying the claim might be time-consuming. Judging claims might require expertise that a security expert cannot be expected to have. If the security expert cannot reasonably ascertain the truth or falsity of an evidence claim, should instead challenge the applicant to replace the evidence with a sub-argument supported by simpler evidence. For example, the claim might be replaced by an appeal to an independent and qualified third party's assessment of whether the evidence supports the claim. Unnecessary argument elements. A security argument might contain unnecessary elements. For example, elements that are not necessary in the final argument might be left behind as the applicant extends and revises an initial argument. Unnecessary elements should be discarded.

- **Assumption Necessity and Reasonableness:** Assumptions are critical elements of a security argument. For example, securing information access is a process therefore it always assumes that the operation platform and supporting services beneath the application is secure when discussing the security argument of an application. All assumptions need to be checked for necessity and reasonableness. If it is practical to replace an assumption with evidence and argument, the assumption is not necessary and the security expert should ask the software architect to replace it. An assumption is reasonable if it is plausible and if the security experts can construct no remotely plausible argument that the assumption is false. Security experts should consider accident and incident experience when attempting to rebut assumptions: an assumption that proved false in practice should not be accepted in a similar context.

- **Freedom from Well-Known Fallacies:** A fallacy is an instance of unsound or invalid reasoning. Because fallacious reasoning in a security argument can lead to belief in a false proposition, fallacies must be removed from security arguments. A taxonomy of well-known fallacies has been developed for safety arguments (W. Greenwell 2006). In the same, these well-know fallacies can be used in the inspection of security arguments. Guided by such a list, the security experts should systematically examine the selected fragment for well-known forms of fallacious reasoning.

Establishing Essential Quality of Security Architecture

In previous section, we have already discussed the criteria of good security architecture. Related to the security argument, there are some extra quality measurements required. They are consistency and traceability.

The evidences to support the security argument are mapped to the security features in the security architecture. The consistency of security architecture requires that the mapping relationships between security evidence in the argument and security feature in the architecture are consistent, i.e. same security feature in the entire project corresponds to the same security evidence. In addition, it is necessary that the incremental security architecture is traceable in order to ensure the quality of entire security architecture.

Summary

Above all, we have already answered one and a half questions listed at the beginning of this monograph, which are:

- How can developers satisfy themselves that security mechanisms, which may be scattered through the system, provide useful system level security features?
- What factors have to be considered in an iteratively developing system, to ensure that new security features are not prohibitively expensive?

The iterative development of an enterprise system is based on its service oriented architecture, and we introduced a mechanism of security argument to justify the quality of security in the up-front security architecture during each iterations. In the next section, we will demonstrate how these techniques can help the judgement what sufficient and necessary security features should be implemented in the system.

CASE STUDY

The system to be developed in our case study is a medical record management system, which is a part of hospital information system of PKUP Hospital in Beijing, China. PKUP hospital is one of the first hospital established in China. It was built in 1918. By the end of 2009, the hospital has developed to a comprehensive hospital with 1448 beds in the in-patient department, more than 100 people discharged from in-patient department everyday, and 38 clinical departments, more than 4100 patients (including emergency department) treated everyday. Nowadays, PKUP Hospital has become one of the biggest hospitals in Beijing city, with multiple functions including medical care, scientific research, and teaching. For a hospital as large as PKUP Hospital, the information system used in the hospital is large in terms of its scale, and complex in terms of its business logic. It provides a platform for us to study various issues of large complex information systems. The medical record management system is one of recent major changes in the entire hospital information system since electronic medical record (EMR) is introduced into the hospital. In emphasise our approach in this monograph, we demonstrate the development of security argument and incremental security architecture of EMR system, which is a part of whole hospital management system. And we may not address entire functional requirements of EMR system.

Brief Introduction of Functionality Development

Figure 6 illustrates services interacted with service of medical record.

An electronic medical record contains patient basic information from patient registration service; it will contain information of doctor's diagnosis after inspected by a doctor; it also may have data that record the results of various tests or operations the patient has done. In addition to these information, it is necessary to keep some cross-references of other objects in the system, for example the doctor's ID and test/operation' ID. To protect the data in the EMR, a preliminary risk analysis has to be done to identify all vulnerabilities in the system. Then security goals and features are summarised in next section.

Security Goals and Security Feature

The security goals of EMR system mainly came from user requirements of hospital and government regulations. Initially, the security goals are as follows:

1. Information in EMR system is labeled, and sensitive information should be protected with a higher level of security.
2. Medical records should be protected from loss, theft, unauthorized access, disclosure, copying, use, or modification, regardless of their format.
3. Meanwhile, from the point of availability, the data should be accurate, up-to-date, and accessible when needed.
4. Auditing is a big part of medical practice, and accountability is to make sure access is based on a legitimate need to know, and no collision exists.
5. Last, integrity and non-repudiation of medical data are also required. In order to achieve these security goals, the EMR management system is designed to reach evaluation assur-

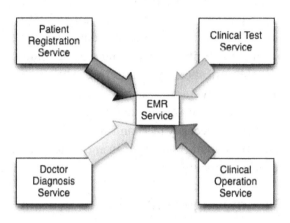

Figure 6. Services interacted with EMR

ance level 4 (EAL4-methodically designed, tested, and reviewed) in Common Criteria. Defined in Common Criteria, EAL4 permits a developer to gain maximum assurance from positive security engineering based on good commercial development practices which, though rigorous, do not require substantial specialist knowledge, skills, and other resources. EAL4 is the highest level at which it is likely to be economically feasible to retrofit to an existing product line.

In assurance class of development in EAL4 there are 4 assurance components: ADV_ARC.1 (security architecture description), ADV_FSP.4 (complete functional specification), ADV_IMP.1 (implementation representation of the TSF), and ADV_TDS.3 (basic modular design). All these components are defined clearly in Common criteria, thus we do not explain them in more details. Meanwhile, there is also a set of security functions listed in Common Criteria. In the case study, we focus on the protection of unauthorized access information. Therefore, we must adopt a set of proper mechanisms to reach the goal. The protection mechanisms we planned (based on the layered security architecture (Ge 2007)) include but are not limited to the following: physical security protection, such as separate room with access control to run database servers; network security protection, such as firewall and intrusion detection system, secure communication; operation security, such as database encryption, user authentication; application security, such as application-level access control; and staff security, such as separation of duty and job sharing.

Once the security mechanisms are planned in the system architecture, we can argue the system security explicitly in GSN.

Security Argument of Entire System

In general, there are a few argument patterns identified (Kelly 1998) to help the construction of arguments. In the case study, the security argument is built on the argument pattern and modular argument architecture (see Figure 5). Figure 7 illustrates the argument of application security of EMR system (i.e., the security mechanisms implemented in the application). The legend of GSN can be found in (Kelly 1998).

In the argument, the top claim is that the EMR system is free from unauthorised access. Based on its service oriented architecture, to support that claim goal, we can argue that there are no unauthorised access from linked services. These arguments are modular arguments which should be expended in a separate argumentation. Now the only thing left in the security argument is the argument about secure communication between services. In next section, we will demonstrate the incremental security architecture of secure communications.

Incremental Security Architecture of Secure Communications

Figure 6 shows the initial service architecture. However when considering security mechanisms to secure communications, we have to consider these services are operating in different security domain. Usually, EMR service, along with doctor diagnosis service, clinical test service, and clinical operation service are in higher-level security domain where operators are strictly authorized users. But patient registration service may be used by patients for self-registration. Thus, they are in different security domain (Shown in Figure 8), and the communications are classified into two groups: communication channels crossed the boundary and communication channels within one security domain.

For the first group of communication channels, we used policy based cryptography (Bagga 2005), and for the second group of communication channels, we used identity based cryptography (Boneh 2003) which can guarantees no medical data can be used outside to the hospital.

The system developed in the case study is a security critical system. Based on the original security argument (illustrated in Figure 7), the argument for the second iteration of security architecture focus on the *G2. Communication channel are secure.* Here, we do not show the detailed argumentation for it.

Above all, we demonstrate how the approach of incremental security architecture works in the case study of developing an EMR system. The description of case study is brief because the development and implementation of system's functional requirements are not the focus of this monograph. However, in the paper, we listed the key artifacts produced in the development process. Based on the observation in the case study development process, it is reasonable to conclude the argument based approach is feasible to development security critical system. The next thing is to argue this approach is an agile development process.

EVALUATION OF PROPOSED APPROACH

In this paper, we discussed how to introduce agile development process in the security critical system projects. The focus of our research is the first two

Figure 7. Security argument of EMR system

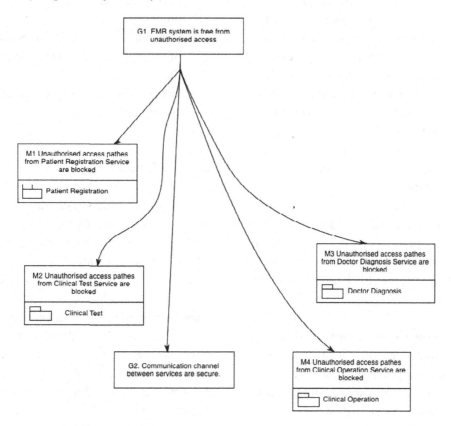

Figure 8. Service oriented architecture of EMR system with concerns of security domain

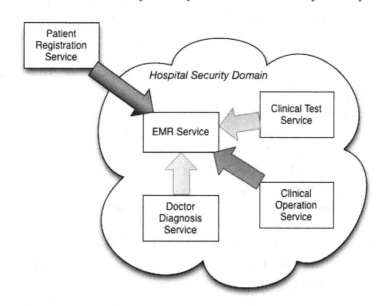

stages of the development process: preparation and planning. The techniques introduced in this paper are nothing new: some are from different engineering domain; and some have been existing in software engineering from many years. However, we integrated these mature techniques into a new package in order to develop security critical systems in a simple and iterative manner. It has been accepted that new technique always builds on existing techniques. Being aware that there is nothing new in agile software development, it is just packing of existing techniques which work really well (Ambler 2002). Although we do not introduce brand new techniques, we still can claim that the approach we proposed is an agile development process not only because it satisfies all characteristics of existing agile processes:

- **Incremental (Small Software Releases, with Rapid Cycles):** With help of argument based approach, the security architecture can be create incrementally so does the software system that implements the security architecture.
- **Cooperative (Customer and Developers Working Constantly Together With Close Communications):** We do not address the customer involvement in the approach because it is not the key problem of integrating agile development and security engineering. Since the system, especially the security architecture can be built in an iterative manner, the existing agile development process can be applied to complete the development of system's functions.
- **Straightforward (The Method Itself is Easy to Learn and to Modify, Well Documented):** The method itself is easy, at least the successful development of case study demonstrates this.
- **Adaptive:** It is difficult to claim the development of a security-critical system can be adaptive because the security requirements

are often fixed up-front of the development process. However, the approach itself is very adaptive since it solves the problems of security architecture and planning so that the users of our approach can choose any existing agile process to complete the system development.

CONCLUSION

A key issue in agile system development is the prospect for incremental security, and the possibility that refactoring security is inherently difficult. In order to integrate security in an agile development environment it is necessary for the team as a whole to have an overview of the security approach, and a trigger that causes them to consider and refactor the security design. This places security in the mainstream of agile development practices, and has strong parallels with the way that quality functional designs are produced. We have shown that this can be achieved by using iterative security architectures. Such an architecture includes only what is necessary for the present delivery, but provides the necessary communication mechanisms and design triggers to ensure that the security solution remains well structured. The questions listed at the beginning are answered:

- Developers can satisfy themselves that security mechanisms, which may be scattered through the system, provide useful system level security features by constructing a security argument of entire system.
- Techniques, including argument based development, incremental security architecture, and feature oriented domain analysis, can support an iteratively way of developing system, and ensure that security features are not prohibitively expensive?

This paper outlines criteria for an incremental security architecture and describes how it can be used in system implementation. A concrete example shows that iterative architectures are superior to top-down architectures: they defer design costs until features are needed, and reduce the danger of cultural commitment to a faulty design.

REFERENCES

Abrahamsson, P., & Salo, O. (2002). *Agile software development methods: Review and analysis.* Technical Research Centre of Finland.

Abrahamsson, P., Warsta, J., et al. (2003). New directions on agile methods: A comparative analysis. The *25th International Conference on Software Engineering ICSE 2003,* Portland, Oregon, (pp. 244-254).

Ambler, S. (2002). *Agile modeling: Effective practices for eXtreme programming and the unified process.* John Wiley & Sons.

Amey, P., & Chapman, R. (2003). Static verification and extreme programming. *Proceedings of the 2003 Annual ACM SIGAda International COnfernce on Ada: The Engineering of Correct and Reliable Software for Real-Time and Distributed Systems Using Ada and Related Technologies* (pp. 4-9).

Amoroso, E. (1994). *Fundamentals of computer security technology.* Prentice & Hall.

Anderson, R. J. (2001). *Security engineering: A guide to building dependable distributed systems.* Wiley.

Apvrille, A., & Pourzandi, M. (2005). Secure software development by example. *IEEE Security & Privacy, 3*(4), 10–17. doi:10.1109/MSP.2005.103

Bagga, W., & Molva, R. (2005). Policy-based cryptography and application. In *Proceedings of in FC' 2005, 9th International Conference on Financial Cryptography and Data Security*, LNCS Volume 3570, 28 February-03 March 2005, Roseau, The Commonwealth of Dominica.

Baskerville, R. (1993). Information systems security design methods: Implications for information systems development. *ACM Computing Surveys, 25*(4), 375–414. doi:10.1145/162124.162127

Baskerville, R. (2004). Agile security for information warfare: A call for research. *Proceedings of the European Conference on Information System, ECIS2004*, Turku, Finland.

Beck, K. (2004). *Extreme programming explained: Embrace change.* Addison-Wesley.

Beznosov, K. (2003). Extreme security engineering: On employing XP practices to achieve 'good enough security' without defining it. *Proceedings of First ACM Workshop on Business Driven Security Engineering BizSec,* Fairfax, VA.

Boneh, D., & Frankliny, M. (2003). Idnetity-based encryption from the Weil pairing. *SIAM Journal on Computing, 32*(3), 586–615. doi:10.1137/S0097539701398521

Booch, G., & Cockburn, A. (2004). *Balancing agility and discipline: A guide for the perplexed.* Addison-Wesley.

Chivers, H., Paige, R. F., & Ge, X. (2005). Lecture Notes in Computer Science: *Vol. 3556. Agile security using an incremental security architecture extreme programming and agile processes in software engineering* (pp. 1325–1327).

Criteria Common. (2005). *Common criteria for information technology security evaluation*, version 2.5.

Fisch, E. A., & White, G. B. (2000). *Secure computers and networks: Analysis, design, and implementation*. CRC Press.

Fowler, M., & Beck, K. (1999). *Refactoring: Improving the design of existing code*. Addison-Wesley Professional. doi:10.1007/3-540-45672-4_31

Ge, X. (2007). *Agile security for Web applications*. Department of Computer Science, University of York, PhD.

Ge, X., Chivers, H., et al. (2005). *Adapting security risk analysis to the design of database-centric Web-based information system*. 18th International Conference of Software and System Engineering and Their Applications (ICSSEA), CNAM, Paris.

Grance, T., Hash, J., et al. (2003). *Security considerations in the information system development life cycle*. National Institute of Standards and Technology (NIST), Special Publication 800-64.

Graydon, P. J. (2010). *Assurance based development*. Department of Computer Science, University of Virginia, PhD.

Greenwell, W., Holloway, J. C., & Pease, J. (2006). *A taxonomy of fallacies in system safety arguments*. 2006 International System Safety Conference (ISSC 06), Albuquerque, NM, USA.

Hawkins, R. D. (2006). *Using safety contracts in the development of safety critical object oriented systems*. Department of Computer Science, University of York, PhD.

Jaquith, A. R., Soo Hoo, K., & Sudbury, A. W. (2001). Tangible ROI through secure software engineering. *Secure Business Quarterly, 1*(2).

Kelly, T. P. (1998). *Arguing safety -A systematic approach to managing safety cases*. Department of Computer Science, University of York.

Kelly, T. P. (2004). *A systematic approach to safety case management*. Society for Automotive Engineers 2004 World Congress, Detroit, Michigan, USA.

Kelly, T. P. (2007). *Reviewing assurance arguments — A step-by-step approach*. Workshop on Assurance Cases for Security -The Metrics Challenge, Dependable Systems and Networks (DSN).

McGraw, G. (2006). *Software security: Building security in*. Addison Wesley Professional.

Murru, O., & Deias, R. (2003). Assessing XP at a European internet company. *IEEE Software, 20*(3), 37–43. doi:10.1109/MS.2003.1196318

Paige, R., Cakic, J., et al. (2004). Towards agile reengineering of dependable grid applications. *Proceeding of 17th International Conference of Software and System Engineering and Their Applications* (ICSSEA). CNAM, Paris.

Palmer, S. R., & Felsing, J. M. (2002). *A practical guide to feature-driven development*. Prentice Hall.

Pfleeger, C. P., & Pfleeger, S. L. (2003). *Security in computing*. Prentice Hall.

Shore, J. (2004). Continuous design. *IEEE Software, 21*(1), 20–22. doi:10.1109/MS.2004.1259183

Siponen, M., Baskerville, R., et al. (2005). *Integrating security into agile development methods*. 38th Hawaii International Conference on System Sciences.

Stoneburner, G., Goguen, A., et al. (2002). *Risk management guide for information technology systems*. National Institute of Standards and Technology (NIST), Special Publication 800-30.

Viega, J., & McGraw, G. (2002). *Building secure software*. Addison-Wesley.

Wasson, K. (2006). *CLEAR requirements: Improving validity using cognitive linguistic elicitation and representation*. Department of Computer Science, University of Virginia, PhD.

Wayrynen, J., & Boden, M. (2004). Security engineering and eXtreme programming: An impossible marriage? *Extreme Programming and Agile Methods -XP/Agile Universe 2004 (XP2004)* [Springer.]. *LNCS, 3134*, 117–128.

KEY TERMS AND DEFINITIONS

Agile Development: Agile development is a concept which is made up by a set of agile principles in Agile manifesto and concrete practices.

Security Architecture: Security architecture is a system architecture but emphasises the deployment of security features.

Security Argument: Security argument is a document that explicitly explain how the system is secure by giving evidences that the system satisfies its security requirement.

Security Critical System: Security-Critical systems are those where any breach of security is likely to result in huge loss. Security engineering: security engineering is a sub-field of software engineering and it focuses on how to the build secure software system.

Security: Information security means protecting information and information systems from unauthorised access, use, disclosure, disruption, modification, or destruction in order to provide security goals, which are often summarised as confidentiality, integrity and availability.

Service Oriented Architecture: Service oriented architecture (SOA) is an architectural style promoting the concept of business-aligned enterprise service as the fundamental unit of designing, building, and composing enterprise business solutions.

Chapter 10
Analyses of Evolving Legacy Software into Secure Service-Oriented Software using Scrum and a Visual Model

Sam Chung
Institute of Technology, University of Washington, USA

Conrado Crompton
Institute of Technology, University of Washington, USA

Yan Bai
Institute of Technology, University of Washington, USA

Barbara Endicott-Popovsky
University of Washington, USA

Seung-Ho Baeg
Korea Institute of Industrial Technology, Korea

Sangdeok Park
Korea Institute of Industrial Technology, Korea

ABSTRACT

This chapter explores using service-oriented computing to reengineer non-secure legacy software applications to create new secure target applications. Two objectives of this chapter are: (1) to analyze the architectural changes required in order to adopt new web technologies and cope with resultant vulnerabilities in source code; and (2) to measure the level of effort required to modernize software by adopting new web technologies and adding security countermeasures. To meet these objectives, a model-driven Scrum for Service-Oriented Software Reengineering (mScrum4SOSR) methodology was chosen and applied to a reengineering project. Scrum is employed to manage the reengineering project, as well as to measure implementation effort related to the modernization process. Further, a re-documentation technique called 5W1H Re-Doc is used to re-document the non-secure software application at a high level of abstraction in order to help project participants comprehend what is needed to identify candidate services for service-oriented reengineering. Case studies with and without security features are created for different types of applications - a desktop graphical user interface, a web application, a web services application, a restful web services application, and an enterprise service bus application.

DOI: 10.4018/978-1-4666-2503-7.ch010

INTRODUCTION

The collected empirical results in this chapter show that the combination of Scrum and the visual model can help software reengineers to conduct, not only project management and candidate service identification, but also comparisons of modernization efforts in service-oriented reengineering: New architectures that incorporate web technologies do not, necessarily, bring serious complexity to a well-architected legacy system. Modernization from a web application to a Simple Object Access Protocol web services application requires less effort, compared to migrating to a Representational State Transfer web services application. When we incorporated security countermeasures to mitigate known vulnerabilities in a given legacy system, the requirements did not result in major architectural changes.

This chapter discusses how new web technologies and security requirements affect the process of reengineering non-secure and non-service-oriented legacy applications into secure and service-oriented target applications. Software reengineers are interested in understanding how new web technologies and application security requirements affect various software architectures and how much effort is needed to modernize legacy systems into target systems that use Service-Oriented Computing (SOC) (Erl, 2005, Papazoglou & Heuvel, 2007). The process for reengineering a non-service-oriented legacy system into a service-oriented target system is called Service-Oriented Software Reengineering (SOSR) (Chung, Davalos, An, & Iwahara, 2008), a special purpose software reengineering process (Chikofsky & Cross, 1990). It is different from other reengineering problems. SOSR requires identifying the components of a legacy system to be converted into services and how they should be converted. The method used for converting services depends on how the services are implemented. Further, converted services also should be rendered secure during this process.

SOSR can be done at an application, organizational, or cross-organizational level. In this chapter, we are interested in SOSR at the application level for service producers: software reengineering practitioners, who are interested in modernizing legacy applications, want to know what architectural changes new web services technologies bring to an existing desktop or web application. They also want to understand the level of effort required to migrate a legacy application to a target application that embraces web technologies and mitigates vulnerabilities in source code. Meeting these objectives requires methods for collecting information about the software architecture changes and the effort expended during reengineering.

To manage a software engineering project, several agile methods, such as Scrum (Schwaber & Beedle, 2002, Sander, 2007), XP (Hayes, 2003), etc. (Highsmith, 2002), have been broadly used by the software development community. Documentation methods such as 5W1H Re-Doc (Chung, Won, Baeg, & Park, 2009), ICONIX (Rosenberg & Scott, 2001, Rosenberg, Stephens, & Collins-Cope, 2005), etc., have been employed to help development participants comprehend a given application. Several other methods have been proposed to identify candidate services from a given legacy application by Gomaa and Shin (2009), Shin and Gomaa (2006), Peterson (2006), and Chung et al. (2009). Among these approaches, we chose a software reengineering methodology called Model-Driven Scrum for Service-Oriented Software Reengineering (mScrum4SOSR), which was proposed by Chung et al. (2009). The mScrum4SOSR guides the reengineering process using burn down charts and re-documents each system at a high level of abstraction through a visual model. It also allows us to conduct analysis of the impact of new web technologies on the development process and identify vulnerabilities in legacy system code.

In mScrum4SOSR, both Scrum agile software development and 5W1H Re-Doc documentation methods are used. Scrum's unique agile method visualizes the reengineering process through burn down charts. These allow project participants to have a clear understanding of how much the project has progressed and what has blocked progress. Using the burn down charts, we can measure how much effort is needed in order to modernize architecture and implement security countermeasures. 5W1H Re-Doc visualizes multiple architectural views and is designed first and foremost for reverse engineering. The outcome of 5W1H Re-Doc, a visual model, allows participants to understand the software architecture clearly and to identify service candidates in the visual model that are reusable for other applications.

In this chapter, we discus several reengineering case studies we designed that begin with software that has no security features. We assume that an organization wishes to modernize a desktop graphical user interface application to a web application, then to Simple Object Access Protocol (SOAP) web services (Erl, 2005, Papazoglou & Heuvel, 2007), Representational State Transfer (REST) web services (Laitkorpi, Selonen, & Systa, 2009), and finally to an Enterprise Service Bus (ESB) application (Chappell, 2004, Robision, 2004), respectively. Once all of these are complete, these cases are further reengineered to include security countermeasures. All of these reengineering processes are managed using mScrum4SOSR. During the reengineering process, we collected Unified Modeling Language (UML) diagrams showing architecture changes due to evolving technologies and security requirements. We recorded the level of effort required during the process by totaling the burn down points of each Scrum agile process. Empirical results demonstrate how implementing a new web technology affects the architecture of a legacy application, how the application's vulnerabilities affect the architecture of the legacy system, and how much effort is required to make both the architectural and security-driven changes. By studying our examples, software re-engineering practitioners

will discover the benefits of using Scrum and 5W1H Re-Doc for more than visualization of process and application software.

BACKGROUND

Four key concepts, essential to our work, are discussed in this section: (1) the software architecture documentation technique - 5W1H Re-Doc, (2) the agile software development process - Scrum, (3) the scrum-governed and visual model-driven methodology for service-oriented software reengineering - mScrum4SOSR, and 4) service implementation technologies –SOAP Web Services, REST Web Services, and ESB.

5W1H Re-Doc Software Architecture Documentation Method

Re-documentation methods such as 5W1H Re-DOC (Chung et al., 2009) and ICONIX (Rosenberg & Scott, 2001, Rosenberg et al., 2005) are very useful for comprehending legacy systems and user requirements. They allow a software architect to produce either a semantically equivalent representation of the legacy code in high level abstraction or the specified and constructed visual model for user requirements. 5W1H Re-Doc was proposed in our previous work (Chung et al., 2009). It uses standard UML diagrams, emphasizes reverse software engineering, and guides development of simple software documentation. We chose 5W1H Re-Doc for this project.

The 5W1H Re-Doc approach asks, "Who, What, Where, When, Why, and How," hence the name "5W1H". We apply the 5W1H concept to software re-documentation by answering the following questions: (1) Who was involved in re-documentation?; (2) What was re-documented?; (3) Where did re-documentation take place?; (4) When did re-documentation occur?; (5) Why was re-documentation undertaken?; 6) How did re-documentation happen? The concepts of 5W1H Re-Doc were proposed by Chung et al. (2009), and applied to service-oriented software reengineering for case studies (Chung et al., 2009).

The 5W1H Re-Doc is particularly well suited to reverse engineering, compared to other methods like ICONIX (Rosenberg & Scott, 2001, Rosenberg et al., 2005) because it assumes that a legacy application has limited information - such as source code or executable components - which is likely the case in the real world. These artifacts are often essential for reengineering participants to comprehend a given legacy application. The main inputs of 5W1H Re-Doc in the reverse software engineering phase are source code, executable components, and any available documentation. Its output is an abstraction of the legacy system at a high level, i.e., a visual model in UML. In the second forward software engineering phase, new requirements are designed and added into the model. The model generation in this phase is also guided by the 5W1H Re-Doc. Outcomes of the forward phase are a modernized system and its visual model. Until a satisfactory target application is delivered, these two phases are iterated in sequence and the sizes of its model and target application are incremented whenever each phase is over.

When conducting the 5W1H Re-Doc process, the first W defined is "When" which refers to identifying a set of sub-phases for either the reverse or forward software engineering phase. For example, reverse engineering sub-phases could include deployment, implementation, static design, dynamic design, and analysis, in that order; for forward software engineering, the order is opposite. The order is a general guideline and can be iterated in parallel as the reverse engineering process progresses. The second W addressed, "Who," identifies the primary, driving role specific to each sub-phase. There are five different roles to choose from - system administrator, programmer, static designer, dynamic designer, and analyst. For example, the driving role at the deployment sub-phase is typically "system administration." The third W tackled, "Where," refers to 4+1 views - the deployment, implementation, design, process, and use case views created for each role at a specific sub-phase. The strength of the 4+1 view model, proposed by Krunchten (1995) is that it separates software architecture into four concurrent views based upon a shared set of scenarios, giving a comprehensive picture of the system. For example, the deployment view describes the hardware used by the system as well as any communication between nodes. Each view is explicitly represented as a package in the visual model. The fourth W in the process, "What," describes which UML diagrams are used for each view. For example, the deployment view package contains a set of nodes and links. Their relationships are shown in a deployment diagram. The H (How), undertaken next, describes how to draw a UML diagram for each view. For example, within a visual model consisting of the five 4+1 views packages, the implementation view package contains components representing physical files of the legacy application. Relationships among them are represented in a component diagram subordinate to the package where components can be accessed from the deployment view. The last W (Why) describes the purpose of documentation. For example, the purpose of drawing a component diagram under the implementation view package is to represent the concerns of programmers.

Since the 5W1H Re-Doc approach does not depend on a specific set of tools or technologies, it can be used in many documentation or re-documentation processes for software architecture. In addition, many Computer Aided Software Engineering (CASE) tools support generation of classes and their packages for the design view, with minimized human intervention.

Scrum Agile Software Development Process

There are many available agile software development methods such as Scrum, XP, etc., (Hayes, 2003, Highsmith, 2002, Sander, 2007, Schwaber & Beedle, 2002). We chose Scrum because of the strengths of Scrum: (1) visible progress can be demonstrated through the use of burn down charts and (2) constant inspection can be implemented through daily standup and retrospective meetings. Using burn down charts in Scrum allows us to compare our efforts in reengineering.

A Scrum team is made up of several distinct roles, Scrum Master, Product Owner, and Development Team with Quality Assurance. The Scrum Master is responsible for keeping the team moving, facilitating collaboration and making sure iterations are time-boxed correctly; the Product Owner must be available to answer questions, clarify requirements and prioritize tasks; The Development Team is responsible for self-organizing to effectively complete the work.

The Scrum process begins with a sprint planning meeting. In the meeting, a product backlog is created containing all the tasks that the development team must complete before the product can be shipped. A sprint back log is created that contains all the tasks that must be completed during a specific sprint. Once a sprint begins, the Scrum team participates in daily meetings where progress is examined and problems are discussed. The outcome of a sprint is deliverable artifacts such as code, visual models, burn down charts, etc. At the end of every sprint, a sprint demo of the tasks completed during the sprint, along with a retrospective meeting, is held where the team's execution of the process is examined, along with the burn down charts.

Model-Driven Scrum for SOSR: mScrum4SOSR

In order to modernize a legacy system without SOC to a secure target system with SOC, we need a methodology that guides the software reengineering project. For this purpose, we chose mScrum4SOSR, which was proposed in our previous work (Chung et al., 2009). The mScrum4SOSR supports both 5W1H Re-Doc and Scrum that generates visual models and burn down charts.

The mScrum4SOSR is shown in Figure 1. It consists of a pair of reverse and forward software engineering phases that are governed by 5W1H and Scrum. The main tasks in the reverse engineering phase are to (1) generate the visual model, (2) identify candidate services, (3) discover vulnerabilities, and (4) find the corresponding countermeasures from the given legacy source code. Through the reverse engineering phase, we gain comprehension of a given legacy system which is non-secure and not service-oriented. That comprehension is captured in a high level abstraction through 5W1H Re-Doc, i.e., a UML visual

Figure 1. Scrum-governed, model-driven, service-oriented software reengineering

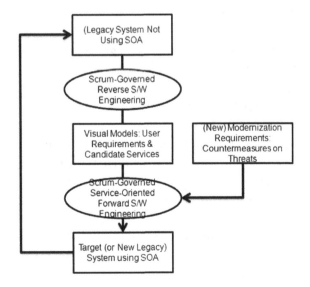

model. By analyzing the visual model, a software reengineer understands the architecture, discovers vulnerabilities, and identifies service candidates that need to be implemented as services. Both a product backlog and a burn down chart with estimated burn points are prepared and updated. For each Sprint, tasks and actual burn points are added or reprioritized.

The main tasks in the forward software engineering phase are to (1) update the visual model according to new requirements, (2) implement a target system based upon the new designs, and (3) update the model again for the new implementation. A software reengineer updates the generated visual model for correct design, based upon new requirements such as service identification and security countermeasures. In parallel with the model updates, the software reengineer converts the components that were identified as candidate services into actual services by using one among several web service implementation technologies. In addition, countermeasures are implemented that mitigate discovered vulnerabilities in the target system in order to create a secure target application. Like in the reverse engineering phase, the product backlog and the burn down chart are constantly updated at each sprint.

Service Implementation Technologies

SOC is an emerging computing paradigm. In SOC, software is a service, which can be combined with other services to create a new service (Erl, 2005, Papazoglou & Heuvel, 2007). Currently, there are three possible implementation approaches - SOAP web services (Erl, 2005, Papazoglou & Heuvel, 2007), REST web services (Laitkorpi et al., 2009), and ESB (Chappell, 2004, Robision, 2004).

SOAP is a protocol designed to exchange structured information using eXtensible Markup Language (XML). It is a message framework of choice for many different web services. The struc-

ture of a SOAP message is as follows. The root node of a SOAP message is the *Envelope* element. Contained within the envelope are a mandatory *Body* element and an optional *Header* element. The *Body* element contains the message payload. The *Header* element is used for the purposes of processing messages at intermediary nodes, extension, and authentication, to name a few.

SOAP is associated with Service Oriented Architecture (SOA), in which a service is published with a standard interface by a service producer, discovered by a service consumer, and advertised at a service registry. SOA is geared towards applications that are activity-based, such as banking, where users are interested in performing transactions. SOA has many distinct characteristics including, loose-coupling between client and server, binding to a service interface, full interface and payload descriptions in the interface contract, support for request/response and message-passing systems, and works well for "shared" systems that cross organizational boundaries.

The most common alternative to SOAP is REST. REST web services are resource-oriented (as opposed to SOAP which is operation-oriented). They are invoked through a standard interface with HTTP, not SOAP. These qualities require special consideration at the design stage. REST web services are simple to implement with no contract to define a REST service. They rely on a simple set of "verbs" and put all complexity into "nouns" that specify the resource, receiving HTTP GET, POST, PUT, and DELETE requests. REST web services only require HTTP, not SOAP.

REST is often associated with Resource Oriented Architecture (ROA). ROA is ideal for applications that are resource-based where feeds are the "resource" that users seek information about and then update the status of that resource. ROA has characteristics such as loose-coupling between client and server, binding to resource data, cacheability of resource data, repeatable operations, and results returned within an expiration period.

An ESB is a layer of communication and integration logic between the client and server units used to solve technology and information model mismatches when building an extended SOA. For an ESB, three distinct roles of a developer are defined: service producer, consumer, and broker. The goal of ESB is to automate the business process. It achieves this by offering orchestration and choreographic technologies using Web Service Business Process Execution Language (WS-BPEL), along with message routing and message binding. The result is a heterogeneous environment where service units can be integrated or replaced quickly.

ESB has the following characteristics: it encourages loosely coupled architecture; it decouples via message passing mechanisms (Java Messaging Service (JMS)) versus direct network connections (Hyper Text Transfer Protocol (HTTP)); it provides integration of business applications and processes quickly and easily; it supports multiple protocols and data transformation; and it provides reliable and secure messaging and queuing through straight forward configuration rather than coding. The latter allows the exposure of legacy systems as services, without the need for programming, through the use of adapters that support only one-to-one request-reply communication through traditional HTTP-based services. This allows asynchronous, one-way messaging to multiple subscribers using topic-based messaging, and employing built-in mediation, orchestration, transformation, or integration to legacy systems.

RELATED WORK

In order to discover which software engineering methodology works best for our analyses, we explored existing methodologies and chose one that satisfied the following criteria: first, it needed to be a software reengineering methodology that starts with reverse engineering for comprehending a given legacy application, as well as identifying candidate services and vulnerabilities from the source code of the given legacy system. Second, we were particularly interested in a methodology that used metrics to trace the level of effort invested during reengineering. Third, we were interested in a methodology that would migrate a legacy system not using web services into a target system that uses web services - either simple or composite. In other words, we were interested in an application level SOSR, not an organizational or cross-organizational level SOSR.

Many existing methodologies do not satisfy all of the criteria above. Some requirements engineering methodologies - such as ProSecO (Breu, Hafner, Innerhofer-Oberperfler, & Wozak, 2008, Bertino, Martino, Paci, & Squicciarini, 2010), OCTAVE[1], and CORAS[2] - start with forward engineering to discover security issues from given requirements. These methods focus on SOSR at the organizational or cross organizational levels.

Bertino and et al. (2010) provide a comprehensive guide to security for web services. Their book focuses on service level security. Another book "Security Engineering for Service-Oriented Architectures," by Hafner and Breu (2009), describes a security analysis process called ProSecO and a framework for domain model-driven security for inter-organizational workflow called SECTET. Those approaches highlight organizational level SOSR. We are interested in counter measuring the source code itself.

Other approaches, discussed below and in (Gomaa & Shin, 2009, Shin & Gomaa, 2006, Peterson, 2006), do not provide either a clear explanation for re-documentation, or metrics for invested effort. Gomaa and Shin (2009) explain an approach for modeling complex applications by modeling application requirements independently from security requirements, using case models. Consequently, this separation of requirements reduces system complexity, therefore making the system more maintainable; however, when the two requirements are improperly woven back together into an application, this method could potentially introduce security flaws.

Shin & Gomaa (2006) also proposed a method for describing the evolution of an application system to a secure application system. This approach also separates the concerns of security from concerns for the application. The software architecture for supporting security services is modeled using UML notation, which is separated from application concerns. Security requirements are captured in security use cases and are encapsulated in security objects as the non-secure system evolves to a secure system. Security services are encapsulated in connectors, separated from components providing application system functionality, and are activated if the security requirement conditions are satisfied. The disadvantage of this approach is that not all connectors and components become secure ones, making those remaining prospective targets for attackers. Furthermore, the output data from components is not validated for rigidity, therefore infected components could feed invalid or corrupted data to a component that is not secure, creating vulnerability to a chain-link attack on the system.

Peterson (2006) introduces Service-Oriented Security Architecture (SOSA) which views security as a service that is decoupled and can be composed. The SOSA provides a set of software architecture viewpoints that allow security architects to construct a holistic system design. The SOSA consists of the following different views: identity, service, message, deployment environment, and the transaction use case life cycle view. Each view is mapped to a particular section of the architecture, and consequently demonstrates the security and design decisions made. The views are composed of domain specific elements, constraints, threats, risks, vulnerabilities, and countermeasures.

Although other diverse SOSR methodologies may be further explored, based upon the best knowledge of the authors, mScrum4SOSR satisfies the given criteria: the methodology combines (1) the 5W1H re-documentation technique (Chung et al., 2009) supporting Kruchten's 4+1 architectural views (Krunchten, 1995) and (2) the Scrum

agile software development method equipped with its built-in metric system (Schwaber & Beedle, 2002, Sander, 2007). In addition, this combined methodology focuses on an application level SOSR with emphasis on the reverse software engineering phase.

DESIGN OF EXPERIMENTS

In this section, we first describe the legacy system to be modernized, and then provide several examples of two types of reengineering projects conducted to modernize this legacy system: (1) four non-secure legacy systems evolved into four non-secure target systems using different web technologies and (2) five non-secure legacy systems evolved into five secure target systems using this same series of web technologies. Finally, we describe our approach used to conduct these reengineering projects.

Legacy System to be Modernized

For our experiment, a desktop application called 'Intelligent Business (iBusiness) Suite' is modernized to a series of target systems using different web technologies. The system is currently used by a small company in Pierce County, Washington. It maintains information about the company employees, meeting minutes, and power point slides presented during community events. This type of legacy system is considered an invaluable corporate asset, in and of itself, because the embedded business logic represents an investment of many years of coding, development, enhancement, and modification; however, the system was developed without a consistent underlying architecture, resulting in overlapping and redundant functionality and data.

Figure 2 shows the iBusiness Suite use case, design, and deployment views. The use case view of Figure 2 shows the interactions between two actors (user, administrator) and the 'iBusiness'

Figure 2. Use case, design, and deployment views of the non-secure 'iBusiness suite' legacy system

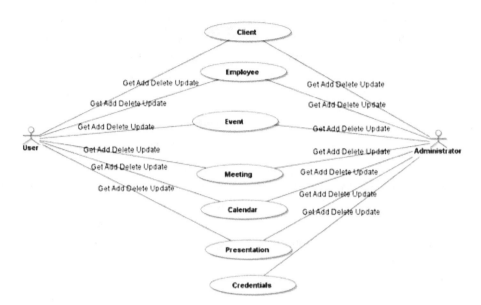

system; the design view of Figure 3 shows the high level packages, classes within each package, and their relationships among three different layers—the presentation, business logic, and data access layers. The deployment view of Figure 4 represents the deployment of executable components of 'iBusiness Suite,' a non-secure application written in C#. It uses a layered architecture, backed by an MS SQL Server Express database with Open Data Base Connectivity (ODBC).

ODBC uses 2-tier client/server architecture. The entity-relationship diagram for 'IBusinessDB' is shown in Figure 5.

Reengineering Projects

Our goal in our experiment was to determine (1) how the application architecture would change due to incorporation of a web technology and (2) the level of effort required for this modernization

Figure 3. High level packages, classes within each package, and their relationships among three different layers

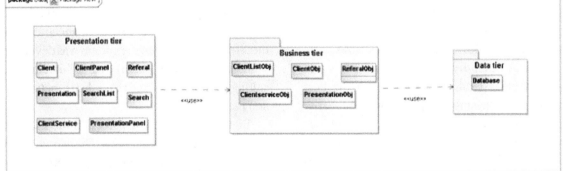

Figure 4. Deployment of executable components of "iBusiness Suite"

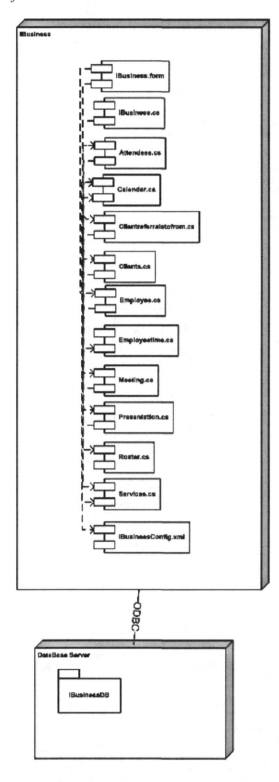

activity. We set up four reengineering projects in Table 1 and followed a standard procedure for each project. First the desktop legacy system was reengineered to a target web application using layered and 3-tier architectures. The web legacy system is then modernized into two web services applications using SOAP and REST technologies, supporting different architectures, SOA and ROA, respectively. The SOAP web services application is further reengineered into an ESB application. This sequence of evolutions was adopted because this reflects the order in which those technologies emerged. Many desktop applications were first migrated to web applications, then SOAP, REST, and then ESB for any services.

We used Java technologies - such as Java Server Page (JSP), Servlet, and Java. We selected 'openESB' (found at http://openesb-dev.org) which integrates 'NetBeans' IDE, and thus provides a set of SOC tools for development, testing and deployment. At this stage, REST web services could not be invoked from the 'openESB.'

Microsoft .NET technology could have been used for migration instead of Java technology; however, Microsoft's ESB engine, BizTalk, does not support WS-BPEL for service composition at this stage. In addition, current MS Visual Studio Pro, 2007, supports the SOAP web services development environment, but not the REST web services development environment.

Our legacy system, iBusiness Suite, was designed without considering security requirements. Thus, for our next series of experiments, we modernized five non-secure versions of our legacy system into secure target systems in order to determine (1) how the architecture of each system was changed for mitigating vulnerabilities found in each legacy system version and (2) the level of effort required to implement these security countermeasures. To identify our security requirements, we referred to the Open Web Application Security Project (OWASP) top 10 risks which names SQL injection and Cross-Site Scripting (XSS) as, by far, the top two risks[3]. Therefore,

Figure 5. IBusinessDB entity-relationship diagram

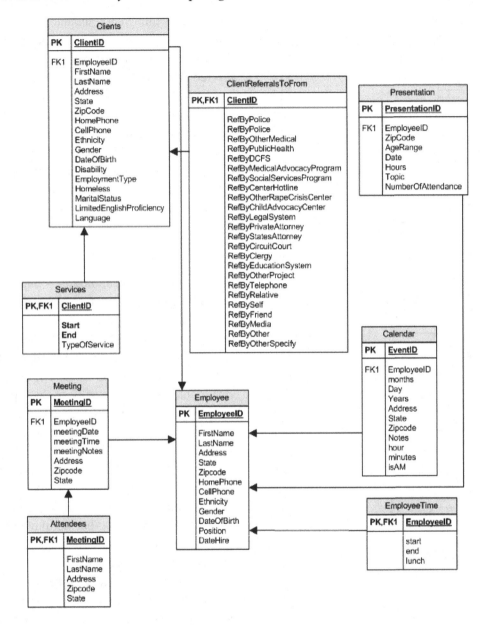

Table 1. Reengineered non-secure legacy to non-secure target systems by Web technology

Reengineering Project	Legacy System	Target System	Technology
1	Non-Secure Desktop app.	Non-Secure Web app.	Desktop to Web
2	Non-Secure Web app.	Non-Secure SOAP Web Services app.	Web to SOAP Web Services
3	Non-Secure Web app.	Non-Secure REST Web Services app.	Web to REST Web Services
4	Non-Secure SOAP Web Services app.	Non-Secure ESB app.	SOAP to ESB

the security countermeasures introduced into our legacy system examples were designed to mitigate these two types of attacks from non-trusted data sources. Table 2 enumerates the five projects we conducted that migrate a non-secure version of our legacy system to a secure system using several different web technologies.

The Reengineering Process

Each of the nine reengineering projects consisted of 20 Sprints; each Sprint taking 1 week. The Scrum team for each project consisted of 3 people assuming the 4 different roles: Product Owner, Scrum Master, Developer, and Quality Assurance. One person took the role of Product Owner, the second person the roles of Developer and Quality Assurance, the third person the roles of Scrum Master and Quality Assurance. (Note that two were assigned to Quality Assurance.) The Developer was educated and trained in Scrum, 5W1H Re-Doc, Microsoft .NET technology, and Java technology before starting the project. He had more than 4 years of development experience within the business domain of the legacy system and holds a bachelor degree in Computer Science.

The Product Owner expected the Scrum team to develop an initial desk top application that remained vulnerable to invalid input data - thus separating the web modernization effort from the security modernization effort so that we could analyze the impacts of each. The Scrum Master supervised each Sprint. A Sprint took one week instead of two or four weeks since the projects were limited to two academic quarters. Also, instead of a daily Scrum standup meeting, two Scrum standup meetings were usually held per Sprint due to team member availability. A burn down chart was reviewed at each Sprint. In Figure 6, the X axis shows a total of 20 Sprints and the Y axis the burn points. To estimate burn points, a product back log, which consisted of modernization tasks, was first constructed. An estimated burn point was assigned to each task according to its difficulty level. The starting burn point, 650, was calculated by summing the estimated burn points of tasks in the product back log. Before starting each reengineering project, we estimated how many points would be burned at the end of each Sprint. Whenever a Scrum meeting occurred during a reengineering project, actual burn points were recorded.

Figure 6 shows (1) the optimum pace (in blue) for the expected burn points for all modernization efforts, (2) the actual burn points (in red) required to develop all of the system versions under comparison, and (3) the actual burn points (in green) required to mitigate certain common vulnerabilities. Actual burn points are compared to estimates in order to show results of our reengineering efforts. If an actual burn point (in red) for a specific Sprint appears below the estimate, it indicates that the project performed better than estimated. Further, if an actual burn point (in green) for a non-secure to secure reengineering project is higher than the estimated burn point, it means that the reengineering project experienced delays.

Table 2. Reengineered non-secure legacy to secure target systems by Web technology

Reengineering	Legacy System	Target System	Technology
1	Non-Secure Desktop app.	Secure Desktop app.	Desktop
2	Non-Secure Web app.	Secure Web app.	Web
3	Non-Secure SOAP WS app.	Secure SOAP WS app.	SOAP WS
4	Non-Secure REST WS app.	Secure REST WS app.	REST WS
5	Non-Secure ESB app.	Secure ESB app.	ESB

Figure 6. A burn down chart for the modernization of 'iBusiness' suites

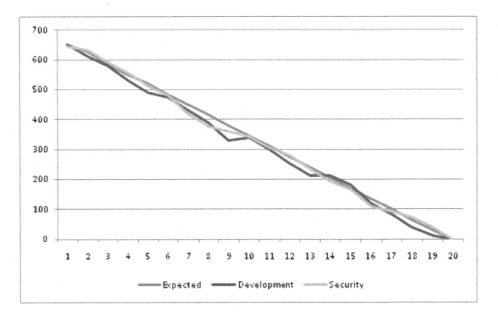

The Developer conducted the 5W1H Re-Doc process for each system version. The outcomes of the 5W1H Re-Doc process - the visual models - were discussed and reviewed during Sprint meetings. The Quality Assurance team members tested both the source code and the visual models for each system version. Due to space limitation in this article, we only provide conclusions drawn from among the 4+1 views developed for each system. Once developed, the non-secure system versions were reengineered further into secure target systems by adding countermeasures designed to mitigate the identified vulnerabilities.

Factors under Study

During the mScrum4SOSR activities, we collected visual models and a burn down chart for each system version. The visual models were used to analyze:(1) how implementing various web technologies into legacy systems affects the architectures of the target systems and (2) how mitigating web system vulnerabilities affects architectures of secure target systems. In order to know the degree of architectural change, the following information was collected from the visual models: the programming languages used for implementation, the number of tiers used for deployment, the relationship between the layers and n-tiers, the protocols employed between two tiers, and the conceptual architecture for the design. A burn down chart was used to analyze: (1) the level of effort required to modernize non-secure legacy systems using various different web technologies and (2) the level of effort required to modernize non-secure legacy systems into secure target systems in order to mitigate against common web application vulnerabilities.

ANALYSIS OF RESULTS

Effects of New Technologies on Architectural Changes when Migrating from Non-Secure Legacy Systems to Non-Secure Target Systems

In order to understand how new web technologies affect architectural changes in non-secure systems, we first collected the 4+1 architecture views for each respective visual model and made comparisons. We summarize the results in Table 3 which provides information about each legacy system: the programming languages used for implementation, the number of tiers implemented, the relationship between the 3 layers (P: Presentation, B: Business Logic, and D: Data Store) and n-tiers, the protocols employed between two tiers, and the conceptual architecture.

Based upon information gleaned from architectural comparisons summarized in Table 3 and the corresponding visual models, we gained understanding of how implementing new web technologies affects the architecture of a target system. Table 4 summarizes our findings from our four reengineering project examples about the impacts of implementing different web technologies on system architecture. First, a very small change occurs at the data store layer, compared to both the presentation and the business logic layers. These changes arise from the change of database engine. If this change were not required by the web application, this layer would not be affected. The design view of the database was not changed during all migrations. The data store layer was not affected by choice of web services technologies.

We also found that the web application can be migrated to a web services application - regardless of whether SOAP, REST, or ESB is implemented - with only small changes to the presentation layer. The discovered changes came from the client side implementation of the web application as a result of applying the HTTP protocol. Moreover, the use case view in each visual model was not changed at all, regardless of which new web technology was implemented.

Table 3. Reengineered non-secure legacy to secure target systems by Web technology

Target Application	Non-Secure Desktop	Non-Secure Web	Non-Secure SOAP WS	Non-Secure REST WS	Non-Secure ESB
Legacy Application		Non-Secure Desktop	Non-Secure Web	Non-Secure Web	Non-Secure SOAP Web
Language	C#	Java, Servlet	JSP, Java	JSP, Java, Servlet	JSP, Java
# of tiers	2	3	3	3	3
Tier # (Layer)	1(P/B), 2 (D)	1 (P), 2 (B), 3 (D)	1 (P), 2 (B), 3 (D)	1 (P), 2 (B), 3 (D)	1 (P), 2 (B), 3 (D)
Protocol between client and tier 1		HTTP	HTTP	HTTP	HTTP
Protocol between tiers 1 and 2		HTTP	SOAP	HTTP	SOAP
Protocol between tiers 2 and 3	ODBC	JDBC	JDBC	JDBC	JDBC
Application Engines		Web Server	SOAP Engine	Web Server	SOAP & ESB Engine
Database Engines	MS SQL Server Express	MySQL	MySQL	MySQL	MySQL
Architecture Type	3 Layered, 2-tier	3 Layered, 3-tier, C/S	3 Layered, 3-tier, C/S, SOA	3 Layered, 3-tier, C/S, ROA	3 Layered, 3-tier, C/S, Extended SOA

Table 4. Analyses of architectural changes for non-secure versions 'iBusiness' suite

Relative Changes	Layers	Desktop to Web	Web to SOAP WS	Web to REST WS	SOAP to ESB
Very Small Changes	Data Store Layer	Not Changed	Not Changed	Not Changed	Not Changed
	Protocol between tiers 2 and 3	Changed (ODBC to JDBC)	Not Changed (JDBC to JDBC)	Not Changed (JDBC to JDBC)	Not Changed (JDBC to JDBC)
	Database Engines	Changed (MS SQL Server Express to MySQL)	Not Changed (MySQL to MySQL)	Not Changed (MySQL to MySQL)	Not Changed (MySQL to MySQL)
Small	Presentation Layer	Changed (2 components added)	Not Changed (no change)	Not Changed (no change)	Not Changed (no change)
	Protocol between a client and tier 1	Changed (none to HTTP)	Not changed (HTTP to HTTP)	Not changed (HTTP to HTTP)	Not changed (HTTP to HTTP)
Somewhat	Business Layer	Changed (2 components replaced)	Not Changed (no change)	Changed (6 added)	Changed (1 replaced, 4 added)
	Protocol between tiers 1 and 2	Changed (none to HTTP)	Changed (HTTP to SOAP)	Not changed (HTTP to HTTP)	Not Changed (SOAP to SOAP)
	Application Engines	Changed (None to Web Server)	Changed (SOAP engine added)	Not Changed (Web Server to Web Server)	Changed (ESB Engine added)
	Architecture Type	No change (C/S to C/S)	Changed (SOA added)	Changed (ROA added)	Changed (SOA to Extended SOA)

Lastly, most changes occur at the business logic layer due to the different architecture requirements for SOA, ROA, and an extended SOA. In our analysis, we noted which components were replaced or added and also counted how many components were changed at the business layer. The REST web services application needed more changes, compared to the SOAP web services application. Many specifications of REST web services are done manually due to the lack of REST tool support. Modernization from SOAP web services to the ESB application requires some change in order to employ the ESB engine. When a desktop application is migrated to a web application, the web application required some changes to existing components in the desktop application; however, the migration from a web application to a SOAP services application did not cause any addition to the physical components, except for adding a SOAP engine. This implies that

the current infrastructure of SOAP web services is well-supported, compared to REST and ESB. Since the current computing environment supports a built-in SOAP engine, the modernization process can be performed easily, although the developer must understand two different roles - that of service consumer and that of service producer.

Effects of Mitigating Security Vulnerabilities on Architectural Changes when Migrating from Non-Secure Legacy to Secure Target Systems

We then studied how mitigating the security vulnerabilities affected architectures of the various target systems created in the first phase of our experiment. We again collected the 4+1 architectural views for each respective visual model and made architectural comparisons. Prior to migration, we noted whether the deployment view of the legacy system had input data validation features. If the features did not exist in the visual model, the legacy system was determined to be vulnerable to SQL injection and XSS. We then added input validation countermeasures to create secure target systems. As an example, the secure SOAP web application was determined to be vulnerable to XSS and SQL injection. By adding client and server-side input data validation components to the legacy system, the system was secured. All network protocols were also secured. In Table 5, we summarize information from each migration of a non-secure version of 'iBusiness' Suite to a secure target system.

Table 6 summarizes the architectural changes required for securing each non-secure version of iBusiness Suite. All resulting target systems, regardless of web technology employed, implemented the same security countermeasures - input data validation at both the client and server sides and the addition of secure protocols. For example, when a non-secure web application was reengineered to a secure web services application using SOAP, REST, or ESB, the presentation at tier 1 was secured with its client-side validation. The business layer was modified by adding a validation utility class for input data validation to its legacy system. Those validation components, for

both the presentation and the business logic layers, sanitize all incoming data, thus verifying the validity of the data before it is used at each layer. The communication between the presentation and business tiers was modified to use HTTP over Secure Sockets Layer (SSL) called HTTPS. HTTPS protects against eavesdropping and man-in-the-middle attacks. The communication between the business tier and the database was also upgraded to use HTTPS.

Level of Effort Required for New Web Technology Adoption

In order to understand the level of effort required to migrate a non-secure legacy systems to a web application, the modernization effort was evaluated using Scrum burn points. Figure 7 shows the actual percentage of burn points required for modernization by web technology used. The amount of effort applied to modernizing the C# desktop application to a Java web application is almost the same. Reusing existing design, database, and core classes from C# to Java saves burn points. These artifacts were used to create object relational mapping for Hibernate, and web application Java files.

The level of effort needed to modernize the web application to a SOAP web service is com-

Table 5. Analysis of architectural changes for secure versions of 'iBusiness' suite

Target Application	Secure Desktop	Secure Web	Secure SOAP WS	Secure REST WS	Secure ESB
Legacy Application	Non-Secure Desktop	Non-Secure Web	Non-Secure SOAP WS	Non-Secure REST WS	Non-Secure SOAP WS
Security for Presentation	Validate.cs	Validate.js HTTPS	Validate.js HTTPS	Validate.js HTTPS	Validate.js HTTPS
Security for Business		Validate.java HTTPS	Validate.java HTTPS	Validate.java HTTPS	Validate.java HTTPS
Security for Data	ODBC/HTTP	JDBC/HTTPS	JDBC/HTTPS	JDBC/HTTPS	JDBC/HTTPS
Architecture Type	3 Layered, 2-tier	3 Layered, 3-tier, Client/Server	3 Layered, 3-tier, C/S, SOA	3 Layered, 3-tier, C/S, ROA	3 Layered, 3-tier, C/S, Extended SOA

Table 6. Architectural changes required to create secure 'iBusiness' suite by Web technology

Relative Changes	Layer	Desktop to Web	Web to SOAP WS	Web to REST WS	SOAP to ESB
Very minimal changes	Presentation Layer	Change (Validate.cs to Validate.js & HTTPS)	No change (Validate.js & HTTPS kept)	No change (Validate.js & HTTPS kept)	No change (Validate.js & HTTPS kept)
No	Business Logic Layer	Change (Validate.cs to Validate.java HTTPS)	No change (Validate.java HTTPS kept.)	No change (Validate.java HTTPS kept.)	No change (Validate.java HTTPS kept.)
No	Data Store Layer	Change (ODBC/HTTP to JDBC/HTTPS)	No change (JDBC/HTTPS kept)	No change (JDBC/HTTPS kept)	No change (JDBC/HTTPS kept)

Figure 7. Level of effort required to modernize 'iBusiness' suite with Web technologies

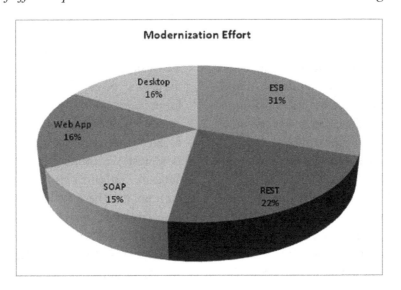

paratively less than that for modernizing the desktop application to a web application. All existing Java classes were reused, including the database and the Hibernates object relational mapping. The majority of the effort was spent creating the WSDL file and implementing the services; however, compared to modernization to a SOAP web services application from a web application, the modernization to a REST web services application requires more effort due to the process of defining restful web services. From our analysis, the amount of effort to modernize a web application to a REST web services application is greater than modernizing a web application to a SOAP web services application.

The level of effort to modernize the web SOAP application to an ESB application is significantly greater than any of the other modernization projects due to the effort expended on understanding how to use the ESB engine and BPEL for composition; however, after the ESB application is created, updating it with new functionality takes the least amount of time, compared to developing the equivalent functionally for each of the other web technologies.

Level of Effort Required for Implementing Security Countermeasures

Using the burn down chart, the level of effort required to implement security countermeasures was recorded and analyzed. Figure 8 illustrates the percentage of effort used to secure each of the target systems under comparison. Effort to implement countermeasures to secure the web application was relatively higher than that required for securing the desktop application since it required server-side validation and protocol changes. Further, as the chart clearly shows, securing SOAP and REST web services consumed the most effort; meanwhile the least effort was required to protect the desktop application. Effort to implement countermeasures to secure the SOAP and the REST web services applications was relatively greater than securing the web application, which we attributed to the design of web services. When modernizing a web service to a secure web service, the security framework used to protect the web application is ported over to the web service and used as a foundation to secure the web service, requiring

more and stricter validation rules, error and exception handling, along with system-level logging. This would account for the additional eight or nine percent increased effort required to protect the REST and the SOAP systems, respectively.

In contrast, when transitioning to a secure ESB application from a non-secure ESB application, the level of effort to implement security countermeasures was proportionally less than for any of the other systems, because the ESB framework manages the majority of the countermeasures which are already provided by the SOAP web service. Thus, the level of effort required to implement any remaining security countermeasures for the ESB application was less than for other migrations.

LIMITATION OF VALIDITY

We caution readers to consider the limitations of our study. Internally, any experiment of the sort we just outlined is dependent on the quality of the Scrum team assembled to execute the project, the experience and knowledge of participating team

Figure 8. Level of incorporation effort required to secure 'iBusiness' suite

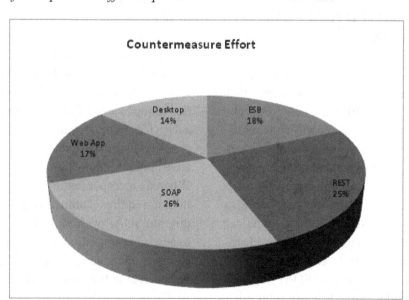

members, and the length of the project period. Our study is biased to an academic setting, rather than an industrial one. Project participants consisted of a graduate student as an experienced developer and tester who has worked in a business area related to the project, a product owner who supervised the student at his work place, and an instructor who conducted roles of both Scrum Master and quality assurance. Further, the student was trained in many of the concepts and skills critical to the experiment - such as Scrum, UML modeling, and web services, etc., before starting the project. Externally, since this project was conducted as the student's capstone project, the selected project period was limited, artificially, to the 2 quarters of the academic calendar that the capstone was offered and to 1-week time increments chosen arbitrarily for each Sprint. An extrapolation of our results to industry should be seen in light of these limitations; however, we are optimistic that our findings will prove useful to software reengineering practitioners who are considering implementing new web services technologies in legacy systems or who are concerned with implementing security countermeasures to mitigate software vulnerabilities.

LESSONS LEARNED AND FUTURE RESEARCH DIRECTIONS

In summary, this chapter has discussed a study designed to determine how modernization - that includes either (1) implementing new web technologies or (2) mitigating web security vulnerabilities, respectively - affects architectural changes and the level of effort expended on reengineering projects. Four reengineering projects were conducted, based on a single use case scenario for modernizing a non-secure desktop graphical user interface application to a non-secure web application, then to SOAP web services and REST web services, respectively. The SOAP services were then migrated to an ESB application. Five

additional reengineering projects were conducted that incorporated security countermeasures into these newly derived web applications.

This service-oriented software reengineering activity was guided by 'mScrum4SOSR' that uses the Scrum process for managing and visualizing the process and UML modeling for re-documenting each system version at a high level of abstraction. During each Sprint, we collected data about the architectural changes that occurred due to incorporating either evolving web technologies or security requirements. We then recorded the level of effort required by totaling the burn down points for all Sprints employed for managing each of the software reengineering projects.

We discovered that the layered and multi-tier architecture of a system plays a key role in affecting the level of effort required for modernization. Although new technologies need new engines such as web server, SOAP engine, and ESB to support new architectures such as SOA, ROA, or extended SOA, the level of effort required to accommodate the necessary architectural changes can be minimized as long as a given legacy system is designed with layered and n-tier architecture. This implies that new architectures that incorporate web technologies do not, necessarily, bring serious complexity to a well-architected legacy system. In our examples, the majority of architectural changes occurred at the business layer by adding components that ensure that the new engines work.

Secondly, we learned that modernization from a web application to a SOAP web services application requires less effort, compared to migrating to a REST web services application. In other words, we concluded that the current REST development environment requires more effort for migration. When we incorporated an ESB engine, we learned that it requires comparatively more effort to migrate SOAP web services to ESB, compared to any other migration. ESB requires that the reengineer understand service composition and the ESB server at the outset, consuming resources.

Thirdly, when we incorporated security countermeasures to mitigate known vulnerabilities in a given legacy system, the requirements for input data validation did not result in major architectural changes. We discovered that protocols must be secured and that architectural layers must be validated in a non-secure application when adding an input validation module. Through the design of our experiments, we were able to separate the architectural effects of implementing security requirements from that of implementing new web technologies. Further, we documented that a secure web application can migrate seamlessly to a secure target application using advanced web technologies such as SOAP, REST, and ESB.

Fourthly, we learned that securing web applications requires an increased level of effort compared to securing a desktop application using monolithic computing, since an architectural tier is added. Each individual tier, and all the connections between tiers, must be secured in order for the application to be secure. Further, securing an ESB application requires relatively less effort compared to securing SOAP or REST web service applications. For the ESB transformation, the web services are first secured and then the ESB engine applied, which typically has a management system that handles implementation of the majority of security countermeasures.

Lastly, we learned that migrating a legacy system to a service-oriented application through the use of Scrum and 5W1H Re-Doc aids in comparing the effects on architectural change of adopting new web technologies or adding security countermeasures. Scrum also facilitates the collection of level of effort measures through the burn down chart feature. By using burn down charts that visualize reengineering progress, we can compare how much effort has been expended toward migration. In parallel with Scrum, 5W1H Re-Doc allowed comparison of visual models for each system required to produce the necessary architectural changes. Table 7 shows the best practices and things to avoid when applying a model-driven Scrum to an SOSR project.

For future research, we plan to develop additional diverse examples, using different programming languages and architectures. The initial non-secure legacy system was designed using good architecture, for example, a 2-tier, layered architecture. This made migration to a web application relatively easier and candidate services for service-orientated architectures more discoverable. Also, the initial legacy system was implemented in a well-defined, object-oriented programming language, C#, which is comparatively easy to modernize to a target system using another well-defined object-oriented programming language, Java. If we start with a legacy system

Table 7. The best practices and things to avoid when applying a model-driven Scrum to an SOSR project

Purpose	Best Practices	Things to Avoid
To visualize reengineering progress and architectural changes	Use both a burn down chart for visualizing agile process and a visual model for visualizing software architecture	Using burn down charts and visual models without knowing their complementary effects
To minimize the necessary architectural changes due to new web technologies	Start to design a system using good architecture	Develop a system without a consistent underlying architecture
To minimize the modernization effort due to new web technologies	Use SOAP instead of REST web services if you need less modernization effort with object orientation	Using ESB without understanding service composition and the business itself
To minimize the incorporation effort of security countermeasures to mitigate known vulnerabilities in a given legacy system	Securing your system does not need major architectural change	Not considering security at the beginning

that uses the procedural language, C, and that does not employ good architecture, the adoption of service-oriented software reengineering is expected to be more challenging. We plan to study the effects of Scrum-governed, service-oriented software reengineering in this unfavorable set of circumstances to offer a comparison to our current study.

In addition, we plan to collect more examples subject to different types of threats. In this current set of experiments, we studied the effects on architecture and level of effort expended for implementing countermeasures that mitigate against the most frequently encountered web application threats - SQL injection and XSS. In future work, we will consider implementing countermeasures for other threats such as buffer overflow, denial of service (DOS), etc. These threats are expected to require additional secure coding measures for modernization into a secure application.

ACKNOWLEDGMENT

This research is funded by both NSF/SFS Capacity Building grant: DUE-0912109 and Dual Use Projects of MKE (Ministry of Knowledge and Economy) contract titled "Development of Quadruped Legged Robot Platform Technology."

REFERENCES

Bertino, E., Martino, L., Paci, F., & Squicciarini, A. (2010). *Security for Web services and service-oriented architectures*. Berlin, Germany: Springer-Verlag. doi:10.1007/978-3-540-87742-4

Breu, R., Hafner, M., Innerhofer-Oberperfler, F., & Wozak, F. (2008). *Model-driven security engineering of service oriented system* (pp. 59–71). Information Systems and E-Business Technologies, Lecture Notes in Business Information Processing. doi:10.1007/978-3-540-78942-0_8

Chappell, D. E. (2004). *Enterprise service bus*. O'Reilly Media, Inc.

Chikofsky, E. J., & Cross, H. J. II. (1990). Reverse engineering and design recovery: A taxonomy. *IEEE Software*, 7(1), 13–17. doi:10.1109/52.43044

Chung, S., Davalos, S., An, J., & Iwahara, K. (2008). Legacy to Web migration: Service-oriented software reengineering (SoSR) methodology. *International Journal of Services Sciences*, 1(3/4), 333–365. doi:10.1504/IJSSCI.2008.021769

Chung, S., Won, D., Baeg, S., & Park, S. (2009). *A model-driven scrum process for service-oriented software reengineering: mScrum4SOSR*. The 2nd International Conference on Computer Science and its Applications (CSA 2009), December 10-12, 2009, Jeju Island, Korea.

Chung, S., Won, D., Baeg, S., & Park, S. (2009). *Service-oriented reverse reengineering: 5W1H model-driven re-documentation and candidate services identification*. IEEE International Conference on Service-Oriented Computing and Applications (SOCA'09), Taipei, Taiwan.

Erl, T. (2005). *Service-oriented architecture concepts, technology, and design*. Prentice Hall.

Gomaa, H., & Shin, M. E. (2009). Separating application and security concerns in use case models. *Proceedings of the 15th Workshop on Early Aspects (EA)*. Charlottesville, VA: ACM.

Hafner, M., & Breu, R. (2009). *Security engineering for service-oriented architectures*. Berlin, Germany: Springer-Verlag.

Hayes, S. (2003, May 21). *An introduction to extreme programming*. ZDNet Australia.

Highsmith, J. (2002). *Agile software development ecosystems*. Boston, MA: Addison-Wesley.

Krunchten, P. (1995). The 4+1 view model of software architecture. *IEEE Software*, 12(6), 42–50.

Laitkorpi, M., Selonen, P., & Systa, T. (2009). Towards a model-driven process for designing ReSTful Web services. *IEEE International Conference on Web Services (ICWS '09)*, (pp. 173–180).

Papazoglou, M., & Heuvel, W. (2007). Service oriented architectures: Approaches, technologies and research issues. *The VLDB Journal, 16*(3), 389–415. doi:10.1007/s00778-007-0044-3

Peterson, G. (2006). *Security architecture blueprint*. Arctec Group, LLC. Retrieved March 29, 2011, from http://arctecgroup.net/pdf/ArctecSecurityArchitectureBlueprint.pdf

Robision, R. (2004). *Understand enterprise service bus scenarios and solutions in service-oriented architecture, Part 1*. Retrieved March 29, 2011, from https://www.ibm.com/developerworks/library/ws-esbscen/

Rosenberg, D., & Scott, K. (2001). *Introduction to the ICONIX process of software modeling*. informIT. Retrieved March 29, 2011, from http://www.informit.com/articles/article.aspx?p=167902#
Rosenberg, D., Stephens, M., & Collins-Cope, M. (2005). *Agile development with ICONIX process people, process, and pragmatism*. Apress.

Sander, D. (2007). Using Scrum to manage student projects. *Journal of Computing Sciences in Colleges, 23*(1), 79.

Schwaber, K., & Beedle, M. (2002). *Agile software development with Scrum*. Upper Saddle River, NJ.

Shin, M. E., & Gomaa, H. (2006). Modeling of evolution to secure application system from requirements model to software architecture. *Proceedings of the International Conference on Software Engineering Research and Practice Conference on Programming Languages and Compilers*, Vol. 2, SERP 2006, Las Vegas, Nevada, USA.

KEY TERMS AND DEFINITIONS

4+1 Views: Architecture of a software application represented by four multiple and current views including design, process, implementation, and deployment views in order to represent one common view, the use case view.

5W1H Re-Doc: A software re-documentation technique using the concepts of 5W1H (When, Who, Where, What, Why, and How).

Forward Software Engineering: A software engineering process that generates software source code from given user requirements.

mScrum4SOSR: A model-driven Scrum for a service-oriented software reengineering process. It is guided by an agile software development process, Scrum, and a re-documentation technique using UML visual models, 5W1HRe-Doc.

Reverse Software Engineering: A software engineering process that generates user requirements and discovers designs from given software source code.

Software Reengineering: Modernizing or maintaining a legacy software system to a target software system based upon new corrective, preventive, perfective, and adaptive requirements.

Software Vulnerability: Common types of software flaws that allow an attacker to compromise the information assurance of a system.

ENDNOTES

[1] OCTAVE Method http://www.cert.org/octave/octavemethod.html
[2] CORAS Method http://coras.sourceforge.net/index.html
[3] OWASP Top 10 2010 http://www.applicure.com/blog/owasp-top-10-2010

Chapter 11
Adapting Test–Driven Development to Build Robust Web Services

Nuno Laranjeiro
Universidade de Coimbra, Portugal

Marco Vieira
Universidade de Coimbra, Portugal

ABSTRACT

Web services are increasingly being used in business critical environments as a mean to provide a service or integrate distinct software services. Research indicates that, in many cases, services are deployed with robustness issues (i.e., displaying unexpected behaviors when in presence of invalid input conditions). Recently, Test-Driven Development (TDD) emerged as software development technique based on test cases that are defined before development, as a way to validate functionalities. However, programmers typically disregard the verification of limit conditions, such as the ones targeted by robustness testing. Moreover, in TDD, tests are created before developing the functionality, conflicting with the typical robustness testing approach. This chapter discusses the integration of robustness testing in TDD for improving the robustness of web services during development. The authors requested three programmers to create a set of services based on open-source code and to implement different versions of the services specified by TPC-App, using both TDD and the approach presented in this chapter. Results indicate that TDD with robustness testing is an effective way to create more robust services.

DOI: 10.4018/978-1-4666-2503-7.ch011

INTRODUCTION

Web services are increasingly being used in Service Oriented Environments as a strategic vehicle for data exchange and software component interoperability, providing a simple interface between a service provider and a consumer. Interaction between service consumers and providers is achieved by exchanging messages that comply with the SOAP protocol, which, along with WSDL and UDDI, constitute the core of the web services technology (Curbera et al., 2002).

Web services are frequently complex software components that can implement a composite service, in some cases using a set of external web services. Software faults (i.e., program defects or bugs) (Kalyanakrishnam, Kalbarczyk, & Iyer, 1999; Lee & Iyer, 1995) are a relevant cause of computer failures and, research indicates that web services are not different from other types of software, in this matter (Vieira, Laranjeiro, & Madeira, 2007a). With the increase of the software complexity, the weight of software faults also tends to increase.

Interface faults are related to problems in the interaction among software components or modules (Weyuker, 1998) and are of utmost importance in web services environments. Web services must provide a robust interface to client applications even when clients misuse the service by providing invalid input calls. Such invalid inputs may result from bugs in the client applications, data corruption caused by silent network failures, or even security attacks. Obviously, in web services compositions (a set of web services that work together to achieve a goal), when a component fails (by, for instance, throwing an unexpected exception), the entire composition may be affected. In fact, the execution results of subcomponents (i.e., external services) can be seen as inputs for the main service and are, in fact, a potential source of robustness issues. Additionally, a particular web service composition may use services provided by external entities, which emphasizes the importance

of mitigating unexpected inputs to improve the robustness of the overall composition.

Creating robust web services is a challenging task. In fact, research and practice show that many web services are being deployed on the web with robustness problems (Vieira, Laranjeiro, & Madeira, 2007a), i.e., displaying unforeseen behaviors when handling invalid inputs. Among other effects, these robustness issues can result in security vulnerabilities due to the lack (or incorrect use) of input validation. A frequently observed case is the presence of SQL Injection vulnerabilities, where unchecked inputs are exploited by hackers with the goal of modifying the structure of a SQL command (Stuttard & Pinto, 2007).

Test-Driven Development (TDD) (Beck, 2003) is an agile software development technique based on test cases that define new software functionalities or improvements (i.e., unit tests specify the requirements and are created before writing the functionality code itself). Development then follows in short iterations, where the developer creates the code that is required for the tests to pass. The process explicitly incorporates changes (via refactoring) as a means to improve code quality. Despite this, the definition of test cases that assure high coverage is quite demanding and developers tend to focus on the creation of tests that satisfy the requirements in normal situations, while often disregarding the verification of limit condition, such as the ones targeted by robustness testing.

Robustness testing can characterize the behavior of a particular system in presence of invalid input conditions (Mukherjee & Siewiorek, 1997). Web services robustness testing is an after-development technique that has its origin in traditional robustness testing approaches (Koopman & DeVale, 1999; Rodríguez, Salles, Fabre, & Arlat, 1999), typically used to assess of robustness of operating systems and microkernels. The fact that this testing technique was designed to be executed after development conflicts with the Test-Driven Development approach, which requires the tests to be created before developing the software functionalities.

In previous work we presented a preliminary approach that illustrates how to use robustness testing in a Test-Driven Development environment (Laranjeiro & Vieira, 2009) and focuses on basic required adaptations on both techniques. In this paper we present a thorough methodological view on how Test-Driven Development can be extended to include robustness testing. The approach is discussed in detail from a software development process point-of-view, while still including the theoretical and technical aspects related with robustness testing. In summary, the technique consists of introducing fully automated robustness testing in the development process, allowing developers to focus on the implementation of the functionalities and providing them with a way of verifying their services robustness before deployment. In the proposed approach, the creation and execution of the robustness tests is an automated process. The developer needs only to define the web service interface (i.e., which operations the service provides and their corresponding parameters and domains), which is sufficient to automatically generate the robustness tests.

To demonstrate the proposed approach we invited three senior developers to implement a set of services based on open-source code and to implement three different versions of the web services specified by the TPC-App benchmark (Transaction Processing Performance Council, 2008). The inclusion of the open-source services represents a broader experimental scenario than the one presented in previous work (Laranjeiro & Vieira, 2009), allowing for a more detailed discussion of the results. Regarding the TPC-App benchmark implementation, two of the developers followed the typical Test-Driven Development approach (one of these two developers was instructed about web services robustness and the importance of robustness testing), while the third developer used TDD combined with robustness testing. The results observed indicate that our approach can be a practical way to prevent the deployment of services carrying robustness issues.

This chapter is organized as follows. The next section presents background on web services and Test-Driven Development. We present, in the follow-up sections, the proposed extension to the TDD development process. We then conclude with an experimental demonstration of the framework and summarize the chapter, presenting possible topics for future research.

BACKGROUND AND RELATED WORK

The web services framework is divided into three major areas: communication protocols, service descriptions, and service discovery. The main specifications for each area, SOAP, WSDL, and UDDI, are all XML-based. XML is now firmly established as a language that enables information and data encoding, platform independence, and internationalization (Curbera et al., 2002). SOAP (Simple Object Access Protocol) is a protocol for messaging that can be used along with existing transport protocols, such as HTTP, SMTP, and XMPP. WSDL (Web Services Description Language) is used to describe a web service as a collection of communication endpoints that can exchange particular types of messages. That is, a WSDL document describes the interface of the service and provides users (e.g., the web service's clients) with a point of contact. Finally, UDDI (Universal Description, Discovery, and Integration) offers a unified way to find service providers through a centralized registry (Curbera et al., 2002). Figure 1 presents a typical web services environment.

In each interaction the consumer (client) sends a request SOAP message to the provider (the server). After processing the request, the server sends a response message to the client with the results. A web service may include several operations (in practice, each operation is a method with zero or more input parameters).

Figure 1. Typical web services environment

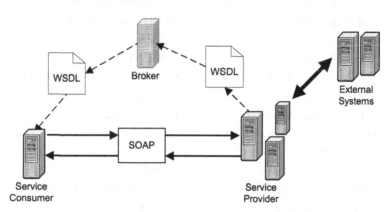

The process of creating web services, and software in general, involves a large set of basic tasks that can be organized, controlled, and evaluated in many distinct ways. The software industry has used, since its inception, multiple methodologies or processes with the goal of creating high quality software. Along the years, these methodologies also evolved into forms that adapt better to the type of software being created, the type of physical and human resources involved, the programming techniques involved, among other aspects.

Currently, software development processes range from highly structured to mostly informal. These different classes of methodologies are frequently referred to as prescriptive and agile, respectively (Janzen & Saiedian, 2005). A prescriptive methodology prescribes how a new software system should be developed. Prescriptive software development methodologies are used as guidelines or frameworks to organize and structure how software development activities should be carried out, and in what order (Scacchi, 2001). On the other hand, an agile methodology is typically a lightweight process for developing software (in terms of level of formality and also degree of documentation). It values individuals and interactions, working software, customer collaboration and change response over aspects like processes, documentation, contracts, and plans, respectively (Highsmith & Cockburn, 2001).

There are several types of software development lifecycles such as waterfall, spiral, incremental and iterative, or evolutionary. Iterative development is based on the repetition of a set of development tasks, which use a set of requirements as basis. These requirements typically increase with time providing ground for a new iteration. Evolutionary software development methodologies imply adaptive and lightweight iterative development. Such techniques use feedback from earlier iterations as a way to improve the software being built (i.e., they are adaptive). They are lightweight in the sense that complete requirements or specifications are not required at the starting point of development, which essentially allows the use of the iterations to guide future development. The spiral model is an evolutionary methodology with strong emphasis on risk assessment and that applies the cyclic nature of iterative development. Milestones and iterations that take risk into account are used in this model. The incremental methodology can be characterized as a process that typically delivers a set of software releases (i.e., increments), where each release provides more functionality (Janzen & Saiedian, 2005).

Agile methodologies have roots in the iterative, incremental, and evolutionary process models. Test-Driven development appeared within the rise of agile methodologies. Extreme Programming (XP) is a well-known agile methodology that supports the creation of software in very short iterations. Test-Driven Development was early described as a XP practice necessary for analysis, design, and testing. In fact, Extreme Programming recommends programmers to adopt Test-Driven Development, among other practices like frequent releases or pair programming (Chromatic, 2003).

TDD has received a considerable amount of individual attention in recent years. A singular characteristic of TDD is the fact that tests are defined before the actual functionality development takes place. Tests and development proceed in an iterative fashion (in short iterations) and the combined whole makes the development task more productive, reduces response time to requirements changes, and facilitates continuous regression testing. The tests specify the requirements and contain assertions that can be true or false. Running the tests allows developers to quickly validate the expected behavior as code development evolves. It is important to emphasize that Test-Driven Development is a software design method and not simply a testing technique. Tests actually drive the development and are continuously applied by developers to validate if the implementation fulfills the software requirements (that are specified by the tests themselves). As in other agile software development techniques, the short iterations facilitate managing requirements changes (Beck, 2003). TDD is also frequently applied in projects whose goal is to improve legacy code developed with older techniques and technologies (Feathers, 2004).

With the rise of TDD, developers started to create tools specifically to support this methodology across a wide range of languages. A large number of unit testing frameworks are currently available for developers to create and automatically run sets of test cases, e.g., JUnit (http://junit.org/), CppUnit (http://sourceforge.net/projects/cppunit/), and JUnitEE (http://www.junitee.org/) and this obviously can have impact on the adoption of a development methodology. Despite the fact that these frameworks support unit testing, the defini-

tion of the test cases is typically a manual (and difficult) task. A key problem is that developers tend to focus on the functionality itself, disregarding limit conditions (e.g., testing both extreme points in a integer domain). In addition, it is frequent to find test suites that do not provide 100% coverage, indicating that they may be incomplete. Despite the obvious difficulty in creating a test case suite that has a complete coverage, frequently there is also time-to-market pressure that can make developers disregard important tests (or part of tests).

Robustness can be defined as the response of a system in the presence of invalid inputs (Koopman & DeVale, 1999). As referred earlier, current research indicates that web services are being deployed on the web with robustness problems, indicating the absence of testing (or the presence of incomplete testing). A first approach to assess the behavior of web services in the presence of invalid input messages was proposed in (Vieira, Laranjeiro, & Madeira, 2007b). It consists of a set of robustness tests based on invalid web services call parameters. The services are classified using an adaptation of the CRASH robustness scale, proposed by Koopman and DeVale for operating systems (Koopman & DeVale, 1999). Robustness testing is an effective way to characterize a given system in the presence of invalid inputs, and the results of this technique can be used to effectively correct issues in the developed software.

Robustness testing is a technique that is to be applied after development, which implies that, in its original form, it cannot be used along with TDD. However, considering the benefits of both, it can be beneficial to provide developers with a way of using the robustness testing approach in a Test-Driven Development context. This chapter discusses precisely this topic, presenting an approach to integrate TDD and robustness testing. The following section describes the TDD methodology in detail and the specific process adjustments required to provide integration with robustness testing.

INTEGRATING ROBUSTNESS TESTING IN TEST-DRIVEN DEVELOPMENT FOR WEB SERVICES

Test-driven development requires developers to follow a set of steps in an iterative fashion. The steps that compose this software development methodology are the following (adapted from the book "Test-Driven Development by Example") (Beck, 2003):

Step 1: Add a Test: A developer starts by defining or modifying a test (or a set of tests). This test will serve as a validation point for the feature that will be implemented (or modified). Since, at this point, the corresponding feature has not yet been implemented; the execution of this test must obviously fail. If the test does not fail, this is an indicator that either the test is incorrect and does not specify or validate the desired requirement, or the feature has already been implemented. This type of issue highlights the fact that there must be a clear understanding of the requirements before the test can be written. Requirements specification techniques like user stories (Cohn, 2004) and use cases (Bittner & Spence, 2003) can be used as a support for understanding the requirements. An important aspect is that the pre-definition of the tests focuses the developer on the requirements before developing the code. This contrasts with typical unit testing where the developer writes tests only after creating the code. Certainly, in this latter case tests can be influenced by the code that has already been created.

Step 2: Run All Tests and Verify if the New Ones Fail: The goal of this step is to certify that the testing infrastructure is operating correctly and that the newly created tests effectively fail (and do not pass without requiring any new code). The new tests should effectively fail because the feature has not yet been implemented and not due to any existing problem in the testing infrastructure or development environment. Note that this step validates the tests as it guarantees that the new tests do not pass until the developer creates the required code.

Step 3: Write Code: The developer writes the code required for the tests to pass. Frequently, the code written in this step is not final and may, for example, pass the tests in an inelegant manner. Despite this, the TDD process explicitly reserves space for improvement in a later step. An important aspect is that the developer should write code with the only goal of passing the tests; no additional functionality should be implemented, as it would not be covered by any written tests (i.e., it would not be tested).

Step 4: Run the Automated Tests: If all written test cases pass then the code fulfills all the tested requirements. In the case of failure of some tests, the development process should return to step 3. Furthermore, in some exceptional cases, developers may understand at this step that the tests do not accurately describe the requirement (in the same manner tests can validate code, code can also be used to validate the tests). In such case, the developer should review the tests, which results in going back to step 1.

Step 5: Refactor Code: After passing the tests, the code undergoes an improvement step. The goal is to improve the global code quality in terms of typical quality requirements, such as readability, complexity, and modularity, among others). The refactoring procedure itself may affect the actual code functionality, which means that programmers should re-execute the existent test cases, as needed. This refactoring step is, in fact, only concluded when all tests cases are executed successfully.

The steps presented above form a complete iteration. A new iteration starts with the act of writing another new test (or a new set of tests) that specifies a new feature. The size of the steps is adjustable and is not predefined in any way. In fact, this size should be the one the developer is more comfortable with. Frequently, less experienced developers choose to use shorter iterations that get larger as their development confidence increases.

An approach for evaluating web services in terms of robustness was proposed in (Vieira, Laranjeiro, & Madeira, 2007b). That work is limited in some aspects: tests are designed to be applied after development, robustness testing does consider external web services responses (typically present in complex compound services), and the identification of robustness issues requires human intervention. In the current work we adopted and extended the approach proposed in (Vieira, Laranjeiro, & Madeira, 2007b), focusing on these three problems. In practice, the integration of robustness testing in the Test-Driven Development methodology requires an extra step, related with the web service interface specification:

Step 0: Specifying the Web Service: This new step must be performed before any of the abovementioned and consists of specifying the web service interface in detail. The developer should indicate which operations are provided by the web service and include information about their input and output parameters, in particular data types and domains. These definitions will be used later to generate robustness tests and detect robustness issues (see the following sections for details).

Concerning the integration of the robustness tests in the overall procedure, and starting with the information obtained in Step #0, robustness tests can be generated at Step #1 (see Section "Generating Robustness Tests") and can be later executed during Steps #2 and #4 of TDD (see Section "Executing Robustness Tests"). We provide an automated tool, available at (Laranjeiro, Vieira, & Madeira, 2009a), that implements the proposed approach and can be easily integrated in software projects. Currently, the tool can be used in any software development project that uses Maven (Apache Software Foundation, 2008) as building tool.

Specifying the Web Service

As mentioned before, the specification of the web service is the first step of the procedure. A web service interface is described as a WSDL document. This XML-based file contains a list of all operations, their corresponding input and output parameters and associated data types. The description of the structure and type of all inputs and outputs of each operation is usually defined in a XML Schema file (also frequently referred to as simply XSD file). The XML Schema can be used to describe the structure of an XML object, and, in web services, the WSDL file references this structure (Curbera et al., 2002). Nowadays, developers do not have to spend effort in creating these files. Although it is possible to define them manually, in many cases developers simply compile the web service code and deploy it in an application server that automatically generates these files at runtime.

After defining the service interface it is necessary to specify, for each operation, the valid domains of all input and output objects. As referred, the XSD file (W3C, 2008a), that describes all service parameters, can be used to keep this information. However, developers typically use this file to include only very basic information about valid values of each parameter, based on XML schema restrictions. In fact, WSDL and XSD do not support the definition of complex domains and the specification of dependencies between two (or more) parameters of a given web service operation. This lacking feature prevents the full definition of a given domain and, in terms of robustness, a domain that is only partially defined is ultimately of no use.

With the goal of providing a way for service applications to fully express and announce business logic domains, we propose the use of an extension to WSDL/XSD description documents (Laranjeiro, Vieira, & Madeira, 2009b). This extension can be used by service developers to provide complete information regarding the valid domains for each parameter, and provides strong semantics for expressing domain dependencies between multiple parameters. As explained in the following paragraphs we make use of current XSD features to provide the aforementioned semantics, which enables us to maintain retro-compatibility not only with existing service implementations but also with supporting stack tools.

Basic domain information is expressed by means of standard XSD restriction elements (W3C, 2008a). In our case, these elements must have an *id* attribute (it is an optional attribute in the XSD reference) so that they can be referenced when defining parameters inter-dependencies. To state parameters inter-dependencies, while maintaining retro-compatibility with any XSD schema reader, we make use of the XSD element *appinfo*, in which we include our extended domain

representation. Figure 2 shows an example of the proposed syntax (Extended Domain Expression Language - EDEL). A schema describing the complete language can be found at (Laranjeiro, Vieira, & Madeira, 2009a).

As we can see, the extended domain representation consists of a set of dependencies, each one expressing a relation between two or more parameters. Keep in mind that, at this point, parameters already have their individual domains defined in standard XSD restrictions and are identified by a unique id attribute.

Each relation (the *function* element in the figure) is a function that uses individual restrictions to ultimately produce a Boolean output and is composed by three attributes: an *id* that uniquely identifies it; a *name* that indicates the behavior to apply to each restriction argument (each subelement of the function element); and a *strategy* that specifies how the named function should be applied. The sub-elements of the function element (*param* elements) are basically arguments for its parent. Each *param* element specifies the name of a restriction (by referring the restriction's *id*) and, optionally, an *index* attribute for the cases where a service accepts multiple complex objects of the same type.

Figure 2. Extended domain expression language example

```
...
<dependencies>
  <dependency id="1">
    <function id="f1" name="aggregator" strategy="and">
      <param index="0" name="r1" />
      <param index="0" name="r3" />
    </function>
  </dependency>
<dependency id="2">
    <function id="f2" name="starts-with" strategy="or">
      <param index="0" name="r2" />
      <param index="0" name="r4" />
      <param index="0" name="r5" />
    </function>
  </dependency>
</dependencies>
...
```

For instance, in Figure 2, the aggregator function with the *and* strategy indicates that a logical AND must be applied to the values of parameters associated with restrictions r1 and r3. r1 could, for example, define that some numeric parameter must be greater than zero and r3 could define that a string parameter must match a given regular expression. In this two-element case, the strategy attribute has no effect and could be removed (it is *and* by default). However, the strategy element makes a significant difference in the next dependency (*id* 2 in the figure). Here, we are defining that at least one of the parameters associated with r4 and r5 must start with the value obtained in runtime for the parameter associated with r2. The first *param* element in all functions is the one that serves as reference for applying the function through all the remaining children.

In order to reuse programmers' knowledge we aim to provide a comprehensive set of functions based on the XPath 2.0 and XQuery 1.0 function reference list (W3C, 2008b). In this way, programmers do not need to learn another new language when specifying domain dependencies. Virtually any XPath reference function that returns a result is a candidate function that can be used in EDEL. However, the final result of a dependency element must be a Boolean so that our EDEL engine can logically evaluate it. This means that, all non-Boolean results provided by XPath functions that are used to express the domains of a web service must also be used as parameters of other functions that can compute a Boolean result. For instance, two substring functions can be used to return a sequence of characters over two different parameters. However, an extra aggregator function must be defined, so that we can compute a logical result over these two functions. The result of this last function will be the one effectively used to validate the service domain.

As previously mentioned, compound services use other web services (i.e., external services) to execute a particular function. The execution results of these external components are, in fact, inputs

for the main service and, as such, are a potential source of robustness issues. Thus, we need to collect information concerning the response domains of the external web services. Relevant information regarding those web services responses can be extracted from the WSDL document. If this document already specifies the valid domains (using EDEL) then this information is used. If there is no information regarding the external services, the programmer must provide the valid response domains for each component service being used. These domains should be defined in EDEL and are appended to a local copy of the WSDL file. If the developer does not possess information regarding those domains (for instance, a third-party service is being used and there is no available information about the service) the full domain of the response data type is assumed as valid.

Generating Robustness Tests

Our proposal to identify robustness issues consists of executing a set of tests on web services inputs, including both public operations call parameters and external web services responses. As described earlier, in a web service interaction, a client sends a SOAP message to a server that is responsible for providing a given service. This SOAP message is essentially an XML document that contains, among other elements, the name of the web service operation that is to be executed and the necessary parameter values.

Testing web services for robustness consists of substituting original parameter values by invalid values at execution time. Regular values are generated according to the data types and input domains of each public operation parameter (defined in Step 0). Additionally, this generation process can follow three strategies: *Deterministic*, where values are generated according to a set of algorithms provided by our testing tool (e.g., fixed increment, variable increment); *Stochastic* (e.g., random generation, random generation following an exponential distribution); and *Hybrid* (a mixture of the previous strategies). The tool can be configured to use any of the available strategies for value generation (Laranjeiro, Vieira, & Madeira, 2009a). Using the generated workload as basis, it is then possible to generate the robustness tests, which essentially involves the application of our mutation rules (see Table 1 for details) to the generated workload. The robustness tests are, in this way, automatically created and are based on combinations of exceptional and acceptable input values.

The mutation rules used in our approach are presented in Table 1 and were adopted from previous work on web services robustness testing (Vieira, Laranjeiro, & Madeira, 2007a). These rules are designed to focus on difficult input validation aspects (which are the typical origin of robustness issues), such as:

- Null and empty values (e.g., null string, empty string).
- Valid values with special characteristics (e.g., nonprintable characters in strings, valid dates by the end of the millennium).
- Invalid values with special characteristics (e.g., invalid dates using different formats).
- Maximum and minimum valid values in the input domain (e.g., maximum value valid for the parameter, minimum value valid for the parameter).
- Values exceeding the maximum and minimum valid values in the input domain (e.g., maximum value valid for the parameter plus one).
- Values that cause data type overflow (e.g., add characters to overflow string max size, duplicate the elements of a list, and replace by maximum number valid for the type plus one).

For illustrative purposes, we present a possible instantiation of the parameter mutation rules in Table 2. In this example, the rules are applied to

an integer parameter in a fictitious SOAP web service operation that accepts an integer between 10 and 20 (inclusively) and is initialized with the value "15".

An important aspect is that we should also test responses of external web services (and try to trigger robustness issues at this point). Thus, we again define tests based on invalid input values, similarly to the general guidelines presented above, but we extend this concept to the injection of exceptions. In this case, we explicitly define tests that throw exceptions at particular points (invocations of external web services), with the goal of exercising any existing error handling. As an example, Table 3 presents possible exceptions to be thrown for web services created in the Java programming language. Other languages (e.g., C#, Python, etc.) have similar constructs that can be used in the tests in a similar manner.

In the example presented above, it is possible to observe that the exception injection rules include the injection of all exceptions declared by the external service (i.e., checked exceptions, that are a subclass of *Exception*) and a set of runtime exceptions. The latter set includes *RuntimeException* (the superclass of those exceptions that can be thrown during the normal operation of the virtual machine) and all of its direct known subclasses.

Executing Robustness Tests

The execution of the robustness tests generated earlier takes place in Steps 2 and 4 of the TDD process. The developer defines the tests, by defining the operations domains. The tests are then executed to exercise the web service operation and the original parameter values are replaced by the invalid values generated in Step 1, according to the robustness testing rules (see previous section).

The execution of the robustness tests requires the use of a fault injection tool (the general use is illustrated in Figure 3). This tool is essentially a

Table 1. Parameters values mutation rules, adapted from (Vieira, Laranjeiro, & Madeira, 2007a)

Type	Test Name	Parameter Mutation
String	StrNull	Replace by null value
	StrEmpty	Replace by empty string
	StrPredefined	Replace by predefined string
	StrNonPrintable	Replace by string with nonprintable characters
	StrAddNonPrintable	Add nonprintable characters to the string
	StrAlphaNumeric	Replace by alphanumeric string
	StrOverflow	Add characters to overflow max size
Number	NumNull	Replace by null value
	NumEmpty	Replace by empty value
	NumAbsoluteMinusOne	Replace by -1
	NumAbsoluteOne	Replace by 1
	NumAbsoluteZero	Replace by 0
	NumAddOne	Add one
	NumSubtractOne	Subtract 1
	NumMax	Replace by maximum number valid for the type
	NumMin	Replace by minimum number valid for the type
	NumMaxRange	Replace by maximum value valid for the parameter
	NumMinRange	Replace by minimum value valid for the parameter
	NumMaxRangePlusOne	Replace by maximum value valid for the parameter plus one
	NumMinRangeMinusOne	Replace by minimum value valid for the parameter minus one
List	ListNull	Replace by null value
	ListRemove	Remove element from the list
	ListAdd	Add element to the list
	ListDuplicate	Duplicate elements of the list
	ListRemoveAllButFirst	Remove all elements from the list except the first one
	ListRemoveAll	Remove all elements from the list
Date	DateNull	Replace by null value
	DateEmpty	Replace by empty date
	DateMaxRange	Replace by maximum date valid for the parameter
	DateMinRange	Replace by minimum date valid for the parameter
	DateMaxRangePlusOne	Replace by maximum date valid for the parameter plus one day
	DateMinRangeMinusOne	Replace by minimum date valid for the parameter minus one day
	DateAdd100	Add 100 years to the date
	DateSubtract100	Subtract 100 years to the date
	Date31-12-1999	Replace by the last day of the previous millennium
	Date1-1-2000	Replace by the first day of this millennium
Boolean	BooleanNull	Replace by null value
	BooleanPredefined	Replace by predefined value

Table 2. Example of the application of the parameter mutation rules

Data type	Test name	Parameter mutation
Integer	NumNull	Non-existent XML SOAP tag
	NumEmpty	Empty XML SOAP tag
	NumAbsoluteMinusOne	-1
	NumAbsoluteOne	1
	NumAbsoluteZero	0
	NumAddOne	16
	NumSubtractOne	14
	NumMax	2147483647
	NumMin	-2147483648
	NumMaxPlusOne	2147483648
	MumMinMinusOne	-2147483649
	NumMaxRange	20
	NumMinRange	10
	NumMaxRangePlusOne	21
	NumMinRangeMinusOne	9

Table 3. Exception injection rules and examples

Exception superclass	Exception to be injected
Exception	Any Exception declared in by the web service operation
RuntimeException	ArithmeticException
	BufferOverflowException
	BufferUnderflowException
	ClassCastException
	IndexOutOfBoundsException
	NullPointerException
	...
	WebServiceException

proxy application that, at server side, intercepts all incoming client requests, performs a set of parameter mutations in the incoming request message and forwards the altered request to the server. After this set of steps, execution proceeds normally. The service consumer is responsible for executing the tests defined by the developer while the service provider essentially executes the web service.

In the present work we have used AspectJ (Eclipse Foundation, 2008), a widely known AOP framework, to create a fault injection tool that is able to inject faults into any web service implementation that uses the reference JAX-WS API.

Using AOP involves understanding a few key concepts, namely (see (Kiczales et al., 1997) for details):

- **Aspect:** A concern that cuts across multiple objects.
- **Joinpoint:** A point during the execution of a program (e.g., the execution of a method or the handling of an exception).
- **Advice:** Action taken by an aspect at a particular joinpoint. Types of advice include: "before", "after", and "around" (i.e., before and after).
- **Pointcut:** A predicate that matches joinpoints. An advice is associated with a pointcut expression and runs at any joinpoint matched by the pointcut (e.g., the execution of a method with a certain name).

In our specific case, the pointcut is, of course, the execution of any given web service operation. The technique and concepts used here are also applicable to other major programming languages

Figure 3. Required test configuration

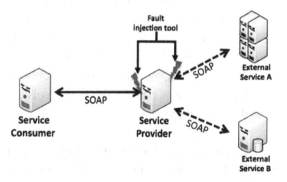

and web service platforms. In fact, many AOP implementations exist for languages like C/C++, the .NET framework languages, Delphi, Python, among others.

The fault injection tool creates a log with detailed information during the execution of the robustness tests. This log consists of several entries, and each of these entries has information regarding a single execution of a web service operation. This execution information includes the input values, the injected fault and the web service response. The fault injection toolset identifies robustness problems by analyzing this log and by looking for responses that violate the valid output domain of the operation (as defined in Step 0), including unexpected exceptions. Whenever the tool identifies an invalid response, it registers the injected fault and the problematic input parameter or service output. This data is then presented to the programmer, who has the responsibility of correcting the disclosed robustness issue.

EXPERIMENTAL EVALUATION

This section presents the application of the software development approach proposed before. To illustrate the approach, we have invited three senior developers, with more than two years of experience in developing web services, to participate in the following experimental scenarios:

- A single development cycle involving the creation of a set of web services, adapted from existing publicly available code;
- A complete multi-cycle implementation of several versions of a set of web services specified by the TPC-App performance benchmark (Transaction Processing Performance Council, 2008), involving distinct developers.

The goal of the first experimental scenario described above was to understand if the simple integration of the robustness testing procedure

in TDD is feasible, and if it can be used to detect robustness issues. One developer was requested to adapt open-source code, publicly available on the Internet (Exhedra Solutions, Inc., 2010), and create four web services, consisting of a total of 20 service operations. These open-source services perform the following functions: manage student information; manage phone book addresses; and simulate bank operations (in 2 versions). It is important to mention that a single cycle was sufficient to create the services, since the actual code of the services was already implemented and available as open-source. The developer's tasks consisted of changing the existing code so that it could be deployed as web services, in a proper container (i.e., an application server). A key aspect is that there was no domain information available, so the developer had to infer the valid domains from the source code and database contents, in order to create the robustness tests.

Table 4 presents the results obtained. The "Robustness Problems" column presents a detailed view of the issues found in each tested operation. The number of problematic parameters is also indicated between parentheses in this column. The last table column indicates the number of problematic parameters (P) with respect to the total number of parameters for the operation (T). Each robustness problem identified represents either a regular result that falls outside of the specified valid response domain, or an exceptional result that is not one of the declared web service exceptions.

The integration of robustness testing was, in fact, successful. We can easily observe that the technique revealed the presence of numerous robustness issues, from which we highlight several null pointers and SQL exceptions. Also relevant, was the presence of misrepresented data types (numbers defined as strings at the service interface, but later handled internally as numbers), a typical source of robustness problems.

These initial experiments indicated a clear utility of using robustness testing along with TDD. However, we still wanted to study its applicability in a more realistic and complex scenario. In

Table 4. Results obtained for the single-cycle creation of web services

Web Service	Operation	Robustness problems	P/T
JamesSmith	login	-	0/2
	add	-	0/11
	update	-	0/12
	delete	-	0/1
	search	Null pointer (1); SQL exceptions (3)	3/9
Bank3	deleteAcc	Null pointer (1); Conversion issues (1)	1/1
	deposit	Null pointer (4); Conversion issues (1)	4/4
	displayDeposit	SQL exceptions with database vendor disclosure (1)	1/2
	displayInfo	Null pointer (1)	1/2
	newAccount	-	0/4
	Withdrawal	-	0/4
Bank	balance	-	0/1
	create	-	0/2
	deposit	Null pointer (1); Conversion issues (1)	2/2
	sign	-	0/1
	withdraw	Null pointer (1); Conversion issues (1)	2/2
PhoneDir	addNewRecord	-	0/2
	deleteInput	-	0/1
	firstNameWithIt	-	0/1
	modify	SQL exceptions with database vendor disclosure (2)	2/2

the second experimental scenario tested, we considered the implementation of a set of web services specified by the TPC-App performance benchmark (Transaction Processing Performance Council, 2008), a benchmark for web services and application servers widely accepted as representative of real environments. The goal was to try to assess the impact of integrating robustness testing in a typical and relatively complex TDD environment, and verify if the approach is helpful in preventing the creation of web services with robustness problems.

Three Java programmers (Dev1, Dev2, and Dev3) were requested to implement three versions of the TPC-App web services. As the implementation of these services require more coding effort, development was completed in four iterations (using one iteration for each implemented ser-

vice) and there was no shared data or information between the three developers, with the exception of the TPC-App specification document. Dev1 and Dev2 were responsible for creating the web services using the standard TDD process, while Dev3 used the extension proposed in this chapter. Prior to development, Dev2 was instructed about the importance of robustness and robustness testing. However, Dev1 did not receive any kind of instruction or information regarding these topics.

The TPC-App specification document describes all web services in detail, but also includes a workload generator that is responsible for creating web services calls. In our experiments we provided an implementation of this emulator to the three developers. The calls generated by this emulator can be seen as functional tests that can be used during the development of the web services. Despite of the presence of this emulator, developers were free to create any additional test they understood as necessary to verify the implemented web services.

A set of new independent robustness tests was conducted, after development, over each of the three versions. The goal was to verify the robustness of the code created by the developers. Notice that Dev3 had already used robustness testing during the implementation of the services, however, in order to verify its implementation, we used a new set of robustness tests. The generation and outcome of the tests is not a deterministic process. In fact, this procedure can have different outcomes, depending on the generated workload (and also on the type of service being tested). This justifies the need for executing new robustness tests to verify the implementation, or most likely the results would have been the same as the ones observed by Dev3. Table 5 presents a detailed view of the results obtained.

As shown in Table 5, we did not identify robustness issues in the version created using the extended TDD methodology presented in this chapter. Instead, we detected robustness problems in the remaining two solutions (including the one implemented by the developer that had been previously tutored about robustness and robust-

Table 5. Robustness problems observed for each TPC-App implementation

Web service	Target parameter	Dev1 Robustness problems	Dev2 Robustness problems	Dev3 Robustness problems
changePayment	customerID	null pointer	null pointer	-
	paymentMethod	null pointer	null pointer	-
	creditInfo	null pointer	-	-
	poId	null pointer	-	-
newCustomer	billingAddr1	null pointer	null pointer	-
	billingAddr2	null pointer	null pointer	-
	BillingCity	null pointer	null pointer	-
	billingCountry	null pointer	-	-
	billingState	null pointer	null pointer	-
	billingZip	null pointer	null pointer	-
	businessInfo	null pointer	-	-
	businessName	null pointer	-	-
	contactEmail	stack overflow	-	-
	contactFName	null pointer	-	-
	contactLName	null pointer	-	-
	contactPhone	null pointer	-	-
	creditInfo	null pointer	-	-
	Password	null pointer	-	-
	paymentMethod	null pointer	null pointer	-
	poId	-	-	-
newProducts	subjectString	-	-	-
	cutOffDuration	-	null pointer	-
	itemLimit	-	null pointer	-
productDetail	itemIds	-	null pointer	-

ness testing). Although the results, in this scenario, cannot be used to extract generic conclusions, they are a strong indicator that the integration of robustness testing in the Test-Driven Development process can be an effective technique to avoid robustness issues. Obviously, the alternative scenario, where robustness testing is carried out after development, can also be an effective way to disclose robustness issues, however it requires an additional step that has impact on development time and costs. Moreover, it does not fit well the TDD concept, in which tests guide the development and should be defined first, as part of the requirements specification (and applied afterwards). As a final note, regard that we do not draw conclusions considering the development time as it can be strongly influenced by the individual developers' expertise and capabilities. In these experiments, dev3 took a few minutes less than the other two developers.

The results presented in Table 5 were forwarded to the developers, with the goal of correcting and improving the implementations that revealed issues. This is a typical task executed by developers when code defects are found. After a thorough analysis of the results, both programmers identified solutions for the detected software faults and two new versions were implemented. A new set of independent robustness tests were executed for the new versions and no robustness issues were disclosed. This shows the utility of this type of testing and emphasizes the importance of robustness testing in development environments.

The *newCustomer* service in Dev1 implementation revealed an appealing robustness issue. Although this operation had specific code to validate the *contactEmail* parameter, a large email address caused the service to throw a *StackOverflowException*. After a detailed code analysis we concluded that the issue resided in an external (and popular) tool that was being used to validate email addresses – Jakarta Commons Validator 1.3.0 (Apache Software Foundation, 2010). This essentially shows that robustness issues may occur even when the

code correctness is a major goal. In fact, the use of third party software (as in this case) can raise problems that are not obvious for developers. Moreover, this kind of errors can easily appear or disappear when an apparently harmless update is done to external libraries commonly required by software projects. Despite this, developers can use robustness testing during development to easily detect such issues, which emphasizes the importance of integrating robustness testing in the software development process.

CONCLUSION

In this chapter we presented an approach that integrates robustness testing and Test-Driven Development in a software development process tailored for creating robust web services. The integration consists of adding a step to the standard TDD, with the goal of gathering information regarding the web service interface (i.e., operations, parameters, and input and output domains). This initial step enables the automatic generation and execution of robustness tests that are used in later steps to identify robustness problems. The approach presented includes using an extension to XML Schema that allows web service developers to define valid parameter domains, including domain dependencies between distinct parameters.

An initial robustness testing and TDD integration experiment was executed using a single development cycle and open-source code as basis. Results provided a strong indicator of the utility of the proposed approach. Despite this initial indicator, we executed a set of experiments in a typical (and also more complex) web services development scenario. We invited experienced developers to implement three distinct versions of the TPC-App performance benchmark. Two developers followed the typical Test-Driven Development process while one used the approach proposed in this chapter. Results indicate that the integrated use of TDD and robustness testing is an effective way to prevent the development of services with robustness problems. No issues were disclosed in the TPC-App version developed using the approach proposed in this chapter, while several problems were disclosed in the remaining two versions.

Future work may include the improvement of a recent Java Specification Request (Bernard, 2010), whose goal is currently to specify class level constraint declaration and validation facilities for Java developers. It is possible to extend the concepts described in this JSR with our domain description language (which introduces dependency constraints and connects validation aspects to the web service technology). Ideally, in the near future, developers will be able to use their favorite programming language to automatically generate EDEL code for domain expression and announcement. This means that robustness tests can be executed faster (as the domains will be already fully specified), resulting overall in a more agile Test-driven development process, with clear benefits for developers but also for end users that will be in possession of more robust software.

REFERENCES

W3C. (2008a). *W3C XML schema*. Retrieved December 15, 2008, a from http://www.w3.org/XML/Schema

W3C. (2008b). *XQuery 1.0 and XPath 2.0 functions and operators*. Retrieved December 15, 2008, from http://www.w3.org/TR/xquery-operators/

Apache Software Foundation. (2008). *Apache Maven Project*. Retrieved February 14, 2008, from http://maven.apache.org/

Apache Software Foundation. (2010). *Apache commons validator*. Retrieved December 8, 2007, from http://commons.apache.org/validator/

Beck, K. (2003). *Test-driven development: By example*. Addison-Wesley Professional.

Bernard, E. (2010). *JSR 303: Bean validation*. Retrieved February 27, 2010, from http://jcp.org/en/jsr/detail?id=303

Bittner, K., & Spence, I. (2003). *Use case modeling*. Addison-Wesley Professional.

Chromatic. (2003). *Extreme programming pocket guide* (1st ed.). O'Reilly Media.

Cohn, M. (2004). *User stories applied*. Boston, MA: Addison-Wesley.

Curbera, F., Duftler, M., Khalaf, R., Nagy, W., Mukhi, N., & Weerawarana, S. (2002). Unraveling the Web services web: An introduction to SOAP, WSDL, and UDDI. *Internet Computing*, *6*(2), 86–93. doi:10.1109/4236.991449

Eclipse Foundation. (2008). *The AspectJ Project*. Retrieved December 8, 2007, from http://www.eclipse.org/aspectj/

Exhedra Solutions, Inc. (2010). *Planet source code*. Retrieved February 25, 2010, from http://www.planet-source-code.com/

Feathers, M. (2004). *Working effectively with legacy code*. Prentice Hall PTR.

Highsmith, J., & Cockburn, A. (2001). Agile software development: The business of innovation. *Computer*, *34*(9), 120–127. doi:10.1109/2.947100

Janzen, D., & Saiedian, H. (2005). Test-driven development concepts, taxonomy, and future direction. *Computer*, *38*(9), 43–50. doi:10.1109/MC.2005.314

Kalyanakrishnam, M., Kalbarczyk, Z., & Iyer, R. (1999). Failure data analysis of a LAN of Windows NT based computers. *Proceedings of the 18th IEEE Symposium on Reliable Distributed Systems* (p. 178). IEEE Computer Society.

Kiczales, G., Lamping, J., Mendhekar, A., Maeda, C., Lopes, C., Loingtier, J. M., & Irwin, J. (1997). Aspect-Oriented Programming. *11th European Conference on Object-Oriented Programming,* Jyväskylä, Finland.

Koopman, P., & DeVale, J. (1999). Comparing the robustness of POSIX operating systems. *Twenty-Ninth Annual International Symposium on Fault-Tolerant Computing* (pp. 30-37). Retrieved from http://ieeexplore.ieee.org/iel5/6328/16917/00781031.pdf

Laranjeiro, N., & Vieira, M. (2009). Extending test-driven development for robust Web services. *International Conference on Dependability (DEPEND 2009)* (pp. 122-127). Athens/Vouliagmeni, Greece: IEEE Computer Society. doi:10.1109/DEPEND.2009.25

Laranjeiro, N., Vieira, M., & Madeira, H. (2009a). *Robustness improvement for Web services.* Retrieved a from http://eden.dei.uc.pt/~cnl/papers/2009-icws-edel.zip

Laranjeiro, N., Vieira, M., & Madeira, H. (2009b). Improving Web services robustness. *IEEE International Conference on Web Services (ICWS 2009)* (pp. 397-404). Los Angeles, CA: IEEE Computer Society. doi:10.1109/ICWS.2009.27

Lee, I., & Iyer, R. K. (1995). Software dependability in the tandem GUARDIAN system. *IEEE Transactions on Software Engineering, 21*(5), 455–467. doi:10.1109/32.387474

Mukherjee, A., & Siewiorek, D. P. (1997). Measuring software dependability by robustness benchmarking. *Transactions on Software Engineering, 23*(6), 366–378. doi:10.1109/32.601075

Rodríguez, M., Salles, F., Fabre, J.-C., & Arlat, J. (1999). MAFALDA: Microkernel assessment by fault injection and design aid. *The Third European Dependable Computing Conference on Dependable Computing* (pp. 143-160). Springer-Verlag. doi:10.1007/3-540-48254-7_11

Scacchi, W. (2001). Process models in software engineering. In Marciniak, J. J. (Ed.), *Encyclopedia of software engineering* (2nd ed.). New York, NY: John Wiley & Sons Inc.

Stuttard, D., & Pinto, M. (2007). *The web application hacker's handbook: Discovering and exploiting security flaws.* John Wiley & Sons, Inc.

Transaction Processing Performance Council. (2008). *TPC BenchmarkTM app (application server) standard specification,* Version 1.3. Retrieved July 5, 2008, from http://www.tpc.org/tpc_app/

Vieira, M., Laranjeiro, N., & Madeira, H. (2007a). Benchmarking the robustness of Web services. *13th IEEE Pacific Rim Dependable Computing Conference (PRDC 2007)* (pp. 322-329). Melbourne, Australia: IEEE Computer Society. doi:10.1109/PRDC.2007.56

Vieira, M., Laranjeiro, N., & Madeira, H. (2007b). Assessing robustness of Web-services infrastructures. *37th Annual IEEE/IFIP International Conference on Dependable Systems and Networks (DSN 2007)* (pp. 131-136). Edinburgh, UK: IEEE Computer Society. doi:10.1109/DSN.2007.16

Weyuker, E. J. (1998). Testing component-based software: a cautionary tale. *Software, 15*(5), 54–59. doi:10.1109/52.714817

ADDITIONAL READING

Astels, D. (2003). *Test driven development: A practical guide.* Prentice Hall Professional Technical Reference.

Augustine, S. (2005). *Managing agile projects.* Prentice Hall PTR.

Beizer, B. (2002). *Software testing techniques.* Dreamtech Press.

Bhat, T., & Nagappan, N. (2006). Evaluating the efficacy of test-driven development: Industrial case studies. *Proceedings of the 2006 ACM/IEEE International Symposium on Empirical Software Engineering* (pp. 356–363).

Canfora, G., Cimitile, A., Garcia, F., Piattini, M., & Visaggio, C. A. (2006). Evaluating advantages of test driven development: A controlled experiment with professionals. *Proceedings of the 2006 ACM/IEEE International Symposium on Empirical Software Engineering* (pp. 364–371).

Cohn, M. (2004). *User stories applied: For agile software development.* Addison-Wesley Professional.

Crispin, L. (2006). Driving software quality: How test-driven development impacts software quality. *Software, 23*(6), 70–71. doi:10.1109/MS.2006.157

Damm, L.-O., & Lundberg, L. (2006). Results from introducing component-level test automation and test-driven development. *Journal of Systems and Software, 79*, 1001–1014. doi:10.1016/j.jss.2005.10.015

Desai, C., Janzen, D. S., & Clements, J. (2009). Implications of integrating test-driven development into CS1/CS2 curricula. *ACM SIGCSE Bulletin. SIGCSE, 09*, 148–152. doi:doi:10.1145/1508865.1508921

Fu, C., Ryder, B. G., Milanova, A., & Wonnacott, D. (2004). Testing of Java Web services for robustness. *ACM SIGSOFT Software Engineering Notes. ISSTA, 04*, 23–34. doi:10.1145/1007512.1007516

George, B., & Williams, L. (2003a). An initial investigation of test driven development in industry. *Proceedings of the 2003 ACM Symposium on Applied Computing* (pp. 1135–1139).

George, B., & Williams, L. (2004b). A structured experiment of test-driven development. *Information and Software Technology, 46*(5), 337–342. doi:10.1016/j.infsof.2003.09.011

Geras, A., Smith, M., & Miller, J. (2004). A prototype empirical evaluation of test driven development. *Proceedings of the Software Metrics, 10th International Symposium,* (pp. 405–416). doi:10.1109/METRICS.2004.2

Hanna, S., & Munro, M. (2008). Fault-based Web services testing. *Proceedings of the Fifth International Conference on Information Technology: New Generations,* (pp. 471–476). doi:10.1109/ITNG.2008.182

Highsmith, J. (2004). *Agile project management: Creating innovative products.* Redwood City, CA: Addison Wesley Longman Publishing Co., Inc.

Janzen, D. S, & Saiedian, H. (2006). *On the influence of test-driven development on software design.*

Jeffries, R. E., Anderson, A., & Hendrickson, C. (2000). *Extreme programming installed.* Boston, MA: Addison-Wesley Longman Publishing Co., Inc.

Laranjeiro, N., Canelas, S., & Vieira, M. (2008). WSRbench: An on-line tool for robustness benchmarking. *Proceedings of the 2008 IEEE International Conference on Services Computing, Vol. 2,* (pp. 187–194). doi:10.1109/SCC.2008.123

Martin, E., Basu, S., & Xie, T. (2007). WebSob: A tool for robustness testing of Web services. *Companion to the Proceedings of the 29th International Conference on Software Engineering,* (pp. 65–66). doi:http://dx.doi.org/10.1109/ICSECOMPANION.2007.84

Maximilien, E. M., & Williams, L. (2003). Assessing test-driven development at IBM. *Proceedings of the 25th International Conference on Software Engineering* (pp. 564–569).

Myers, G. J. (2008). *The art of software testing.* Wiley-India.

Nagappan, N., Maximilien, E. M., Bhat, T., & Williams, L. (2008c). Realizing quality improvement through test driven development: Results and experiences of four industrial teams. *Empirical Software Engineering, 13*(3), 289–302. doi:10.1007/s10664-008-9062-z

Newkirk, J. W., & Vorontsov, A. A. (2004). *Test-driven development in Microsoft. Net.* Redmond, WA: Microsoft Press.

Poppendieck, M., & Poppendieck, T. (2006). *Implementing lean software development: From concept to cash.* Addison-Wesley Professional Signature Series.

Schwaber, K. (2007). *The enterprise and Scrum.*

Williams, L., Maximilien, E. M., & Vouk, M. (2003). *Test-driven development as a defect-reduction practice.*

KEY TERMS AND DEFINITIONS

Agile Software Development: A largely informal software development methodology. It is lightweight and emphasizes teamwork and customer involvement. It typically implies frequent and short iterations that aim first at the creation of small working components of the complete system being developed.

Robustness: The behavior of a given system in the presence of invalid input parameters.

Robustness Testing: A testing technique that can characterize a system in terms of robustness. Characterization is frequently carried out using failure mode scales.

Software Development Methodology: A framework designed to structure plan, and control the complete process of developing a software system.

Software Fault: A computer program defect or bug that can lead to an error (a perturbation of system state), which in turn can result in a failure (an event that occurs when the delivered service deviates from correct service).

Test-Driven Development: A software development methodology that is based on short development iterations. In each iteration the developer writes a test case to validate a specific functionality (or functionality improvement) that will be implemented after the test is written. Development of the functionality follows (so that the test can pass) and finally code is refactored to an acceptable level.

Web Services: Self-Describing components that can be used by other software across the web in platform-independent manner. Web services supported by standard protocols such as SOAP (Simple Object Access Protocol), WSDL (Web Services Description Language), and UDDI (Universal Description, Discovery, and Integration).

Chapter 12

An Agile and Tool-Supported Methodology for Model-Driven System Testing of Service-Centric Systems

Michael Felderer
University of Innsbruck, Austria

Philipp Zech
University of Innsbruck, Austria

Ruth Breu
University of Innsbruck, Austria

ABSTRACT

In this chapter, the authors present an agile and model-driven system testing methodology for service-centric systems called Telling TestStories. The methodology has a tool implementation and is based on separated system, requirements, and test models that can be validated in an integrated way. Test models contain test stories describing test behavior and test data in an integrated way. The underlying testing process is iterative, incremental, and supports a test-driven design on the model level. After a general overview of the artifacts and the testing process, the authors employ the methodology and the tool implementation on a case study from the healthcare domain.

INTRODUCTION

The number and complexity of service-centric systems for implementing flexible inter- and intra-organizational IT based business processes is steadily increasing. Arising application scenarios have demonstrated the power of service-centric systems that consist of peers providing and re-quiring services (Breu, 2010). These range from the cross-linking of traffic participants, over new business models like Software-as-a-Service, to the exchange of health related data among stakeholders in healthcare. Elaborated standards, technologies and frameworks for realizing service-centric systems have been developed, but system testing tools and methodologies have been neglected so far (Canfora & Di Penta, 2008).

DOI: 10.4018/978-1-4666-2503-7.ch012

The trend in industrial software development is going towards agile development processes that provide continuously growing executable systems. Agile processes (Fowler & Highsmith, 2001) are based on iterative and incremental development and testing, where requirements and solutions evolve through collaboration between cross-functional teams and support for (semi-) automatic system testing is highly important.

Agile system testing methodologies for service-centric systems, i.e., methods for evaluating the system's compliance with its specified requirements, have to consider specific issues that limit their testability including the integration of various component and communication technologies, the dynamic adaptation and integration of services, the lack of service control, the lack of observability and structure of service code, the cost of testing, and the importance of Service Level Agreements (SLA).

A system testing methodology which considers model-driven testing and agile methods is particularly suitable for system testing of service-centric systems. Such a methodology supports the definition of requirements by modeling tests in a very early phase of the development process and on a high level of abstraction. The assignment of tests to requirements on the model-level makes requirements executable and enables the definition plus the modification of requirements and tests in a collaborative way by various stakeholders. Modeled tests can be adapted easily to changing requirements, they support the optimization of test suites without a running system, they provide an abstract technology and implementation independent view on tests, and they allow the modeling and testing of service level agreements. The latter especially allows for defining test models in a very early phase of system development even before or simultaneous with system modeling supporting test-driven development on the model level.

In this chapter we introduce an agile and model-driven system testing methodology called Telling TestStories (TTS) that is based on tightly integrated platform-independent requirements, system and test models. The approach is capable of iterative and incremental test-driven development on the model level, and guarantees high quality system and test models by checking consistency, completeness and coverage. Additionally, TTS provides full traceability between the requirements, the system and test models, and the executable services of the system. The collaboration between stakeholders for defining and adapting tests is supported by test models and the tabular representation of test data and test results as in the Framework for Integrated Testing (FIT). Our approach is therefore not only model-driven but also tabular. The tool environment of TTS supports these features in a stringent way and integrates domain experts, test experts, and system experts into a process of collaborative requirements, system and test design. The TTS framework adheres to a test-driven development approach, thus it allows the execution of test stories in early stages of system development and supports the evolution of the underlying system. Our methodology can also be employed for acceptance testing because we consider it as system testing performed by a customer.

There are several system testing methodologies and tools available. Unlike TTS, these frameworks do not combine tabular and model-driven system testing.

FIT/Fitnesse (Mugridge & Cunningham, 2005) is the most prominent framework which supports system test-driven development of applications allowing the tabular specification, observation and execution of test cases by system analysts. TTS is due to its tabular specification of test data based on the ideas of FIT/Fitnesse. But additionally, TTS is model-driven supporting validation, maintenance and traceability of test designs on the model level. Tests in TTS are also more expressive than FIT tests because TTS supports to model control flows in tests.

A model-driven approach to testing SOA with the UML 2.0 Testing Profile (OMG, 2005) is defined in (Baker et al., 2007). It focuses on web services technology and uses the whole set of U2TP concepts. Our approach can be mapped to that approach but additionally it is designed for arbitrary service technologies, provides a service-centric view on tests, supports the tabular definition of tests and guarantees traceability between all involved artifacts.

In (Margaria & Steffen, 2004) a system testing method whose test model is based on test graphs similar to our test stories is presented. Therein consistency and correctness is validated via model checking but the relationship to system models and traceability such as in our approach are not considered.

Test sheets (Atkinson et al., 2010) provide a semantically self-contained tabular representation of tests that has been employed for testing service-centric systems (Atkinson et al., 2008). Differing from TTS, tests are not modeled and therefore there is no validation support, graphical representation of tests or relationship to a system model.

This chapter is structured as follows. We first give an overview of the Telling TestStories methodology. We then apply our tool-based methodology on a case study from the healthcare domain, and evaluate our approach. We finally draw conclusions and discuss future work.

TELLING TESTSTORIES SYSTEM TESTING METHODOLOGY

The TTS methodology defines a testing process and its underlying artifacts. In this section we first give an overview of the TTS artifacts and then present the TTS testing process.

An overview of the TTS artifacts and their relationship is shown in Figure 1. Based on the *Informal Requirements*, a *Requirements Model* is defined. The requirements are traceable to model elements of the *System Model* and the *Test Model*. The system model is needed for validation, coverage checks and generation of the test model. The test model is used for validating the system model. From the test model *Test Code* is generated. The

test code is executed by the *Test Controller* using *Adapter* classes to invoke operations on the *System Under Test*.

On the model level TTS defines a requirements model, a system model containing services as core elements, and a test model. The test model contains so called *test stories* which are controlled sequences of service calls and assertions plus test data. In the table assigned to each test story, data for the service calls and the assertions is defined. Each test case corresponds to one line in that table. The notion of a test story is very clear and claimed to be defined by domain experts rather than testers. The models are designed in UML, and checks in OCL are applied to check their consistency, coverage and completeness.

The test stories are automatically transformed to Java code. Its service calls are executable on the running services of the SUT via adapters. We have introduced the term "test story" for our way of defining tests to show the analogy to the agile term "user story" also defining a manageable requirement together with system tests (Felderer, Breu et al., 2009). Test stories are hierarchical, and a top-level sequence of test stories is called a test sequence. In the following paragraphs we explain the artifacts of Figure 1 in more detail.

On the informal level there is only one type of artifact defined, namely Informal Requirements, i.e., written or non-written capabilities and properties. Informal requirements are not discussed in detail because they are not in the main focus of our testing methodology and cannot be validated automatically.

On the model level there are three models defined: requirements, system and test model. The models are formally defined by a metamodel. Based on the metamodel inter-model and intra-model relationships are defined, namely traceability, validation, coverage, and transformation. For readability reasons in Figure 1 only the inter-model relationships are depicted, but in each of the models it is possible to define validation, coverage and transformation rules based on their metamodel.

Figure 1. TTS artifacts

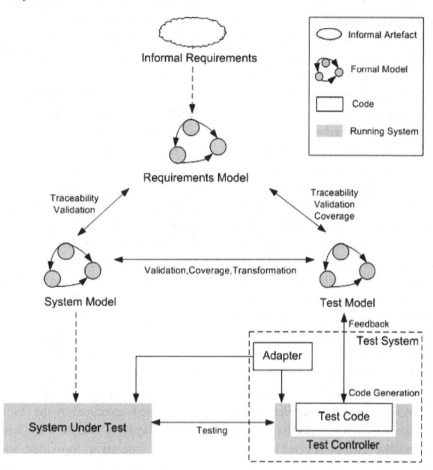

Requirements Model: The Requirements Model contains the functional and non-functional requirements for system development and testing. Its structured part consists of a requirements hierarchy. The requirements are based on informal requirements depicted as a cloud. The requirements model provides a way to integrate textual descriptions of requirements needed for communication with non-technicians into a modelling tool.

System Mode: The system model describes the system structure and system behaviour in a platform independent way. Its *static structure* is based on the notion of services. Each (business) service or even each operation is assigned to a requirement. We assume that each service in the system model corresponds to an execut-

able service in the running system to guarantee traceability. Additionally, configuration services for configuring the system or modifying types and information services providing information about the business objects may be defined. The latter two types of services do not correspond to requirements. Nevertheless, all requirements, (business) services and executable services are traceable. The *dynamic structure* is based on local processes controlled by a specific service that correspond to an orchestration, and global processes which integrate several services and correspond to a choreography.

Test Model: The test model defines the test requirements, the test data and the test scenarios as so called test stories. We use the terms "test story" and "test" interchangeably in this chapter depending on the context. To convey the more abstract view, we use the term "test, and to convey the more application-oriented and process-oriented view we use the term "test story". *Test stories* (i.e. tests) are controlled sequences of service operation invocations defining the interaction of services and assertions for computing verdicts. Tests may be generic in the sense that they do not contain concrete objects but variables which refer to test objects provided in tables. Tests can also invoke configuration services for the system setup and tear down. The concept of a test is in principle of its representation. We apply UML sequence diagrams (Felderer, Agreiter et al., 2010) and UML activity diagrams (Felderer, Zech et al., 2010) but are not restricted to these notations. Tests include references to a table of test data including values for all free parameters of the test. Each line in this table defines test data for one test case. The test data elements are stored in a *data pool*. *Test Requirements* can contain global arbitrations that define when a test is successful by restrictions on the verdicts, or coverage constraints that define what parts of a model have to be inspected by a test.

If tests are designed manually, the test stories tool has to guarantee that the tests are consistent with each other and that the set of tests in the test model fulfils some coverage criteria with respect to the system model. Alternatively, if the system model is complete, then tests can be generated by a model-to-model transformation between the system and the test model. If the system model is not complete, then the test model can be regarded as an integrated part of the system specification, a so called *partial system specification*. This model-driven approach can therefore be applied in a system-driven way by deriving tests from the system model or in a test-driven way by integrating tests into the system. In all application scenarios, the system model can be used to validate the test model and vice versa. The approach also supports classical *test-driven development* because from

test models and adapters it is possible to derive executable tests even before the system implementation has been finished. Tests are linked to requirements and associated with services of the systems by service calls. Tests can additionally be transformed from an abstract workflow representation to a concrete test representation from which test code can be generated.

Each test is linked to a requirement and can therefore be regarded as an executable requirement by analogy with FIT tests (Mugridge & Cunningham, 2005). Tests in our sense can also be used as testing facets (Canfora & Di Penta, 2008) defining built-in test cases for a service that allows potential actors to evaluate the service. Together with appropriate requirements the tests may serve as executable SLAs.

- **Test Code:** The test code is generated by a model-to-text transformation from the test model to test code in Java (Felderer, Fiedler et al., 2009). The generated test code is executed by the test controller.
- **Adapters:** Adapters are needed to access the operations provided and required by components of the system under test. For a service implemented as a web service, an adapter can be generated from its WSDL description. Adapters for each service are the link for traceability between the executable system, the test model and the requirements.
- **Test Controller:** The test controller executes the generated test code and accesses the system services via adapters. The current implementation of the test controller executes test code in Java.
- **Test System:** The test controller, the adapter and the test code form the test system.
- **System Under Test:** The system under test (SUT) is a service-centric system with service interfaces that provide and require operations.

In TTS, traceability is guaranteed between all artefacts. Requirements, tests and services are associated on the model level via links between model elements. Each modelled service is associated with an executable service in the system. The adapter link service calls in the model to executable services. Every service invocation is thereby traceable to a requirement.

The TTS testing process depicted in Figure 2 consists of a design, validation, execution, and evaluation phase and is processed in an iterative and incremental way under customer support.

The first step is the definition of requirements. Based on the requirements, the system model containing services and the test model containing test stories are designed. The test model design includes the definition of tests, i.e., test stories or test sequences, the data pool definition and the

definition of test requirements, i.e., specific validation, coverage or assertion criteria.

The system model and the test model, the data pool and the test requirements, can be validated for consistency and completeness and checked for coverage. This validity checks allow for an iterative improvement of the system and test quality.

Test stories are normally modeled manually, but in specific cases it is also possible to transform system traces to test stories. The methodology does not consider the system development itself but is based on traceable services offered by the system under test (SUT). As soon as adapters which may be - depending on the technology - generated (semi-)automatically or implemented manually are available for the system services, the process of test selection and test code generation can take place. Test stories can be created in a test-driven

Figure 2. TTS testing process

way even before the system model has been completed. Therefore the system and test model share concepts, are business-oriented, not considering the test architecture and the underlying technology, and support the tabular description of data.

In the tool implementation, adapters for web services can be generated automatically based on a WSDL description, adapters for RMI access can only be generated semi-automatically. The generated test code is then automatically compiled and executed by a test controller which logs all occurring events into a test log.

The test evaluation is done offline by a test analysis tool which generates test reports and annotations to those elements of the system and test model influencing the test result. Additionally, the lines of the test table are colored green, yellow or red depending whether the corresponding test passes, is inconclusive or fails. Pass indicates that the SUT behaves correctly for the specific test case. Fail indicates that the test case has been violated. Inconclusive is used where the test neither passes nor fails. The verdict inconclusive may for instance be assigned when the test data is insufficient or the network connection to a service is broken. An error verdict indicates exceptions within the test system itself. In the model itself only a pass or a fail can be specified. Inconclusive or error is

assigned automatically. This definition of verdicts originates from the OSI Conformance Testing Methodology and Framework (ISO/IEC, 1994).

The separation of the test behavior and the test data has been influenced by the column fixture of FIT which allows the test designer to focus directly on the domain because tests are expressed in a very easy-to-write and easy-to-understand tabular form also suited for data-driven testing.

The manual activities in the TTS testing process are performed by specific roles. Figure 3 shows these roles and their activities which are the manual or semi-automatic activities in the TTS testing process of Figure 2. Note that the activities can also be performed by testers but the roles are defined independently of test specific roles.

A Domain Expert or Customer, which are represented by one role in Figure 3, is responsible for the test design and the requirements definition. Additionally, domain experts or customers may initiate the test execution and all related automatic activities (validation, test code generation, test analysis). Domain experts and customers are responsible for the same activities but have different views on testing, i.e., domain experts represent the internal view performing system tests and customers represent the external view performing acceptance tests.

Figure 3. Roles in the TTS testing process

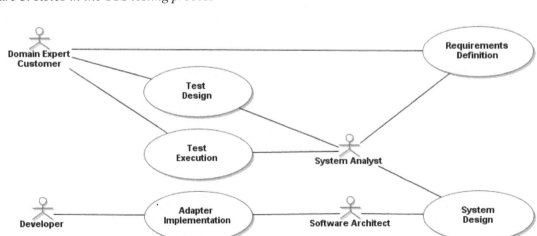

A System Analyst is partially responsible for the test design, the requirements definition, and the system design. Additionally, the system analyst may also initiate the test execution and all related activities. The system analyst is especially responsible for the definition of non-functional requirements, e.g., for security or performance and corresponding tests.

A Software Architect is partially responsible for the system design and the adapter implementation. The software architect defines interfaces and component technologies in coordination with the system analyst and the developer.

A Developer implements adapters if they have to be developed manually.

TOOL-BASED CASE STUDY

In this section we apply the TTS methodology and its tool (all figures in this section are screenshots or exports from our tool implementation) in an industrial case study from the healthcare domain. The system under test makes medical data available in the right place and at the right time for authorized users. Due to the system's complexity and its application field in the area of patients' data storage, data management, and advanced medical diagnostics, reliability and scalability are of high importance. Reliability, scalability, and the functional behavior are guaranteed by extensive testing. So far the application has solely been tested with JUnit (ObjectMentor, 2009). However, testing the complete application in a scenario-driven way starting from the model level requires a more enhanced approach such as TTS.

In our methodology first, the requirements and static parts of the system are designed. Requirements are typically modeled in a hierarchy of functional and non-functional requirements such as reliability or scalability. To make this chapter readable we only consider one requirement and its assigned test story for retrieving patient's specific data by his given ID.

The system model contains specific data types, e.g., for medical data, and service components providing and requiring interfaces, e.g., a service component called Source providing various operations like findPatientByID or findDocuments. The types are modeled inside UML class diagrams and the services are abstracted as components inside UML component diagrams. For a more detailed explanation of the system model, the interested reader is advised to take a look at (Felderer, Zech et al., 2009). The requirements and the system are defined in an iterative way. In the following we only consider the test model which is the most innovative and critical model artifact of our methodology in more detail.

The test model consists of two packages, named *Teststories* and *Testsequences*, containing all test related information. In the former, the various test stories, depicting test cases, are located, whereas the latter one contains the various test sequences, defining how the various test cases are executed during a test run. Allowing the usage of multiple test sequences enhances our approach with the capability to distinctively test different usage scenarios exhaustively.

Figure 4 shows a basic test story FindAndRetrieveDocumentsTest modeled as a UML activity diagram, enhanced with stereotypes for service calls and assertions.

As shown in Figure 4, a test story consists of a flow of service calls and assertions, used to define the behavior of a test case. Beneath, a story may also be separated into different partitions, each representing one of the system's services. Inside these partitions service calls represent invocations of operations on the represented service. Additionally, test stories contain assertions. The idea of an assertion is to be used to define a condition to hold after a single test run. Yet, assertions may not only be defined once at the end of a test run, as can be seen in Figure 4, they may also be defined between different service calls. This allows aborting a test prior to finishing similar as with JUnit's various assert statements.

The reason why those assertions rely outside of any swim lanes is due to the fact that they represent general test activities not assigned to a specific service. Hence, as they are to be evaluated by the TTS runtime, they logically rely outside of any service domain.

The basic test story depicted in Figure 4 is used to examine whether the SUT's functionality to search for a patient, based on his/her ID (service call findPatientByID on the service Consumer). Further on, if the patient is found, it is tested whether the SUT properly returns the patient's specific documents (service call findDocuments on the service Consumer). The representation of a test story is very abstract and can be defined by customers or domain experts to integrate them into the test definition process. Test stories can be defined as soon as the structural elements of the system, i.e., services are defined.

Table 1 shows the test data table assigned to the test story FindAndRetrieveDocumentsTest of Figure 4. Each line of that table represents one test case and has columns for each input variable of all service calls and for the free parameters of assertions.

In its nature, the test data sheet shown above is unique compared to other current approaches. Despite offering the capability to provide simple types like String or Boolean values, as it is the case for findPatientByID_patientID or findPatientByID_searchByExternalDomains, we also allow to incorporate complex instances of object structures as test data values, referenced by their unique bean IDs. In the test data table Table 1 this is the case with all the remaining parameters of the table, passed to the test runs, e.g.: findPatientByID_sessionInfo. The beans stored inside Spring's IoC (Inversion-of-Control) container and are retrieved during executing a test case by their unique bean ID, as shown in the above test data table.

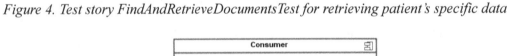

Figure 4. Test story FindAndRetrieveDocumentsTest for retrieving patient's specific data

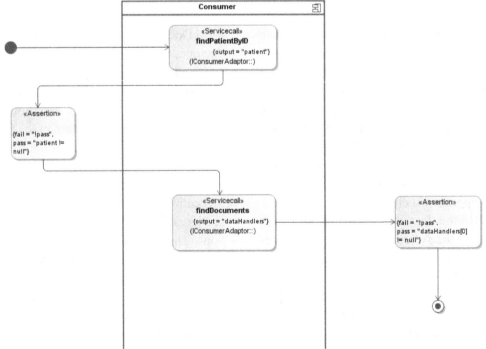

Table 1. Test data table for FindAndRetrieveDocumentsTest

TestID	findPatientByID_patientID	findPatientByID_sessionInfo	findPatientByID_searchExternalDomains	findDocuments_patientInfo	findDocuments_filter	findDocuments_sessionInfo
1	1354230267	sessionInfo1	true	patient.patientInfo	nullFilter	sessionInfo1
2	3417111066	sessionInfo2	true	patient.patientInfo	nullFilter	sessionInfo2
3	4567121285	sessionInfo3	false	patient.patientInfo	nullFilter	sessionInfo3

For instance, in each test run, a complex object containing session specific information is required by means of sessionInfo01, sessionInfo02 and sessionInfo03, respectively. Another interesting feature contained in the above test data table is the possibility to access intermediary test values. This actually happens in each test run in the case of findDocuments_patientInfo, where the information of the patient instance, retrieved by the former findPatientById service call, is used.

Taking a closer look at Figure 4 reveals, that the object, returned by the service call shall be stored with the unique variable name patient (output = "patient"). At this point it shall be mentioned, that each test run has its unique context of related test data to store such intermediary values. Finally, to conclude the discussion of this sample test story and its artifacts, Table 1 contains no assertion specific columns. This comes due to the fact that the used assertions inside the test story only check, whether the returned objects are not null. Hence, as null actually has no value, it does not need to be provided. However, if declared parameters are to be used in assertions, providing values for them is analogous to the schema for test data values of service calls and also done inside the test data tables.

Figure 5 shows a test sequence that contains two sequence elements which call the two test stories, CreateFolderWithDocumentsTest and FindAndRetrieveDocumentsTest. Each sequence element contains an arbitration defining a global condition to determine whether a set of test cases passes or fails.

Test stories can be defined as soon as the underlying requirements and the invoked services are defined. Test stories are checked for consistency and are iteratively adapted. These consistency checks are implemented using OCL and are used to assure the consistency of the test stories. In other words, the consistency checks assure that the test model contains no errors by means of

Figure 5. Test sequence including CreateFolderWithDocumentsTest and FindAndRetrieveDocumentsTest

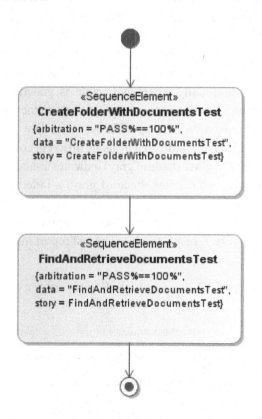

referencing non-existent services, and the like. However, these consistency checks are also used to assure the validity of a test story, put another way, to assure that only valid features and requirements are tested. For example, the OCL query of Listing 1 is used to assure, whether a service call is valid, in other words, whether all parameters are properly set and the invoked service operation actually is offered by the SUT and testable.

If the test model passes all the checks, test stories are transformed to executable test code and as soon as adapter implementations are available, they can be executed.

The result of the test execution is annotated to model elements. As shown in Figure 6, the sequence elements are colored based on the test result and linked to comments visualizing detailed test results. The first sequence element Create-FolderWithDocumentsTest is colored in green to indicate a pass, and the second sequence element FindAndRetreiveDocumentsTest is colored in red to indicate a fail. Note that in the gray scale images of Figure 6 and Figure 7 the color red is represented by the darker shade of gray, and green by the brighter one. The direct model feedback and the assignment of test stories to requirements guarantees the executability of requirements.

Additionally, an HTML table is generated, which shows each test data line and whether the test execution of a specific test data line succeeded or not (indicated by using different colors, green (brighter shade of gray) indicates a successful test, red (darker shade of gray) a failed test execution – as it would be the case with the second run of the FindAndRetrieveDocumentsTest in Figure 7, respectively). The test report in Figure 7 shows possible results of the execution of the test sequence of Figure 5 using a tabular notation similar to FIT. Besides, if a test run fails due to some exception triggering error, the complete information provided by the exception is included in the HTML log in a separate additional column, containing this very exception related information (in the example, no exception was thrown, hence this column is not visible).

Under the bottom line, using TTS allowed us to develop and perform system tests, resembling different usage scenarios and workflows. In the TTS approach requirements, the system, and tests are developed in a model-driven, iterative and incremental way fostering agile development on the model level.

EVALUATION

The design science paradigm (Hevner et al., 2004) in computer science essentially advocates the construction of a demonstration implementation of a proposed new approach followed by an evaluation of its usability and effectiveness. According to the paradigm of explanatory design theory (Baskerville & Pries-Heje, 2010) in design science, only two elements are essentially necessary for a complete design theory: requirements, i.e., the definition of a tabular and model-driven system testing approach for service-centric systems in our context, and a solution, i.e., the contributing results evaluated by a tool implementation and its application to a case study in our context.

We have implemented a tool for the TTS methodology that supports a tabular and model-driven approach which can be employed in an iterative and incremental way integrating customers. We have applied the methodology and its tool implementation in an industrial case study from the healthcare domain. The application of the TTS tool and the TTS methodology on a case study is an indicator for the usability of the approach.

Listing 1. OCL query for validity of service calls

```
context Model
    query checkIsValidServicecalls:
    severity 0
    let result:Set(CallOperationAction)=CallOperationAction.
        allInstances()
    message result.isValidServiceCall() endmessage
```

Figure 6. Test result annotated to test sequence elements

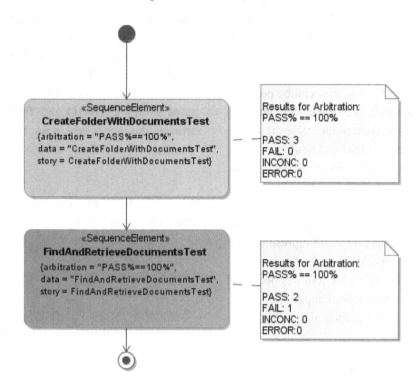

Figure 7. Test result report in tabular form

TestWorkflow
06-15-2011/12:35:48

System Under Test
Name: eHealth App
Version: 1.0

CreateFolderWithDocumentsTest

ID	addDocumentsToFolder folder	addDocumentsToFolder documents	addDocumentsToFolder submissionInfo	addDocumentsToFolder swessionInfo
1	folder1	docs1	submissionInfo1	sessionInfo1
2	folder2	docs2	submissionInfo2	sessionInfo2
3	folder3	docs3	submissionInfo3	sessionInfo3

FindAndRetrieveDocumentsTest

ID	findPatientByID_patientID	findPatientByID_sessionInfo	findPatientByID_searchExternalDomains	findDocuments_patientInfo	findDocuments_filter	findDocuments_sessionInfo
1	1354230267	sessionInfo1	true	patient.patientInfo	nullFilter	sessionInfo1
2	1417111066	sessionInfo2	true	patient.patientInfo	nullFilter	sessionInfo2
3	1567121285	sessionInfo3	false	patient.patientInfo	nullFilter	sessionInfo3

The implementation is available online at http://www.teststories.info [accessed: March 17, 2011].

The effectiveness of our approach stems from several reasons. Our methodology supports the model-driven definition of tests in an incremental and iterative way. Test stories can be defined before behavioral artifacts of the system and are used to validate the system model. Therefore our approach can be considered as test-driven. The OCL validation between the requirements, system and test model supports high quality tests already in a very early phase of the software development lifecycle. The approach also supports convenient tabular definition of test data and represents the test results in these tables. Due to the positive feedback of the TTS users, the tool has been assessed as usable in its practical application.

As in many agile projects, JUnit has been employed for system testing in our case study. In model-driven approaches, TTS has several advantages compared to JUnit. Test stories can already be defined on the model level and due to their relationship to the system and requirements model provide validation support. Additionally, the graphical notation of test stories (see Figure 4) is more intuitive than tests in JUnit, and especially for complex systems the test design is supported more effectively.

To show the applicability of our approach, we have implemented the same tests with JUnit and TTS. Therefore the test results are equal and also the test execution time is not critical in both approaches. Nevertheless already the test design with TTS has several advantages, considering that a requirements hierarchy and the static structure of the system are predefined. For service-centric systems which are considered by TTS this should not be critical because at least WSDL interfaces for the services are available. As mentioned before the graphical representation of test stories supports early definition of tests, validation of tests, definition of tests by non-technicians like domain experts, and the intuitive definition of tests.

The graphical representation of a test story is transformed into test code which is the basis for test execution. In Listing 2 the generated TTS test code of the test story FindAndRetrieveDocumentsTest (see Figure 4) is shown.

The test code in Listing 2 invokes the operations findPatientByID and findDocuments, retrieves the necessary data from the context, computes the verdicts based on the assertion, and

Listing 2. Test code of a test story FindAndRetrieveDocumentsTest

```
1 public void sequence1() throws Exception {

2 context.storeValue("patient", ConsumerAdaptier.invoke(

3 "findPatientByID",

4 context.retrieveValue("findPatientByID_patientID"),

5 context.retrieveValue("findPatientByID_sessionInfo"),

6 context.retrieveValue("findPatientByID_searchExternalDomains")));

7

8 verdict = evaluator.evaluateAssertion("patient != null", "!pass",

9 context.getData());

10 LOGGER.log(Verdict.fromValue(verdict.name()),

11 EnactmentRuntimeProperties.getInstance().getProperty(

12 IProjectRuntimeProperties.TTS_RUNTIME_TABLE_CURRENT_ROW),"");

13

14 context.storeValue("dataHandlers", ConsumerAdaptier.invoke(

15 "findDocuments",

16 context.retrieveValue("findDocuments_patientInfo"),

17 context.retrieveValue("findDocuments_filter"),

18 context.retrieveValue("findDocuments_sessionInfo")));

19

20 verdict = evaluator.evaluateAssertion("dataHandlers[0] != null",

21 "!pass", context.getData());

22 LOGGER.log(Verdict.fromValue(verdict.name()),

23 EnactmentRuntimeProperties.getInstance().getProperty(

24 IProjectRuntimeProperties.TTS_RUNTIME_TABLE_CURRENT_ROW),"");

25 }
```

logs the data of the test run. The test generator for generating this test code out of the test story is explained in (Felderer, Fiedler et al., 2009). The generated test code contains 26 method invocations or read operations on class variables.

Listing 3 shows the JUnit code corresponding to the test story CreateFolderTest and its test code representation in Listing 2.

The JUnit code in Listing 3 first retrieves the patient by invoking findPatientByID needed as input for the findDocuments operation, which is then invoked to retrieve the patient's documents The JUnit code contains 39 method invocations or read operations on class variables, whereas the TTS test code only contains 26 invocations and read operations. The main reason for this difference is that TTS separates the test behavior and the test data definition while in the JUnit code also test objects are generated. In principle it is possible to transform test stories into JUnit code. The TTS approach and JUnit are therefore compatible. In general the definition of test stories is more intuitive and due to the validation support also less error-prone than the definition of tests in JUnit.

CONCLUSION AND FUTURE WORK

In this chapter we have presented an agile, tabular and model-driven methodology for system testing called Telling TestStories. After an overview of the TTS artifacts and the TTS testing process, we have provided a case study from the healthcare domain and evaluated it.

The TTS methodology is a system testing approach for service-centric systems. Tests are modeled as so called test stories integrating test behavior and test data. TTS supports the early definition of high-quality test by validation and coverage checks. The visual definition of test stories is suited for test definition by domain experts because it is simple and intuitive. After the

Listing 3. JUnit code for CreateFolderTest

```
1 @Test
2 public void testFindAndRetrieveDocuments() throws Exception {
3 LOGGER.info("\n\n -- Start " + this.getClass().getSimpleName()
4 + "# testFindAndRetrieveDocuments");
5
6 LOGGER.info("Setting patient data");
7 ID patientId = new ID();
8
9 patientId.setExtension(TestPatients.
10 PATIENT_SCHWARZ_SOCIAL_SECURITY_NUMBER_AS_STRING);
11 patientId.setOid(ConnectivityConstants.OID_OF_SSN_DOMAIN);
12
13 LOGGER.info("Call 'findPatientByID(...)'");
14 PatientInfo foundPatient = findPatientByID(consumerAdaptorStub,
15 patientId);
16
17 LOGGER.info("check response");
18 Assert.assertNotNull("Patient not found.", foundPatient);
19
20 LOGGER.info("Call 'findDocuments(...)' with patient global-ID: '"
21 + foundPatient.getHomeCommunityPatientID().getExtension() + "'");
22
23 DocumentMetaInformation[] foundDocumentEntries = findDocuments(
24 consumerAdaptorStub, foundPatient);
25
26 for (DocumentMetaInformation documentEntry: foundDocumentEntries) {
27 LOGUtil.printDocumentMetadata(documentEntry.
28 getDocumentMetadata());
29 }
30
31 LOGGER.info("Select first found Document to retrieve");
32 DocumentMetadata[] documentEntriesToRetrieve = new DocumentMetadata[] {
33 foundDocumentEntries[0].getDocumentMetadata() };
34
35 LOGGER.info("Retrieve the first found Document");
36 DataHandler[] dataHandlers = retrieveDocumentSet(consumerAdaptorStub,
37 documentEntriesToRetrieve);
38
39 LOGGER.info("Write First Document to Harddisk");
40 String fileName = "testOutput" + System.getProperty("file.separator")
41 + this.getClass().getSimpleName() + ".dat";
42 writeDocumentToDisk(dataHandlers[0], fileName);
43 }
```

initial effort of modeling the relevant parts of the system, TTS is usable, effective and has several advantages compared to JUnit.

In future we plan further extensions of the TTS methodology. We want to integrate additional test types (regression testing, risk-based testing) and consider also risk-based security testing. Additionally, we plan to evaluate our test design approach by a comparison to FIT which is also a framework widely used in agile system testing and by controlled experiments.

ACKNOWLEDGMENT

This work was partially funded by the research project "QE LaB - Living Models for Open Systems" (FFG 822740).

REFERENCES

Atkinson, C., Barth, F., & Brenner, D. (2010). *Software testing using test sheets.*

Atkinson, C., Brenner, D., Falcone, G., & Juhasz, M. (2008). *Specifying high-assurance services. IEEE Computer, 41.* Los Alamitos, CA: IEEE.

Baker, P., Dai, P. R., Grabowski, J., Haugen, O., Schieferdecker, I., & Williams, C. E. (2007). *Model-driven testing - Using the UML testing profile.*

Baskerville, R., & Pries-Heje, J. (2010). Explanatory design theory. *Business & Information Systems Engineering, 2*(5), 271–282. doi:10.1007/s12599-010-0118-4

Breu, R. (2010). *Ten principles for living models - A manifesto of change-driven software engineering.* Paper presented at CISIS 2010, The Fourth International Conference on Complex, Intelligent and Software Intensive Systems.

Canfora, G., & Di Penta, M. (2008). Service-oriented architectures testing: A survey. In L. Andrea De & L. C. Filomena Ferrucci (Eds.), *International Symposium on Signals, Systems and Electronics* (Vol. 5413, pp. 78-105).

Felderer, M., Agreiter, B., Breu, R., & Armenteros, A. (2010). *Security testing by telling TestStories.*

Felderer, M., Breu, R., Chimiak-Opoka, J., Breu, M., & Schupp, F. (2009). Concepts for model-based requirements testing of service oriented systems. *Proceedings of the IASTED International Conference* (Vol. 642, p. 18).

Felderer, M., Fiedler, F., Zech, P., & Breu, R. (2009). *Towards adaptive test code generation for service oriented systems.* Paper presented at the Ninth International Conference on Quality Software (QSIC 2009).

Felderer, M., Zech, P., Fiedler, F., & Breu, R. (2010). *A tool-based methodology for system testing of service-oriented systems.* Paper presented at the The Second International Conference on Advances in System Testing and Validation Lifecycle (VALID 2010).

Felderer, M., Zech, P., Fiedler, F., Chimiak-Opoka, J., & Breu, R. (2009). *Model-driven system testing of a telephony connector with telling test stories.* Paper presented at the Software Quality Engineering. Proceedings of the CONQUEST 2009.

Fowler, M., & Highsmith, J. (2001). The agile manifesto. *Software Development, 9*(8), 28–35.

Hevner, A. R., March, S. T., Park, J., & Ram, S. (2004). Design science in information systems research. *Management Information Systems Quarterly, 28*(1), 75–105.

ISO/IEC. (1994). *Information technology -- Open systems interconnection -- Conformance testing methodology and framework*.

Margaria, T., & Steffen, B. (2004). *Lightweight coarse-grained coordination: A scalable system-level approach* (Vol. 5, pp. 107-123).

Mugridge, R., & Cunningham, W. (2005). *Fit for developing software: Framework for integrated tests*.

ObjectMentor. (2009). *Junit*. Retrieved March 18, 2011, from http://www.junit.org/

OMG. (2005). *UML testing profile*, Version 1.0.

KEY TERMS AND DEFINITIONS

Model-Driven Testing: Model-driven testing considers the derivation of executable test code from test models by analogy to Model Driven Architecture (MDA).

Service-Centric System: A service-centric system consists of a set of independent peers providing and calling services.

System Testing: Testing a system for compliance with specified requirements. System Testing performed by customers is called acceptance testing.

Telling TestStories: The name of a methodology which is used for incremental and iterative model-driven testing of service-centric systems. In telling teststories (tts) tests are defined in models and test data is defined in tables.

Section 3
Practice

Chapter 13
Improving Lean, Service–Oriented Software Development at Codeweavers Ltd

Paul Shannon
7digital Ltd, UK

Neil Kidd
Codeweavers Ltd, UK

Paul Barrett
Codeweavers Ltd, UK

Chris Knight
Codeweavers Ltd, UK

Sam Wessel
Esendex Ltd, UK

ABSTRACT

Following a successful adoption of lean and agile practices, the development team at Codeweavers Ltd has furthered its approach to service-oriented software development for the motor finance and insurance industry. Through iteratively inspecting and adapting their processes over the last twelve months, the team members have seen a change from their Kanban-style single piece flow to multiple work cells developing with separate swim lanes on a work in progress board and within fixed length iterations. The arrival of strong competition to their market led to a positive shift towards customer service and interaction with increased attention on lean planning and agility. This chapter reports on improvement in software craftsmanship with a focus on quality, largely achieved by the use of service-oriented architecture, combined with increased use of mocking for unit-testing. The perspective taken is from software team members, and in the chapter, the developers chart their own observations, improvements, and failures over the course of a year.

DOI: 10.4018/978-1-4666-2503-7.ch013

1. INTRODUCTION TO CODEWEAVERS AND THEIR AGILE ADOPTION PROCESS

Codeweavers Ltd is a software solutions provider based in Staffordshire, UK. The company has around twenty-five employees, including a development team of around twelve developers. Smaller teams of two or three are responsible for infrastructure, design, sales and client support. Since 2001 the company has delivered applications and web services for the automotive financial and insurance industries, and in that time has grown to become the market leader in its specialised field. Its client-base includes leading car manufacturers and dealer groups.

In late 2007 the company began a gradual journey of agile process adoption, in response to a chaotic working environment and a period without profit. At this time, developers at Codeweavers were divided into two teams of four, working on separate applications with specialised knowledge and no shared code base. Each developer worked alone from his own to-do list. Planning and development were unpredictable, code quality was poor and deadlines were often missed. Almost half of the developers' time was devoted to fixing bugs and making small, ad hoc changes.

In response to these problems, the teams adopted Scrum. They each compiled their to-do lists into a backlog and began using planning poker to estimate tasks. They began working to fixed-length sprints, holding daily stand-up meetings and weekly retrospectives. They also began implementing Test Driven Development and Pair-Programming in an attempt to raise code quality. To assist with these changes, the company hired an Agile Coach, who introduced work in progress boards to replace sprint management software, and a continuous integration server to automate builds and unit test runs.

As a result of the improvements to planning and development gained from these actions, the developers' focus shifted to reducing specialisation and knowledge silos. This was accomplished by merging the two teams together and swapping pairs more frequently, which helped to share knowledge across all the developers, and helped the whole team to agree on common standards and domain language.

By mapping the value stream through the company the team was able to identify bottlenecks on which they could swarm. Responding to one such bottleneck in deploying releases, the developers began grouping tasks into marketable features of predictable sizes. These were specified with criteria for their acceptance and only deployed when all developers were satisfied with their quality. These changes noticeably improved the quality and speed of development.

A brief bottleneck in development led the team to begin recording causes of wasted time, increasing the frequency of stand-up meetings and encouraging developers to stop the whole team when a problem was encountered. This action increased communication, reduced downtime, and improved the flow of value through the business.

By Spring 2010, the business was transformed both financially and culturally. Codeweavers Ltd was a vastly more relaxed, sociable and productive environment, with a self-organising development team and a healthy profit from regular feature releases with dramatically fewer bugs. Details on the company's transformation from chaos to Kanban via the Scrum, and the approach used, are provided in Rutherford et al. (Rutherford et al., 2010).

2. FURTHER IMPROVEMENTS IN SOFTWARE CRAFTSMANSHIP AT CODEWEAVERS

2.1 Codeweavers' Understanding of Agility and Leanness

Codeweavers, and in particular the development team, experienced a positive feedback loop by reporting on the way the company inspect, adapt and continually try to improve their practices and processes.

This chapter emerged in the same vein and reports on further improvements, new observations and additional changes to the software development process. It covers the overall increase in code quality, and the changes to practices that helped foster these improvements.

Codeweavers Ltd arrived at the following understanding of agility Highsmith(Highsmith, 2002):

Agility is the ability to both create and respond to change in a turbulent business environment. Agility is the ability to balance flexibility and stability

With this understanding of agility, Codeweavers' goal to produce a stable, ethical and profitable company that has a positive effect on people, society and the environment is facilitated. In addition a set of Agile principles and practices was adopted so that the organisation could respond to customer requirements easily and deliver high quality, feature-rich software to their customers without wasting effort. This consciousness to avoid waste led to a focus on lean principles. Codeweavers' definition of Lean is the elimination of waste through concentrating on process improvement and intelligent planning to ensure that decisions can be made as late as possible.

The inspect and adapt cycle employed by Codeweavers empowers the team to change so that the end product can be delivered as quickly as possible; team empowerment and fast software delivery are key concepts of the lean principles. Other lean practices promote knowledge sharing and software integrity, through testing and refactoring, which are fundamental to the way the development team works.

2.2 Observations and Responses

The techniques used to identify issues were, and remain to be, deliberately lightweight, using a qualitative approach rather than quantitative collection and analysis of data. On occasion data has been collected, where such information was deemed necessary, however the record keeping has been confined to the visibility and ease of use of a whiteboard. Weekly retrospectives are held where the team identifies areas for process improvement - the most valuable points are then selected to be addressed in the following week. It should be noted that improvements are not confined to retrospective outcomes, the team practices Kaizen[1] whereby continuous improvements may be implemented immediately.

The following chapter details the most significant observations and responses that the team used to adapt their processes over that period. The format of this section is a description of an observed problem, labelled '*Problem*', directly followed by a description, labelled '*Response*', of the actions taken to solve or improve the perceived issue.

2.2.1 Initial Efforts to Become Leaner

Problem: During the Spring of 2010 we found that the flow of development was being negatively affected by a continually growing backlog of upcoming work. Despite the backlog being visible, represented by index cards pinned to a wall board, it was virtually full and time was being wasted prioritising the cards. The large and unorganised backlog meant it was often unclear what the next work item was and therefore a smooth work-flow was difficult to sustain. We estimated how much work the backlog contained, and discovered it represented roughly two years of development effort. In addition, the value of each item to both clients and the internal organisation was not easily identified and it was becoming more difficult to accurately estimate the delivery time for customer requests.

Response: The Development Director attended a course, "Leading Lean Software Development", delivered by Mary and Tom Poppendieck, and based on their book of the same title(2010). The major action point brought back from the course aligned with our Agile Coach's view that our large backlog was wasteful, so all of the backlog items were removed from the wall board and the Urgent/Important Matrix technique (Covey, 2008) was applied to prioritise them.

The Urgent/Important Matrix prescribes that a workspace is split into quarters with the following labels placed on the axes: Urgent - Not Urgent and Important - Not Important. We decided that an optimal backlog was four weeks of development work - significantly less than the two years we previously had queued up. With a shorter target in mind, each backlog item was then pinned back on the board relative to its perceived importance and urgency. Any item placed in the least important / least urgent quartile was discarded. The process was then repeated, with the remaining backlog items being removed and reprioritised, until our target estimate of four weeks of work remained.

We immediately saw the benefits of reducing our backlog, and not just in development. The flow of client requests through to delivery was improved. The upstream queue of work items became clearer to developers. Communication with our clients was improved, as we could more accurately estimate delivery times. Sometimes, when a client had a non-urgent request, we had to push back, advising them that we could not carry out the work right now. While this response was often against their expectations, it removed superfluous or low value work from the backlog.

Problem: The improved view of upcoming feature requests meant that we started to notice

downsides to our team merger the previous year, when our two previously isolated teams had been combined. There were now frequent conflicts when committing work, and attempts to avoid this led to critical paths in development, which meant there could sometimes be pairs left without work to do towards the end of a minimum marketable feature (MMF)(Rutherford et al., 2010). In some cases development was taking longer than expected due to the learning curve required by half the team, who were now working on unfamiliar products. All of these factors meant the backlog began to build up again.

Response: The team was divided into two work cells so that two features could be worked on at a time. We maintained single piece flow by having each team work on separate projects and on separate work in progress boards. The work cells were not two distinct teams, as they stayed together only for the duration of an MMF's development. Developers were also able to swap between cells as appropriate. When both cells had finished their MMFs the team members were mixed up again and the cells reallocated which maintained our efforts to share knowledge and improve and standardise the code, while avoiding conflicts and the blocking of pairs.

Problem: While increased knowledge sharing was improving our code quality, we found that it was often laborious to maintain our test code. Developers were resistant to large scale changes and refactoring because of close coupling and dependencies between classes, which often resulted in long test setup methods and rigid code.

Response: Early moves toward a service-oriented codebase came with investigations into mocking. By creating lightweight mock versions of an object's dependencies we could separate the larger application into smaller, well-defined services that interacted with other aspects of the application. We found we could test the messages and collaborations between objects, based on real world interactions, rather than testing the inputs and outputs. We began to use dependency injection for our tests, producing lightweight, verifiable service objects that could be mocked and injected from within unit tests, helping us model collaborations and allowing improved designs to emerge as responsibilities became separated and objects were decoupled. We tried the mars lander kata from Rainsberger (2009) and invited Brian Marick to visit and present his talk on testing object interactions using mocks (2010). This style of testing from an outside-in point of view integrated well with our use of CRC[2] (Beck & Cunningham, 1989) sessions - a technique to identify objects and their responsibilities using index cards and role-play.

Problem: To handle any defects that made it to our live applications, the team would nominate one or two developers each day to a support role. The role mainly consisted of responding to clients and investigating defects. While it was intended to allow developers to focus on development, it often had the opposite effect. Familiar clients would email and phone the developers they knew directly. Colleagues from outside the team would approach the most knowledgeable developers because it wasn't clear who was assigned to support. Time was wasted handing over support issues each day, and developers would often continue handling a particular support issue for days after leaving their support role.

Response: We set up a dedicated support desk, away from the developers' room, in close proximity to the Client Support, Infrastructure and Management teams. All telephone and email support requests were directed to this desk. Two people would man the desk for the duration of the MMF (around a week), rather than just a day. The defined time-box for support allowed the designated developers to see a support ticket through to completion, and to work more closely with the Client Support and Infrastructure teams. It also allowed the developers to focus their efforts on the work in progress board and removed additional streams of work that were previously hidden

Problem: Defects that required development time were reported via the two developers assigned to support. These were noted on red index cards and pinned to the work in progress board. Any bugs would get added to the "In Development" column and would be investigated or fixed during the development of an MMF, regardless of their severity. This process resulted in low priority bugs slowing down the delivery of high value MMFs.

Response: We introduced an 'Urgent' box to our work in progress boards. When a bug report came in, the work cells would check with the Operations Manager if the bug was considered urgent. If so, one pair of developers would stop work on the MMF and fix it. Otherwise it could be fixed once the MMF was complete. There was a work in progress limit of one for this box, so that genuinely urgent defects could be fixed quickly but less urgent problems didn't impede the delivery of the MMF.

2.2.2 Focus on Improvement

Problem: We began to see the benefit of moving to two work cells, separating support from development and concentrating on code quality. Features were being delivered consistently on time and with fewer defects. Around the beginning of the Summer period our Agile Coach spent less time with us as he worked on other commitments. We knew that without his input the onus was on the team to ensure we continually inspected and adapted our process. At this time we held retrospective meetings on a Friday, one hour before the end of each working week. These took the form of a round table open forum. We had previously tried structured approaches to retrospectives but these had been dropped when we moved away from Scrum. Alarm bells began to sound when the same problems were brought up week after week, suggesting that we could effectively inspect but not adapt.

Response: At each meeting someone was nominated to take minutes and post them to the group over the weekend as the points of discussion were often forgotten by Monday morning. The format for these minutes soon evolved into a list of action points that we would target in the following week. This change helped us to focus the discussion into thinking up simple, actionable solutions.

Problem: At this time attendance at the retrospective was mandatory for members of the development team, while members of other departments would make sporadic appearances. A number of issues that were raised required discussion with the other teams, but they were rarely present as, at the time, they were focused on preparing for our impending office move. We also had concerns that some of our limited retrospective time was being wasted as some issues under discussion weren't relevant to the company as a whole.

Response: We made the retrospective a meeting for the development team along with at least one member of the management team. The intention was to then hold a separate meeting with representatives from each department present. This was successful for a period and helped the organisation work as one larger team.

Problem: Regular inspections of our work in progress boards revealed that MMFs were taking longer to complete. By discussing possible causes, we realised that we were not always sure exactly what was required to fulfil a particular MMF, and as a result we would sometimes work on improvements and functionality that was not required. The development team felt like they were adding value, but this wasn't as important as the delivery of the features to our customers.

Response: When a pair was unsure of the validity of a task they would place it on a card and put it in a space on the board labelled "to be evaluated". This space was reviewed by the whole team in the morning and afternoon stand-up meetings and the tasks were either added to the current MMF or placed into a "don't" section of the board. This enabled us to clarify what work wasn't necessary as part of the current feature. At the end of the MMF these "don't" cards were reviewed again to see if it was appropriate to add them to the next MMF.

Problem: Since the beginning of our agile adoption we had held regular coding dojos (Bossavit, n.d.) using a variety of formats, including katas[3], videos and presentations. An early technique that worked for us was to rotate the person responsible for preparing and presenting the dojo. However, this led to incoherence between sessions and a lack of structure over time. We noticed that dojos were sometimes unprepared and didn't add value.

Response: One team member volunteered to organise and oversee dojos, to help keep a consistent theme running between sessions. We alternated the format between a technical dojo (investigating new tools or process improvements) and a code dojo (performing either a randori or prepared kata). We were able to tailor the chosen kata to be relevant to the week's work. For example, in one week, the team encountered difficulties encapsulating primitive lists in classes, so we tried a kata where this could be practised in isolation, in order to see the benefits.

Problem: The organisation's client base is both broad and disparate, ranging from individual car dealerships to finance and insurance underwriters, so it was impractical for the process to utilise an "On-site customer" (Shore & Warden, 2008). The Development Director had therefore assumed the role of a Proxy Product Owner (Pilcher, 2010). As the business expanded, the Development Director's responsibilities grew, and he was promoted to Managing Director. With new responsibility meaning he had less time to dedicate to a Product Owner role, the development team found that they were often unable to obtain timely feedback, which occasionally led to us making incorrect assumptions. These assumptions were then fed into the development process creating considerable wasted effort.

Response: To fill the void, an Operations Manager was appointed from within the development team. The primary responsibilities of this position were: to assume the role of the Product Owner, providing continual feedback to the development team; to be a consistent, first point of contact for clients; to assist the Managing Director in the assessment and prioritisation of the development backlog.

Problem: The changing roles and responsibilities of the management team meant that the planning of MMFs was largely being carried out by the development team. We were not utilising the new Product Owner effectively; he was being treated more like an external customer.

Response: Involvement of the product owner in the planning of MMFs. This was merely a refinement of the Product Owner role. We started to utilise simple techniques such as printing screen-shots and collaboratively producing rough drawings of user interface changes. These artefacts were then pinned to the work in progress board alongside the MMF card, to be used as part of the acceptance criteria. We were pleasantly surprised at how often, and how quickly, misunderstandings were discovered by using such low ceremony techniques.

2.2.3 Reducing Defects and Increasing Code Quality

Problem: We took on a large project for a customer who worked in a domain with a complex, domain-specific language. The customer also had a number of existing prototypes for the application we were to produce. The best approach seemed to be to implement the pseudo-code provided by the customer and refactor this into a workable, clean solution. However, it quickly emerged that the problem was too complex for this approach, so we started to test drive each section of the code in isolation, rebuilding the application core as a test-driven module. While this afforded us better test coverage, much of the code quality was still low from our previous efforts of implementing

the pseudo-code, and developers moving onto the project for the first time had trouble understanding the code and consequentially the problem domain.

Response: The team decided that we should focus more on code quality, especially around this piece of functionality. There had been recent incidents of defective code being released to customers and not caught in the shorter feedback cycles of integration testing and user acceptance testing. A holistic approach to code quality meant that more code smells were removed and we were able to communicate the intent of the code more effectively. This allowed developers to swap more often and understand the code to a greater extent.

Problem: The drive to quickly deliver MMFs to the customer had exposed other aspects of our development process that were not given sufficient care. Although we were defining small enough features, to allow for delivery every few days, the team found that this rhythm was causing a race to the next feature. Essential activities such as internal demonstrations, defect resolution and waste reduction were not being apportioned sufficient development time, leading to a decrease in delivered quality. We also noticed that the weekly retrospectives would often over-run and some issues were discussed in far too much detail.

Response: Codeweavers' agile journey has, on a number of occasions, demonstrated that the development team has a visual mind-set. This meant to avoid forgetting something, it simply has to be on an index card placed on a work in progress board. The short iterative process that we follow was also adjusted to permit time on each MMF for a mini retrospective, defect resolution and waste reduction.

A complete MMF cycle contained the following stages: planning, development, internal demonstration, deployment to customer acceptance environment, deployment to live environment, defect resolution, mini retrospective, waste identification and resolution. The work in progress boards were updated to reflect the planning, development, customer acceptance and live stages.

The weekly retrospective format was changed to a more traditional voting system. We would begin each session by asking the questions, "What went well?" and "What could go better?" Each attendee was invited to identify points for discussion, write them on sticky notes and attach them to the wall. After removing duplicates, each person would have three votes on what to discuss. The top three sticky notes would then become the agenda for the retrospective. Discussion of each issue was time-boxed to fifteen minutes to prevent overrun. Previous attempts to time-box the discussion of complex issues had had a detrimental effect, but by limiting the retrospective to the three most important issues, we were able to focus the discussion and produce actionable activities for the following week.

Problem: The development team help maintain a focus on delivery using a build monitor, situated in the corner of the office. Ideally it shows a soothing, green screen. If a build becomes broken, for example due to a failing automated test or a compilation error, the build monitor plays a sound indicating failure and the screen turns red. We found the build monitor useful, but noticed that occasionally members of the development team would ignore failure warnings. In the worst cases, one pair might cause the build to fail but ignore the warning, and another pair would commit further changes that compounded the issue, to the extent that the build took several days to get back into a successful "green" state. This meant that our codebase could not be deployed and any emergency fixes were bottlenecked behind our failing build.

Response: If the build monitor announced a failing build all developers were asked to immediately stand up and discuss the cause. Someone could then volunteer to resolve the problem. In order to ingrain this practice we initially appointed a "build czar" to ensure that everybody downed tools immediately when a failure was reported. Using this approach, fixes could be addressed immediately by one pair, allowing the rest of the team to continue adding value.

Problem: Despite this response, it seemed that the frequency of failed builds still hadn't fallen. The whole team soon developed a Pavlovian response to the fail sound. We had noticed that some failures would go away if the failing build was simply re-run, and so we often took this approach without taking the time to understand or solve the underlying problem.

Response: The cause of each build failure was recorded on a whiteboard, with a tally for each time the same problem re-occurred. Prior to the weekly retrospective, we would discuss each of these causes of failures and, if appropriate, raise an action point to investigate or produce a fix. The listed item would not be removed from the board if the issue hadn't been resolved. These fixes improved the code quality and stability of our projects, reduced the number of build failures, and ensured that we could spend more time adding value rather than maintaining fragile tests.

2.2.4 Increased Customer Collaboration for Improved Delivery

Problem: Following our focus on code quality, we found that some MMFs were taking too long. By attempting to improve the code we had lost sight of the goal, and the team were not delivering value to our customers as quickly as we would have liked.

Response: We identified that the problem was not due to the amount of time spent on refactoring, but that the team didn't have a clear understanding of the service-oriented architecture we wanted to move towards, in order to ensure we could easily extend and maintain our code-base. We therefore held a series of technical language dojo sessions where we discussed and defined naming schemes, architectural concepts and object interactions.

All of these were recorded on a wiki which we could then update as we evolved. The naming strategies were a revelation, as we could now name objects easily and consistently, based on how they fit into a design pattern or architectural concept, or how they represented the real world. Objects like mappers, adapters, persistence records and value objects were all defined. We discussed hexagonal architecture (Cockburn, 2005) and ensured that we all knew why we wanted to keep business logic in our core project with web service endpoints, web site views and database persistence logic outside the core.

Problem: Imprecise and vague requirement definitions were leading to a lack of focus directed on business value.

We realised we were not collaborating effectively with our customers. Contrary to the agile manifesto, we had begun working to acceptance criteria defined solely by the developers, rather than discussing a customer's needs and iteratively delivering working software to meet them. With a rush to code, clamouring to get features released, it was very easy to take the wrong path. Legacy code was a magnet for developers tempted to clean up sections of old code that did not add direct value.

Response: The disconnection between development and our customers was reduced by involving our product owner more heavily in the planning of a feature and working with him to produce acceptance criteria, which were defined using "given, when, then" syntax. This Behaviour Driven Development (BDD) style of test definition describes the requirements concisely and in a demonstrable form, using a non-technical business language. We also modified the definition of our MMFs to explicitly express the intention of the feature. This ensured there was no ambiguity in our understanding of the customer's higher level expectations and ensured the team could focus only on the functionality required. To maintain focus on delivering value each cell began electing a team leader for the duration of an MMF's development. This person was responsible for ensuring we swapped pairs and held stand up meetings twice a day, and that we continued to collaborate with the customer. The product owner could then easily convey and educate the development team of the value for customers.

Problem: To really extend our collaboration with customers we wanted to investigate their end users' experience when using our applications. We were already responsive to the needs of our business clients, as they found it simple to report issues to us, but end users would rarely give us feedback as there was no easy way for them to do so.

Response: We added an "ask us" tab to the side of all our web applications which enabled our customers to raise defects directly. Improvements were made to the application error logging so that emails could be sent to the support desk when an end user experienced a failure. This meant we had immediate visibility of the error the user encountered and didn't need to rely on them to contact us.

Problem: By inviting more feedback while our customer base was already growing, the number of requests for support increased considerably. Our main Client Support Administrator was replaced around this time by two people who had no experience in our business domain. Often we would receive support requests for tasks that were relatively simple for someone with knowledge of our administration tools, yet we still required two developers on support preventing them from adding value in development. Other tasks could be easily automated if they had specific administration pages. An example that highlighted the inefficiency was the process of setting up a new account. This was slowed down as it required opening up lines of communication between the Sales Team, the customer, Client Support and Developer Support.

Response: A greater focus was put into improving our internal administration tools by working closely with the Client Support team to understand and improve areas of the process that slowed them down. We also built GUIs to enable non-technical staff to perform tasks that developers previously achieved through more complex means. In order to make the balance between internal improvements and marketable features more visible, we represented internal improvements with yellow cards on the work in progress board. The Sales Team spent a day working alongside Client Support in order to understand what the role involved, and a meeting was held between Sales, Client Support and the management team to define a less chaotic process. All members of the Sales Team were extremely positive about how they could now deal directly with the clients without needing to wait for further information to be conveyed from the office. It also gave the Sales Team a stronger sense of how our products could be used.

2.2.5 A Leaner Service Oriented Architecture

Problem: At the start of a two week sprint our Operations Manager informed us that there were three high value MMFs for one of the cells to complete on one application, and that it was important for these to be done by an externally set deadline. The other cell was working on non time critical MMFs for a separate application,.

Response: Feeling that lessons had been learned from, and practices put into place to resolve earlier issues with multiple cells working on a single application, the team decided to split into three cells, each working on the same application, on one of the time-critical MMFs. Improved communication between cells, smaller, more regular commits and better defined, more vertically sliced MMFs resulted in fewer conflicts and bottlenecks.

Problem: Our improved code architecture helped with multiple work cells but we still found it difficult to identify work that would not result in conflicts because of the nature of the applications. We had improved the separation of behaviour between objects in our two main applications through the changes we had made to testing and the use of lightweight service objects. We were happy with the increasing quality of newly written code, but teasing out a similar quality in our legacy code was more difficult.

Response: A suggestion from a team member to start a book group, and the decision for a number of team members to attend Software Craftsmanship 2010 highlighted the relevance of object-oriented design to us. We read and discussed chapters from Agile Principles, Patterns, and Practices in C# (Martin, 2006) which gave a good understanding of the S.O.L.I.D. principles (Martin, 2003) to apply to any legacy code classes that we worked around while adding new features. A good example of how this helped is our use of the Single Responsibility Principle. This technique allowed us to break complex classes into smaller, more coherent objects that perform smaller amounts of work, enabling us to test previously untestable code. The more modular object model facilitated code reuse in the rest of the application.

Problem: We were increasingly bottlenecked by the need to wait for three streams of development to complete before we could safely deploy related features, even though the features were based in separate areas of the application (for example; web services, control panel and customer forms). We attempted to work as two larger cells again but the same bottlenecks recurred.

Response: A new project afforded us the opportunity to separate the web application from the service object core. We introduced a core API object in the web application to communicate and use the functionality of the core business objects by defining the contract by which the objects could be used. Previously, the notion of separation was achieved via projects in the same solution, but this extra step now separated the two object worlds distinctly into two solutions, which allowed us to develop and deploy either project independently of the other. There were fewer conflicts between development streams allowing features to be added more quickly, while preventing deployment bottlenecks. Faster deployments resulted in smaller customer feedback loops and faster delivery of working software to our clients.

3. DISCUSSION

Looking back on the observed period it is clear to see that there have been far fewer radical changes in comparison to the period documented in 'From Chaos to Kanban'. This conservative approach emerged because our processes matured, beyond initial churn, to a level that we were comfortable with. Instead we have focused on implementing smaller changes that have simply evolved and refined existing processes.

While the rate of change has slowed, the effectiveness of any adjustment appears to have increased. We now have the confidence to allow changes time to bed in by making minor tweaks to fine tune processes. We have identified that earlier in our journey we seemed to rush to correct problems with wholesale changes that could easily result in losing some of the positive aspects of the outgoing process.

The most radical change in this period was implemented following a set of one-to-one meetings between the Managing Director and the development team. He observed that several developers raised similar concerns regarding the current process. He therefore suggested an overhaul of the work in progress boards. This situation highlighted the fact that we had lost the perspective that our Agile Coach brought to the team and that we were finding it more difficult to adapt without his authority.

Our reaction to this was to change the way that we inspect and adapt by continually evaluating our retrospective meetings to ensure that they always deliver direct value. We also "pushed out" and became more active in the agile community by attending conferences and courses, while welcoming third parties into our environment.

Since the start of the period discussed in this paper, five new people have joined the development team. Each of the new team members committed production code to the trunk within their first few days, and saw their work deployed to a live environment soon after. The level of entry has been significantly reduced which is hugely beneficial

to both Codeweavers and the new staff. This is largely due to pairing, the improved consistency of the team's coding style, and the descriptive language of the test and production code. This uniformity and group knowledge is a direct result of regular dojos, katas and discussions focusing on a ubiquitous language and shared ideals.

The organisation has become more sensitive to flow, whereby anything that negatively affects the delivery of value is attacked with vigour. This is demonstrated by a number of activities: the dramatic trimming of the backlog to just those features of highest value; extending the cycle of the support rota to reduce interruptions in both development and support cycles; reacting to the state of the backlog by restructuring the development team into two or three cells depending on the urgency and value of the work in hand. All of this has helped to achieve and maintain a consistent flow and rhythm within the organisation.

We had attempted to eradicate knowledge silos by merging the development team into one cell, but this change was not as effective as we had envisioned. We found that a move back towards smaller cells with regular swapping was more effective, resulting in higher throughput. Although the single team approach initially helped to share knowledge, it actually led to knowledge being spread too thinly resulting in some features being developed without any member of the team having complete understanding of it.

The focus of the development team regularly seems to wander between quality, value and flow. There are short periods of concentration on each area, whereupon it becomes apparent that a slight correction back towards the neglected areas is required. Although we have achieved improvements in most aspects of our work, we still feel that a satisfactory balance in all of the areas has not yet been reached.

An important consideration for the development team is to continually and regularly return to basics. We have found that it is too easy to forget some of the valuable lessons learned early on in the agile journey. For example, our failure to fully utilise the Product Owner as an on-site customer now seems a very obvious mistake. New team members bring fresh perspective and ideas, often questioning practices that senior members take for granted, reminding us to revisit our previous lessons.

The changes that have been introduced have resulted in both our working practices and software artefacts becoming increasingly lean. The software was forced to change with every adaptation to our daily work and the emergent focus on service oriented architecture is a good example of how we facilitated improvements by adhering to good code design principles. The first foray into SOA, through collaboration testing, helped modularise areas of our larger systems so that bottlenecks and waste could be reduced.

When customer collaboration was improved we then improved flow, both in planning and development, by increasing system granularity and reducing coupling so that features could be developed and deployed independently.

3.1 Future Directions

The scale of changes has adjusted so that small modifications to processes are made rather than large overhauls. This trend seems likely to continue as we refine rather than redefine how we work. We still need to extend our agile practices to other departments and suppliers through larger scale changes to ensure the business benefit is felt throughout the organisation. The team have accepted that some defects will still occur and the focus should now be on minimising these effectively while maintaining development pace.

3.2 Summary of Themes

While reviewing the changes that have occurred in Codeweavers' agile journey, six themes of targeted improvement stood out. What follows is a brief summary of some of the improvements that were made and the theme that each of these helped to address.

3.2.1 Planning

Reduction of the backlog, along with, improvements in how it was maintained and regular re-prioritising of MMFs, helped clarify their urgency for both the organisation and clients. This allowed clients to reassess the features they had requested and whether they are still needed. Improved communication between the organisation and clients, and also within the organisation, helped increase understanding of the requirements for MMFs, resulting in better acceptance criteria.

3.2.2 Flow

Clearer understanding and improved management of upcoming work, together with restructuring the support teams, lead to fewer interruptions to the development team, which in turn reduced delivery times. Increasing the number of development streams reduced bottlenecks which meant developers were able to spend more time working on a direct value stream rather than having to subordinate to a bottleneck.

3.2.3 Knowledge

The spreading of knowledge within the organisation came with changes to team sizes and the introduction of technical language dojos. Highlighting areas that reduced flow during an MMF allowed the entire team to address and improve coding standards. There was knowledge lost when our Agile Coach left as he would observe the whole team and give valuable input throughout his visits.

3.2.4 Technique

Improved standardisation across the development team came with the introduction of tools to help abide by the team's coding standards, together with technical language dojos and regular, practical, hands-on dojos with code reviews at the end.

3.2.5 Quality

It was identified that there was an adverse relationship between improved quality and flow, that the team needed to regularly assess to gain an appropriate balance. It was observed that quality was being sacrificed when knowledge was spread too thinly when there was one large team; the introduction of multiple streams helped to improve quality again, as it was decided that every developer did not need to work on every feature. This was aided by improvements to coding standards so that developers could easily be reassigned to features they were not originally involved in. Recording the reasons for build monitor failures meant that any related issues could be identified and addressed, therefore improving quality within various departments.

3.2.6 Value

Changes in the number of streams depending on the urgency of upcoming work resulted in a faster throughput of MMFs to both internal and external clients. Changes to the support structure meant that developers covered incoming tickets for an extended period, this offered better value to clients as they were always dealing with the same people throughout a ticket's life-cycle. Developer flow was also increased as there were fewer interruptions to those not on support, therefore increasing the time developers could spend delivering value.

4. CONCLUSION

The development team at Codeweavers have successfully improved their practices and processes to enable them to deliver high quality software more quickly and with fewer defects. The series of changes we made to the planning procedures, work in progress boards, cell sizes and acceptance criteria helped us maintain focus on only adding value that the customer required. Changes to

support, increasing customer collaboration and inviting wider feedback led to quicker delivery of valued features and a reduced feedback loop.

All these improvements to the flow of business value were coupled with the identification early on that having multiple, simultaneous value streams working on one application improved our ability to deliver features to customers. Subsequent changes to software architecture, separation of behaviour and a focus on small batch sizes meant that we could have the whole team develop a number of related features on one application - meeting our customer's needs in a more reactive manner.

Our improved ability to separate our applications' dependencies through applying service-oriented engineering techniques has made the flow of business value more lean, which has already had a positive effect on the profitability of the organisation and the satisfaction of our customers. We hope that we can continue to maintain this level of throughput to better serve our customers and sustain the business well into the future.

REFERENCES

Beck, K., & Cunningham, W. (1989, October). A laboratory for teaching object oriented thinking. *ACM SIGPLAN Notices, 24*(10), 1–6. doi:10.1145/74878.74879

Bossavit, L. (n.d.). *Coding dojo*. Retrieved from http://www.codingdojo.org/

Cockburn, A. (2005). Hexagonal architecture. Retrieved from http://alistair.cockburn.us/Hexagonal+architecture

Covey, S. R. (2008). *The 7 habits of highly effective people*. London, UK: Simon & Schuster Ltd. doi:10.1002/pfi.4170301009

Highsmith, J. (2002). *Agile software development ecosystems* (p. 17). Boston, MA: Pearson Education, Inc.

Marick, B. (2010). *I think I finally understand mocks*. Retrieved from http://video2010.scottishrubyconference.com/show_video/2/0

Martin, R. C. (2003). *Principles of OOD*. Retrieved from http://butunclebob.com/ArticleS.UncleBob.PrinciplesOfOod

Martin, R. C. (2006). *Agile principles, patterns, and practices in C#*.

Pilcher, R.(2010). Agile Product Management with Scrum. (pp 19). Boston: Pearson Education, Inc.

Poppendieck, M., & Poppendieck, T. (2010). *Leading lean software development: Results are not the point*. Boston, MA: Addison-Wesley.

Rainsberger, J. B. (2009). *Integration tests are a scam*. Retrieved from http://www.infoq.com/news/2009/04/jbrains-integration-test-scam

Rutherford, K., Shannon, P., et al. (June 2010). *From chaos to Kanban, via Scrum*.

Shore, J., & Warden, J. (2008). *The art of agile development* (p. 28). Sebastpol, CA: O'Reilly Media, Inc.

KEY TERMS AND DEFINITIONS

Continuous Improvement: Repeated application of insect-adapt all of the time through regular retrospective analysis and through constant awareness of bottlenecks and potential improvements.

Inspect-Adapt: To examine recent actions and make adjustments for future reduction of waste and the improvement of principles and practices.

Kanban: Visualisation of work in progress by pulling customer value through the system from the customer's perspective. From the Toyota Production system - used at Codeweavers in the form of index cards on a pin board.

Kata: A usually trivial programming problem that is selected to perform deliberate practice. The solution is usually deleted with a focus on the practice and improvement of technique through repetition.

Lean: To work in a manner that produces minimum waste, amplifies learning and empowers the team. Enabling the team to deliver as fast as possible by making decisions as late as possible. Building into the software enough integrity to ensure the systems produced are stable and documented through clean, tested code.

Service Oriented Software Development: Separation of behaviour between objects within a software system defined by contracts and interfaces. Separation of behaviour between sub-systems using clearly defined APIs to promote system granularity, reuse, abstraction, standardisation and loose coupling.

Software Craftsmanship: Assuming personal responsibility for maintaining and improving software quality in the industry.

Software Quality: Maintaining a high standard in code structure, test coverage, descriptive code and alignment to the S.O.L.I.D. principles.

ENDNOTES

[1] Kaizen: a Japanese management term meaning continuous improvement.

[2] CRC: Class Responsibility Collaboration.

[3] Kata: Japanese term for a set routine of movements. Used by developers for deliberate practice.

Chapter 14
Test Driven Decomposition of Legacy Systems into Services

David Parsons
Massey University, New Zealand

Manfred Lange
EFI, New Zealand

ABSTRACT

A number of questions have been raised by both practitioners and researchers regarding the compatibility of service oriented architectures and agile methods. These are compounded when both approaches are combined to maintain and migrate legacy systems. In particular, where test driven development is practiced as a core component of an agile development process, both legacy systems and service oriented architectures can present an incongruous set of development challenges. In this chapter, the authors provide experience reports on how legacy systems have been adapted to an agile, test driven development context by a process of decomposition into testable services. They describe two domains and technology contexts where automated agile testing at multiple interface layers has improved both quality of service and functionality.

INTRODUCTION

A service oriented architecture (SOA) is a collection of self-contained services that communicate with each other, passing data or coordinating some activity. Each service has a provider and one or more consumers. The primary aim of a service is to support business processes; implementing services is not an end in itself, but rather a means to deliver agile systems to support a business (Wilkes & Veryard, 2004). Nevertheless beyond this core requirement there are a number of general principles that can be applied to service oriented architectures. These principles include that a service should have explicit boundaries, be based on schemas and wire formats, not classes and APIs, and be policy-driven, autonomous, document-oriented, loosely coupled, standards-compliant,

DOI: 10.4018/978-1-4666-2503-7.ch014

vendor independent and metadata-driven (Tilkov, 2007). Unfortunately few of these criteria can easily be applied to the interface of a legacy system. In particular, the boundaries and coupling of a legacy system may be problematic. However the value of services in the context of legacy systems is that services do not have to be brand new. They can be fragments of old applications that were adapted and wrapped, or combinations of new and legacy code (Papazoglou & van den Heuvel, 2007).

Though we can perhaps bridge legacy systems and service oriented architectures, there are other questions raised about how effectively an agile software development approach can be applied when working with these systems. Service oriented and agile approaches may conflict in areas such as architecture, team organisation and feedback (Elssamadisy, 2007). It has also been suggested that service orientation encourages upfront architecture while agile does not, though service oriented architectures can be incrementally introduced into an existing system. On the other hand it does pay to understand the strategic direction in advance, including layers and main system components such as infrastructure services. There are also potential conflicts in terms of organizing teams, where a service oriented approach encourages teams to split along functional lines while agile approaches encourage cross-functional teams. This can be a challenge in maintaining perspectives, for example ensuring that business logic is not added to the codified structure of a schema or document. In terms of feedback, a service oriented approach does not have the same focus on frequent feedback at both a technical and personal level. There may also be tensions in terms of the level of ceremony required for different types of software development. Chung et al. (2008) suggest that the mainstream agile methods focus on forward engineering new systems, and claim that a more formal approach related to the Unified Process is required to integrate legacy systems and services. Agile assumptions about delivering potentially shippable code at the end of every iteration are also challenged when dealing with live external services that may require extensive performance and stress testing (Puleio, 2006).

Despite these reservations, the experience reports in this chapter offer a different perspective to some degree. Perhaps the key aspect of the agile approach is flexibility or adaptability, so it is the flexibility aspect of services that assists agile transformation (Sucharov, 2007). Flexibility is required in order to address ever-changing market and customer expectations, and the move to an agile service oriented approach provides the capability to adapt to these ever-changing expectations.

In addressing both the mapping between legacy systems and service oriented architecture, and the relationship between both of these and agile methods, it is testing that can provide the overall glue to the process, providing that a test driven approach is taken. Test driven development drives design, as well as providing unit tests, and therefore enables us to define the interfaces between services and legacy systems. Sharing tests between client and service developers enables the two layers to be developed and maintained effectively. The internal design of services can also be performed in an agile way, once the outer interface to the service has been defined. In particular the interface concept already goes a long way towards making a legacy system more agile, for example by being able to componentize functionality into services, making testing easier or enabling it in the first place, or by plugging in different flavours of infrastructure services (security, transactions, logging, etc.) Tests provide a way of specifying the boundaries of vertical slices of functionality that might be decomposed into services. They also provide a way of defining the service's external contracts prior to those contracts being implemented. A unit testing philosophy also emphasizes testing services in isolation. The service under test can be provided with meaningful mocks for other services that it may depend on.

In the organisations used as the basis for this experience report, the generic approach taken was to gradually identify legacy features that could be specified by a set of interface tests, and then extract these into independent services. Though not initially test driven, since the module functionality was already in place, the extracted services could then be developed in a test driven manner as they were subsequently refactored. Feature identification was driven both by the requirements of other product components and services and customers who wanted to integrate with in-house or 3rd party systems. Therefore it was driven by external requirements, rather than trying to identify features in isolation. In addition, the development teams also used a service oriented approach for all new functionality, thus creating a hybrid architecture between a 2-tier legacy and a 3-tier service oriented architecture. From another perspective, testability was enhanced by an architecture that allowed interoperability with plugins for integrating external services. Again, plugins could be individually tested. This chapter provides a number of practical experiences and lessons learned in using tests to drive the wrapping of legacy systems into discrete, testable services.

WORKING WITH LEGACY CODE

Legacy systems are commonplace in software supported industries, and these systems can take many forms. They may be acceptable to their regular users even when they have significant bugs, as users become familiar with the required workarounds, and are aware of current 'characteristics' of the system. Sometimes customers do not characterise issues as bugs, but rather are aware of what they regard as usability problems. On the other hand the cost of customer-impacting errors on systems that are already deployed is high (Feathers, 2002). Given that legacy systems are typically the result of significant investment, and probably in live use, development teams

considering tacking underlying issues such as large, complex and flawed legacy systems need to balance a number of trade-offs.

Thomas (2006) describes the problem of large systems with defective but poorly understood modules, making developers approach each fix or feature with great trepidation. As he indicates, the general solution to this kind of problem is to incrementally replace the faulty components, one component at a time. There are, however a number of problems with this approach. Legacy systems sometimes include legacy testing frameworks that may themselves need to be refactored or replaced before progress can be made (Puleio, 2006). It can also be difficult to find any inflection points where parts of the legacy system can be broken apart. Feathers (2002) refers to techniques such as dependency inversion to create such inflection points, but this is only possible if the legacy system is written in a language that makes such interventions feasible. Sometimes the only inflection point that you can find is the system boundary which can encompass the GUI, calls to other external libraries and the database (Feathers, 2002). However simply adding a large wrapper around monolithic legacy systems does not help address possible underlying issues of on-going maintenance costs and lack of flexibility (Sucharov, 2007). Furthermore having large monolithic blocks of code with many service interfaces interacting with them will not yield the full benefits of a service oriented architecture, where conceptually each single service can be replaced with a different implementation without the need to change any other part of the system.

Given the problems of trying to tackle monolithic systems, and the likelihood that adding a service wrapper alone does not address underlying problems, there needs to be a systematic approach to converting legacy systems to robust, maintainable and modular service oriented systems. This requires techniques of discovery and transformation rather than classical design and development. The first step in the process is to bring test coverage and code modularity to the point where transformations can be applied frequently and with confidence (Thomas, 2006).

Visaggio (2001) asserts that when a legacy system has poor quality it is said to be *old* or *aged*. This perspective emphasises the quality issues in legacy systems. Feathers' (2002) definition of legacy code also relates to quality, but from a different perspective, that it is code without tests. The fundamental assumption, therefore, is that to bring legacy code into line with current development we must start with a complete test suite, which will both externalise the current quality of the system and provide a lever for improving it. Feathers also lays out a general strategy for the management of legacy code for which tests are essential, namely:

1. **Identify Change Points:** Decide where the changes should be made. Ideally the approach chosen should be the one that requires the fewest changes.
2. **Find an Inflection Point:** Identify a narrow interface to a set of classes where any changes to those classes can be detected; like a façade to part of the system.
3. **Add a Test Covering to the Inflection Point:** This means writing a set of tests for the interface identified above. Of course this cannot be test driven since the unit under test already exists. The tests for the inflection point should be unit tests, not integration tests, so both external and internal dependencies may have to be broken. This phase consists of the following steps:
   a. **Break External Dependencies:** It may be necessary to break dependencies on other components. Feathers suggests using dependency inversion, where the language of the legacy system allows this. Otherwise some kind of mocking layer would have to be used.
   b. **Break Internal Dependencies:** Some code under test may create concrete components that are outside the scope

of the units under test. Feathers suggests a combination of subclasses and null classes to avoid these orthogonal components being created.
   c. **Write Tests:** The tests need to cover the inflection point as comprehensively as possible. Starting with boundary values is appropriate.
4. **Make Changes:** After an initial test covering is in place, further tests should become evident as changes are made to the legacy system. This takes the process into a more test driven mode as each change can be preceded by writing the test for the change.
5. **Refactor the Covered Code:** As is normal practice in test driven development, each change to the code must first pass the test, and then be refactored to improve its design, while still passing the test.

While this strategy provides a general guideline for the steps of a test driven process for working with legacy code, we need to also take into consideration a number of contextual issues such as commercial aspects. Perhaps the most significant of these is the extent to which this is seen as a process that aims to eventually replace the legacy codebase, or whether it becomes more of a mechanism to better control and leverage legacy systems. The extent to which the legacy system is changed and refactored depends on issues such as the current reliability and maintainability of the legacy system, the extent of new requirements, and the potential costs versus the payback of replacing legacy components.

EXPERIENCE REPORTS: FROM LEGACY SYSTEMS TO AGILE SERVICES

This article reflects on some real world experiences of a number of the issues introduced thus far, in the context of two different types of legacy systems, written in different languages in different domains. In both cases the lessons learned are similar. However experience has shown the limitations of over-simplistic models of the use of services as a half-way house to refactoring underlying systems. Such models advocate the use of a service wrapper to encapsulate a legacy system as the first step to re-engineering or replacing that system. In many cases, however, for practical, financial and pragmatic reasons, it is enough to build a testable service wrapper around a legacy system without extensive rewriting or refactoring. Thus we should not approach the wrapping of legacy systems with an assumption that the system itself will be extensively modified. Rather, the service wrapper enables the system to be safely refactored in cases where business requirements for such changes are identified.

The first experience report, which is relatively brief, may be regarded as setting the scene for the second, in that it provided the context for a service oriented approach that began by making conventional assumptions about the gradual replacement of a legacy system by means of inflection points and testable wrappers, as described by Feathers (2002). The second report, which is somewhat more detailed and elaborated, may be regarded as putting into practice some of the learning that took place in the context of the first report. It certainly takes a more circumspect view of the process within which legacy code may be changed and refactored, driven by pragmatic requirements and considerations.

Experience Report 1: The Green Pen and the Blue Code

The first system described here was in the context of a customer relationship management system for the utility industry. In this case the legacy system had a billing engine written in a 4GL as its core component, with some Java connectors for integration with other functionality implemented in Java. In order to render this system more easily interoperable with client facing systems, it was originally intended to replace this system with a full Java implementation. However this task was made more complicated because the legacy system was still under maintenance, so was a moving target in terms of attempting to replace it with a new system. Therefore, despite an original intent to replace the old system, this was adapted over time into a more pragmatic approach. To provide the development team with a strategic direction, the vision of a target system design was created. This was referred to as the 'green' system design, while the legacy system was coded 'blue'. The team adopted the metaphor of the 'green pen' based on this; Everyone gets a green pen. Colour in as much as you can, but no more than makes business sense. Practically, it meant that when the 'green' pen was used the resulting design and implementation was expected to be in line with the target design. The colour coded approach also recognised some of the more valued features of the 'blue' legacy system, including its transactional support, which was exposed via Java connectors to enable the integration of transactions across the blue and green components. This aspect of the system enabled a transaction started in the client facing layer to propagate into the billing engine. This represented a business critical feature of the legacy system that also assisted the service orientation of that feature via its external connectors. In terms of the metaphor the introduction of this cross-cutting transaction mechanism itself was an example of using the 'green' pen as it was designed and implemented in line with the target system design, but provided a service view of the 'blue' functionality in the legacy system.

Despite the limitations of working with a live legacy system under maintenance, and the impracticality of replacing this system, the overall approach of developing a service oriented wrapper enabled the green and the blue code to work effectively together within an agile development approach. In time, with the green pen colouring in all the external interfaces, the whole system looked service oriented, regardless of the legacy components behind the service layer. All the blue code eventually had a green interface. In addition, new features were developed completely using the green pen. The result was a hybrid system design proving that a legacy system (the 'blue' parts) and a service oriented architecture (as in the 'green' design) can co-exist.

The main driver for compromise in the extent of replacing legacy systems turns out to be a combination of marketing and risk, so in the end it comes down to commercial considerations. What sells is what can be well presented to decision makers, which is not necessarily the same as daily functionality for users. Sometimes a new wrapping (e.g. updated user interface) is all that is required to present a product or a feature as 'new' to the market. Quality of itself is not the key selling point. Given that quality is not an absolute, only when software failures affect a customer's bottom line does quality become the most important issue. However the risk to quality of rewriting the entire billing engine was also a significant consideration.

Experience in the first context revealed that the most important factor in any approach to moving a project forward from a legacy past is to choose the overall direction. The original intent to replace the legacy system turned out, for various reasons, not to be economically practical, nor indeed particularly valuable. An embodiment, perhaps, of the agile phrase 'YAGNI' ('you ain't gonna need it'). This experience underlined the concept that a simple replacement of a legacy system with new code is often not the most realistic or economical approach. Therefore a disciplined way of bringing legacy systems into more managed, service oriented architectures is important, along with an agile mindset that promotes 'the simplest thing that could possibly work' as the default technical architecture, maintained and refactored as needed. This was the approach that was brought forward into the second experience report.

Experience Report 2: The Big Picture – Interfaces over Business Logic

The second domain described in this article is production management for the printing industry. In this case, the legacy system was written in C++ with some portions written in C#. It lacked a sufficiently clear strategic design, with code written from disparate perspectives. There were also known problems with the existing codebase, with customers experiencing problems that could be serious enough to affect their productivity. However, despite these issues, given the experience at the previous organisation, replacing the entire existing legacy system was not considered an option. Instead, the first priority was to regain control over the system by introducing adequate test coverage so that a solid foundation could be created for future development.

The system had been developed over a long period of time by many people, so although there were islands of consistency in the way the code was written, there were also many inconsistencies, including different approaches to C++ metadata, and seven different ways of any two product components talking to each other (database, files, COM etc.) The most challenging feature was the management of database schema upgrades which were part of the native client, thus occasionally causing avoidable issues in live deployments. As a first step to taking the system into a service oriented architecture, the Web UI was moved from a 2-tier to a 3-tier architecture, at the same time introducing an application server as a new product component. Upgrade code for the database was moved to the application server installer to solve the brittle update problem, replacing it with a solid and reliable mechanism.

Over time, the legacy system has been encapsulated behind a series of service wrappers, each one with comprehensive test suites. Legacy unmanaged C++ has become managed, with new code in C#, but all residual unmanaged code behind managed wrappers. For the native client, a hybrid approach was established to allow features using services to co-exist with features using a 2-tier approach, i.e. talking directly to the database.

Although there was no overall requirement to re-engineer the entire legacy system, there were business drivers that triggered steps 6 and 7 in Feather's strategy for legacy code; to fix and refactor. The time when this most urgently had to be done was when the code had failed, particularly if a customer suffered a major software issue. When this happened with unmanaged legacy code, a testable wrapper was added to enable the code to be fixed and refactored. As a result of having these testable wrappers around the legacy code, the number of these reactive emergency fixes having to be done inside legacy code dropped to practically zero. In the longer term process of tackling less critical legacy issues, there are on-going quality improvements of 10%-20% a year in reported errors. In that less urgent context, tests are added to the test suite as needed. Whilst new code is continuously refactored, legacy code is not refactored as a matter of course, but only for major issues or where it is 'obvious'. Some of the more obvious refactorings that have proved worthwhile have been related to the inconsistencies of past coding practices. The large product codebase has 70 projects, and 5,000 files, with a build that used to take an hour. There were many reasons for this, including empty files left in the system and the same code appearing in binaries more than once. Visaggio (2001) defines 'useless components' as those that provide worthless output, but it is also the case that a legacy system may contain useless components that do nothing at all, and these should certainly be refactored out of a system. A related feature of a legacy system may be useless duplication. One of the important pieces of test code added to the system does not test functionality but consistency. It tests all the source header files to check that the first line is the '#pragma once' pre-processor directive that causes the current source file to be included only once

in a single compilation. Other tests were added that eliminate risks from non-code related items such as preventing the introduction of business logic to the service interfaces (service contracts, data contracts, etc.).

Other important refactorings relating to header files included using the correct syntax for including library headers versus programmer defined headers to optimise the search path and removing multiple includes. As a result of refactoring the system's naming and header conventions, the build time has now been reduced from over 1.5 hours to 25 minutes (of which about 5 minutes are running the suite of developer tests), with further improvements restricted by the linker being single threaded rather than by the compilation stage. This, however, is still not seen as a final destination. Further improvements will be applied in the future.

Figure 1 provides an architectural view of the use of testable service wrappers around legacy code, and the various communication and testing inflection points in this particular experience context. Windows Communication Foundation (WCF) is used to expose services behind URLs, giving a range of communications options to services. The communications protocol can be configured without changing the server or the client. The most efficient protocol can therefore be chosen both for testing and deployment. Tests can even bypass the WCF proxy/stub code where appropriate to speed up testing. Each service can be tested in isolation. The legacy system features are encapsulated in services that expose interfaces, give additional testability and overall system consistency. From the service consumer perspective, it makes no difference if the underlying code is new or legacy. There is the capacity to replace legacy code with new code if required without affecting the client interface. Figure 1 shows that there are a series of test inflection points; the native client (which still has some legacy features to be refactored out, such as direct database connections), the Web UI, the service interface and the services themselves. This enables tests to be

Figure 1. Service oriented architecture, inflection points, and tests

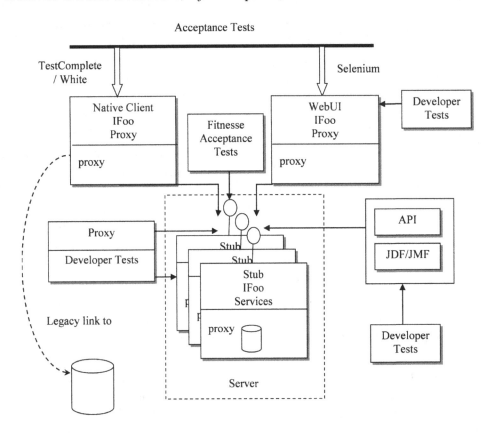

written in TestComplete or White for the native UI, Selenium for the Web UI, direct developer tests on the various APIs and service endpoints, and Fitnesse acceptance tests for business processes using the service interfaces. The loosely coupled service oriented architecture also enables integration with non-Microsoft systems, and with the standard Job Definition Format (JDF) and Job Messaging Format (JMF) used within the printing industry.

COMMERCIAL AND OTHER BENEFITS

While it is important to give sufficient weight to the technical perspective on transforming legacy systems into services through test driven development, the key drivers behind the approaches

described in this chapter are commercial aspects. With the approach now taken it is possible to drive the system in any direction that may be required by the market and/or customers. Integration with partner products, support of mobile clients, plugging-in customer-specific functionality, and other outcomes of this architecture are the means to help the company and the product to address new markets.

The benefits of service oriented architectures also include scalability. The product in the second experience report started with a target of 5 to 25 users many years ago. With the new approach it scales to hundreds or thousands of users. Again, this creates additional commercial options.

The 2-tier approach also had a security challenge as a web application, which is typically deployed in a demilitarized zone (DMZ), needs direct visibility to the database server. With the new design in place for the web user interface, the product has eliminated this requirement thus resulting in strengthened security in live deployments.

By standardizing on service oriented integration the system becomes more consistent and easier to maintain. Code and design that does not conform to the coding and design conventions is easier to spot and eliminate, further enhancing quality.

Finally by using an agile approach, in particular through the support of automated tests and builds, the service oriented architecture can be rolled out incrementally, focusing first on the most important areas of the product. This maximizes customer satisfaction and has a positive impact on the bottom line of the company.

FUTURE WORK

Going forward, areas for further exploration include further decoupling using services. For example certain infrastructure elements such as security, transactions, logging, monitoring, etc. could be provided using a combination of services, aspect oriented programming (AOP) and a dependency injection framework. With this in place a test-driven approach towards implementing these cross cutting concerns is expected to become even easier. Applied to legacy systems it could mean that code that is related to these infrastructure elements can be removed to separate these concerns from the business functionality.

RELATED WORK

Legacy systems provide a number of challenges to enterprises. They may be poor quality, monolithic and difficult to update and reuse. Approaches to the refactoring of legacy systems stress the importance of testing, though the types of testing recommended may vary. Feathers (2002) addresses common issues of working with legacy code,

including the agile approach of test driven development, but a number of the specific strategies he suggests are only appropriate to legacy systems coded in object oriented languages. In contrast, renewing more traditionally coded systems may need to rely more on acceptance testing. Visaggio (2001) outlines three tasks in the process of legacy systems renewal, covering both reverse engineering and restoration; automatic processes performed by tools, reading code and documentation, and interviewing the users, maintainers or managers of the system. The key goal is to isolate stable information (embodied in some consistent entity) and unstable information (implicitly held by people), and then to transform the unstable information into stable information. One important feature of this is the role of acceptance testing in rendering the unstable, stable. Service oriented architectures have also been analysed in the context of legacy systems by a number of authors, including Heckel et al (2008) who also stress the importance of automation on some reengineering processes, extracting layered service oriented architectures from monolithic legacy systems. The theme of reengineering a legacy system into a 3 layer architecture is also highlighted by the SOSR approach (Chung et al., 2008)

Table 1. The relationship between traditional software maintenance and agile development (from Thomas, 2006)

Traditional Software Maintenance	Agile Development
Understanding the essence of the system	Metaphor and Stories
Customer defect and feature requests	Customer and Stories
Test suites	Test first, Unit test, Acceptance test
Regression testing	Continuous integration and test
Fixes and "Dot" Release	Small Increments
Change Management	Scrum, Planning Game, Stand Up

In terms of agile, we see two areas where agile methods relate to the various aspects of legacy systems of service oriented architecture. First, we see agile techniques such as test driven development and refactoring being applied to legacy systems renewal. Second, we see the role of services in supporting more organisational agility. As Papazoglou & van den Heuvel (2007) indicate, an agile approach is needed to support the rapid construction and assembly of business services into larger architectures. Thomas (2006) also notes that many agile practices actually map well to more traditional aspects of the maintenance of legacy systems, such as regression testing and change management (Table 1).

SUMMARY AND CONCLUSION

In this experience report we have reported on two different contexts in which legacy systems have been integrated into service oriented architectures using an agile test driven approach. Despite the two contexts being in very different domains using very different technologies, in both cases the wrapping of legacy systems with test driven wrappers not only exposed the legacy systems as more flexible and interoperable services, but also enabled them to be substantially improved and refactored.

Being an experience report this chapter is not intended to present new approaches to test driven decomposition of legacy systems into services. It does, however, provide an opportunity to reflect on how the work of others has been applied to this particular context. It also gives an opportunity to consider how an individual enterprise might adopt and adapt a particular approach to the renewal of legacy systems via an agile service oriented architecture taking into account factors such as the nature of the original legacy system, the quality of that system and the market forces that

may or may not require complete refactoring of such systems once they have been encapsulated as services. The concept of automation, as outlined by Visaggio (2001) and Heckel et al (2008), and going beyond simply wrapping systems to increase their quality, as indicated by Sucharov (2007), have been shown to be important, while the general approach of Feathers (2002) has been shown to be a useful framework but one that has to be adapted to the nature of the legacy system.

In the introduction to this chapter we reported on a number of issues that some authors claim make the integration of legacy systems, service oriented architectures and agile software development problematical. In this experience report we have endeavoured to suggest that in fact these three very different axes of software can be effectively integrated, with the primary means to do so being a comprehensive approach to testing, applied at every level of the system from the UI, to acceptance tests, to service interface tests to developer (unit) tests. With these tests in place the agile ability to dynamically refactor live services provides the kind of responsiveness that more traditional methods could not deliver.

REFERENCES

Chung, S., Davalos, S., An, J., & Iwahara, K. (2008). Legacy to web migration: Service-oriented software reengineering methodology. *International Journal of Services Sciences*, *1*(3/4), 333–365. doi:10.1504/IJSSCI.2008.021769

Elssamadisy, A. (2007). SOA and agile: Friends or foes? *InfoQ*. Retrieved March 29th, 2011, from http://www.infoq.com/articles/SOA-Agile-Friends-Or-Foes

Feathers, M. (2002). *Working effectively with legacy code*. Retrieved March 29, 2011, from http://www.objectmentor.com/resources/articles/WorkingEffectivelyWithLegacyCode.pdf

Heckel, R., Correia, R., Matos, C., El-Ramly, M., Koutsoukos, G., & Andrade, L. (2008). Architectural transformations: From legacy to three-tier and services. In Mens, T., & Demeyer, S. (Eds.), *Software evolution* (pp. 139–170). Springer. doi:10.1007/978-3-540-76440-3_7

Papazoglou, M., & van den Heuvel, W. (2007). Service oriented architectures: Approaches, technologies and research issues. *Journal on Very Large Data Bases, 16*, 389–415. doi:10.1007/s00778-007-0044-3

Puleio, M. (2006). How not to do agile testing. *Proceedings of the Conference on Agile, 2006* (pp. 305-314).

Sucharov, T. (2007). Mainframe makeovers. *Information Professional, 4*(6), 36–38. doi:10.1049/inp:20070606

Thomas, D. (2006). Agile evolution: Towards the continuous improvement of legacy software. *Journal of Object Technology, 5*(7), 19–26. doi:10.5381/jot.2006.5.7.c2

Tilkov, S. (2007). 10 principles of SOA. *InfoQ.* Retrieved March 29, 2011, from http://www.infoq.com/articles/tilkov-10-soa-principles

Visaggio, G. (2001). Ageing of a data-intensive legacy system: symptoms and remedies. *Journal of Software Maintenance and Evolution, 13*, 281–308. doi:10.1002/smr.234

Wilkes, L., & Veryard, R. (2004). *Service-oriented architecture: Considerations for agile systems.* CBDI Forum, April 2004.

ADDITIONAL READING

Astels, D. (2003). *Test-driven development: A practical guide.* Upper Saddle River, NJ: Prentice Hall.

Beck, K. (2003). *Test driven development by example.* Boston, MA: Pearson.

Beck, K., & Andres, C. (2004). *Extreme programming explained: Embrace change* (2nd ed.). Addison Wesley.

Channabasavaiah, K., Tuggle, E., & Holley, K. (2003). *Migrating to a service-oriented architecture.* IBM Developer Works. Retrieved March 28th, 2011, from http://www.ibm.com/developerworks/library/ws-migratesoa/

Feathers, M. (2004). *Working effectively with legacy code.* Upper Saddle River, NJ: Prentice Hall.

KEY TERMS AND DEFINITIONS

Agile Software Development: Building software using the methods and techniques outlined by the agile manifesto, which values individuals and interactions over processes and tools, working software over comprehensive documentation, customer collaboration over contract negotiation and responding to change over following a plan.

Inflection Point: In the definition used by Feathers (2002), an inflection point is a narrow interface to a set of classes behind which meaningful changes to the code base can be detected.

Job Definition Format (JDF): A standard domain specific XML messaging format developed by the graphic arts industry to assist the development of workflow systems including multiple vendors.

Job Messaging Format (JMF): An XML messaging format that is part of the Job Definition Format specification, used to communicate events, status information and results between JDF agents and controllers.

Legacy System: Systems that may be technically obsolete but are still mission critical. Often too frail to modify and too important to discard, they must be reused.

Refactoring: Improving the design of existing code without changing its behaviour.

Service: A software component that consists of business logic, the data it operates on and an interface to access both. A service also has meta-information, e.g. its interface.

Service Oriented Architecture: A loosely coupled architecture of interoperable services that may be implemented in different languages on different platforms, but communicate using common messaging formats over standard protocols.

Test Covering: A set of tests that covers the behaviour of a small area of a system just well enough to provide some 'invariant' that can indicate if the behaviour of the system has changed.

Test Driven Development: Designing units of code by starting with unit tests and then writing the unit under test, incrementally building units of code using both black box and white box testing techniques. The key is to drive the design by carefully selecting tests and mercilessly refactoring code.

Compilation of References

Aalto, J. M. (2008). *Large scale agile development of S60 product software: A few hundred synchronized scrums –setup and experiences*. Finland: OO Days at Tampere University of Technology.

Abbas, N. (2009). *Software quality and governance in agile software development*. PhD thesis, School of Electronics and Computer Science, University of Southampton.

Abrahamsson, P., Oza, N., & Siponen, M. (2010). Agile software development methods: A comparative review. In T. Dingsøyr, T. Dyb́a, & N. B. Moe (Eds.), *Agile software development*, (pp. 31–59). Berlin, Germany: Springer.

Abrahamsson, P., Warsta, J., Siponen, M. T., & Ronkainen, J. (2003). New directions on agile methods: A comparative analysis. In *Proceedings 25th International Conference on Software Engineering* (ICSE).

Abrahamsson, P. (2008). *End of agile. VTT Olio-päivät '08*. Tampere: VTT Research Center of Finland.

Abrahamsson, P., Conboy, K., & Wang, X. (2009). Lots done, more to do- The current state of agile method research: Challenges and opportunities. *European Journal of Information Systems*, *18*(4), 281–284. doi:10.1057/ejis.2009.27

Abrahamsson, P., & Salo, O. (2002). *Agile software development methods: Review and analysis*. Technical Research Centre of Finland.

Abrahamsson, P., Salo, O., Ronkainen, J., & Warsta, J. (2002). *Agile software development methods: Review and analysis. Number 478 in VTT Publications*. Espoo, Finland: VTT Technical Research Centre of Finland.

Adomavicius, G., & Tuzhilin, A. (2005). Personalization technologies: A process-oriented perspective. *Communications of the ACM*, *48*, 83–90. Retrieved from http://doi.acm.org/10.1145/1089107.1089109doi:10.1145/1089107.1089109

Agarwal, S., & Studer, R. (2006). Automatic matchmaking of Web services. *Proceedings of the IEEE International Conference on Web Services* (pp. 45-54).

Agile Manifesto. (2001). *Manifesto for agile software development*. Retrieved from http://www.agilemanifesto.org/

Aho, A. V., Lam, M. S., Sethi, R., & Ullman, J. D. (2006). *Compilers: Principles, techniques, and tools* (2nd ed.). Prentice Hall.

Akkiraju, R., Farrell, J., Miller, J., Nagarajan, M., Schmidt, M.-T., Sheth, S., & Verma, K. (2005, November 7). *Web service semantics - WSDL-S*. Retrieved from http://www.w3.org/Submission/WSDL-S/

Akkiraju, R., Srivastava, B., Ivan, A.-A., Goodwin, R., & Syeda-Mahmood, T. (2006). SEMAPLAN: Combining planning with semantic matching to achieve Web service composition. *Proceedings of the IEEE International Conference on Web Services* (pp. 37-44).

Alter, S. (2009). Mapping the domain of service science. *Proceedings of the Fifteenth Americas Conference on Information Systems*, San Francisco, California.

Alter, S. (2008). Service system fundamentals: Work system, value chain, and life cycle. *IBM Systems Journal*, *47*(1). doi:10.1147/sj.471.0071

Amber, S. (2012). *Surveys exploring the current state of information technology practices*. Retrieved from http://www.ambysoft.com/surveys/

Amber, S. (2002). *Agile modeling: Effective practices for extreme programming and the unified process*. New York, NY: John Wiley & Sons, Inc.

Ambler, S. W. (2007). *Agile software development: Definition*. Retrieved from http://www.agilemodeling.com/essays/agileSoftwareDevelopment.htm

Ambler, S. W. (2009). *Inclusive modeling: User centered approaches for agile software development*. Retrieved from http://www.agilemodeling.com/essays/inclusive-Models.htm

Ambler, S. (2002). *Agile modeling: Effective practices for eXtreme programming and the unified process*. John Wiley & Sons.

Amey, P., & Chapman, R. (2003). Static verification and extreme programming. *Proceedings of the 2003 Annual ACM SIGAda International COnfernce on Ada: The Engineering of Correct and Reliable Software for Real-Time and Distributed Systems Using Ada and Related Technologies* (pp. 4-9).

Amoroso, E. (1994). *Fundamentals of computer security technology*. Prentice & Hall.

Anderson, D. J. (2004). *Agile Management for software engineering*. Prentice Hall PTR.

Anderson, D. J. (2010). *Kanban, successful evolutionary change for your technology business*. Blue Hole Press.

Anderson, R. J. (2001). *Security engineering: A guide to building dependable distributed systems*. Wiley.

Andrews, T., Curbera, F., Dholakia, H., Goland, Y., Klein, J., & Leymann, F. … Weerawarana, S. (2003). *Business process execution language for Web services, version 1.1*. Technical report, BEA Systems, International Business Machines Corporation, Microsoft Corporation.

Andrikopoulos, V. (2010). *A theory and model for the evolution of software services*. The Netherlands: Tilburg University.

Aoyama, M. (1998). Web-based agile software development. *IEEE Software, 15*(6), 56–65. doi:10.1109/52.730844

Apache Software Foundation. (2008). *Apache Maven Project*. Retrieved February 14, 2008, from http://maven.apache.org/

Apache Software Foundation. (2010). *Apache commons validator*. Retrieved December 8, 2007, from http://commons.apache.org/validator/

Apvrille, A., & Pourzandi, M. (2005). Secure software development by example. *IEEE Security & Privacy, 3*(4), 10–17. doi:10.1109/MSP.2005.103

Armbrust, M., Fox, A., Griffith, R., Joseph, A. D., Katz, R., & Konwinski, A. (2010). A view of cloud computing. *Communications of the ACM, 53*, 50–58. doi:10.1145/1721654.1721672

Arsanjani, A. (2004). *Service-oriented modeling and architecture*. Retrieved from http://www-128.ibm.com/.

Arsanjani, A., Ghosh, S., Allam, A., Abdollah, T., Ganapathy, S., & Holley, K. (2008). SOMA: A method for developing service-oriented solutions. *IBM Systems Journal, 47*(3). doi:10.1147/sj.473.0377

Astels, D. (2003). *Test driven development: A practical guide*. Prentice Hall Professional Technical Reference.

Atkinson, C., Barth, F., & Brenner, D. (2010). *Software testing using test sheets*.

Atkinson, C., Brenner, D., Falcone, G., & Juhasz, M. (2008). *Specifying high-assurance services. IEEE Computer, 41*. Los Alamitos, CA: IEEE.

Auerswald, P. (2009). Creating social value. *Stanford Social Innovation Review, 7*, 50–55.

Badr, Y., & Caplat, G. (2010). Software-as-a-service and versionology: Towards innovative service differentiation. *24th IEEE International Conference on Advanced Information Networking and Applications* (pp. 237–243). IEEE.

Bagga, W., & Molva, R. (2005). Policy-based cryptography and application. In *Proceedings of in FC' 2005, 9th International Conference on Financial Cryptography and Data Security*, LNCS Volume 3570, 28 February-03 March 2005, Roseau, The Commonwealth of Dominica.

Bajec, M., Damjan Vavpotič, D., Furlan, S., & Krisper, M. (2007). Software process improvement based on the method engineering principles. *IFIP International Federation for Information Processing, 244*, 283–297. doi:10.1007/978-0-387-73947-2_22

Baker, P., Dai, P. R., Grabowski, J., Haugen, O., Schief-erdecker, I., & Williams, C. E. (2007). *Model-driven testing - Using the UML testing profile.*

Baker, F. T. (1972). Chief programmer team management of production programming. *IBM Systems Journal, 11*(1), 56–73. doi:10.1147/sj.111.0056

Balkundi, P., & Kilduff, M. (2006). The ties that lead: A social network approach to leadership. *The Leadership Quarterly, 17,* 419–439. doi:10.1016/j.leaqua.2006.01.001

Bandara, A., Payne, T., De Roure, D., Gibbins, N., & Lewis, T. (2008). A pragmatic approach for the semantic description and matching of pervasive resources. *Proceeding of the 3rd International Conference on Grid and Pervasive Computing* (pp. 434-446).

Banerjee, P., Friedrich, R., Bash, C., Goldsack, P., Huberman, B., & Manley, J. (2011, March). Everything as a service: Powering the new information economy. *Computer, 44*(3), 36–43. doi:10.1109/MC.2011.67

Banerji, A., Bartolini, C., & Beringer, D. Chopella. V., Govindarajan, K., Karp, A., … Williams, S. (2002, March 14). *Web services conversation language* (WSCL) 1.0. Retrieved from http://www.w3.org/TR/wscl10/

Baniassad, E., & Clarke, S. (2004). *Finding aspects in requirements with theme/doc.* Workshop on Early Aspects (AOSD 2004), Lancaster, UK.

Barry, D. K. (2003). *Web services and service-oriented architectures (The savvy manager's guides).* San Francisco, CA: Morgan Kaufmann Publishers.

Baskerville, R. (2004). Agile security for information warfare: A call for research. *Proceedings of the European Conference on Information System, ECIS2004,* Turku, Finland.

Baskerville, R. (1993). Information systems security design methods: Implications for information systems development. *ACM Computing Surveys, 25*(4), 375–414. doi:10.1145/162124.162127

Baskerville, R., & Pries-Heje, J. (2001). Racing the e-bomb: How the Internet is redefining information systems development methodology. In Fitzgerald, B., Russo, N., & DeGross, J. (Eds.), *Realigning research and practice in IS development.* New York, NY: Kluwer.

Baskerville, R., & Pries-Heje, J. (2010). Explanatory design theory. *Business & Information Systems Engineering, 2*(5), 271–282. doi:10.1007/s12599-010-0118-4

Beck, K. (2000). *eXtreme programming explained, embrace change.* Addison Wesley.

Beck, K. et al. (2001). *Manifesto for agile software development.* Retrieved November 29, 2011, from agilemanifesto.org

Beck, K., et al. (2001). Principles behind the agile manifesto. *Agile Manifesto.* Retrieved August 4, 2009, from http://agilemanifesto.org/principles.html

Becker, J., & Krcmar, H. (2008). Integration von Produktion und Dienstleistung – Hybride Wertschöpfung. *Wirtschaftsinformatik, 50*(3). doi:10.1365/s11576-008-0044-y

Beck, K. (2000). *Extreme programming explained.* Boston, MA: Addison-Wesley Pearson Education.

Beck, K. (2002). *Test driven development by example* (1st ed.). Addison-Wesley Professional.

Beck, K. (2004). *Extreme programming explained: Embrace change.* Addison-Wesley.

Beck, K., & Andres, C. (2004). *Extreme programming explained: Change.* Boston, MA: Addison-Wesley.

Beck, K., & Cunningham, W. (1989, October). A laboratory for teaching object oriented thinking. *ACM SIGPLAN Notices, 24*(10), 1–6. doi:10.1145/74878.74879

Benbya, H., & McKelvey, B. (2006). Using coevolutionary and complexity theories to improve IS alignment: A multi-level approach. *Journal of Information Technology,* (n.d.), 21.

Bennett, S., McRobb, S., & Farmer, R. (2006). *Object-oriented system analysis and design using UML.* McGraw Hill.

Berkovich, M., Esch, S., Leimeister, J. M., & Krcmar, H. (2009). Requirements engineering for hybrid products as bundles of hardware, software and service elements – A literature review. *Wirtschaftinformatik Proceedings 2009.*

Berkowitz, S. D. (1982). *An introduction to structural analysis: The network approach to social research.* Toronto, Canada: Butterworth.

Bernard, E. (2010). *JSR 303: Bean validation*. Retrieved February 27, 2010, from http://jcp.org/en/jsr/detail?id=303

Bertino, E., Martino, L., Paci, F., & Squicciarini, A. (2010). *Security for Web services and service-oriented architectures*. Berlin, Germany: Springer-Verlag. doi:10.1007/978-3-540-87742-4

Bertolino, A. (2007). Software testing research: Achievements, challenges, dreams. In *FOSE '07: 2007 Future of Software Engineering* (pp. 85–103). Washington, DC: IEEE Computer Society. doi:10.1109/FOSE.2007.25

Beydoun, G., Gonzalez-Perez, C., Low, G., & Henderson-Sellers, B. (2005). Synthesis of a generic MAS metamodel. *4th International Workshop on Software Engineering for Large-Scale Multi-Agent Systems,* St. Louis, Missouri.

Beydoun, G., Hoffmann, A., Fernandez-Breis, J. T., Martinez-Bejar, R., Valencia-Garcia, R., & Aurum, A. (2005). Cooperative modelling evaluated. *International Journal of Cooperative Information Systems, 14*(1), 45–71. doi:10.1142/S0218843005001080

Beynon-Davies, P., & Holmes, S. (1998). Integrating rapid application development and participatory design. *IEE Proceedings. Software, 145*(4). doi:10.1049/ip-sen:19982196

Beznosov, K. (2003). Extreme security engineering: On employing XP practices to achieve 'good enough security' without defining it. *Proceedings of First ACM Workshop on Business Driven Security Engineering BizSec,* Fairfax, VA.

Bianco, P., Lewis, G. A., Merson, P., & Simanta, S. (2011). *Architecting service-oriented systems.* Carnegie Mellon University, Software Engineering Institute, CMU/SEI-2011-TN-008.

Bianculli, D., Ghezzi, C., & Pautasso, C. (2009). *Embedding continuous lifelong veri☐cation in service life cycles.* In Principles of Engineering Service Oriented Systems (PESOS 2009), co-located with ICSE 2009, DOI 10.1109/PESOS.2009.5068828

Bittner, K., & Spence, I. (2003). *Use case modeling*. Addison-Wesley Professional.

Boehm, B. (1986). A spiral model of software development and enhancement. *ACM Software Engineering Notes*, August.

Boehm, B., & Lane, J. A. (2007, October). Using the incremental commitment model to integrate systems acquisition, systems engineering, and software engineering. *Cross Talk*, (pp. 4-9)

Boehm, B., & Lane, J. A. (2008). *Incremental commitment model guide*, Version 0.5. Center for Systems and Software Engineering Technical Report. Retrieved August 4, 2009, from http://csse.usc.edu/csse/TECHRPTS/2009/usc-csse-2009-500/usc-csse-2009-500.pdf

Boehm, B., Lane, J. A., Koolmanojwong, S., & Turner, R. (2010). *Architected agile solutions for software-reliant systems*. Paper presented at the 20th International Symposium of INCOSE, Chicago, IL.

Boehm, B. (1984). Verifying and validating software requirements and design specifications. *IEEE Software, 1*(1), 75–88. doi:10.1109/MS.1984.233702

Boehm, B. (1996, July). Anchoring the software process. *IEEE Software, 13*(4), 73–82. doi:10.1109/52.526834

Boehm, B. (1998, May). A spiral model of software development and enhancement. *IEEE Computer, 21*(5), 61–72. doi:10.1109/2.59

Boehm, B., & Bhuta, J. (2008, November). Balancing opportunities and risks in component-based software development. *IEEE Software, 25*(6), 56–63. doi:10.1109/MS.2008.145

Boehm, B., & Turner, R. (2004). *Balancing agility and discipline: A guide for the perplexed*. Addison-Wesley. doi:10.1007/978-3-540-24675-6_1

Bogsnes, B. (2008). *Implementing beyond budgeting: Unlocking the performance potential*. London, UK: John Wiley & Sons.

Boneh, D., & Frankliny, M. (2003). Idnetity-based encryption from the Weil pairing. *SIAM Journal on Computing, 32*(3), 586–615. doi:10.1137/S0097539701398521

Booch, G., & Cockburn, A. (2004). *Balancing agility and discipline: A guide for the perplexed*. Addison-Wesley.

Bossavit, L. (n.d.). *Coding dojo*. Retrieved from http://www.codingdojo.org/

Botha, R. A., & Eloff, J. H. P. (2001). Access control in document-centric workflow systems an agent-based approach. *Computers & Security, 20*(6), 525–532. doi:10.1016/S0167-4048(01)00613-7

Braun, I., Strunk, A., Stoyanova, G., & Buder, B. (2008). ConQo - A context- and QoS-aware service discovery. *Proceedings of the IADIS International Conference WWW/Internet* (pp. 432-436).

Brazier, F. M. T., Kephart, J. O., Parunak, H. V. D., & Huhns, M. N. (2009). Agents and service-oriented computing for autonomic computing: A research agenda. *IEEE Internet Computing, 13*(3), 82–87. doi:10.1109/MIC.2009.51

Breu, R. (2010). *Ten principles for living models - A manifesto of change-driven software engineering.* Paper presented at CISIS 2010, The Fourth International Conference on Complex, Intelligent and Software Intensive Systems.

Breu, R., Hafner, M., Innerhofer-Oberperfler, F., & Wozak, F. (2008). *Model-driven security engineering of service oriented system* (pp. 59–71). Information Systems and E-Business Technologies, Lecture Notes in Business Information Processing. doi:10.1007/978-3-540-78942-0_8

Brinkkemper, S., Saeki, M., & Harmsen, F. (1998). Assembly techniques for method engineering. *Proceedings Advanced Information Systems Engineering, 10th International Conference, CAiSE'98, LNCS1413,* Pisa, Italy, (pp. 381-400). Springer Verlag.

Brinkkemper, S. (1996). Method engineering: Engineering of information systems development methods and tools. *Information and Software Technology, 38,* 275–280. doi:10.1016/0950-5849(95)01059-9

Brooks, F. P. (1975). *The mythical man month.* Addison Wesley.

Bruegge, B., Dutoit, A. H., & Wolf, T. (2006). *Sysiphus: Enabling informal collaboration in global software development.* International Conference on Global Software Engineering. Florianopolis, Brazil.

Bryman, A. (2000). *Research methods and organization studies.* Routledge. (first published 1989 by Unwin Hyman)

Bucchiarone, A., Cappiello, C., Nitto, E. D., Kazhamiakin, R., Mazza, V., & Pistore, M. (2009). *Design for adaptation of service-based applications: Main issues and requirements.* In Engineering Service-Oriented Applications: Supporting Software Service Development Lifecycles (WESOA) co-located with ICSOC/ServiceWave

Bunker, D., & Smith, S. (2009). *Disaster management and community warning (CW) systems: Inter-organisational collaboration and ICT innovation.* Pacific Asia Conference on IS.

Burg, S., Jonge, M., Dolstra, E., & Visser, E. (2009). Software deployment in a dynamic cloud: From device to service orientation in a hospital environment. *ICSE Workshop Software Engineering Challenges of Cloud Computing* (pp. 61-66). ACM.

Canfora, G., & Di Penta, M. (2008). Service-oriented architectures testing: A survey. In L. Andrea De & L. C. Filomena Ferrucci (Eds.), *International Symposium on Signals, Systems and Electronics* (Vol. 5413, pp. 78-105).

Cao, L., & Ramesh, B. (2008). Agile requirements engineering practices: An empirical study. *IEEE Software, 25*(1), 60–67. doi:10.1109/MS.2008.1

Capiluppi, A., Fernandez-Ramil, J., Higman, J., Sharp, H., & Smith, N. (2007). An empirical study of the evolution of an agile-developed software system. In 29th International Conference on Software Engineering, ICSE 2007, (pp. 511–518). DOI 10.1109/ICSE.2007.14

Cardellini, V., & Iannucci, S. (2010). Designing a broker for QoS-driven runtime adaptation of SOA applications. *Proceedings of the 2010 IEEE International Conference on Web Services* (pp. 504-511). Miami, Florida, USA.

Carmel, E., Whitaker, R. D., & George, J. F. (1993). PD and joint application design: A transatlantic comparison. *Communications of the ACM, 36*(4).

Carroll, N., Whelan, E., & Richardson, I. (2010). Applying social network analysis to discover service innovation within agile service networks. *Service Science, 2*(4), 225–244. doi:10.1287/serv.2.4.225

Castro, V. D., Marcos, E., & Cáceres, P. (2004). A user service oriented method to model web information systems. *WISE 2004: Web Information Systems, LNCS: Vol. 3306. 2004, Brisbane, Australia* (pp. 41 52). Berlin, Germany: Springer.

CDW. (2009). *Introduction to cloud computing architecture.* Retrieved March 1, 2011, from http://webobjects.cdw.com/webobjects/media/pdf/Sun_CloudComputing.pdf

Chabbra, B., Verma, D., & Taneja, B. (2010). Software engineering issues from the cloud application perspective. *International Journal of Information Technology Knowledge Management, 2*(2), 669–673.

Chakraborty, D., Perich, F., Avancha, S., & Joshi, A. (2001). Dreggie: Semantic service discovery for m-commerce applications. *Proceedings of the Workshop on Reliable and Secure Applications in Mobile Environment, Symposium on Reliable Distributed Systems.*

Chappell, D. E. (2004). *Enterprise service bus.* O'Reilly Media, Inc.

Charette, R. N. (2002). *Foundations of lean development: The lean development manager's guide*, Vol. 2. Spotsylvania, VA: The Foundation Series on Risk Management (CD), ITABHI Corporation.

Chau, T., Maurer, F., & Melnik, G. (2003). Knowledge sharing: Agile methods vs. tayloristic methods. *Proceedings of the 12th IEEE International workshop on Enabling Technologies: Infrastructure for Collaborative Enterprises,* Linz, Austria, (pp. 302-307).

Chen, H.-M., Kazman, R., & Perry, O. (2010). From software architecture analysis to service engineering: An empirical study of methodology development for enterprise SOA implementation. *IEEE Transactions on Services Computing, 3*(2).

Cheng, B., de Lemos, R., Giese, H., Inverardi, P., Magee, J., & Andersson, J. … Whittle, J. (2009). Software engineering for self-adaptive systems: A research roadmap. In B. Cheng, R. de Lemos, H. Giese, P. Inverardi, & J. Magee (Eds.), *Software Engineering for Self-Adaptive Systems, Lecture Notes in Computer Science, vol 5525*, (pp. 1–26). Berlin, Germany: Springer.

Chesbrough, H. (2011). Bringing open innovation to services. *MIT Sloan Management Review, 52*(2), 85–90.

Chikofsky, E. J., & Cross, H. J. II. (1990). Reverse engineering and design recovery: A taxonomy. *IEEE Software, 7*(1), 13–17. doi:10.1109/52.43044

Chivers, H., Paige, R. F., & Ge, X. (2005). Lecture Notes in Computer Science: *Vol. 3556. Agile security using an incremental security architecture extreme programming and agile processes in software engineering* (pp. 1325–1327).

Chong, F., & Carraro, G. (2006). *Architecture strategies for catching the long tail.* Retrieved from http://msdn.microsoft.com/en-us/library/aa479069.aspx

Christensen, E., Curbera, F., Meredith, G., & Weerawarana, S. (2001, March 15). *Web services description language* (WSDL) 1.1. Retrieved from http://www.w3.org/TR/wsdl

Chromatic. (2003). *Extreme programming pocket guide* (1st ed.). O'Reilly Media.

Chung, L., Nixon, B. A., Yu, E., & Mylopoulos, J. (2000). *Non-functional requirements in software engineering.* Kluwer Academic Publishers, 2000.

Chung, S., Won, D., Baeg, S., & Park, S. (2009). *A model-driven scrum process for service-oriented software reengineering: mScrum4SOSR.* The 2nd International Conference on Computer Science and its Applications (CSA 2009), December 10-12, 2009, Jeju Island, Korea.

Chung, S., Won, D., Baeg, S., & Park, S. (2009). *Service-oriented reverse reengineering: 5W1H model-driven re-documentation and candidate services identification.* IEEE International Conference on Service-Oriented Computing and Applications (SOCA'09), Taipei, Taiwan.

Chung, S., Davalos, S., An, J., & Iwahara, K. (2008). Legacy to web migration: Service-oriented software reengineering methodology. *International Journal of Services Sciences, 1*(3/4), 333–365. doi:10.1504/IJSSCI.2008.021769

Clement, L., Hately, A., von Riegen, C., Rogers, T., Bellwood, T., Capell, S., et al. (2004, October 19). *UDDI spec technical committee draft.* Retrieved from http://uddi.org/pubs/uddi_v3.htm

CMMI Product Team. (2009). *CMMI for services,* Version 1.2. Retrieved January 11, 2010, from ftp://ftp.sei.cmu.edu/pub/documents/09.reports/09tr001.doc

Coad, P., Lefebvre, E., & De Luca, J. (1999). *Java modeling in color with UML: Enterprise components and process.* Upper Saddle River, NJ: Prentice Hall.

Cockburn, A. (2002). *Agile software development.* Addison-Wesley / Pearson.

Cockburn, A. (2005). Hexagonal architecture. Retrieved from http://alistair.cockburn.us/Hexagonal+architecture

Cockburn, A., & Highsmith, J. (2001). Agile software development: The people factor. *IEEE Computer,* November.

Cockburn, A. (2005). *Crystal clear: A human-powered methodology for small teams.* Addison-Wesley.

Cockburn, A. (2006). *Agile software development: The cooperative game.* Addison-Wesley.

Cockburn, A., & Highsmith, J. (2001). Agile software development: The people factor. *Computer, 34*(11), 131–133. doi:10.1109/2.963450

Cohen, D., Lindvall, M., & Costa, P. (2004). An introduction to agile methods. *Advances in Computers, 2004,* 2–67.

Cohn, M. (2004). *User stories applied.* Boston, MA: Addison-Wesley.

Cohn, M. (2005). *Agile estimating and planning.* Prentice Hall.

Cohn, M. (2006). *Agile estimating and planning.* Prentice Hall PTR.

Coleman, G., & Verbruggen, R. (1998). A quality software process ofr rapid application development. *Software Quality Journal,* (n.d), 7.

Comuzzi, M., & Pernici, B. (2009). A framework for QoS-based web service contracting. *ACM Transactions on Web, 3*(3)

Conboy, K. (2009). Agility from first principles: Reconstructing the concept of agility in information systems development. *Information Systems Research, 20*(3), 329–354. doi:10.1287/isre.1090.0236

Conboy, K., & Fitzgerald, B. (2004). Toward a conceptual framework of agile methods: A study of agility in different disciplines. In *Proceedings of XP/Agile Universe.* Springer Verlag. doi:10.1007/978-3-540-27777-4_11

Conboy, K., & Morgan, L. (2011). Beyond the customer: Opening the agile systems development process. *Information and Software Technology, 53,* 535–542. doi:10.1016/j.infsof.2010.10.007

Cooper, R. G., Edgett, S. J., & Kleinschmidt, E. J. (2002). *Portfolio management for new products* (2nd ed.). Basic Books.

Coulin, C., Zowghi, D., & Sahraoui, A. (2006). A situational method engineering approach to requirements elicitation workshops in the software development process. *Software Process Improvement and Practice, 11*(5), 451–464. doi:10.1002/spip.288

Covey, S. R. (2008). *The 7 habits of highly effective people.* London, UK: Simon & Schuster Ltd. doi:10.1002/pfi.4170301009

Criteria Common. (2005). *Common criteria for information technology security evaluation,* version 2.5.

Cross, R. L., & Parker, A. (2004). *The hidden power of social networks: Understanding how work really gets done in organizations.* Harvard Business Press.

CSCI577ab (2011). *CSCI577ab – USC software engineering course.* Retrieved June 11, 2011, from http://greenbay.usc.edu/csci577/spring2011/

Cunsolo, D. V., Distefano, S., Puliafito, A., & Scarpa, M. (2010). Applying software engineering principles for designing cloud@home. *10th IEEE/ACM International Conference on Cluster, Cloud and Grid Computing* (pp. 618-624). Washington, DC: IEEE.

Curbera, F., Duftler, M., Khalaf, R., Nagy, W., Mukhi, N., & Weerawarana, S. (2002). Unraveling the Web services web: An introduction to SOAP, WSDL, and UDDI. *Internet Computing, 6*(2), 86–93. doi:10.1109/4236.991449

Curtis, B., Hefley, W. E., & Miller, S. (1995). *People capability maturity model.* (CMU/SEI-95-MM-002), Software Engineering Institute, Carnegie Mellon University, September.

Dahl, O. J., Dijkstra, E. W., & Hoare, C. A. R. (1972). *Structured programming*. New York, NY: Academic Press.

Davenport, T. H., & Short, J. E. (1990, July 15). The new industrial engineering: Information technology and business process redesign. *Sloan Management Review*.

Davis, A. (1992). Operational prototyping: A new development approach. *IEEE Software*, *9*(5). doi:10.1109/52.156899

de Lemos, R., Giese, H., Müller, H., Shaw, M., Andersson, J., & Baresi, L. … Wuttke, J. (2011). Software engineering for self-adaptive systems: A second research roadmap. In R. de Lemos, H. Giese, H. Müller, & M. Shaw (Eds.), *Software Engineering for Self-Adaptive Systems*, Schloss Dagstuhl -Leibniz-Zentrum für Informatik, Germany, Dagstuhl, Germany, no. 10431 in Dagstuhl Seminar Proceedings

Demirkan, H., Kauffman, R. J., Vayghan, J. A., Fill, H., Karagiannis, D., & Maglio, P. P. (2008). Service-oriented technology and management: Perspectives on research and practice for the coming decade. *Electronic Commerce Research and Applications*, *7*, 356–376. doi:10.1016/j.elerap.2008.07.002

Dey, A. K., & Abowd, G. D. (2000). *Towards a better understanding of context and context-awareness*. In Workshop on The What, Who, Where, When, and How of Context-Awareness

Di Nitto, E., Ghezzi, C., Metzger, A., Papazoglou, M., & Pohl, K. (2008). A journey to highly dynamic, self-adaptive service-based applications. *Automated Software Engineering*, *15*(3-4), 313–341. doi:10.1007/s10515-008-0032-x

DOD. (1988). *Military standard, Defense system software development*. DOD-STD-2167A, Washington, US, 29 February.

Dourish, P., Edwards, K. K., Lamarca, A., Lamping, J., Petersen, K., & Salisbury, M. (2000). Extending document management systems with user-specific active properties. *ACM Transactions on Information Systems*, *18*(2), 140–170. doi:10.1145/348751.348758

Dove, R. (2001). *Response ability – The language, structure, and culture of the agile enterprise*. New York, NY: Wiley.

DSDM Consortium. (1997). *Dynamic systems development method, Version 3*. Ashford, UK: DSDM Consortium.

Dubey, A., & Wagle, D. (2007). Delivering software as a service. *The McKinsey Quarterly*, May.

Dubois, D. J. (2008). *An approach for improving business process management in agile service networks*. Minor Research Report. Retrieved from http://home.dei.polimi.it/dubois/papers/bpm4asn09.pdf

Ebert, C. (2009). Software product management. *Cross-Talk, The Journal of Defense Software Engineering*, January.

Eckstein, J. (2004). *Agile software development in large. Diving into the deep*. New York, NY: Dorset House Publishing.

Eclipse Foundation. (2008). *The AspectJ Project*. Retrieved December 8, 2007, from http://www.eclipse.org/aspectj/

Eidelson, R. J. (1997). Complex adaptive systems in the behavioral and social sciences. *Review of General Psychology*, *1*(1). doi:10.1037/1089-2680.1.1.42

Elssamadisy, A. (2007). SOA and agile: Friends or foes? *InfoQ*. Retrieved March 29th, 2011, from http://www.infoq.com/articles/SOA-Agile-Friends-Or-Foes

Endrei, M., Ang, J., Arsanjani, A., Chua, S., Comte, P., & Krogdahl, P. (2004). *Patterns: Service-oriented architecture and web services*. IBM Redbooks.

Ensell, J. (2011, April 12). *Agile development in the cloud*. Retrieved May 1, 2011, from http://www.agilejournal.com/articles/columns/column-articles/6018

Erdogmus, H. (2003). Let's scale agile up. *Agile Times*, *2*(1), 6–7.

Erl, T. (2004). *Service-oriented architecture*. Prentice Hall.

Erl, T. (2005). *Service-oriented architecture: Concepts, technology, and design*. Upper Saddle River, NJ: Pearson Education Inc.

ESI/SFE. (2012). *System family engineering*. European Software Institute. Retrieved from http://www.esi.es/Families/famOverview.html

Exhedra Solutions, Inc. (2010). *Planet source code.* Retrieved February 25, 2010, from http://www.planet-source-code.com/

Feathers, M. (2002). *Working effectively with legacy code.* Retrieved March 29, 2011, from http://www.objectmentor. com/resources/articles/WorkingEffectivelyWithLegacy-Code.pdf

Feathers, M. (2004). *Working effectively with legacy code.* Prentice Hall PTR.

Felderer, M., Agreiter, B., Breu, R., & Armenteros, A. (2010). *Security testing by telling TestStories.*

Felderer, M., Breu, R., Chimiak-Opoka, J., Breu, M., & Schupp, F. (2009). Concepts for model-based requirements testing of service oriented systems. *Proceedings of the IASTED International Conference* (Vol. 642, p. 18).

Felderer, M., Fiedler, F., Zech, P., & Breu, R. (2009). *Towards adaptive test code generation for service oriented systems.* Paper presented at the Ninth International Conference on Quality Software (QSIC 2009).

Felderer, M., Zech, P., Fiedler, F., & Breu, R. (2010). *A tool-based methodology for system testing of service-oriented systems.* Paper presented at the The Second International Conference on Advances in System Testing and Validation Lifecycle (VALID 2010).

Felderer, M., Zech, P., Fiedler, F., Chimiak-Opoka, J., & Breu, R. (2009). *Model-driven system testing of a telephony connector with telling test stories.* Paper presented at the Software Quality Engineering. Proceedings of the CONQUEST 2009.

Fellbaum, C. (Ed.). (1998). *WordNet.* Cambridge, MA: MIT Press.

Feuerlicht, G. (2006). System development life-cycle support for service-oriented applications. In Fukita, H., & Mejri, M. (Eds.), *New trend in software methodologies, tools and techniques (Vol. 147,* pp. 116–126). Quebec, Canada: IOS Press.

Fisch, E. A., & White, G. B. (2000). *Secure computers and networks: Analysis, design, and implementation.* CRC Press.

Fitzgerald, B., Hartnett, G., & Conboy, K. (2006). Customising agile methods to software practices at Intel Shannon. *European Journal of Information Systems, 15*(2), 200–213. doi:10.1057/palgrave.ejis.3000605

Fowler, M., & Beck, K. (1999). *Refactoring: Improving the design of existing code.* Addison-Wesley Professional. doi:10.1007/3-540-45672-4_31

Fowler, M., & Highsmith, J. (2001). The agile manifesto. *Software Development, 9*(8), 28–35.

Freeman, L. C., White, D. R., & Romney, A. K. (1992). *Research methods in social network analysis.* New Brunswick, NJ: Transaction Publishers.

Ge, X. (2007). *Agile security for Web applications.* Department of Computer Science, University of York, PhD.

Ge, X., Chivers, H., et al. (2005). *Adapting security risk analysis to the design of database-centric Web-based information system.* 18th International Conference of Software and System Engineering and Their Applications (ICSSEA), CNAM, Paris.

Geyer, R. (2003). *Europeanisation, complexity, and the British welfare state.* Paper presented to the UACES/ESRC Study Group on The Europeanisation of British Politics and Policy-Making, Department of Politics, University of Sheffield, September 19.

Gilb, T. (1989). *Principles of software engineering management.* Addison Wesley Longman.

Gill, A. Q., & Bunker, D. (2011). *Conceptualization of a context aware cloud adaptation (CACA) framework.* Ninth IEEE International Conference on Dependable, Autonomic and Secure Computing, Sydney.

Goguen, J., & Linde, C. (1993). Techniques for requirements elicitation. *1st IEEE International Symposium on Requirements Engineering (RE'93),* San Diego, USA, (pp. 152-164).

Goldman, S. L., Nagel, R. N., & Preiss, K. (1995). *Agile competitors and virtual organizations: Strategies for enriching the customer.* Van Nostrand Reinhold.

Goldratt, E. (1999). *Theory of constraints.* North River Press.

Goldratt, E. (2004). *The goal: A process of ongoing improvement* (3rd ed.). North River Press.

Gollery, S. (1999). *Re-engineering a software development organization as a complex adaptive system.* InterSymp-99, Baden-Baden, Germany, August.

Gomaa, H., & Shin, M. E. (2009). Separating application and security concerns in use case models. *Proceedings of the 15th Workshop on Early Aspects (EA).* Charlottesville, VA: ACM.

Gottesdiener, E. (1995). RAD realities: Beyond the hype to how RAD really works. *Application Development Trends,* August.

Grance, T., Hash, J., et al. (2003). *Security considerations in the information system development life cycle.* National Institute of Standards and Technology (NIST), Special Publication 800-64.

Grant, T. (2012). *What is the value of agile in your organization*? Retrieved from http://blogs.forrester.com/tom_grant/11-11-08-what_is_the_value_of_agile_in_your_organization

Graydon, P. J. (2010). *Assurance based development.* Department of Computer Science, University of Virginia, PhD.

Greenwell, W., Holloway, J. C., & Pease, J. (2006). *A taxonomy of fallacies in system safety arguments.* 2006 International System Safety Conference (ISSC 06), Albuquerque, NM, USA.

Grigori, D., Corrales, J. C., & Bouzeghoub, M. (2006). Behavioral matchmaking for service retrieval. *Proceedings of the IEEE International Conference on Web Services* (pp. 145-152).

Grogono, P., & Shearing, B. (2008). *Preparing for paradigm shift.* Montreal, Canada: ACM. ISBN 978-1-60558-101-9/08/05

Gudgin, M., Hadley, M., Mendelsohn, N., Moreau, J.-J., Nielsen, H. F., Karmarkar, A., & Lafon, Y. (2007, April 27). *SOAP version 1.2 part 1: Messaging framework* (2nd ed.). Retrieved from http://www.w3.org/TR/soap12-part1/

Guha, R., & Al-Dabass, D. (2010). Impact of web 2.0 and cloud computing platform on software engineering. *International Symposium on Electronic System Design* (pp. 213-218). IEEE.

Hafner, M., & Breu, R. (2009). *Security engineering for service-oriented architectures.* Berlin, Germany: Springer-Verlag.

Hamilton, M., & Zeldin, S. (1976). *Integrated software development system / higher order software conceptual description.* Technical Report ECOM-76- 0329-F. Fort Monmouth, NJ: US Army Electronics Command.

Hansen, M. (1999). The search-transfer problem: The role of weak ties in sharing knowledge across organization subunits. *Administrative Science Quarterly, 44*(1), 82–111. doi:10.2307/2667032

Hassan, N. R. (2009). Using social network analysis to measure IT-enabled business process performance. *Information Systems Management, 26*(1), 61–76. doi:10.1080/10580530802557762

Hassine, I., Rieu, D., Bounaas, F., & Seghrouchni, O. (2002). *Towards a resuable business components model.* A Workshop of the 8th International Conference on Object-Oriented Information Systems OOIS, Montpellier, France.

Hawkins, R. D. (2006). *Using safety contracts in the development of safety critical object oriented systems.* Department of Computer Science, University of York, PhD.

Hayes, S. (2003, May 21). *An introduction to extreme programming.* ZDNet Australia.

Heckel, R., Correia, R., Matos, C., El-Ramly, M., Koutsoukos, G., & Andrade, L. (2008). Architectural transformations: From legacy to three-tier and services. In Mens, T., & Demeyer, S. (Eds.), *Software evolution* (pp. 139–170). Springer. doi:10.1007/978-3-540-76440-3_7

Henderson-Sellers, B. (2003). Method engineering for OO system development. *Communications of the ACM, 46*(10), 73–78. doi:10.1145/944217.944242

Hevner, A. R., March, S. T., Park, J., & Ram, S. (2004). Design science in information systems research. *Management Information Systems Quarterly, 28*(1), 75–105.

Hielscher, J., Kazhamiakin, R., Metzger, A., & Pistore, M. (2008). A framework for proactive selfadaptation of service-based applications based on online testing. In *ServiceWave 2008, LNCS 5377*. Springer.

Highsmith, J. (2002). *Agile software development ecosystems*. Addison-Wesley / Pearson.

Highsmith, J., et al. (2001), *Manifesto for agile software development*. Retrieved from http://agilemanifesto.org/

Highsmith, J. (2000). *Adaptive software development: A collaborative approach to managing complex systems*. New York, NY: Dorset House.

Highsmith, J. (2002). *Agile software development ecosystems* (p. 17). Boston, MA: Pearson Education, Inc.

Highsmith, J. (2004). *Agile project management, creating innovative products*. Pearson Education Inc.

Highsmith, J. A. I. (2000). *Adaptive software development: A collaborative approach to managing complex systems*. New York, NY: Dorset House Publishing.

Highsmith, J., & Cockburn, A. (2001). Agile software development: The business of innovation. *Computer*, *34*(9), 120–122. doi:10.1109/2.947100

Hofer, T., Schwinger, W., Pichler, M., Leonhartsberger, G., & Altmann, J. (2002). Context-awareness on mobile devices: The Hydrogen approach. In *36th Annual Hawaii International Conference on System Sciences*, (pp. 292–302).

Holcombe, M. (2008). *Running an agile software development project*. Wiley-Blackwell.

Hooper, M. J., Steeple, D., & Winters, C. N. (2001). Costing customer value: An approach for the agile enterprise. *International Journal of Operations & Production Management*, *21*(5/6), 630–644. doi:10.1108/01443570110390372

Hope, J., & Fraser, R. (1997). *Beyond budgeting...Breaking through the barrier to 'the third wave'. Management Accounting*. UK: Chartered Institute of Management Accountants.

Hull, E. (1995). *Systems at speed – Rapid application development in 1995. Computer Audit Update*. Elsevier Science Ltd.

Hunt, A., & Thomas, D. (2000). *The pragmatic programmer*. Addison Wesley.

IBM. (2009, April). *Staying aloft in tough times*. Retrieved March 1, 2011, from ftp://ftp.software.ibm.com/common/ssi/ecm/en/ciw03059usen/CIW03059USEN.PDF

ICSM. (2010). *26th IEEE International Conference on Software Maintenance* (ICSM 2010), September 12-18, 2010, Timisoara, Romania. IEEE Computer Society.

IEEE. (1990). *IEEE standard glossary of software engineering terminology*. (IEEE Std 610.12-1990 ed). New York, NY: Institute of Electrical and Electronics Engineers.

IEEE. (2007). *Draft recommended practice for the customer-supplier relationship in agile software projects*. P1648/D5.

IfM and IBM. (2007). *Succeeding through service innovation: A discussion paper*. Cambridge, UK: University of Cambridge Institute for Manufacturing.

Iivari, J., Hirschheim, R., & Klein, H. K. (1998). A paradigmatic analysis contrasting information systems development approaches and methodologies. *Information Systems Research*, *9*(2). doi:10.1287/isre.9.2.164

Ikonen, M. (2011). *Impacts of Kanban on lean software development*. PhD Thesis, Department of Computer Science, University of Helsinki, Series of Publications A, Report A-2011-4.

Irmert, F., Fischer, T., & Meyer-Wegener, K. (2008). Runtime adaptation in a service-oriented component model. *Proceedings of the 2008 International Workshop on Software Engineering for Adaptive and Self-Managing Systems* (pp. 97-104). Leipzig, Germany.

ISO/IEC. (1994). *Information technology -- Open systems interconnection -- Conformance testing methodology and framework*.

ISO/IEC. (1997). *International standard ISO/IEC TR 15504, Information technology – Process assessment-Parts 1- 5*. International Standardization Organization.

ITIL. (2012). *IT infrastructure library, Office of Government Commerce, UK*. Retrieved from http://www.itil-officialsite.com/

itSMF. (2007). *An introductory overview of ITIL*, v3. The UK Chapter of the itSMF, itSMF Ltd.

Izumi, N., Takaki, O., & Hasida, K. (2009). Service system development based on web process ontology. *Proceedings of the 4th International Conference on Software Engineering Advances (ICSEA 2009)*, (pp. 222-228). IEEE Computer Society Press.

Izumi, N., & Yamaguchi, T. (2002). Integration of heterogeneous repositories based on ontologies for EC applications development. *International Journal of Electronic Commerce Research and Applications*, *1*(1), 77–91. doi:10.1016/S1567-4223(02)00007-8

Jackson, M. (2001). *Problem frames: Analysing and structuring software development problems*. New York, NY: Addison-Wesley.

Janzen, D., & Saiedian, H. (2005). Test-driven development concepts, taxonomy, and future direction. *Computer*, *38*(9), 43–50. doi:10.1109/MC.2005.314

Jaquith, A. R., Soo Hoo, K., & Sudbury, A. W. (2001). Tangible ROI through secure software engineering. *Secure Business Quarterly, 1*(2).

Jiang, L., Eberlein, A., Far, B. H., & Mousavi, M. (2008). A methodology for the selection of requirements engineering techniques. *Software Systems Models, 7*(3), 303–328. doi:10.1007/s10270-007-0055-y

Josuttis, N. (2007). *SOA in practice: The art of distributed system design*. O'Reilly Media.

Ju, J., Wang, Y., Fu, J., Wu, J., & Lin, Z. (2010). Research on key technology in saas. *International Conference on Intelligent Computing and Cognitive Informatics* (pp. 384-387). IEEE.

Kalyanakrishnam, M., Kalbarczyk, Z., & Iyer, R. (1999). Failure data analysis of a LAN of Windows NT based computers. *Proceedings of the 18th IEEE Symposium on Reliable Distributed Systems* (p. 178). IEEE Computer Society.

Karlsson, F., & Ågerfalk, P. J. (2008). Method configuration: The eXtreme programming case. *Agile Processes in Software Engineering and Extreme Programming. Lecture Notes in Business Information Processing, 9*, 32–41. doi:10.1007/978-3-540-68255-4_4

Karlström, D., & Runeson, P. (2006). Integrating agile software development into stage-gate managed product development. *Empirical Software Engineering*, (n.d.), 11.

Kautz, K., & Madsen, S. (2010). 47P. Understanding agile software development in practice. *CONF-IRM 2010, Proceedings*, Paper 21. Retrieved from http://aisel.aisnet.org/confirm2010/21

Kawalek, P., & Greenwood, R. W. (2000). The organization, the process, and the model. In Bustard, D., Kawalek, P., & Norris, M. (Eds.), *Systems modeling for business process improvement* (pp. 61–80). Artech House Publishers.

Kaye, D. (2003). *Loosely coupled: The missing pieces of web services*. RDS Press.

Keller, E., & Rexford, J. (2010). The "Platform as a service" model for networking. *INM/WREN'10 Proceedings of the 2010 Internet Network Management Conference on Research on Enterprise Networking*, USENIX Association Berkeley, CA, USA.

Kelly, T. P. (2004). *A systematic approach to safety case management*. Society for Automotive Engineers 2004 World Congress, Detroit, Michigan, USA.

Kelly, T. P. (2007). *Reviewing assurance arguments — A step-by-step approach*. Workshop on Assurance Cases for Security -The Metrics Challenge, Dependable Systems and Networks (DSN).

Kelly, T. P. (1998). *Arguing safety - A systematic approach to managing safety cases*. Department of Computer Science, University of York.

Kettunen, P. (2009). *Agile software development in large-scale new product development organization: Team-level perspective*. Doctoral Dissertation, Helsinki University of Technology, Department of Computer Science and Engineering.

Kiczales, G., Lamping, J., Mendhekar, A., Maeda, C., Lopes, C., Loingtier, J. M., & Irwin, J. (1997). Aspect-Oriented Programming. *11th European Conference on Object-Oriented Programming*, Jyväskylä, Finland.

Kitchenham, B., & Charters, S. (2007). *Guidelines for performing systematic literature reviews in software engineering*. Keele University and Durham University Joint Report. EBSE 2007-001.

Kniberg, H., & Skarin, M. (2010). *Kanban and Scrum, making the most of both. C4Media Inc.* InfoQ.

Knoke, D., & Kuklinski, J. H. (1991). Network analysis: Basis concepts. In G. Thompson, J. Frances, R. Levačić, & J. Mitchell (1991). *Markets, hierarchies and networks: The coordination of social life.* Sage Publications.

Kodali, R. R. (2005). *What is service-oriented architecture: An introduction to SOA.* Retrieved from www.javaworld.com

Kontogogos, A., & Avgerio, P. (2009). *An overview of software engineering approaches to service oriented architectures in various fields.* 18th IEEE International Workshops on Enabling Technologies: Infrastructures for Collaborative Enterprises.

Koolmanojwong, S. (2010). *The incremental commitment spiral model process patterns for rapid-fielding projects.* Doctoral dissertation, Department of Computer Science, University of Southern California.

Koopman, P., & DeVale, J. (1999). Comparing the robustness of POSIX operating systems. *Twenty-Ninth Annual International Symposium on Fault-Tolerant Computing* (pp. 30-37). Retrieved from http://ieeexplore.ieee.org/iel5/6328/16917/00781031.pdf

Koschmider, A., Hornungb, T., & Oberweis, A. (2011). Recommendation-based editor for business process modeling. *Data & Knowledge Engineering, 70*(6), 483–503. doi:10.1016/j.datak.2011.02.002

Koskela, L., & Howell, G. (2002). *The underlying theory of project management is obsolete.* Project Management Institute. doi:10.1109/EMR.2008.4534317

Krebs, J. (2005). *Dissecting business from software requirements.* Retrieved from www.ibm.com/developerworks/rational/library/aug05/krebs

Krishnan, R., Munaga, L., & Karlapalem, K. (2002). XDoC-WFMS: A framework for document centric workflow management system. [Springer.]. *Conceptual Modeling for New Information Systems Technologies, LNCS, 2465,* 348–362. doi:10.1007/3-540-46140-X_27

Krogdahl, P., Luef, G., & Steindl, C. (2005). *Service-oriented agility, Methods for successful service-oriented architecture (SOA) development,* Part 1. IBM. Retrieved from http://www-128.ibm.com/

Krogdahl, P., Luef, G., & Steindl, C. (2005). Service-oriented agility: An initial analysis for the use of agile methods for SOA development. In *IEEE International Conference on Services Computing,* (pp. 93–100). Los Alamitos, CA: IEEE Computer Society.

Kruger, I. H., Gupta, D., Mathew, R., Praveen, M., Phillips, W., Rittmann, S., & Ahluwalia, J. (2004). *Towards a process and tool-chain for service-oriented automotive software engineering.* ICSE 2004 Workshop on Software Engineering for Automotive Systems, Edinburgh.

Krunchten, P. (1995). The 4+1 view model of software architecture. *IEEE Software, 12*(6), 42–50.

Kuhn, T. S. (1962). *The structure of scientific revolutions.* University of Chicago Press.

Kumar, K., & Welke, R. J. (1992). Method engineering: A proposal for situation-specific methodology construction. In Senn, C. A. (Ed.), *Systems analysis and design: A research agenda* (pp. 257–269). John Wiley and Sons.

La, H. J., & Kim, S. D. (2009). A systematic process for developing high quality SaaS cloud services. *1st International Conference on Cloud Computing* (pp. 278-289). Berlin, Germany: Springer-Verlag.

La, H. J., Choi, S. W., & Kim, S. D. (2009). Technical challenges and solution space for developing SaaS and mash-up cloud services. *IEEE International Conference on e-Business Engineering* (pp. 359-364). IEEE.

Ladas, C. (2009). *Scrumban - Essays on Kanban systems for lean software development.* Modus Cooperandi Press.

Laitkorpi, M., Selonen, P., & Systa, T. (2009). Towards a model-driven process for designing ReSTful Web services. *IEEE International Conference on Web Services (ICWS '09),* (pp. 173–180).

Lane, S., & Richardson, I. (2011). Process models for service-based applications: A systematic literature review. *Information and Software Technology, 53,* 424–439. doi:10.1016/j.infsof.2010.12.005

Lankhorst, M., & van Drunen, H. (2007). *Enterprise architecture development and modelling, Combining TOGAF and ArchiMate.* Retrieved from www.via-nova-architectura.org

Laranjeiro, N., & Vieira, M. (2009). Extending test-driven development for robust Web services. *International Conference on Dependability (DEPEND 2009)* (pp. 122-127). Athens/Vouliagmeni, Greece: IEEE Computer Society. doi:10.1109/DEPEND.2009.25

Laranjeiro, N., Vieira, M., & Madeira, H. (2009). *Robustness improvement for Web services.* Retrieved a from http://eden.dei.uc.pt/~cnl/papers/2009-icws-edel.zip

Laranjeiro, N., Vieira, M., & Madeira, H. (2009). Improving Web services robustness. *IEEE International Conference on Web Services (ICWS 2009)* (pp. 397-404). Los Angeles, CA: IEEE Computer Society. doi:10.1109/ICWS.2009.27

Lari, E., Beach, J., Mazzachi, T. A., & Sarkani, S. (2010). Allocating resources in multi-project programs: Lessons Learned from the trenches. *CrossTalk, The Journal of Defence Software Engineering*, May/June.

Larman, C. (2004). *Agile and iterative development: A manager's guide.* Addison-Wesley / Pearson.

Larman, C., & Vodde, B. (2009). *Lean primer*, Version 1.5.2009. Retrieved from www.leanprimer.com

Larman, C., & Basili, V. R. (2003). Iterative and incremental development: A brief history. *Computer*, 36(6), 47–56. doi:10.1109/MC.2003.1204375

Larman, C., & Vodde, B. (2008). *Scaling lean & agile development: Thinking and organizational tools for large-scale Scrum.* Addison-Wesley Professional.

Larson, R. C. (2008). Service science: At the intersection of management, social, and engineering sciences. *IBM Systems Journal*, 47(1). doi:10.1147/sj.471.0041

Laumann, E. O., Marsden, P., & Prensky, D. (1989). The boundary specification problem in network analysis. In Freeman, L. C., White, D. R., & Kimball Romney, A. (Eds.), *Research methods in social network analysis*. Fairfax, VA: George Mason University Press.

Lee, J. Y., Lee, J. W., Cheun, D. W., & Kim, S. D. (2009). A quality model for evaluating software-as-a-service in cloud computing. *ACIS International Conference on Software Engineering Research, Management and Applications* (pp. 261-266). ACIS.

Lee, L.L., Padmanabhan, V., & Whang, S. (1997). The bullwhip effect in supply chains. *Sloan Management Review*, Spring.

Lee, S. P., Chan, L. P., & Lee, E. W. (2006). *Web services implementation methodology for SOA application.* IEEE International Conference on Industrial Informatics, August.

Lee, I., & Iyer, R. K. (1995). Software dependability in the tandem GUARDIAN system. *IEEE Transactions on Software Engineering*, 21(5), 455–467. doi:10.1109/32.387474

Leffingwell, D. (2009). *Thoughts on lean thinking.* Retrieved from http://scalingsoftwareagility.wordpress.com/2009/09/15/thoughts-on-lean-thinking/

Leffingwell, D. (2010). *Agile software requirements: Lean requirements practices for teams, programs, and the enterprise.* Addison-Wesley Professional.

Lei, L., & Duan, Z. (2005). Transforming OWL-S process model into EDFA for service discovery. *Proceedings of the IEEE International Conference on Web Services* (pp. 137-144).

Lenk, A., Klems, M., Nimis, J., Tai, S., & Sandholm, T. (2009). What's inside the cloud? An architectural map of the cloud landscape. *ICSE Workshop on Software Engineering Challenges of Cloud Computing* (pp. 23-31). ACM.

Lewis, T. G. (2009). *Network science – Theory and application.* Hoboken, NJ: John Wiley & Sons.

Li, E. Y., Chen, H.-G., & Lee, T.-S. (2002). Software process management of top companies in Taiwan: A comparative study. *Total Quality Management*, 13(5). doi:10.1080/0954412022000002081

Li, J. (2006). An empirical study of variations in COTS-based software development processes in Norwegian IT industry. *Journal of Empirical Software Engineering*, 11(3), 433–461. doi:10.1007/s10664-006-9005-5

Liker, J. K. (2004). *The Toyota way: 14 management principles from the world's greatest manufacturer.* New York, NY: McGraw-Hill.

Linder, J. C., & Cantrell, S. (2000). *Changing business models: Surveying the landscape.* Institute for Strategic Change, Accenture. Retrieved from http://www.riccistreet.net/dwares/lane/mba600/linder.pdf

Lindvall, M., & Rus, I. (2000). Process diversity in software development. *IEEE Software, 17*(4), 14–18. doi:10.1109/MS.2000.854063

Liu, F., Tong, J., Mao, J., Bohn, R., Messina, J., Badger, L., & Leaf, D. (2011). *NIST cloud computing reference architecture.* National Institute of Standards and Technology, US Department of Commerce.

Lusch, R. F., & Varg, S. L. (2006). Service-dominant logic: Reactions, Reflections and refinements. *Marketing Theory, 6*(3). doi:10.1177/1470593106066781

Lyytinen, K., & Rose, G. M. (2006). Information system development agility as organizational learning. *European Journal of Information Systems, 15*, 183–199. doi:10.1057/palgrave.ejis.3000604

Maglyas, A., Nikula, U., & Smolander, K. (2011). What do we know about software product management? A systematic mapping study. *IEEE Proceedings of the Fifth International Workshop on Software Product Management* (IWSPM), Trento.

Mahanti, A. (2006). Challenges in enterprise adoption of agile methods – A survey. *Journal of Computing and Information Technology, 14*(3), 197–206.

Maiden, N., & Rugg, G. (1996). ACRE: Selecting methods for requirements acquisition. *Software Engineering Journal, 11*(3), 183–192. doi:10.1049/sej.1996.0024

Mancioppi, M., Carro, M., van den Heuvel, W.-J., & Papazoglou, M. P. (2008). Sound multi-party business protocols for service networks. In *6th International Conference on Service-Oriented Computing (ICSOC 2008), Volume 5364 of Lecture Notes in Computer Science*, (pp. 302–316).

Margaria, T., & Steffen, B. (2004). *Lightweight coarse-grained coordination: A scalable system-level approach* (Vol. 5, pp. 107-123).

Marick, B. (2010). *I think I finally understand mocks.* Retrieved from http://video2010.scottishrubyconference.com/show_video/2/0

Marsden, P. V. (2005). Recent developments in network measurement. In Carrington, P., Scott, J., & Wassermann, S. (Eds.), *Models and methods in social network analysis* (pp. 8–30). Cambridge, UK: Cambridge University Press. doi:10.1017/CBO9780511811395.002

Martin, D., Burstein, M., Hobbs, J., Lassila, O., McDermott, D., McIlraith, S., et al. (2004, November 22). *OWL-S: Semantic markup for Web services.* Retrieved from http://www.w3.org/Submission/OWL-S/

Martin, R. C. (2003). *Principles of OOD.* Retrieved from http://butunclebob.com/ArticleS.UncleBob.PrinciplesOfOod

Martin, R. C. (2006). *Agile principles, patterns, and practices in C#.*

Martin, J. (1991). *Rapid application development.* New York, NY: Macmillan Publishing Company.

Martin, R. C. (2002). *Agile software development: Principles, patterns, and practices* (1st ed.). Prentice Hall, Inc.

McGraw, G. (2006). *Software security: Building security in.* Addison Wesley Professional.

Mei, L., Zhang, Z., & Chan, W. (2009). More tales of clouds: Software engineering research issues from the cloud application perspective. *33rd Annual IEEE International Computer Software and Applications Conference* (pp. 525-530). IEEE.

Mell, P., & Grance, T. (2011). *The NIST definition of cloud computing.* National Institute of Standards and Technology NIST, Information Technology Laboratory, Special Publication 800-145.

Mell, P., & Grance, T. (2011). *The NIST definition of cloud computing.* National Institute of Standards and Technology, US Department of Commerce.

Melnik, G., & Maurer, F. (2006). Comparative analysis of job satisfaction in agile and non-agile software development teams, extreme programming and agile processes in software engineering. *Lecture Notes in Computer Science, Proceedings of the 7th International Conference on Extreme Programming and Agile Processes in Software Engineering.*

Meso, P., & Jain, R. (2006). *Agile software development: Adaptive systems principles and best practices*. Information Systems Management, Summer.

Metzger, A. (2011). Towards accurate failure prediction for the proactive adaptation of service-oriented systems (invited paper). In *Proceedings Workshop on Assurances for Self-Adaptive Systems* (ASAS), collocated with ESEC 2011.

Metzger, A., Schmieders, E., Cappiello, C., Nitto, E. D., Kazhamiakin, R., Pernici, B., & Pistore, M. (2010). *Towards proactive adaptation: A journey along the S-Cube service life-cycle*. In Maintenance and Evolution of Service-Oriented Systems.

Mian, P., Conte, T., Natali, A., Biolchini, J., & Travassos, G. (2005). A systematic review process for software engineering. *3rd International Workshop Guidelines for Empirical Work, Workshop Series on Empirical Software Engineering*, (pp. 1-6). Kaiserslautern, Germany.

Miller, G. (2001). *Sizing up today's lightweight software processes. IEEE IT Professional*. May/June.

Mills, H. D. (1971). Top-down programming in large systems. In Rusting, R. (Ed.), *Debugging techniques in large systems*. Englewood Cliffs, NJ: Prentice Hall.

Moore, G. (1995). *Crossing the chasm*. New York, NY: Harper Business.

Moreira, M. (2011, April 12). *Winning combination of agile and the cloud*. Retrieved May 1, 2011, from Agile Journal: http://www.agilejournal.com/articles/columns/column-articles/6017-winning-combination-of-agile-and-the-cloud

Morgan, J. M., & Liker, J. K. (2006). *The Toyota product development system: Integrating people, process, and technology*. New York, NY: Productivity Press.

Morisio, M., Seaman, C. B., Parra, A. T., Basili, V. R., Kraft, S. E., & Condon, S. E. (2000). Investigating and improving a COTS-based software development. *Proceedings of the 22nd International Conference on Software Engineering* (pp. 32-41).

Moser, O., Rosenberg, F., & Dustdar, S. (2008). Non-intrusive monitoring and service adaptation for WS-BPEL. In *Proceeding of the 17th International Conference on World Wide Web, WWW '08*, (pp. 815–824). New York, NY: ACM Press.

Mugridge, R., & Cunningham, W. (2005). *Fit for developing software: Framework for integrated tests*.

Mukherjee, A., & Siewiorek, D. P. (1997). Measuring software dependability by robustness benchmarking. *Transactions on Software Engineering, 23*(6), 366–378. doi:10.1109/32.601075

Murru, O., & Deias, R. (2003). Assessing XP at a European internet company. *IEEE Software, 20*(3), 37–43. doi:10.1109/MS.2003.1196318

Myers, G. J. (1975). *Reliable software through composite design*. New York, NY: Petrocelli/Charter.

Newbold, R. C. (1998). *Project management in the fast lane: Applying the theory of constraints*. The St. Lucie Press.

NIST. (2011, January). *The NIST definition of cloud computing*. Retrieved April 1, 2011, from http://csrc.nist.gov/publications/drafts/800-145/Draft-SP-800-145_cloud-definition.pdf

Normann, R. (2001). *Reframing business: When the map changes the landscape*. Chichester, UK: Wiley.

Northover, M., Northover, A., Gruner, S., Kourie, D. G., & Boake, A. (2007). *Agile software development: A contemporary philosophical perspective. SAICSIT 2007*. Sunshine Coast, South Africa: Fish River Sun.

Nuseibeh, B. (2001). Weaving together requirements and architectures. *IEEE Computer, 34*(3), 115–117. doi:10.1109/2.910904

O'Connell, E., & Saiedian, H. (2000). Can you trust software capability evaluations? Perspectives. *IEEE Computer, 33*(2).

ObjectMentor. (2009). *Junit*. Retrieved March 18, 2011, from http://www.junit.org/

Omar, W. M., & Taleb-Bendiab, A. (2006). Service oriented architecture for e-health support service based on grid computing overlay. *IEEE International Conference on Services Computing,* (pp. 135-42). IEEE Computer Society.

OMG. (2005). *UML testing profile*, Version 1.0.

Oxford dictionaries. (2012). Retrieved from http://oxford-dictionaries.com/

Paetsch, F., Eberlein, A., & Maurer, F. (2003). Requirements engineering and agile software development. In *Proceedings of the Twelfth international Workshop on Enabling Technologies: Infrastructure for Collaborative Enterprises, WETICE,* (p. 308). Washington, DC: IEEE Computer Society.

Paige, R., Cakic, J., et al. (2004). Towards agile reengineering of dependable grid applications. *Proceeding of 17th International Conference of Software and System Engineering and Their Applications* (ICSSEA). CNAM, Paris.

Palmer, S. R., & Felsing, J. M. (2002). *A practical guide to feature-driven development.* Prentice Hall.

Palmer, S., & Felsing, J. M. (2002). *A practical guide to feature driven development.* Upper Saddle River, NJ: Prentice Hall.

Pant, R. (2009, March 17). *Organizing a Web technology department.* Retrieved March 1, 2011, from http://www.rajiv.com/blog/2009/03/17/technology-department/

Paolucci, M., Kawamura, T., Payne, T. R., & Sycara, K. (2002). Semantic matching of Web services capabilities. *Proceedings of the International Semantic Web Conference* (pp. 333-347).

Papazoglou, M. P., Traverso, P., Dustdar, S., & Leymann, F. (2007). Service-oriented computing: State of the art and research challenges. *IEEE Computer, 40*(11), 38–45. doi:10.1109/MC.2007.400

Papazoglou, M. P., & van den Heuvel, W.-J. (2006). Service-oriented design and development methodology. *International Journal of Web Engineering and Technology, 2*(4), 412–442. doi:10.1504/IJWET.2006.010423

Papazoglou, M., & Heuvel, W. (2007). Service oriented architectures: Approaches, technologies and research issues. *The VLDB Journal, 16*(3), 389–415. doi:10.1007/s00778-007-0044-3

Papazoglou, M., Pohl, K., Parkin, M., & Metzger, A. (Eds.). (2010). *Service research challenges and solutions for the future internet: Towards mechanisms and methods for engineering, managing, and adapting service-based systems.* Heidelberg, Germany: Springer.

Papazoglou, M., & van den Heuvel, W. (2007). Service oriented architectures: Approaches, technologies and research issues. *Journal on Very Large Data Bases, 16,* 389–415. doi:10.1007/s00778-007-0044-3

Parnas, D. L. (1972). On the criteria to be used in decomposing systems into modules. *Communications of the ACM,* (n.d.), 15.

Parveen, T., & Tilley, S. (2010). When to migrate software testing to the cloud? *Third International Conference on Software Testing, Veri□cation, and Validation Workshops* (pp. 424-427). IEEE.

Paulk, M. C., Curtis, W., Chrissis, M. B., & Weber, C. (1993). *Capability maturity model^{sm} for software,* Version 1.1. Carnegie Mellon University, Software Engineering Institute, Technical Report CMU/SEI-93-TR-024, February.

Paulk, M. C., Weber, C. V., Garcia, S., Chrissis, M. B., & Bush, M. (1993). *Key practices of the capability maturity model,* Version 1.1. Software Engineering Institute, Technical Report CMU/SEI-93-TR-25, February.

Payne, A. F., Storbacka, K., & Frow, P. (2008). Managing the co-creation of value. *Journal of the Academy of Marketing Science, 36,* 83–96. doi:10.1007/s11747-007-0070-0

Pelrine, J. (2011). Understanding software agility: A social complexity point of view. *Emergence: Complexity & Organization, 13*(1-2).

Peng, Z., Mei, L., Fei, W., & Fei, Y. (2010). The analisis of gis software engineering pattern under the cloud computing environment. *International Conference on Educational and Information Technology* (pp. 450-452). IEEE.

Peterson, G. (2006). *Security architecture blueprint.* Arctec Group, LLC. Retrieved March 29, 2011, from http://arctecgroup.net/pdf/ArctecSecurityArchitecture-Blueprint.pdf

Pew, R. W., & Mavor, A. S. (2007). *Human-system integration in the system development process: A new look.* Washington, DC: National Academy Press.

Pfleeger, C. P., & Pfleeger, S. L. (2003). *Security in computing.* Prentice Hall.

Pikkarainen, M., Sal, O., & Still, J. (2005). Deploying agile practices in organisations: A case study. *The Proceedings of the EuroSPI, LNCS, 3792*, 16–27.

Pilcher, R.(2010). Agile Product Management with Scrum. (pp 19). Boston: Pearson Education, Inc.

Plummer, K. (2011, March 26). *Enterprise software engineering to the cloud, via agile and DevOps.* Retrieved May 1, 2011, from http://www.maestrodev.com/blogs/enterprise-software-engineering-to-the-cloud-via-agile-and-devops

PMI. (2008). *A guide to the project management body of knowledge* (PMBOK® Guide) — 4th ed. Retrieved from http://www.pmi.org/

PMI. (2012). *PMI agile certified practitioner*[sm]. Retrieved from http://www.pmi.org/Certification/New-PMI-Agile-Certification/PMI-Agile-Toolbox.aspx

Poppendieck, M., & Poppendieck, T. (2003). *Lean software development, an agile toolkit.* Boston, MA: Addison Wesley.

Poppendieck, M., & Poppendieck, T. (2007). *Implementing lean software development: From concept to cash.* Addison-Wesley.

Poppendieck, M., & Poppendieck, T. (2010). *Leading lean software development: Results are not the point.* Addison-Wesley.

Portelli, B. (2010, October 18). *The beauty of agile in the cloud.* Retrieved March 1, 2011, from http://www.cmcrossroads.com/cm-articles/columns/agile-in-the-cloud/13759-the-beauty-of-agile-in-the-cloud

Power, K. (2010). *Stakeholder identification in agile software product development organizations: A model for understanding who and what really counts. AGILE 2010.* IEEE Computer Society.

Programmable Web. (2009). *Mashups.* Retrieved November 11, 2009, from http://www.programmableweb.com/mashups

Puleio, M. (2006). How not to do agile testing. *Proceedings of the Conference on Agile,* 2006 (pp. 305-314).

Qumer, A., & Henderson-Sellers, B. (2010). *Framework as software service (FASS) - An agile e-toolkit to support agile method tailoring.* International Conference on Software and Data Technologies, Athens, Greece.

Qumer, A., & Henderson-Sellers, B. (2008). An evaluation of the degree of agility in six agile methods and its applicability for method engineering. [IST]. *Information and Software Technology, 50*(4), 280–295. doi:10.1016/j.infsof.2007.02.002

Qumer, A., & Henderson-Sellers, B. (2008). A framework to support the evaluation, adoption, and improvement of agile methods in practice. *Journal of Systems and Software, 81*(11), 1899–1919. doi:10.1016/j.jss.2007.12.806

Rainsberger, J. B. (2009). *Integration tests are a scam.* Retrieved from http://www.infoq.com/news/2009/04/jbrains-integration-test-scam

Ralyté, J. (1999). Reusing scenario based approaches in requirements engineering methods: CREWS method base. *Proceedings of the 10th International Workshop on Database and Expert Systems Applications (DEXA'99), 1st International REP'99 Workshop,* Florence, Italy, (p. 305).

Ramollari, E., Dranidis, D., & Simons, A. J. H. (2012). *A survey of service oriented development methodologies.* CiteSeer, April.

Ramsey, R. H., Atwood, M. E., & Campbell, G. D. (1979). *Analysis of software design methodologies.* Science Applications, Incorporated, U.S. Army, Research Institute for the Behavioral and Social Sciences, Technical Report 401.

Ranjan, J. (2011). *SaaS and agile – Match made in heaven.* Retrieved from http://www.mindtree.com/blogs/saas-agile-match-heaven

Rao, J., & Su, X. (2004). A survey of automated Web service composition methods. *Proceedings of the First International Workshop on Semantic Web Services and Web Process Composition.*

Rashid, A., Moreira, A., & Araujo, J. (2003). *Modularisation and composition of aspectual requirements*. International Conference on Aspect Oriented Software Development (AOSD), Boston, USA.

Reifer, D. (2002). How good are agile methods? *IEEE Software*, *19*, 16. doi:10.1109/MS.2002.1020280

Reinertsen, D. G. (1997). *Managing the design factory*. Free Press.

Reinertsen, D. G. (2009). *The principles of product development FLOW: Second generation lean product development*. Celeritas Publishing.

Rellermeyer, J. S., Duller, M., & Alonso, G. (2009). Engineering the cloud from software modules. *ICSE Workshop on Software Engineering Challenges of Cloud Computing* (pp. 32-37). Washington, DC.: IEEE.

Riungu, M. L., Taipale, O., & Smolander, K. (2010). Research issues for software testing in the cloud. *IEEE Second International Conference on Cloud Computing Technology and Science* (pp. 557-564). IEEE.

Robision, R. (2004). *Understand enterprise service bus scenarios and solutions in service-oriented architecture, Part 1*. Retrieved March 29, 2011, from https://www.ibm.com/developerworks/library/ws-esbscen/

Rodríguez, M., Salles, F., Fabre, J.-C., & Arlat, J. (1999). MAFALDA: Microkernel assessment by fault injection and design aid. *The Third European Dependable Computing Conference on Dependable Computing* (pp. 143-160). Springer-Verlag. doi:10.1007/3-540-48254-7_11

Roman, D., Lausen, H., Keller, U., de Bruijn, J., Bussler, C., Domingue, J., et al. Michael Stollberg. (2006, October 21). *D2v1.3. Web service modeling ontology* (WSMO). Retrieved from http://www.wsmo.org/TR/d2/v1.3/

Ron, R. (2011). *XProgramming.com: An agile software development resource*. Retrieved March 1, 2011, from http://www.xprogramming.com

Rosenberg, D., & Scott, K. (2001). *Introduction to the ICONIX process of software modeling*. informIT. Retrieved March 29, 2011, from http://www.informit.com/articles/article.aspx?p=167902# Rosenberg, D., Stephens, M., & Collins-Cope, M. (2005). *Agile development with ICONIX process people, process, and pragmatism*. Apress.

Royce, W. (1970). Managing the development of large software systems. In *IEEE WESCON*, San Francisco, CA, USA, (pp. 1–9).

Royce, W. W. (1970). Managing the development of large software systems. *Proceedings, IEEE WESCON*, August.

Runeson, P., & Höst, M. (2009). Guidelines for conducting and reporting case study research in software engineering. *Empirical Software Engineering*, (n.d), 14.

Rutherford, K., Shannon, P., et al. (June 2010). *From chaos to Kanban, via Scrum*.

Ryan, K. (2008). Engineering the Irish software tiger. *Computer*, *41*(6), 66–71. doi:10.1109/MC.2008.186

Sadiq, W., & Orlowska, M. E. (2000). Analyzing process models using graph reduction techniques. *Information Systems*, *25*(2), 117–134. doi:10.1016/S0306-4379(00)00012-0

Saeki, M. (2003). CAME: The first step to automated software engineering. In C. Gonzalez-Perez, B. Henderson-Sellers & D. Rawsthorne (Eds.), *Proceedings of OOPSLA 2003 Workshop on Process Engineering for Object-Oriented and Component-Based Development*, Anaheim, CA, (pp. 26-30).

Salancik, G. R. (1995). Wanted: A good network theory of organization. *Administrative Science Quarterly*, *40*, 345–349. doi:10.2307/2393642

Salehie, M., & Tahvildari, L. (2009). Self-adaptive software: Landscape and research challenges. *ACM Transactions on Autonomous and Adaptive Systems*, *4*(2).

Salesforce. (2008). *Agile development meets cloud computing for extraordinary results*. Retrieved from salesforce.com

Sander, D. (2007). Using Scrum to manage student projects. *Journal of Computing Sciences in Colleges*, *23*(1), 79.

Scacchi, W. (2001). Process models in software engineering. In Marciniak, J. J. (Ed.), *Encyclopedia of software engineering* (2nd ed.). New York, NY: John Wiley & Sons Inc.

Schneider, M., & Somers, M. (2006). Organizations as complex adaptive systems: Implications of complexity theory for leadership research. *The Leadership Quarterly*, (n.d), 17.

Schuh, P. (2005). *Integrating agile development in the real world*. Charles River Media, Inc.

Schwaber, K. (1996). Controlled chaos: Living on the Edge. *American Programmer, 9*(5).

Schwaber, K. (2004). *Agile project management with Scrum*. Redmond, WA: Microsoft Press.

Schwaber, K., & Beedle, M. (2002). *Agile software development with Scrum*. Upper Saddle River, NJ: Prentice Hall.

Scotland, K. (2012). *Kanban and systems thinking*. Retrieved March 12, 2012, from http://availagility.co.uk/2010/12/22/kanban-and-systems-thinking/

Scott, J. (1991). *Social network analysis: A handbook*. London, UK: Sage.

S-Cube. (2009). *Initial models and mechanisms for quantitative analysis of correlations between KPIs, SLAs and underlying business processes*. Retrieved from http://www.s-cube-network.eu/results/deliverables/wp-jra-2.1

SEI/SPL. (2012). *Software product lines*. Software engineering Institute. Retrieved from http://www.sei.cmu.edu/productlines/

Serhani, M. A., Dssouli, R., Hafid, A., & Sahraoui, H. (2005). A QoS broker-based architecture for efficient web services selection. *Proceedings of the IEEE International Conference on Web Services* (pp. 113-120).

Shahrbanoo, M., Ali, M., & Mehran, M. (2012). An approach for agile SOA development using agile principles. *International Journal of Computer Science & Information Technology, 4*(1).

Shen, Z., & Su, J. (2005). Web service discovery based on behavior signatures. *Proceedings of the IEEE International Conference on Services Computing* (pp. 279- 286).

Shenhar, A. (2004). Strategic project leaderships toward a strategic approach to project management. *R & D Management, 34*(5). doi:10.1111/j.1467-9310.2004.00363.x

Shenhar, A. J. (2001). One size does not fit all projects: Exploring classical contingency domains. *Management Science, 47*(3). doi:10.1287/mnsc.47.3.394.9772

Shin, M. E., & Gomaa, H. (2006). Modeling of evolution to secure application system from requirements model to software architecture. *Proceedings of the International Conference on Software Engineering Research and Practice Conference on Programming Languages and Compilers*, Vol. 2, SERP 2006, Las Vegas, Nevada, USA.

Shore, J. (2004). Continuous design. *IEEE Software, 21*(1), 20–22. doi:10.1109/MS.2004.1259183

Shore, J., & Warden, J. (2008). *The art of agile development* (p. 28). Sebastpol, CA: O'Reilly Media, Inc.

Simon, L., Mallya, A., Bansal, A., Gupta, G., & Hite, T. D. (2005). A universal service description language. *Proceedings of the IEEE International Conference on Web Services* (pp. 824-825).

Singh, A., & Singh, K. (2010). Agile adoption - Crossing the chasm. *Proceedings of the International Conference on Applied Computer Science,* Malta.

Singh, M. P., & Huhns, M. N. (2005). *Service-oriented computing: Semantics, processes, agents*. West Sussex, UK: John Wiley & Sons, Ltd.

Siponen, M., Baskerville, R., et al. (2005). *Integrating security into agile development methods*. 38th Hawaii International Conference on System Sciences.

Sivashanmugam, K., Verma, K., Sheth, A., & Miller, J. (2003). Adding semantics to Web services standards. *Proceedings of the IEEE International Conference on Web Services* (pp. 395-401).

Skoutas, D., Simitsis, A., & Sellis, T. (2007). A ranking mechanism for Semantic Web service discovery. *Proceedings of the IEEE Congress on Services* (pp. 41-48).

Smith, S., & Bunker, D. (2007). *Community warning systems: An information process and ICT architecture approach for emergency incident response*. Issue paper (submitted to the State Emergency Management Committee).

Snowden, D. J., & Boone, M. E. (2007). A leader's framework for decision making. *Harvard Business Review,* November.

Social Intelligence Technology Research Laboratory (SITR). (n.d.). *Outline of AIST-framework*. Retrieved from http://www.sitr.jp/index/activities/aistfw

Solms, F., Gruner, S., & Edwards, C. (2011). *URDAD as quality-driven process*. 10th International Conference on Intelligent Software Methodologies, Tools, and Techniques (SOMET 2011).

Solms, F., & Loubser, D. (2010). URDAD as a semi-formal approach to analysis and design. *Innovations in Systems and Software Engineering, 6*(1-2), 155–162. doi:10.1007/s11334-009-0113-4

Sommerville, I. (2005). Integrated requirements engineering: A tutorial. *IEEE Software, 22*(1), 16–23. doi:10.1109/MS.2005.13

Spohrer, J., & Kwan, S. K. (2009). Service science, management, engineering, and design (SSMED): Outline & references. *International Journal of Information Systems in the Service Sector, 1*(3). doi:10.4018/jisss.2009070101

Spohrer, J., & Maglio, P. P. (2009). Service science: Towards a smarter planet. In Karwowski, W., & Salvendy, G. (Eds.), *Service engineering*. New York, NY: Wiley.

Spohrer, J., Maglio, P. P., Bailey, J., & Gruhl, D. (2007). Steps toward a science of service systems. *IEEE Computer, 40*(1), 71–77. doi:10.1109/MC.2007.33

Sprott, D. (2009). Product overview: OutSystems agile SOA platform. *CBDI Journal*, 15–20.

Srivastava, A., & Sorenson, P. G. (2010). Service selection based on customer rating of quality of service attributes. *Proceedings of the 8th International Conferences on Web Services*.

Stapleton, J. (1997). *DSDM: The method in practice*. Addison-Wesley, Inc.

Stephens, M., & Rosenberg, D. (2003). *Extreme programming refactored: The case against XP*. APress.

Stevens, W. P., Myers, G. J., & Constantine, L. L. (1974). Structured design. *IBM Systems Journal*, (n.d.), 13.

Stiehm, T., Foster, R., & Hulen, R. (2006). *SOA, meet agile: Adopting SOA with agile teams*. Digital Focus – a Command Information Company.

Štolfa, S., & Vondrák, I. (2004). A description of business process modeling as a tool for definition of requirements specification. *Proceedings of System Integration*, (pp. 463-469).

Stoneburner, G., Goguen, A., et al. (2002). *Risk management guide for information technology systems*. National Institute of Standards and Technology (NIST), Special Publication 800-30.

Studer, R., & Benjamins, V. R., & Fensel, D. (1998). Knowledge engineering: Principles and methods. *Data & Knowledge Engineering, 25*, 161–197. doi:10.1016/S0169-023X(97)00056-6

Stuttard, D., & Pinto, M. (2007). *The web application hacker's handbook: Discovering and exploiting security flaws*. John Wiley & Sons, Inc.

Subramaniam, V., & Hunt, A. (2006). *Practices of an agile developer – Working in the real world*. USA: The Pragmatic Bookshelf.

Sucharov, T. (2007). Mainframe makeovers. *Information Professional, 4*(6), 36–38. doi:10.1049/inp:20070606

Takaki, O., Seino, T., Takeuti, I., Izumi, N., & Takahashi, K. (2008). Workflow diagrams based on evidence life cycles. *Proceedings of the 8th Joint Conference on Knowledge - Based Software Engineering 2008 (JCKBSE 2008), Frontiers in Artificial Intelligence and Applications*, (pp. 145-154). IOS Press.

Takaki, O., Takeuti, I., Izumi, N., & Hasida, K. (2010). Syntax and semantics of workflows that include passbacks. *Proceedings of the 5th International Conference on Software Engineering Advances (ICSEA 2010)*, (pp. 169-177). IEEE Computer Society Press.

Takaki, O., Seino, T., Takeuti, I., Izumi, N., & Takahashi, K. (2008). Verification of evidence life cycles in workflow diagrams with passback flows. *International Journal on Advances in Software, 1*(1), 14–25.

Takaki, O., Takeuti, I., Seino, T., Izumi, N., & Takahashi, K. (2009). Incremental verification of consistency properties of large-scale workflows from the perspectives of control flow and evidence life cycles. *International Journal on Advances in Software, 2*(1), 145–159.

Taylor, F. W. (1911). *The principles of scientific management*. New York, NY: Harper & Brothers.

Teasley, S. D., Covi, L. A., Krishnan, M. S., & Olson, J. S. (2002). Rapid software development through team collocation. *IEEE Transactions on Software Engineering, 28*(7). doi:10.1109/TSE.2002.1019481

ter Hofstede, A. H. M., & Verhoef, T. F. (1997). On the feasibility of situational method engineering. *Information Systems, 22,* 401–422. doi:10.1016/S0306-4379(97)00024-0

The MIT process handbook project. (n.d.). Retrieved form http://ccs.mit.edu/ph/

The National Institute of Advanced Industrial Science and Technology (AIST). (2006). *AIST has embarked developments of large scale information systems without vendors' locks-on (in Japanese).* Retrieved from http://www.aist.go.jp/aist_j/press_release/pr2006/pr20061219/pr20061219.html

Thomas, S. (2012). *Agile: I prefer hype to ignorance.* Retrieved from http://itsadeliverything.com/agile-i-prefer-hype-to-ignorance

Thomas, D. (2006). Agile evolution: Towards the continuous improvement of legacy software. *Journal of Object Technology, 5*(7), 19–26. doi:10.5381/jot.2006.5.7.c2

Thomsett, R. (2002). *Radical project management.* Prentice Hall PTR.

Tichy, N. M., Tushman, M. L., & Frombrun, C. (1979). Social network analysis for organizations. *Academy of Management Review, 4,* 507–519.

Tilkov, S. (2007). 10 principles of SOA. *InfoQ.* Retrieved March 29, 2011, from http://www.infoq.com/articles/tilkov-10-soa-principles

Transaction Processing Performance Council. (2008). *TPC BenchmarkTM app (application server) standard specification,* Version 1.3. Retrieved July 5, 2008, from http://www.tpc.org/tpc_app/

Tsai, W. T., Jin, Z., Wang, P., & Wu, B. (2007). *Requirement engineering in service-oriented system engineering.* IEEE International Conference on e-Business Engineering, ICEBE 2007.

Tsai, W. T., Malek, M., Chen, Y., & Bastani, F. (2006). Perspectives on service-oriented computing and service-oriented system engineering. In *Proceedings of the Second IEEE International Symposium on Service-Oriented System Engineering,* (pp. 3-10).

Turk, D., France, R., & Rumpe, B. (2005). Assumptions underlying agile software development processes. *Journal of Database Management, 16*(4), 62–87. doi:10.4018/jdm.2005100104

Tyson, B., Alberts, C. J., & Brownsword, L. (2003). *CMMI for COTS-based systems.* Software Engineering Institute. Retrieved August 4, 2009, from http://www.sei.cmu.edu/publications/documents/03.reports/03tr022.html

Vähäniitty, J., & Rautiainen, K. (2008). Towards a conceptual framework and tool support for linking long-term product and business planning with agile software development. In *Proceedings of the 1st International Workshop on Software Development Governance,* (SDG).

Vähäniitty, J., Rautiainen, K., Heikkilä, V., & Vlaanderen, K. (2010). *Towards agile product and portfolio management.* Aalto University, School of Science and Technology, Software Business and Engineering Laboratory (SoberIT).

Vähäniitty, J. (2012). *Towards agile product and portfolio management. Doctoral Dissertations 15/2012, Software Process Group.* Finland: Department of Computer Science and Engineering, Aalto University School of Science.

van den Heuvel, W. J. A. M. (2009). *Changing the face of the global digital economy: What smart service systems means for people's everday life, enterprises and societies.* Tilburg, The Netherlands: Tilburg University Press.

van der Aalst, W. M. P. (1997). Verification of workflow nets. In *Application and Theory of Petri Nets, LNCS 1248,* (pp. 407-426). Springer.

van der Aalst, W. M. P., Hirnschall, A., & Verbeek, H. M. W. (2002). An alternative way to analyze workflow graphs. In *Proceedings of the 14th International Conference on Advanced Information Systems Engineering (CAiSE), LNCS 2348,* (pp. 535-552). Springer.

van der Aalst, W. M. P. (1998). The application of petri nets to workflow management. *The Journal of Circuits. Systems and Computers, 8*(1), 21–66.

van Lamsweerde, A., Darimont, R., & Letier, E. (1998). Managing conflicts in goal-driven requirements engineering. *IEEE Transactions on Software Engineering, 24*(11), 908–926. doi:10.1109/32.730542

van Oosterhout, M., Waarts, E., van Heck, E., & van Hillegersberg, J. (2007). Business agility: Need, readiness and alignment with IT strategies. In Desouza, K. C. (Ed.), *Agile information systems: Conceptualization, construction, and management*. Elsevier Inc.

Vargo, S. L., & Lusch, R. F. (2004). Evolving to a new dominant logic for marketing. *Journal of Marketing,* (n.d.), 68.

Vargo, S. L., & Lusch, R. F. (2008). From goods to service (S): Divergences and convergences of logics. *Industrial Marketing Management, 37*, 254–259. doi:10.1016/j.indmarman.2007.07.004

Vargo, S. L., & Lusch, R. F. (2008). Service-dominant logic: continuing the evolution. *Journal of the Academy of Marketing Science, 36*, 1–10. doi:10.1007/s11747-007-0069-6

Vargo, S. L., Maglio, P. P., & Akaka, M. A. (2008). On value and value co-creation: A service systems and service logic perspective. *European Management Journal, 26*, 145–152. doi:10.1016/j.emj.2008.04.003

Vidgen, R., & Wang, X. (2009). Coevolving systems and the organization of agile software development. *Information Systems Research, September, 20*(3), 355-376

Vidgen, R., & Wang, X. (2009). Coevolving systems and the organization of agile software development. *Information Systems Research, 20*(3). doi:10.1287/isre.1090.0237

Viega, J., & McGraw, G. (2002). *Building secure software*. Addison-Wesley.

Vieira, M., Laranjeiro, N., & Madeira, H. (2007). Benchmarking the robustness of Web services. *13th IEEE Pacific Rim Dependable Computing Conference (PRDC 2007)* (pp. 322-329). Melbourne, Australia: IEEE Computer Society. doi:10.1109/PRDC.2007.56

Vieira, M., Laranjeiro, N., & Madeira, H. (2007). Assessing robustness of Web-services infrastructures. *37th Annual IEEE/IFIP International Conference on Dependable Systems and Networks (DSN 2007)* (pp. 131-136). Edinburgh, UK: IEEE Computer Society. doi:10.1109/DSN.2007.16

Vijayasarathy, L. R., & Turk, D. (2008). Agile software development: A survey of early adopters. *Journal of Information Technology Management, 19*(2).

Vinekar, V., Slinkman, C. W., & Nerur, S. (2006). Can agile and traditional systems development approaches coexist? An ambidextrous view. *Information Systems Management, 23*(3). doi:10.1201/1078.10580530/46108.23.3.20060601/93705.4

Visaggio, G. (2001). Ageing of a data-intensive legacy system: symptoms and remedies. *Journal of Software Maintenance and Evolution, 13*, 281–308. doi:10.1002/smr.234

V-Model. (2009). *V-model lifecycle process model*. Retrieved October 9, 2009, from http://www.v-modell.iabg.de/kurzb/vm/k_vm_e.doc

Vouk, M. A. (2008). Cloud computing- Issues, research and implementations. *30th International Conference on Information Technology Interfaces* (pp. 31-40). IEEE.

Vu, L.-H., Hauswirth, M., & Aberer, K. (2005). QoS-based service selection and ranking with trust and reputation management. *Proceedings of the Cooperative Information System Conference*.

W3C. (2008). *W3C XML schema*. Retrieved December 15, 2008, a from http://www.w3.org/XML/Schema

W3C. (2008). *XQuery 1.0 and XPath 2.0 functions and operators*. Retrieved December 15, 2008, from http://www.w3.org/TR/xquery-operators/

Wadhwa, S., & Rao, K. S. (2003). Flexibility and agility for enterprise synchronization: Knowledge and innovation management towards flexagility. *Studies in Informatics and Control Journal, 11*(2), 29–34.

Wang, J., & Kumar, A. (2005). A framework for document-driven workflow systems. *Proceeding of 3rd International Conference on Business Process Management (BPM), LNCS 3649*, (pp. 285–301). Springer.

Wang, Y., & Stroulia, E. (2003). Flexible interface matching for web-service discovery. *Proceedings of the 4th International Conference on Web Information Systems Engineering* (pp. 147- 156).

Wang, Y., & Vassileva, J. (2007). Toward trust and reputation based Web service selection: A survey. *International Transactions on Systems Science and Applications, 3*(2), 118–132.

Warnier, J. D. (1974). *Logical construction of programs.* Leiden, The Netherlands: Stenpert Kroese.

Wasserman, S., & Faust, K. (1994). *Social network analysis: Methods and applications.* Cambridge, UK: Cambridge University Press. doi:10.1017/CBO9780511815478

Wasson, K. (2006). *CLEAR requirements: Improving validity using cognitive linguistic elicitation and representation.* Department of Computer Science, University of Virginia, PhD.

Watts, D. J. (2004). The "new" science of networks. *Annual Review of Sociology, 30,* 243–270. doi:10.1146/annurev.soc.30.020404.104342

Watts, D. J., & Strogatz, S. H. (1998). Collective dynamics of 'small-world' networks. *Nature, 393*(6684), 440–442. doi:10.1038/30918

Wayrynen, J., & Boden, M. (2004). Security engineering and eXtreme programming: An impossible marriage? *Extreme Programming and Agile Methods -XP/Agile Universe 2004 (XP2004)* [Springer.]. *LNCS, 3134,* 117–128.

Welke, R., & Kumar, K. (1991). Method engineering: A proposal for situation-specific methodology construction. In *Systems analysis and design: A research agenda.* Wiley.

Wellman, B., & Berkowitz, S. D. (1988). *Social structures: A network approach.* Greenwich, CT: JAI Press.

West, D. (2011). *Water-Scrum-fall is the reality of agile for most organizations today: Manage the Water-Scrum and Scrum-fall boundaries to increase agility.* Forrester report, July 26.

West, D., & Grant, T. (2010). *Agile development: Mainstream Adoption has changed agility.* Forrester report, January 20.

Weyuker, E. J. (1998). Testing component-based software: a cautionary tale. *Software, 15*(5), 54–59. doi:10.1109/52.714817

Wilkes, L., & Veryard, R. (2004). *Service-oriented architecture: Considerations for agile systems.* CBDI Forum, April 2004.

Wirth, N. (1991). Program development by stepwise refinement. *Communications of the ACM,* (n.d.), 14.

Womack, J. P., & Jones, D. T. (2003). *Lean thinking: Banish waste and create wealth in your corporation.* Free press edition.

Womack, J. P., Jones, D. T., & Roos, D. (1991). *The machine that changed the world: The story of lean production.* Harper Perennial.

Wombacher, A., Fankhauser, P., & Mahleko, B. (2004). Matchmaking for business processes based on choreographies. *Proceedings of the IEEE International Conference on e-Technology, e-Commerce and e-Service* (pp. 359-368).

Workflow Management Coalition (WfMC). (2002). *Workflow standard: Workflow process definition interface - XML process definition language (XPDL). (WfMC-TC-1025).* Lighthouse Point, Florida, USA: Technical Report, Workflow Management Coalition.

Xiao, H., Zou, Y., Ng, J., & Nigul, L. (2010). An approach for context-aware service discovery and recommendation. *Proceedings the 8th International Conference on Web Services.*

Yang, Y. (2006). *Composable risk-driven processes for developing software systems from commercial-off-the-shelf (COTS) products.* Doctoral dissertation, Department of Computer Science, University of Southern California, California.

Yara, P., Ramachandran, R., Balasubramanian, G., Muthuswamy, K., & Chandrasekar, D. (2009). *Global software development with cloud platforms* (pp. 81–95). Software Engineering Approaches for Offshore and Outsourced Development.

Ye, L., & Zhang, B. (2006). Web service discovery based on functional semantics. *Proceedings of the Second International Conference on Semantics, Knowledge, and Grid* (pp. 57-57).

Yourdon, E., & Constantine, L. L. (1975). *Structured design*. New York, NY: Yourdon, Inc.

Yu, J., Benatallah, B., Casati, F., & Daniel, F. (2008). Understanding mashup development. *IEEE Internet Computing*, *12*(5), 44–52. doi:10.1109/MIC.2008.114

Zachos, K., & Maiden, N. (2008). Inventing requirements from software: An empirical investigation with web services. In *Proceedings 16th IEEE International Conference on Requirements Engineering*, (pp. 145–154). IEEE Computer Society Press.

Zavala Gutierrez, R. L., Mendoza, B., & Huhns, M. N. (2007). Behavioral queries for service selection: An agile approach to SOC. *Proceedings IEEE International Conference on Web Services*, (pp. 1152-1153).

Zave, P. (1997). Classification of research efforts in requirements engineering. *ACM Computing Surveys*, *29*(4), 315–321. doi:10.1145/267580.267581

Zhao, J. L., Hsu, C., Jain, H. K., Spohrer, J. C., Tanniru, M., & Wang, H. J. (2008). ICIS 2007 panel report: Bridging service computing and service management: How MIS contributes to service orientation. *Communications of the Association for Information Systems*, *22*, 413–428.

Zhong, J. (2001). *Step into the J2EE architecture and process*. Retrieved from www.JavaWorld.com

Zimmermann, O., Schlimm, N., Waller, G., & Pestel, M. (2005). *Analysis and design techniques for service-oriented development and integration*. In INFORMATIK 2005 - Informatik LIVE! Band 2, Beiträge der 35. Jahrestagung der Gesellschaft für Informatik e.V. (GI), Bonn, September

Zimmermann, O., Krogdahl, P., & Gee, C. (2004). *Elements of service-oriented analysis and design*. IBM.

Zowghi, D., Firesmith, D. G., & Henderson-Sellers, B. (2005). Using the OPEN process framework to produce a situation-specific requirements engineering method. *Proceedings of SREP*, Paris, France, (pp. 59-74).

About the Contributors

Xiaofeng Wang is a researcher in Free University of Bozen/Bolzano. Her research areas include software development process, methods, agile software development, and complex adaptive systems theory. Her doctoral study investigated the application of complex adaptive systems theory in the research of agile software development. Her publications include several journal and conference papers in major IS/SE journal and conferences, including *Information Systems Research* (ISR), *Journal of Information Technology* (JIT), *Journal of Systems and Software* (JSS), International Conference on Information Systems (ICIS), and the European Conference on Information Systems (ECIS).

Nour Ali is a Research Fellow at Lero-The Irish Software Engineering Research Centre, Ireland. She graduated in Computer Science from Bir-Zeit University, Palestine and holds a PhD. from the Polytechnic University of Valencia, Spain. She was awarded a grant by the same university, to perform her PhD. under the Researcher training programme (FPI, in Spanish). During her PhD, she was a visiting researcher at University of Leicester, UK. Her PhD. is on specifying software architecture of distributed and mobile systems using model driven engineering techniques for generating and executing their code. She has also been a postdoc at the Politecnico di Milano, Italy. She has been an active member of several research projects focusing on software architecture such as the Microsoft Research Cambridge funded Project: "PRISMA Model Compiler of aspect-oriented component-based software architectures." She serves as reviewer for several venues and journals such as *Journal of Systems and Software, Journal of Information Systems and Technology,* and *IEEE Transactions on Systems, Man, and Cybernetics*. She has co-chaired and co-organized the IEEE International Workshop on Engineering Mobile Service Oriented Systems (EMSOS) and the IEEE Workshop on Future of Software Engineering for/in the Cloud. She is currently co-editing a special issue "The Future of Software Engineering FOR/IN the Cloud - FoSECloud," in the *Journal of Systems and Software*. Her research interests are software architecture, service oriented computing, distributed and mobile systems, aspect-oriented software development, model driven engineering, and global software development.

Isidro Ramos is a full Professor since 1976. He has been teaching during 36 years in several universities. Currently, he is a Lecturer at the Polytechnic University of Valencia and the leader of the Software Engineering and Information Systems research group of the same university. He has been a key researcher in 21 Research Projects, member and president of different Programme Committees of relevant conferences. He has also been the International Coordinator of the VII CYTED Subprogram on Applied Electronics and Computing, and the president of the University of Castilla la Mancha. He has received the Spanish Computer Science National Award 2006. He is currently working in MDE and in Software Architectures fields.

Richard Vidgen is Professor of Systems Thinking in the Hull University Business School. He worked for fifteen years in the IT industry as a programmer, systems analyst, and project manager. On leaving industry he studied for a PhD in Information Systems at the University of Salford and then worked at the School of Management, University of Bath and the Australian School of Business, University of New South Wales. He has published research articles in leading journals including *Information Systems Research, Information & Management, European Journal of Information Systems, Journal of Information Technology, Omega, Journal of Strategic Information Systems*, and the *Information Systems Journal.* His current research interests include: the application of complex adaptive systems theory and social networks to the study of information system development and to organizations in general, Internet quality and Web site usability, and the assessment of scholarly influence and journal quality.

* * *

Seung-Ho Baeg is a Principal Researcher of the Department of Applied Robot Technology (DART) at Korea Institute of Industrial Technology (KITECH) since 1993. His research areas include software engineering, system integration of the unmanned system, such as quadruped walking robots, unmanned ground vehicle, et cetera. Especially, he has focused lots of research on the real time data communication, 3D LIDAR sensor, and INS Sensor in order to build a reliable navigation system.

Yan Bai is an Assistant Professor in the Institute of Technology at University of Washington Tacoma. She received her Ph.D. in Electrical and Computer Engineering from University of British Columbia, Canada in 2003. Her research interests are in the area of computer networking, cybersecurity, eHealth, cloud computing, and multimedia communications.

Paul Barrett, since graduating from the University of Glamorgan in 2000 with a degree in Software Engineering, has worked on a diverse range of projects. These include a Voice over IP client, back-end systems for large insurance companies, finance calculators for the motor industry and a pop quiz website. During his time at Codeweavers Ltd, Paul has played a key role in growing the business from a small start-up to a successful, agile enterprise.

Barry Boehm is the TRW Professor in the USC Computer Sciences and Industrial and Systems Engineering Departments. He is also the Director of Research of the DoD-Stevens-USC Systems Engineering Research Center. He originated the spiral model, the constructive cost model, and the stakeholder win-win approach to software management and requirements negotiation. He is a Fellow of the primary professional societies in computing (ACM), aerospace (AIAA), electronics (IEEE), and systems engineering (INCOSE), a member of the U.S. National Academy of Engineering, and the 2010 recipient of the IEEE Simon Ramo Medal for exceptional achievement in systems engineering and systems science.

Ruth Breu is full Professor at the University of Innsbruck, Institute of Computer Science, since 2002 and head of the research group Quality Engineering. Prior to that she worked for several years as software engineering consultant for companies in the finance and telecommunication sector and passed her academic degrees at Technische Universit%ot M¸nchen and Universit%ot Passau, Germany. Ruth Breu has long year experience in the areas of model-driven software development, requirements engineering, quality management and security engineering. She is co-author of three books and over hundred publications in international journals and conferences. Since 2009, Ruth Breu is scientific head of QE LaB, a private-public partnership competence center. QE LaB focuses on continuous quality management of collaborative systems.

Deborah Bunker is an Associate Professor, BIS and Director of Doctoral Studies at the University of Sydney Business School, having previously held senior academic and administrative positions at UNSW and UOW. Her research interests are in IS philosophy, IS management, and IS adoption and diffusion. Deborah is also Past President, Australasian Association of IS and Vice Chair, International Federation of Information Processing Working Group 8.6 on Innovation, Diffusion, Transfer and Implementation of IS.

Noel Carroll is a PhD student with the Department of Computer Science and Information Systems at the University of Limerick. His research focuses on service science initatives and examines methods to investigate the value of IT on service networks. Noel is a member of Lero – the Irish Software Engineering Research Centre. He is also involved in a European project S-Cube, the European Network of Excellence in Software Services and Systems. He is particularly interested in applying organisational network analysis and actor-network theory to examine the socio-technical influence of IT on service dynamics. He has a number of publications which identifies the need to adopt a new lens towards business process management. His PhD presents theoretical developments on public service science which examines the implementation process of technology in a public service network.

Sam Chung is an Associate and Founding Professor of Information Technology and Systems at the University of Washington, Tacoma. Dr. Chung is also an Associate Director of Cyber Physical Systems at the Center for Information Assurance and Cybersecurity in the University of Washington, Seattle. His Smart and Secure Computing research group focuses on how service-oriented cyber physical systems in a cloud environment can be smart and secure from internal or external attacks. Dr. Chung's research areas include Secure Service-Oriented Software Reengineering in a Cloud Computing environment, Software Assurance, and Attack Aware Cyber Physical Systems. Dr. Chung recently supervised several research grant programs awarded: NSF has supported software reengineering based secure coding curriculum development project. Dr. Chung is also involved in a scholarship program called NSF Scholarship for Services (SFS) supported by NSF through CIAC at the UW, Seattle.

Conrado E Crompton Q. was born in July 25 1977 in Panama city, Republic of Panama in a little town call Alcalde Diaz. He moved together with his family to United States in February 2nd 1989. He attended college at Embry Riddle Aeronautical University (ERAU), receiving a Bachelor of Science in Computer Science in 2004. After ERAU, Mr. Crompton worked at New Tech LLC (NTL), where he was involved in the development of various government related software systems. In 2008, he returned to school, this time receiving a Master's of Science from the University Of Washington, Tacoma. In 2010, he left NTL and worked at Northrop Grumman, Corporation as a Software Engineer. In 2010, he took a position with Motricity a mobile as a service company. He currently works for Expeditors International of Washington, Inc. as a software engineer. He is responsible for the development of logistics software products by the company.

Elisabetta Di Nitto is an Associate Professor at Politecnico di Milano. She is teaching Software Engineering and Foundations of Computer Science. Her expertise lies in the area of software engineering and, in particular, of large-scale, open, service-oriented systems. She has published and presented various papers on the most important international journals and conferences and has served in the program committee of various international conferences and has been program co-chair of ASE 2010 and ServiceWave 2010, workshop co-chair of ICSE 2010 and ICSOC 2006, and demo track chair of ICSE 2007. Moreover, she is member of the Editorial Board of *IEEE Transactions on Software Engineering,* of the *SOCA Journal,* and of the *Journal of Software: Evolution and Process.* She has been involved in various research projects funded by the EU such as S-Cube, SOA4All, SLA@SOI, CASCADAS, and has been Scientific Director of the FP6 SeCSE project.

Barbara Endicott-Popovsky, Ph.D., is Director of the Center for Information Assurance and Cybersecurity at the University of Washington; Academic Director of the Master in Infrastructure Planning and Management; founder of Information Assurance programs at the Universities of Washington and Hawaii Manoa, and holds an appointment as Research Associate Professor with the Information School. Her academic career follows a 20-year industry career in IT executive and consulting positions. Her research interests include enterprise-wide information security, forensic-ready networks, secure coding practices, and digital forensics. She is a member of the American Academy of Forensic Scientists. She earned a Ph.D. in Computer Science/Computer Security from the University of Idaho (2007) under the direction of Dr. Deb Frincke, and holds a Master of Science in Information Systems Engineering from Seattle Pacific University (1987), a Master in Business Administration from the University of Washington (1985), and a Bachelor of Arts from the University of Pittsburgh.

Michael Felderer is a Research Assistant at the Institute of Computer Science at the University of Innsbruck, Austria. He holds a Ph.D. and a M.Sc. degree in computer science. His research interests are model-driven testing, risk-based testing, model engineering, software evolution, and requirements engineering. Michael Felderer leads the research projects Telling TestStories and MATE to define a model-driven testing approach for service-centric systems, and contributes to other research projects. Additionally, he transfers his research results into practice as consultant and speaker on industrial conferences.

Xiaocheng Ge has been a Research Associate at Department of Computer Science, University of York, since 2004. His research interests include agile development of critical systems, model-based secu- rity/safety analysis, and business process analysis. He published several papers in journals and international conferences in these topics.

Asif Qumer Gill is a Research Fellow in Business Information Systems at the University of Sydney. His research interests are in IS strategy, architecture, management and adoption. He is currently researching on agile, cloud, and social computing. Asif has extensive industry experience, primarily in strategic Business-IT projects across several sectors including manufacturing, automotive, educational services, information technology services, financial services, and banking industry.

Koiti Hasida received his Doctoral degree of Science from the University of Tokyo in 1986. He was affiliated with ETL (Electrotechnical Laboratory) from 1986 to 2001, and also with the Institute of New Generation Computer Technology (ICOT) from 1988 to 1992. He is currently at AIST (National Institute of Advanced Industrial Science and Technology). His research co-creations of values, purpose-based (declarative) process modeling, encompasses linguistics, cognitive science, natural language processing, intelligent content, service science, and so forth.

Michael N. Huhns holds the NCR Professorship and is Chair of the Department of Computer Science and Engineering at the University of South Carolina. He also directs the Center for Information Technology. His degrees in electrical engineering are from the University of Michigan (B.S.) and the University of Southern California (M.S. and Ph.D.). He is the author of nine books and more than 200 papers in machine intelligence, including the coauthored textbook "Service-Oriented Computing: Semantics, Processes, Agents." His research interests are in the areas of multiagent systems, ontologies, service-oriented computing, enterprise integration, and cooperative information systems. He serves on the editorial boards for 12 journals, is a Senior Member of the ACM, and is a Fellow of the IEEE.

Noriaki Izumi is a researcher at the National Institute of Advanced Industrial Science and Technology. He received B.E. and M.E. degrees from Osaka Prefecture University in 1992 and 1994, respectively. His research interests include intelligent systems, knowledge modeling, Semantic Web, and Web services. He is a member of JSSST, IPSJ, and JSAI. He also has been developed methods and frameworks for development of large scale information systems, which cover everything from user centered requirement analysis to guidelines of evaluations of system developments. The methods and frameworks have been summarized to be a framework that is called the "AIST-framework," which is used in real developments of large scale information systems.

Neil Kidd graduated from Staffordshire University, in 2001, with a degree in Computing Science during which he gained a year of work experience at CERN in Geneva. Following university he joined Codeweavers Ltd. soon after its inception, developing financial solutions for the vehicle retail, finance underwriting and insurance sectors. He was a key member of the team that elected to introduce agile methods into the company. He gained a Scrum Master qualification and followed this with learning and implementing lean and XP techniques as part of his agile journey. Neil is a co-founder and regular participant in the Agile Staffordshire user group and enjoys attending conferences to continually expand and refine his knowledge.

Chris Knight graduated from Staffordshire University in 2005 with a degree in Business Information Technology. He has since worked on a range of projects at Codeweavers Ltd in the automotive finance and insurance industries. Since the company's adoption of agile and lean practices in 2006, Chris has developed a keen interest in the subject having experienced the advantages they bring. His passion for agile, XP, and lean has helped the company grow into the agile organisation it is today.

Supannika Koolmanojwong is a full-time faculty and a researcher at the University of Southern California Center for Systems and Software Engineering. Her primary research areas are rapid-field software development, service science and engineering, systems and software process improvement, and systems and software engineering education and training. Her dissertation was about the Incremental

Commitment Spiral Model Process Patterns for Rapid-Fielding Projects. Prior to this, she was a Lecturer at Faculty of Science and Technology, Assumption University, Thailand and a RUP/OpenUp Content Developer at IBM Software Group. She received her MS and PhD in software engineering from the University of Southern California.

Jo Ann Lane is a research assistant professor at the University of Southern California Center for Systems and Software Engineering, conducting research in the areas of SoSE, systems engineering, and innovation. She was a co-author of the 2008 Department of Defense Systems Engineering Guide for Systems of Systems. Prior to her academic career, she was a key technical member at SAIC for over 20 years, responsible for the development and integration of software-intensive systems and systems of systems. She received her PhD in systems engineering from the USC and her Master's in Computer Science from San Diego State University.

Manfred Lange is Technical Director for MIS Products for EFI, Auckland, New Zealand. He has worked as a development manager and agile coach across many industries including printing, utilities, enterprise planning and reporting, smart cards, network support and medical systems. His research work has been presented at a number of international conferences including the Agile series, Pattern Languages of Programming and Australasian Conference on Information Systems. He is a member of the Agile Alliance and the Agile Project Leadership Network. He regularly blogs at http://agileleadership.blogspot.com.

Nuno Laranjeiro is an Invited Assistant Professor at the University of Coimbra, Portugal. He submitted his PhD thesis to the University of Coimbra in January 2012, being currently waiting for the final defense. His research focuses on robust software services and his research interests also include experimental dependability evaluation, fault injection, web services security, and enterprise application integration. He has authored more than 20 papers in refereed conferences and journals in the services computing and dependability areas. Nuno Laranjeiro has participated in national and European research projects and acted as referee for several international conferences and journals in the dependability and services areas.

Frank Maurer is a full Professor and is currently an Associate Vice President of Research at the University of Calgary, Canada. He is also the head of the Agile Surface Engineering (ASE) group at the University of Calgary. His research interests are agile software methodologies, engineering digital table applications, executable acceptance test driven development, integrating agile methods & interaction design, framework & API usability, and software engineering for the cloud. He is a member of the Agile Alliance, a Certified Scrum Master, part of the organizers of the Calgary Agile Methods Users Group and was an Associate Editor of *IEEE Software* responsible for the Process and Practices area.

Benito Mendoza is an Assistant Professor in the Computer Engineering Technology Department at the New York City College of Technology. His research interests are in the areas of multiagent systems, situation awareness, and social computing. He was a postdoctoral fellow at ExxonMobil Research and Engineering. He has a PhD. in Computer Science and Engineering from the University of South Carolina and a MSc in Artificial Intelligence and a BSc in Computer Science from the University of Veracruz, Mexico.

Andreas Metzger is Senior Researcher and leader of the "Adaptive Software and Services" research area at Paluno (the Ruhr Institute for Software Technology), at the University of Duisburg-Essen. Since 2008, he is activity and workpackage leader of S-Cube, the European Network of Excellence on software, services & systems, and member of the network's management board. Since 2011, he is the Technical Coordinator of the EU FI PPP use case project FInest. His current research interests include software engineering and service-based systems engineering, focusing on online quality prediction for adaptive systems. Here, Andreas investigates novel techniques that allow anticipating and proactively responding to imminent software failures. He has co-authored over 40 papers, articles and book chapters and acted as member of the program committee for numerous international events.

Sangdeok Park received his M.S. and Ph.D. degrees from the Department of Mechanical Engineering in POSTECH at Pohang, Korea in 1990 and 2000, respectively. Currently he is a Director of the Department of Applied Robot Technology (DART) at Korea Institute of Industrial Technology (KITECH). His research topics include design and control of quadruped walking robots, unmanned aerial vehicles, and wearable robots.

David Parsons holds a senior academic post at Massey University, Auckland, New Zealand. He has a long experience of agile methods in both academia and industry, having previously worked for a number of consulting organisations assisting clients with projects in various domains including healthcare, banking, logistics and the oil industry. He has developed professional courses in agile programming techniques and test driven development for Software Education Associates and provides workshops for startup SMEs in agile methods. His research on various aspects of software engineering has been published in a range of journals and conference proceedings, and he is the author of a number of successful books on software development covering Java, C++, and Web-based applications. He is a professional member of the British Computer Society.

Ita Richardson is Senior Lecturer with the Department of Computer Science and Information Systems at the University of Limerick. She is a Principal Investigator within Lero – the Irish Software Engineering Research Centre and where she is the Competence Leader for Software Process Improvement and Global Software Development research. Dr. Richardson's research focuses on software processes in different environments and domains. She has studied its implementation in the medical device, automotive and financial services domains, and within global software and services development environments. She has over 100 publications in refereed journals and conferences. Dr. Richardson supervises PhD and MSc students, some of whom are part-time and industry-based, and lectures to undergraduate and postgraduate students at the University of Limerick.

Juha Rikkilä is a researcher at the Free University of Bozen-Bolzano. After long career in the industry and the companies NSN, Nokia, and Unisys in different roles in research, quality management, operational development and line management, he is now focusing on research of new approaches to software development, software teams and management of software organizations. This includes study and application of the agile and lean approaches, organizing and enhancing the experimental software factory environment, research of team performance and management, and application of the complexity leadership theory in software organizations. His doctoral thesis deals with managing software development as a complex adaptive system.

Takahiro Seino is a Lecturer of Maebashi Kyoai Gakuen College. He received his Ph.D. in information science from Graduate School of Information Science, Japan Advanced Institute of Science and Technology in 2003. His research interests include large-scale information system developments, software engineering, programming, software testing and formal methods. He also has been occupied on some actual projects which built up large-scale information systems applying his research results.

Paul Shannon graduated from the University of Nottingham with a degree in Computer Science in 2003 and has spent 8 years since then developing software. He has been using agile methods for the last 5 years with a mixture of Scrum, Lean and XP practices. He was pivotal in the adoption of agile and lean practices at Codeweavers Ltd and helped the team improve their service oriented architecture before leaving to join 7digital in August 2011. Paul regularly represented Codeweavers at conferences and published an experience report in 2010. He now leads 7digital's Content Team, runs Agile Staffordshire user group, and continues to share his experiences at other agile events around the country.

Abhishek Sharma is a Master's student in Department of Computer Science at the University of Calgary, Canada. He is a member of Agile Surface Engineering group and is supervised by Dr. Frank Maurer. Before coming to Calgary he finished his Bachelor of Engineering with Honors in Computer Science and Engineering from the Rajiv Gandhi Technical University, India. His research interests include agile software engineering, empirical software engineering, cloud computing, service oriented architecture, testing of web-based applications, automated UI testing, and testing GIS.

Osamu Takaki received his Doctoral degree in Mathematics from Kyoto Sangyo University in 1998. He is currently working in Japan Advanced Institute of Science and Technology. Though he originally studied mathematical logic, his current research interests are theoretical aspects of problems in developing process models and methodologies that address such problems. He is also interested in knowledge modeling and evaluations of medical services, in particular, he is interested in representation of clinical indicators that adequately denote quantitative properties related to quality of medical services by using ontology engineering and formal methods.

Marco Paulo Amorim Vieira is an Assistant Professor at the University of Coimbra, Portugal, and an Adjunct Associate Teaching Professor at the Carnegie Mellon University, USA. Marco Vieira is an expert on experimental dependability and security assessment and benchmarking. His research interests also include robustness assessment and improvement in SOA, fault injection, security in database systems, software development processes, and software quality assurance, subjects in which he has authored or co-authored more than 100 papers in refereed conferences and journals. He has participated in several research projects, both at the national and European level. Marco Vieira has served on program committees of the major conferences of the dependability and databases areas and acted as referee for many international conferences and journals in the dependability and databases areas. Marco Vieira has currently several projects with industry in areas such as service-oriented architectures, databases, decision support systems, and software development processes.

Sam Wessel built his first website in 1994, when he was 12 years old, and has been following the evolution of the web ever since. After graduating from the University of Nottingham with a degree in Computer Science, Sam took his passion for learning to Codeweavers Ltd, where he was able to develop his programming skills while helping to advance the company's adoption of agile practices. He has run several conference workshops on agile approaches to design. In February 2011 Sam joined the development team at Esendex Ltd, where he leads weekly coding dojos and nurtures the company's agile processes. He is currently a co-organiser of the GeekUp Nottingham software group.

Eoin Whelan is a Lecturer in Business Information Systems at the National University of Ireland, Galway. Previously he was on the faculty of the Kemmy Business School at the University of Limerick. He received his PhD from NUI Galway in 2009. His research interests focus upon information networks, with a particular emphasis on open and networked innovation and the role of information and communication technologies within these paradigms. His works have appeared in a variety of journals including *MIT Sloan Management Review, Journal of Information Technology, R&D Management,* and *Information Systems Journal.* Prior to becoming an academic, Eoin held a variety of business analyst positions in Ireland, New Zealand, and the US.

Laura Zavala is a Research Associate in the Computer Science Department at the Medgar Evers College of the City University of New York. Her research interests are in the areas of context aware computing, service oriented computing, ontologies, and Semantic Web. She has a PhD. in Computer Science and Engineering from the University of South Carolina and a MSc in Artificial Intelligence and a BSc in Computer Science from the University of Veracruz, Mexico.

Philipp Zech is a Research Assistant at the Institute of Computer Science at the University of Innsbruck, Austria. He is a member of the Quality Engineering research group, he holds a master degree in computer science, and recently started his PhD. His current research focus lies in the area of risk-based security testing of service-centric systems and cloud testing. Since its initial launch in 2008, he has been a core member and main contributor of the Telling TestStories project.

Index